2012 杭州统计年鉴

HANG ZHOU STATISTICAL YEARBOOK

中国统计出版社
China Statistics Press

（京）新登字041号

图书在版编目（CIP）数据

杭州统计年鉴. 2012 / 杭州市统计局，国家统计局杭州调查队，杭州市社会经济调查局编.
—北京：中国统计出版社，2012.8
ISBN 978-7-5037-6637-4/c.2710

Ⅰ. ①杭… Ⅱ. ①杭… ②国… ③杭…Ⅲ. ①统计资料－杭州市－2012－年鉴

Ⅳ. ①C832.551-54

中国版本图书馆CIP数据核字(2012)第189184号

杭州统计年鉴－2012

作者／杭州市统计局　国家统计局杭州调查队　杭州市社会经济调查局
责任编辑／佘竞雄　郭　栋
责任校对／俞伟锋　陈小国
封面设计／杭州云鼎广告有限公司
出版发行／中国统计出版社
通信地址／北京市西城区月坛南街57号
邮编／100826
办公地址／北京市丰台区西三环南路甲6号
电话／(010)63376907
网址 / http://csp.stats.gov.cn
印刷／浙江新中商务印刷有限公司
经销／新华书店
开本／890 X 1240 毫米　1/16
字数／87万
印张／26.75
印数／1－1200册
版别／2012 年 8 月第 1 版
版次／2012 年 8 月第 1 次印刷
书号／ISBN 978-7-5037-6637-4/c.2710
定价／300.00元

《杭州统计年鉴－2012》编委会和编辑人员

Editorial Board and Staff

编者说明

一、《杭州统计年鉴—2012》是一部信息密集的资料工具书。本书通过大量统计数据，真实地记录了在改革开放中杭州的经济、科技、社会的发展变化。本年鉴在前几年年鉴的基础上作了进一步的调整和改进，充实了数据信息量，并与前几年在版本内容、指标数据等方面基本保持连贯性。

二、本年鉴内容包括：综合；人口和从业人员；农业；工业、能源；建筑业；交通运输、邮电；固定资产投资；国内商业；对外经济、旅游；财政、金融、保险；城市建设、环境保护；科技、教育、文化、卫生、体育；人民生活、物价、民政等十三部分。

三、本年鉴辑入的统计数字，以2011年为主，为方便读者使用，主要指标还列入了1978年以来有关年度的统计数字。

四、2001年3月起，萧山、余杭撤市建区，市区数据为新市区口径，增长速度按同比口径计算。

五、本年鉴表中符号使用说明：“－”表示这一栏没有数字；“…”表示该数字极小，不足计量单位；“#”表示其中的主要项；空白栏表示未掌握资料；“*”表示表下有注解。

六、读者在使用统计资料时，凡与本年鉴有出入的，均以本年鉴为准。

七、《杭州统计年鉴》公开出版以来，受到了广大读者的关心和支持，对此我们深表谢意。欢迎广大读者对年鉴内容、编排等方面提出宝贵意见，以利于我们进一步提高年鉴的编辑工作水平，更好地为广大读者服务。

Editorial Note

Ⅰ. *Hangzhou Statistical Yearbook 2012* covers comprehensive data series of Hangzhou's social and economic development. Through the statistical data, it reflects the changes and development of Hangzhou's economy, science, technology and society since China adopted the policy of reform and opening to the outside world. This book is adjusted and progressed on basis of last years' books. It enriches the data, and keeps the consistency with last years' book in content and indicators.

Ⅱ. The book contains the following thirteen chapters: 1. General Survey; 2. Population and Employment; 3. Agriculture; 4. Industry and Energy; 5. Construction; 6. Transportation, Post and Telecommunication Services; 7. Investment in Fixed Assets; 8. Domestic Trade; 9. Foreign Trade and Tourism; 10. Finance, Banking and Insurance; 11. Urban Construction and Environmental Protection; 12. Science and Technology, Education, Culture, Public Health and Sports; 13. People's Livelihood, Price Indices and Civil Administration.

Ⅲ. The book mainly reflects statistical data in 2011. And it also contains some selected data series in important years after 1978.

Ⅳ. The administrative of area urban district has been adjusted since March 2001, the new administrative area is composed of eight district including Xiaoshan and Yuhang. Data of urban district belong to new administrative area, while indices are calculated at comparable coverage.

Ⅴ. Notations used in this book:"—" indicates that the column has no figure;"…" indicates that the figure is not large enough to be measured with the smallest unit in the table;"blank" indicates that the data not available;"#" indicates the major items of the total;" * " indicates"see footnotes below".

Ⅵ. In any case the data of this book shall be deemed as the authoritative ones.

Ⅶ. Previous editions of Hangzhou Statistical Yearbook have won wide acclaim among the readers. In order to excel, we welcome all candid comments and criticism from our readers.

目　录
Contents

第一篇　综合
Chapter 1　General Survey

第二篇　人口和从业人员

Chapter 2　Population and Employment

第三篇　农业
Chapter 3　Agriculture

第四篇　工业、能源
Chapter 4　Industry and Energy

第五篇　建筑业
Chapter 5　Construction

第六篇　交通运输、邮电
Chapter 6　Transportation, Post and Telecommunications

第七篇　固定资产投资
Chapter 7　Investment in Fixed Assets

第八篇　　国内商业

Chapter 8　Domestic Trade

第九篇　　对外经济、旅游

Chapter 9　Foreign Trade and Tourism

第十篇　财政、金融、保险

Chapter 10　Finance, Banking and Insurance

第十一篇　城市建设、环境保护
Chapter 11　Urban Construction and Environmental Protection

第十二篇　科技、教育、文化、卫生、体育
Chapter 12　Science and Technology, Education, Culture, Public Health and Sports

第十三篇　人民生活、物价、民政

Chapter 13　People's Livelihood, Price Indices and Civil Administration

2011年杭州市国民经济和社会发展统计公报

杭 州 市 统 计 局
国家统计局杭州调查队
杭州市社会经济调查局
（2012年2月）

2011年是“十二五”开局之年，也是加快转型升级、推进科学发展的重要之年。全市坚持以科学发展观统领经济社会发展全局，认真执行中央宏观调控政策，围绕全面建设小康社会、共建共享“生活品质之城”的目标要求，稳增长、调结构、促发展、扩内需、惠民生，实现了“十二五”发展良好开局。

一、综　　合

经济总量

初步核算，全市实现生产总值（GDP）7019.06亿元，按可比价格计算，比上年增长10.1%，连续21年保持两位数增长。其中：第一产业增加值236.77亿元，第二产业增加值3323.79亿元，第三产业增加值3458.5亿元，分别增长2.5%、9.8%和11.0%。全市按常住人口计算的人均GDP达到80478元，按户籍人口计算的人均GDP为101370元，按国家公布的2011年平均汇率折算，分别达到12460美元和15695美元。三次产业结构由上年的3.5∶47.8∶48.7调整为2011年的3.3∶47.4∶49.3。

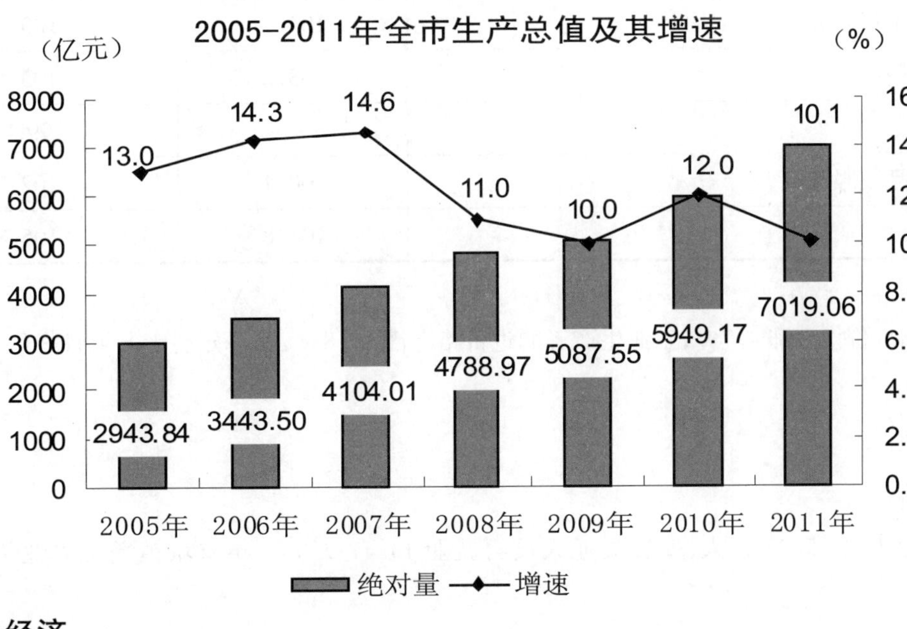

非公经济

初步测算，在全市生产总值中，非公有制经济所占比重已达到66.6%，比上年提高0.6个百分点。个体私营经济持续活跃。年末，全市共有私营企业18.11万户，增长12.0%，从业人员163.67万人，增长12.4%；个体工商户31.17万户，从业人员70.31万人，分别增长4.3%和7.7%。

十大产业

全市文化创意、旅游休闲、金融服务、电子商务、信息软件、先进装备制造业、物联网、生物医药、节能环保、新能源等十大产业实现增加值3010.39亿元，比上年增长13.6%，占全市生产总值的42.9%。

财政收支

全年完成财政总收入1488.92亿元，比上年增长19.6%，其中地方财政一般预算收入785.15亿元，增长17.0%。在税收收入中，增值税407.20亿元，增长14.1%；营业税240.94亿元，增长8.9%；企业所得税327.20亿元，增长31.9%；个人所得税127.65亿元，增长30.2%。全年地方财政支出747.50亿元，比上年增长21.2%。

市场价格

市区居民消费价格总水平比上年上涨4.8%，涨幅高于上年0.9个百分点。八大类商品和服务项目价格呈"七升一降"格局(见下表)。

市区居民消费价格指数(上年=100)

项　　目	2011年	2010年
市区居民消费价格指数	104.8	103.9
1.食品	110.7	107.3
2.烟酒及用品	100.9	101.9
3.衣着	106.1	98.0
4.家庭设备用品及维修服务	104.2	103.6
5.医疗保健和个人用品	103.6	105.5
6.交通和通信	98.4	99.8
7.娱乐教育文化用品及服务	100.1	102.2
8.居住	104.8	105.8

全市工业生产者出厂价格上涨4.7%；工业生产者购进价格上涨10.8%，涨幅分别比上年回落0.2、1.3个百分点。

劳动就业

全年新增城镇就业人员25.27万人，安置失业人员再就业13.17万人。年末城镇登记失业率由上年的2.19%下降为1.86%。

二、人口、人民生活和社会保障

人口

2011年末，全市常住人口873.8万人，比上年末增加3.26万人，其中城镇人口645.74万人，占73.9%。公安部门户籍登记人口 695.71 万人，其中，农业人口 319.68 万人，非农业人口 376.03 万人；全市人口出生率为 10.16‰，人口自然增长率为 4.64‰。

人民生活

据抽样调查，全年市区城镇居民人均可支配收入 34065 元，比上年增长 13.4%，扣除价格因素，实际增长 8.2%。其中人均工资性收入 23760 元、财产性收入 2587 元、转移性收入 10321 元，分别增长 12.7%、18.2% 和 16.0%，经营性收入 1607 元，下降 2.6%。人均生活消费性支出 22642 元，比上年增长 12.0%。市区城镇居民人均住房建筑面积 33.7 平方米，每百户居民家庭拥有家用汽车 31 辆、空调器 212 台、移动电话 211 部、家用电脑 110 台、微波炉 74 台、淋浴热水器 103 台。全市农村居民人均纯收入 15245 元，比上年增长 15.6%，扣除价格因素，实际增长 10.3%，人均生活消费性支出 12125 元，增长 18.1%。全市农村居民人均居住面积 72.5 平方米。每百户农村居民家庭拥有家用汽车 22 辆、空调器 120 台、移动电话 230 部、家用电脑 51 台、微波炉 34 台、淋浴热水器 81 台、洗衣机 78 台、电冰箱 93 台。

年末城乡居民储蓄存款余额达 5547.48 亿元，比上年末增长 11.5%。

社会保障

年末全市参加社会基本养老保险人数达 540.47 万人（其中职工基本养老保险 428.12 万人），比上年末增加 50.20 万人；参加社会基本医疗保险 779.02 万人（其中职工基本医疗保险 386.33 万人），增加 25.46 万人；参加职工失业、工伤、生育保险人数分别达 277.53 万人、355.28 万人、254.38 万人，分别比上年末净增 33.55 万人、40.33 万人、25.85 万人。全年开工建设保障房 47806 套，竣工 48963 套，全面完成省下达目标任务。主城区公开销售经济适用房 7833 套，建筑面积 50.99 万平方米；推出公共租赁住房 4158 套；新增廉租住房保障家庭 3035 户，实现对城镇低保标准 2.5 倍以下的低收入住房困难家庭“应保尽保”。市区最低月工资标准为 1310 元，失业保险金标准为 1048 元/月，分别比上年提高 210 元和 168 元。

社会福利

年末全市拥有各类福利院、敬老院 254 所，比上年增加 38 所，床位 33561 张，收养人员 14768 人，分别增长 44.6% 和 18.7%。全市城镇享受最低生活保障人数 14133 人，农村享受最低生活保障人员 71099 人。农村五保户和城镇“三无”人员集中供养率分别为 96.5% 和 99.9%。开展第十一次“春风行动”，共募集社会帮扶资金 4720.26 万元。

三、城市建设、环境保护和安全生产

城市基础设施建设

全年完成基础设施投资 643.7 亿元。建成东洲综合码头、淳安上江埠大桥等 10 个项目，杭长高速公路、钱江通道及连接线等 15 个续建项目进展平稳。市区地铁 1 号线 31 个车站主体结构全部完工，盾构区间已有 56 段隧道安全贯通。地铁 2 号线东南段全面开工建设。九堡大桥、秋石快速路二期、石德立交西北象限匝道、沪杭甬高速下宁路连接线等工程基本完工；九堡大桥北接线、德胜快速路（上塘河 - 保俶北路）工程、之江大桥及接线工程、彩虹快速路滨江段、彩虹快速路萧山段等快速路在建工程抓紧推进。完成 106 条背街小巷、62 个庭院、309 幢房屋改善项目；提升改建公厕 38 座；完成截污纳管项目 239 个，新增纳管污水 3.02 万吨/日；治理低洼积水 35 处，完成交改项目12个。

公用事业

全年杭州电网建设投入37.92亿元。新开工110千伏及以上项目33项，投产34项，投产变电容量为319万千伏安，线路140.47公里。至2011年末，杭州电网拥有110千伏以上变电所245座，变电容量4736.9万千伏安。全市用电量达到575.28亿千瓦时，比上年增长10.2%，其中城乡居民生活用电69.31亿千瓦时，增长9.2%。市区自来水日供水能力达到320万立方米。年末市区居民家庭天然气用户72.5万户，比上年末增长14.6%。主城区新辟公交线路17条，优化公交线路43条；组织开展错时停车小区107个、单位191家，利用泊位6716个；建成停车泊位59723个，其中公共停车泊位8936个。新增免费单车布点263个，累计建成运行公共自行车租赁点2674个，投入公共自行车6.5万辆。

环境保护

全年单位GDP综合能耗下降4.42%，规模以上工业单位增加值能耗下降7.14%。主要污染物减排任务基本完成。城市污水集中处理率达到94.4%；主要水系监测断面水质三类以上比例由上年的73.2%提高为82.1%。市区空气质量达到二级和好于二级的天数达到333天，比上年增加19天。至年末，市区人均公园绿地面积达15.5平方米，比上年增加0.4平方米，建成区绿化覆盖率为40.0%。

安全生产

全市发生各类安全生产事故次数、死亡人数、受伤人数和直接经济损失分别比上年下降4.1%、3.5%、3.5%和3.4%。亿元GDP安全生产事故死亡人数为0.12人，比上年下降12.4%。全市流通领域食品快速检测合格率由上年的99.1%提高至99.5%，餐饮服务环节食品检测合格率由上年的93.2%上升至94.8%，食品生产加工环节合格率由上年的93.4%提高至93.8%。

四、农　　业

2011年，全市完成农林牧渔业总产值357.07亿元，比上年增长12.9%。其中，农业产值190.79亿元，林业产值34.85亿元，牧业产值83.65亿元，渔业产值39.0亿元，分别增长12.3%、5.8%、18.6%和11.7%。全年粮食总产量97.81万吨，比上年下降2.4%；水产品产量21.23万吨，肉类32.5万吨，禽蛋15.94万吨，水果80.31万吨，分别增长1.6%、2.2%、7.9%和3.3%。全年茶叶、花卉苗木、水产品、节粮型畜禽、蔬菜、竹业等"六大优势产业"和水果、干果、蚕桑、药材、蜂业等"五大特色产业"实现产值247亿元，比上年增长12.5%，占农林牧渔业总产值的69.1%。

五、工业和建筑业

工业生产

2011年，全市实现工业增加值2944.0亿元，按可比价计算增长11.3%。实现全部工业销售产值14710.28亿元，其中规模以上工业销售产值12181.22亿元，增长20.2%。在规模以上工业中：轻工业实现销售产值4774.73

亿元,增长17.3%,重工业实现销售产值7406.49亿元,增长22.2%。全年规模以上工业实现新产品产值2744.74亿元,增长30.1%,新产品产值率由上年的20.6%提高到22.2%。

工业效益

全市规模以上工业企业实现主营业务收入12022.57亿元,比上年增长18.2%;实现利税1330.48亿元,增长15.7%,其中利润795.53亿元,增长14.5%。工业产品产销衔接良好,全年规模以上工业产品产销率为98.63%。

建筑业

全年实现建筑业增加值379.79亿元,比上年下降1.4%。全市有总承包和专业承包资格的建筑企业1373家,完成施工产值3032.5亿元,增长18.0%;房屋建筑施工面积26104.4万平方米,增长15.3%;房屋建筑竣工面积8556.11万平方米,增长4.1%。

六、固定资产投资和房地产开发

固定资产投资

2011年,全市完成固定资产投资3100.02亿元,比上年增长16.9%。从产业投向看,第一产业投资7.69亿元,增长83.3%;第二产业投资748.68亿元,增长8.9%,其中工业投资747.48亿元,增长9.0%;第三产业投资2343.65亿元,增长19.6%。

房地产业

全市完成房地产开发投资1302.72亿元,比上年增长36.2%。房屋施工面积7698.26万平方米,增长23.6%;竣工面积1223.86万平方米,增长11.2%。全年商品房销售面积734.01万平方米,下降25.7%,其中住宅销售597.73万平方米,下降25.1%。

七、国内贸易

2011年,全市实现社会消费品零售总额2548.36亿元,比上年增长18.7%,扣除物价上涨因素,实际增长13.7%。其中城镇消费品零售额2432.51亿元,增长18.8%;乡村消费品零售额115.85亿元,增长18.4%。分行业看,批发零售贸易业零售额2274.84亿元,增长18.6%;住宿餐饮业零售额273.52亿元,增长19.5%。

八、对外经济

对外贸易

2011年,全市完成外贸进出口总额639.72亿美元,比上年增长22.2%。其中进口总额224.5亿美元,增长31.9%;出口总额415.21亿美元,增长17.5%。出口总额中,机电产品出口157.98亿美元,增长15.7%;高新技术产品出口50.02亿美元,增长11.7%。按贸易方式分,一般贸易出口330.27亿美元,比上年增长18.8%;加工贸易出口84.14亿美元,增长12.9%。出口市场中,对欧盟、美国、日本分别出口114.94、77.84和37.57亿美元,增长17.1%、9.0%和19.5%。新兴及周边市场拉美、东盟、非洲、韩国、俄罗斯出口分别增长28.4%、24.0%、27.2%、32.0%和35.3%。

对外合作

至2011年末，全市累计设立各类境外投资企业（机构）700个，其中非贸易企业235个。全年境外协议出资5.82亿美元，其中非贸易性投资4.71亿美元。完成对外承包工程和劳务合作营业额4.47亿美元，增长25.2%。离岸服务外包合同执行额20.34亿美元，比上年增长30.9%。

利用外资

全年批准外商直接投资500项，合同利用外资81.71亿美元，比上年增长6.0%；实际到位外资47.22亿美元，增长8.4%。全市新批总投资3000万美元以上项目91个，总投资64.79亿美元，合同外资36.53亿美元，分别占全市总额的50.2%和44.7%。至2011年末，共有89家世界500强企业来杭投资140个项目。

引进内资

全年共引进内资项目3766个，到位资金720.57亿元，比上年增长10.8%。

开发区建设

杭州经济技术开发区、杭州高新技术产业开发区、萧山经济技术开发区和杭州之江国家旅游度假区等4个国家级开发区全年合同引进外资27.47亿美元，实际利用外资17.07亿美元，分别占全市的33.6%和36.1%。全年实现技工贸总收入4337.67亿元，比上年增长14.5%；实现利税504.97亿元，比上年增长11.8%。

九、交通运输、邮电和旅游

交通运输

2011年，全社会货物运输总量2.88亿吨，比上年增长11.3%；旅客运输量3.48亿人次，比上年增长3.0%。至年末，萧山国际机场已开通航线159条，其中国际航线29条，港、澳、台航线7条；全年民航旅客进出港1751.22万人次，比上年增长2.6%。道路建设快速发展。全年新增公路里程145.87千米，至年末，全市境内公路总里程达到15089千米，其中高速公路503千米。全市行政村客运班车通达率由上年的99.1%提高到99.4%。机动车辆持续增长，年末全市社会机动车拥有量达207.82万辆，其中私人汽车116.29万辆，比上年末分别增长13.4%和23.4%。

邮电通讯

全市完成邮政业务收入10.14亿元，比上年增长23.7%。邮政特快专递辐射230个国家和地区，全年完成国内特快业务1603万件，比上年增长23.3%；国际特快业务38万件，比上年增长26.7%。完成电信业务收入147.22亿元，比上年增长11.0%。年末固定电话用户为353.76万户，比上年下降4.0%，移动电话用户为1218.11万户，增长14.7%；计算机宽带用户达到241.14万户，比上年增长10.7%。

旅游业

全年接待入境旅游者306.31万人次，比上年增长11.1%；接待国内游客7180.96万人次，增长13.9%。旅游总收入达到1191亿元，增长16.1%，其中旅游外汇收入19.57亿美元，增长15.8%。市民出境旅游74.6万人次，比上年增长6.6%。旅游基础设施日趋完善。至年末，全市各类旅行社达562家，比上年增长11.5%；星级宾馆达到230家，其中五星级酒店20家，增加2家；A级景区36个，其中5A景区3个，新增1个。

十、金融、证券和保险

金融

2011年末，全市金融机构本外币存款余额18396.57亿元，比上年末增长8.6%；贷款余额16573.74亿元，比上年末增长11.2%。个人消费贷款余额2497.74亿元，比上年末增长2.9%。

资本市场

全年新增上市公司10家，募集资金101.31亿元。至年末，全市上市公司累计93家，实现上市融资919.9亿元。期货交易所全年代理交易总额24.37万亿元。

保险

全市保费收入211.10亿元，比上年增长18.1%，其中，财产险保费收入96.23亿元，增长19.7%，人身险保费收入114.88亿元，增长16.8%。共支付各类保险赔款62.39亿元，增长37.0%，其中财产险45.24亿元，增长31.2%，人身险17.15亿元，增长55.2%。

十一、教育和科技

教育

2011年末，全市共有小学409所，在校学生46.53万人；初中246所，在校学生22.35万人；普通高中71所，在校学生11.71万人。学前三年幼儿入园率为98.5%，小学入学率和初中升学率均达到100%，初中毕业生升入各类高中比例由上年的99.3%提高到99.5%。优质学前教育覆盖率由上年的65.0%提升到68.3%；优质高中招生比例为82.7%，比上年提高1.9个百分点。普通高等院校38所，在校学生44.67万人，其中在校研究生4.18万人，比上年分别增长2.7%和7.2%。高等教育毛入学率由上年的55.7%提高到56.8%。全市义务教育阶段接纳在读进城务工人员子女20.91万人。

科技

全市研究与试验发展经费(R&D)占GDP的2.88%。专利申请量40892件，专利授权量29249件，分别比上年增长37.5%和10.4%。全年新增高新技术企业302家，累计达到4078家；累计培育认定研发中心774家，其中省级284家；企业技术中心546家，其中国家级20家，省级146家。年内新增9个中国驰名商标，累计已达97个。

十二、文化、卫生和体育

文化

2011年末，全市有各类专业艺术表演团体21个，公共图书馆16个，文化馆15个，博物馆、纪念馆70个，全国重点文物保护单位29处(群)。306件作品获市级广播电视政府奖，67件获省级政府奖，其中10件获省级一等奖。年末全市有线电视用户226.98万户，其中数字电视190.11万户，分别比上年末增长5.5%和41.0%。电视、广播综合覆盖率分别达到99.91%和99.92%。有线电视“村村通”实现全覆盖，有线广播“村村响”实现行政村全覆盖。成功举办第七届中国国际动漫节、第十三届西湖博览会等重大文化活动。杭州市荣获“全国文明城市”称号。西湖文化景观列入世界文化遗产名录。

卫生

年末，全市拥有各类医疗卫生机构2958个，其中医院167个；拥有床位4.53万张，其中医院床位3.9万张。有各类专业卫生技术人员6.59万人，其中执业(助理)医师2.58万人，注册护士2.52万人，分别增长7.8%、5.9%和7.7%。农村卫生服务得到改善。农村自来水普及率提高到99.9%，自来水受益人数达429.82万人。全市婴儿死亡率及5岁以下儿童死亡率分别由上年的3.37‰、4.36‰下降到2.79‰、3.83‰，每十万孕产妇死亡率由上年的6.8人下降为6.37人。

体育

成功举办第八届全国残运会，杭州籍运动员在第十四届世界游泳锦标赛、第七届全国城运会、第八届全国残运会上共获73金48银44铜。组织钱塘江冲浪嘉年华、世界汽车漂移赛、安利纽崔莱健康跑等20余项大型赛事和近600项市级体育赛事。创建省级体育强区1个，强乡镇10个、省级城市体育先进街道1个、社区88个。实施提升城乡公共体育健身设施工程，建设26个农村和社区体育健身中心、体育健身广场，行政村健身苑点建设覆盖率达98%。

国民经济和社会发展存在的主要困难和不足：世界经济走低后外部需求有所减少，投资需求、消费需求对经济增长的拉动作用有待进一步增强；发展方式还没有根本转变、自主创新能力有待加强；基本公共服务资源配置不够均衡，城乡区域发展不够协调；生产要素供给日益趋紧，生态环境约束增强；高物价影响加深，交通“两难”问题仍然突出。

公报注释：

1. 本公报数据为初步统计数。

2. 本公报中增加值为现价，增加值增长速度按可比价格计算。

Statistical Communique of National Economy and Social Development of Hangzhou, 2011

Hangzhou Municipal Bureau of Statistics
Hangzhou survey office of National Bureau of Statistics
Hangzhou Socio – Economic Investigation Bureau

February, 2012

Year 2011 was the beginning of the "twelfth five – year", it was also an important year of accelerating the transformation and upgrading of economy, and to promote the scientific development. The city adhered to make the scientific development concept as the guideline of the economic and social development, earnestly implemented the central government's macro – control policies, focused on the requirements and the goal of building a moderately prosperous society, sharing the "quality of life within a city", steadied the economic growth, adjusted the economic structure, promoted the development, expanded the domestic demand and benefitted the people's livelihood, hence achieved a good start of the "twelfth five – Year".

I. General Situation

Economic Aggregate

According to the preliminary statistics, the Gross Domestic Product (GDP) of Hangzhou was 701.906 billion yuan, up by 10.1% over the previous year at comparable price, which had maintained a double – digit growth for 21 consecutive years. Of the total, the added value of primary industry was 23.677 billion yuan, the added value of secondary industry was 332.379 billion yuan, the added value of tertiary industry was 345.85 billion yuan, up by 2.5%, 9.8%, 11.0%, respectively. The city's per capita GDP (by resident population) was 80,478 yuan, the city's per capita GDP (by household registered population) was 101,370 yuan, according to the average exchange rate in 2011 which published by the country, reached 12,460 U.S. dollars and 15,695 U.S. dollars, respectively. The structure of the three industries was adjusted from 3.5:47.8:48.7 of last year to 3.3:47.4:49.3 in 2011.

Figure 1: **The city's GDP and its annul growth rate, 2005 – 2011**

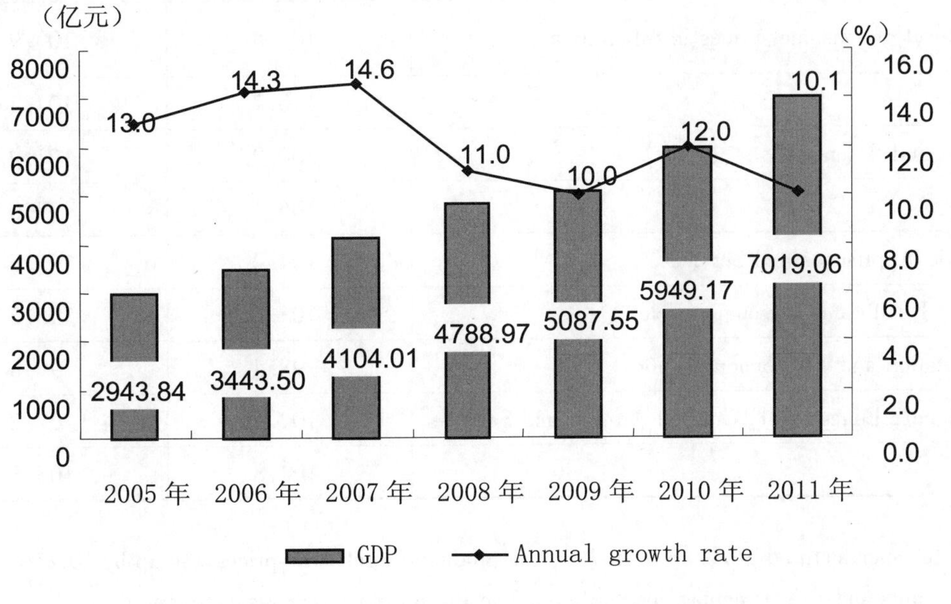

Non – State – Owned Economy

According to the preliminary statistics, the non – state – owned economy accounted for 66. 6% of the city's GDP, increased 0. 6 percentage points over the previous year. At the end of the year, the total private enterprises of the city reached 181. 1 thousand, increased 12. 0% , and employed 1. 6367 million workers, up by 12. 4% over the previous year. The total individual businesses reached 311. 7 thousand, employed total 703. 1 thousand practitioners, up by 4. 3% and 7. 7% respectively.

Ten Major Industries

The added value of the city's cultural and creative industry, tourism and leisure, financial services, e – commerce, information and software, advanced equipment manufacturing industry, the internet of things, biomedicine, energy saving and environment protection, new energy which were also known as the ten major industries reached 301. 039 billion yuan, up by 13. 6% over the previous year, accounting for 42. 9% of the city's GDP.

Fiscal Revenue and Expenditure

The general fiscal revenue of the city totaled 148. 892 billion yuan, up by 19. 6% over the previous year. Of the total, the general budgetary revenue of the local government was 78. 515 billion yuan, up by 17. 0% . In the tax income, the value – added tax amounted to 40. 72 billion yuan, up by 14. 1% , the business tax numbered 24. 094 billion yuan, up by 8. 9% , the enterprises' income tax was 32. 72 billion yuan, up by 31. 9% . The individual income tax was 12. 765 billion yuan, up by 30. 2% . The fiscal expenditure of the local government was 74. 75 billion yuan for the whole year, up by 21. 2% .

Commodity Price

In 2011, the general level of consumer prices in urban area up by 4. 8% compared with the previous year, the increase was 0. 9 percentage points higher than the previous year. The prices of 8 major kinds of commodity and service items presented the layout of "7 Raising and 1 Dropping".

Table1 : Urban consumer price index(previous year = 100)

Item	2011	2010
The general level of consumer prices in urban area	104. 8	103. 9
1. Food	110. 7	107. 3
2. Tobaccos and Alcohols	100. 9	101. 9
3. Clothing	106. 1	98. 0
4. Household Appliances and Services	104. 2	103. 6
5. Medical, Health and Personal Articles	103. 6	105. 5
6. Transportation and Telecommunications	98. 4	99. 8
7. Recreational, Educational, Cultural Articles and Services	100. 1	102. 2
8. Housing	104. 8	105. 8

The producer prices for manufactured goods up by 4. 7% , the producer purchasing prices was up by 10. 8% , the increase was 0. 2 percentage points and 1. 3 percentage points lower than the previous year respectively.

Employment

In 2011, the net increase of job positions reached 252.7 thousand and a total of 131.7 thousand unemployed people were re – employed. The year – end registered urban unemployment rate dropped from 2.19% of the previous year to 1.86%.

II. Population, Living Conditions and Social Security

Population

By the end of 2011, the total number of permanent residents in Hangzhou reached 8.738 million, gained an increase of 32.6 thousand people over the end of the previous year, of which the urban population reached 6.4574 million, accounting for 73.9%. According to the population statistics from the public security department, the number of household registration population reached 6.9571 million, of which the agricultural population was 3.1968 million, the non – agricultural population was 3.7603 million, the city's birth rate was 10.16‰, and the natural population growth rate was 4.64‰.

Living Conditions

According to the sampling survey, the disposable income per capita for urban residents was 34,065 yuan, up by 13.4% over the previous year, after deducting the price factor, the actual increase was 8.2%. In which: the wage income per capita was 23,760 yuan, the property income per capita was 2,587 yuan, the transferred income per capita was 10,321 yuan, up by 12.7%, 18.2%, 16.0%, respectively. The operating income per capita was 1,607 yuan, down by 2.6%. The living expense per capita for urban residents was 22,642 yuan, up by 12.0%. The housing construction area per capita for urban residents was 33.7 square meters, for every 100 urban households, there were 31 family cars, 212 sets of air conditioners, 211 mobile phones, 110 home computers, 74 microwave ovens, and 103 water heaters for shower. The net income per capita for rural residents in Hangzhou was 15,245 yuan, up by 15.6% over the previous year, after deducting the price factor, the actual increase was 10.3%, the living expense per capita for rural residents was 12,125 yuan, up by 18.1%. The living space per capita for rural residents was 72.5 square meters. For every 100 rural households, there were 22 family cars, 120 sets of air conditioners, 230 mobile phones, 51 home computers, 34 microwave ovens, 81 water heaters for shower, 78 washing machines, and 93 refrigerators.

At the end of the year, the balance of savings deposits of urban and rural residents reached 554.748 billion yuan, up by 11.5% over the previous year.

Social Security

At the end of the year, a total of 5.4047 million people participated in the basic social pension insurance (of which 4.2812 million people participated in the employee basic pension insurance), an increase of 0.502 million people over the previous year. A total of 7.7902 million people participated in the basic medical insurance (of which 3.8633 million people participated in the employee basic medical insurance), an increase of 0.2546 million people. A total of 2.7753 million people participated in the unemployment insurance programs, a total of 3.5528 million people participated in the work accident insurance programs, a total of 2.5438 million people participated in the birth insurance programs, increased 0.3355 million, 0.4033 million, 0.2585 million people compared with the previous year respectively. A total of 47,806 sets of security housing were started to construct throughout the year, the construction of 48,963 sets were completed, fully achieved the aim which was issued by the provincial government. A total of 7,833 units of affordable housing were on open sale in the main city, the construction area reached 0.5099 million square meters. The city launched 4,158 units of public rental housing, newly increased 3,035 households of low – rent housing, the coverage of housing security for the families with housing difficulties whose income 2.5 times lower than the urban minimum standard achieved 100%. The minimum monthly wage in urban was 1,310 yuan, the minimum unemployment insurance was 1,048 yuan/month, increased 210 yuan and 168 yuan compared with last year respectively.

Social Welfare

By the end of the year, there were a total of 254 welfare institutions and old people's institutions of various kinds, increased 38 institutions compared to last year, providing 33,561 beds and accommodation for 14,768 inmates, up by 44.6% and 18.7% over the previous year respectively. A total of 14,133 urban residents and a total of 71,099 peasants benefited from the minimum living relief system. The centralized support rate for 5 kinds of rural perfected households and 3 kinds of urban non – working – ability residents reached 96.5% and 99.9% respectively. Carried out the eleventh "Spring Action", a total of 47.2026 million yuan social funds was raised.

III. Urban Construction, Environment Protection and Work Safety

Urban Infrastructure Construction

The total infrastructure investment was 64.37 billion yuan throughout the year. Completed the construction of 10 projects such as Dongzhou integrated dock and Chun'an Shangjiangbu bridge, 15 continued construction projects such as the Hangchang highway, Qianjiang channel and connecting lines were progressing smoothly. The main structure of 31 stations of metro line I was completed, 56 tunnels in the shield zone were linked up safely. The southeast section of Metro Line 2 was in full construction. Fully promoted the construction of the projects such as the North junction of Jiubao Bridge, the Desheng Expressway (Shangtang river – Baoshu north road), the Zhijiang bridge and wiring project, the Caihong Expressway Binjiang section and the Caihong expressway Xiaoshan section. Completed the improvement projects of 106 streets and lanes, 62 courtyards and 309 buildings, Upgraded 38 public toilets, completed 239 projects of sewage interception, newly added 30,200 tons / day of sewer sewage. Managed 35 places of low – lying water, completed 12 reform projects.

Public Utilities

In 2011, a total of 3.792 billion yuan was invested on the construction of power grids. 33 new construction projects which over 110 kV were went into operation, 34 projects were put into production, the power transmission capacity was 3.19 million KVA, and the electrical wiring was 140.47 km. By the end of 2011, there were 245 substations which over 110 kv in Hangzhou, the power transmission capacity reached 47.369 million KVA. The electricity consumption in the whole year reached 57.528 billion kwh, up by 10.2% over the previous year, of which the consumption of residents in urban and rural was 6.931 billion kwh, up by 9.2% over the previous year. The capacity of daily water supply in urban area reached 3.2 million cubic meters. By the end of the year, the number of households used pipeline gas reached 0.725 million, up by 14.6% compared with the end of the previous year. 17 new bus routes were opened in urban area, 43 bus routes were updated. Organized 107 residential quarters and 191 units to carry out the activity of parking in different time, utilized 6,716 parking spaces, completed the construction of 59,723 parking spaces, including 8,936 public parking spaces. Newly increased 263 rental points of free bicycles, the cumulative number of running public bicycle rental points reached 2,674, with a total of 65,000 public bikes.

Environment protection

The comprehensive energy consumption per unit of GDP fell 4.42% throughout the year, the energy consumption per unit added value of above designated size industries fell 7.14%, basically completed the task of emissions of major pollutants. The centralized disposal rate of city sewage reached 94.4%. The proportion of supervised water quality sections which above third level was rose from 73.2% of the previous year to 82.1%. The number of days which air quality in the urban area reached Ⅱ – level or above Ⅱ – level was 333, increased 19 days over the previous year. By the end of the year, the green land area of urban gardens and parks per capita in the urban area reached 15.5 square meters, increased 0.4 square meters over the previous year, the green coverage rate of built – up area was 40.0%.

Production safety

In 2011, the number of accidents, the death toll, the injuring toll and the direct economical loss of accidents decreased 4.1%, 3.5%, 3.5% and 3.4% compared with the previous year respectively. The death toll in production safety accidents per 0.1 billion yuan GDP was 0.12, down by 12.4% over the previous year. The passed rate of food rapid detection in city's circulation area was rose from 99.1% of last year to 99.5%, the passed rate of food in food service area was rose from 93.2% of last year to 94.8%, the passed rate of food in production and processing area was rose from 93.4% of last year to 93.8%.

IV. Agriculture

In 2011, the total output value of farming, forestry, animal husbandry and fishery achieved 35.707 billion yuan, up by 12.9% over the previous year. Of the total, the output value of farming was 19.079 billion yuan, the output value of forestry was 3.485 billion yuan, the output value of animal husbandry was 8.365 billion yuan, the output value of fishery was 3.9 billion yuan, up by 12.3%, 5.8%, 18.6% and 11.7% over the previous year respectively. The total output of grain in 2011 was 0.9781 million tons, down by 2.4% over the previous year. The output of aquatic products was 0.2123 million tons, that of meat was 0.325 million tons, that of poultry and eggs was 0.1594 million tons, that of fruit was 0.8031 million tons, up by 1.6%, 2.2%, 7.9% and 3.3% over the previous year respectively. The "6 Advantageous Industries" of tea, seedling plants, aquatic products, grains – saving livestock & poultry, vegetables and bamboos and the "5 Featured Industries" of fresh fruits, dried fruits, silkworm cocoons&mulberry, medicinal materials and honey achieved an output value of 24.7 billion yuan, up by 12.5%, accounted for 69.1% of the total agricultural output value.

V. Industry and Construction

Industry Production

In 2011, the total Industrial added value was 294.4 billion yuan, up by 11.3% over the previous year at comparable price. The total sales value of the industrial enterprises was 1,471.028 billion yuan, of which the total sales value of the industrial enterprises above designated size reached 1,218.122 billion yuan, up by 20.2%. In the industrial enterprises which above designated size, the sales value of light industry numbered 477.473 billion yuan, up by 17.3% and that of heavy industry amounted to740.649 billion yuan, up by 22.2%. The output value of new products of the industrial enterprises above designated size achieved 274.474 billion yuan in the whole year, up by 30.1%, the proportion of output value of new products which accounted in the total output value of the industrial enterprises above designated size was rose from 20.6% of the previous year to 22.2%.

Industrial efficiency

The sales income of the industrial enterprises above designated size achieved 1,202.257 billion yuan, up by 18.2% over the previous year. The amount of their profits & taxes were 133.048 billion yuan, up by 15.7% over the previous year, of which the amount of profits reached 79.553 billion yuan, up by 14.5% over the previous year. The production and marketing situation was good and the sales rate of industrial enterprises above designated size reached 98.63%.

Construction industry

The total added value of the construction industry achieved 37.979 billion yuan in the whole year, down by 1.4% over the previous year. The number of construction enterprises with the qualification of general contract and special contract was 1,373 and the construction value amounted to 303.25 billion yuan in the whole year, up by 18.0%. The housing construction area was 261.044 million square meters, up by 15.3% and the housing completed area was 85.5611 million square meters, up by 4.1%.

VI. Investment in Fixed Assets and Investment in Real Estate

Investment in Fixed Assets

In 2011, the completed investment in fixed assets was 310.002 billion yuan, up by 16.9%. According to the direction of the investment in fixed assets, the investment in the primary industry was 0.769 billion yuan, up by 83.3%. The investment in the secondary industry was 74.868 billion yuan, up by 8.9%, of which the industrial investment was 74.748 billion yuan, up by 9.0%. The investment in the tertiary industry was 234.365 billion yuan, up by 19.6%.

Investment in Real Estate

In 2011, the development investment of real estate in the whole year totaled 130.272 billion yuan, up by 36.2% over the previous year. The housing construction area was 76.9826 million square meters, up by 23.6%. The housing completed area was 12.2386 million square meters, up by 11.2%. In the whole year, the total area of commercial housing sales was 7.3401 million square meters, down by 25.7% over the previous year, in which the area of residential housing sales was 5.9773 million square meters, down by 25.1%.

VII. Domestic Trade

In 2011, the total retail sales value of the consumer goods in the whole city achieved 254.836 billion yuan, up by 18.7% over the previous year, after detecting the price factor, actually up by 13.7%. Of the total, the retail sales value in urban area was 243.251 billion yuan, up by 18.8% and that of the rural area reached 11.585 billion yuan, up by 18.4%. In terms of the different sectors, the retail sales value of whole sale and retail sector was 227.484 billion yuan, up by 18.6%, and that of the lodging and catering industry retail sales value was 27.352 billion yuan, up by 19.5%.

VIII. Foreign Economy

International Trade

In 2011, the value of import and export totaled 63.972 billion U.S. dollars, up by 22.2% over the previous year. Of the total, the total value of import reached 22.45 billion U.S. dollars, up by 31.9% and that of export amounted to 41.521 billion U.S. dollars, up by 17.5%. In the total exports, the export of electromechanical products was 15.798 billion U.S. dollars, up by 15.7% over the previous year, the export of high - tech products was 5.002 billion U.S. dollars, up by 11.7%. In terms of trading type, the total value of general trading stood at 33.027 billion U.S. dollars, up by 18.8% and that of processing trading numbered 8.414 billion U.S. dollars, up by 12.9%. In terms of exporting countries, the export value to EU was 11.494 billion U.S. dollars, up by 17.1%, that to USA was 7.784 billion U.S. dollars, up by 9.0% and that to Japan was 3.757 billion U.S. dollars, up by 19.5%. In terms of the emerging and neighboring markets in Latin America, ASEAN, Africa, South Korea, Russia, the export values were up by 28.4%, 24.0%, 27.2%, 32.0% and 35.3% respectively.

International Cooperation

By the end of 2011, the number of establishment enterprises (or institutions) by foreign investment was accumulated to 700, of which the number of non - trading enterprises reached 235. The contractual value of the foreign investment reached 0.582 billion U.S. dollars and of which the value of non - trading investment was 0.471 billion U.S. dollars. The turnover of foreign contracted projects and labor cooperation reached 0.447 billion U.S. dollars, up by 25.2% over the previous year. The delivery of offshore outsourcing contract reached 2.034 billion U.S. dollars, up by 30.9% over the previous year.

Utilization of Foreign Capital

There were 500 new foreign direct – funded projects signed in year 2011. The contractual value of foreign investment totaled 8.171 billion U.S. dollars, up by 6.0% over the previous year and the foreign investment actually utilized reached 4.722 billion U.S. dollars, up by 8.4%. The number of new approved projects which the total investment of each over 30 million U.S. dollars amounted to 91, the total investment reached 6.479 billion U.S. dollars, the contracted foreign capital was 3.653 billion U.S. dollars, accounted for 50.2% and 44.7% of the whole city's foreign investment respectively. By the end of 2011, there were 140 projects built in Hangzhou funded by 89 companies of the World Top 500 Companies.

Utilization of Domestic Capital

The number of domestic investment projects was 3,766 throughout the year, the actually utilized investment was 72.057 billion yuan, up by 10.8%.

Development Zone Construction

In 2011, the contractual value of the foreign investment in 4 state – level development zones (such as Hangzhou Economic and Technological Development Zone, Hangzhou High – Tech Development Zone, Xiaoshan Economic & Technological Development Zone and Hangzhou Zhijiang National Holiday Resort Zone) reached 2.747 billion U.S. dollars and the actually utilized investment was 1.707 billion U.S. dollars, accounted for 33.6% and 36.1% of the whole city respectively. The total revenue of technology, industry and trade from the 4 development zones achieved 433.767 billion yuan throughout the year, up by 14.5% over the previous year, the taxes and profits achieved 50.497 billion yuan, up by 11.8% over the previous year.

IX. Transportation, Post & Telecommunications and Tourism

Transportation

In 2011, the annual transported cargo totaled 288 million tons, up by 11.3% over the previous year. The volume of passenger transportation in the whole year reached 348 million person – trips, up by 3.0% over the previous year. By the end of the year, there were 159 flight routes built in the Xiaoshan International Airport, including 29 international routes and 7 routes of HongKong, Macau and Taiwan. The volume of passenger transportation handled by civil aviation amounted to 17.5122 million person – trips, up by 2.6%. The construction of roads sped up. The new increased length of roads totaled 145.87 kilometers. By the end of 2011, the total length of roads within Hangzhou reached 15,089 kilometers, including 503 kilometers expressway. The accessible rate of passenger buses to administrative villagers in the whole city rose from 99.1% of the previous year to 99.4%. The motor vehicles of the city continued to increase drastically. The year – end amount of motor vehicles reached 2.0782 million and of which the private cars were 1.1629 million, up by 13.4% and 23.4% over the previous year respectively.

Post & Telecommunications

The Postal revenue totaled 1.014 billion yuan, up by 23.7% over the previous year. The radiant network of EMS reached 230 countries and regions. During the whole year, 16.03 million items of domestic EMS were completed and 0.38 million items of international EMS were delivered, up by 23.3% and 26.7% over the previous year respectively. The revenue of telecommunications totaled 14.722 billion yuan, up by 11.0%. By the end of 2011, the local telephone users numbered 3.5376 million and there were 12.1811 million mobile phone users, down by 4.0% and up by 14.7% over the previous year respectively. The number of computer broadband users reached 2.4114 million, up by 10.7%.

Tourism

In 2011, the number of oversea visitors to Hangzhou totaled 3.0631 million person – trips, up by 11.1% over the previous year and the domestic tourists to Hangzhou reached 71.8096 million person – trips, up by 13.9%. The income from tourism totaled 119.1 billion yuan, up by 16.1%. Of which the tourism foreign exchange earnings was 1.957 billion U. S. dollars, up by 15.8%. The number of Hangzhou citizens who went abroad for travelling was 0.746 million person – trips, up by 6.6%. The tourist infrastructure facilities had been further perfected. By the end of the year, there were 562 travel agencies of various kinds in the city, up by 11.5%. The number of star – level hotels reached 230, including 20 5 – star hotels, increased 2 5 – star hotels compare to last year. There were 36 sceneries above A – level in the city and of which, 3 scenery were AAAAA – level, increased 1 compare to last year.

X. Banking, Securities and Insurance

Banking

By the end of 2011, the saving deposits of RMB and foreign exchange from all financial institutions in Hangzhou amounted to 1,839.657 billion yuan, up by 8.6% compared with the end of the previous year and loans of RMB and foreign exchange from all financial institutions stood at 1,657.374 billion yuan, up by 11.2%. Of which, the loans for individual consumption reached 249.774 billion yuan, up by 2.9% over the previous year.

Capital Marketing

In 2011, the city newly increased 10 listed companies, raising a total of 10.131 billion yuan funds. By the end of the year, the number of listed companies in Hangzhou accumulated to 93 and money raised through stock markets totaled 91.99 billion yuan. The total trade volume of futures exchanges throughout the year was 24.37 trillion yuan.

Insurance

In 2011, the premiums of insurance companies in the city gained 21.11 billion yuan, up by 18.1% over the previous year. Of the total, the property insurance premiums were 9.623 billion yuan, up by 19.7% and the life insurance premiums were 11.488 billion yuan, up by 16.8%. The insurance companies paid an indemnity worth of 6.239 billion yuan, up by 37.0%. Of which, the indemnity for the property insurance was 4.524 billion yuan, up by 31.2%, and that for the life insurance was 1.715 billion yuan, up by 55.2%.

XI. Education, Science and Technology

Education

By the end of the year 2011, there were a total of 409 elementary schools in the city with 465.3 thousand students. The number of junior middle schools was 246, with a total of 223.5 thousand students. The number of senior secondary schools was 71, with a total of 117.1 thousand students. The enrollment rate of the kindergartens for the children who 3 years younger than the school age reached 98.5%, the enrollment rates of primary school and junior high school all reached 100%, the students from junior middle schools enrolled into senior secondary schools of various sorts rose from 99.3% of the previous year to 99.5%. The coverage rate of quality pre – school education was rose from 65.0% of last year to 68.3%. The enrollment rate of high – quality high school was 82.7%, up by 1.9 percentage points over the previous year. The number of general colleges and universities was 38, a total of 446.7 thousand students were studying in the universities (or colleges), of which 41.8 thousand were graduate students, up by 2.7% and 7.2% over the previous year respectively. The gross enrollment rate of general colleges and universities rose from 55.7% of the previous year to 56.8%. In the whole city, 209.1 thousand children of non – local workers were admitted into the compulsory education.

Science and Technology

The city's research and experimental development (R & D) expenditure accounted for 2.88% of the GDP. A total of 40,892 patent applications were submitted and 29,249 patents were authorized, up by 37.5% and 10.4% over the previous year respectively. Newly added 302 high – tech enterprises throughout the year, accumulated to 4,078. The number of authorized R&D centers added up to 774, including 284 provincial – level centers. The number of enterprise technology centers reached 546, including 20 state – level centers and 146 provincial – level centers. Newly added 9 well – known trademarks in China throughout the year, and accumulated to 97.

XII. Culture, Public Health and Sports

Culture

By the end of the year 2011, there were 21 performing art ensembles, 16 public libraries, 15 cultural stations, 70 museums & memorial halls and 29 state – level protection units of key cultural relics. 306 works won the Municipal Radio and Television Government Award, 67 won the provincial government Award, of which 10 won the first prize at provincial – level. By the end of the year, the number of cable TV subscribers reached 2.2698 million households and of which the number of using digital television was 1.9011 million households, up by 5.5% and 41.0% over the previous year respectively. The coverage rate of TV and that of radio reached 99.91% and 99.92% respectively. The coverage rate of the rural broadcasting and television project of "Extending Radio and TV Coverage to Every Village" reached 100%. Hangzhou successfully hosted the Seventh China International Cartoon and Animation Festival, the Thirteenth West Lake Expo and other major cultural events. Hangzhou City was awarded the title of "National Civilized City". The West Lake Cultural Landscape was included in the World Heritage List.

Public Health

By the end of 2011, there were altogether 2,958 medical treatment institutions of various kinds (including 167 hospitals) and a total of 45.3 thousand beds (including 39 thousand hospital beds). There were a total of 65.9 thousand health workers in the city, including 25.8 thousand licensed doctors and 25.2 thousand registered nurses, up by 7.8%, 5.9% and 7.7% respectively. The condition of health care in rural area was improved. The popularization rate of tap water in the rural area rose to 99.9%, supplying 4.2982 million benefited people. The mortality rate of newborns and that of children below 5 years old dropped from 3.37 and 4.36 of the previous year to 2.79 and 3.83. The death toll per 100,000 pregnant women dropped from 6.8 persons of the previous year to 6.37 persons.

Sports

Successfully hold the Eighth National Games for the Disabled, Hangzhou citizenship athletes won a total of 73 gold, 48 silver and 44 bronze medals in the 14th session of the World Swimming Championships, the Seventh National City Games and the Eighth National Games for the Disabled. Hangzhou Organized the Qiantang River Surfing Carnival, the world's car drift race, Amway Nutrilite Health Run and such more than 20 major events and nearly 600 municipal – level sport events. Created 1 provincial – level sports district, 10 provincial – level sports townships, 1 provincial – level sports sub – district and 88 provincial – level sports communities. Hangzhou implemented the project of enhancing the urban and rural public fitness facilities, constructed 26 rural and community fitness centers, the coverage rate of fitness point construction for the administrative villages reached 98%.

Major difficulties of economic and social development: the foreign demand was decreasing because of the world economic downturn, the roles of investment demand and consumer demand in boosting economic growth need to be further enhanced. The development mode has not been fundamentally changed. The capability of independent innovation needs to be strengthened. The allocation of basic public services resources was uneven. The coordination of development in urban and rural areas was not good enough. The supply of production factors was becoming even tense. The ecological and environmental constraints were enhanced.

The impact of high prices was deepened, and the "two difficulties" in traffic area remain serious.

Communique Notes:

1. Data in the Communique are preliminary statistics.
2. In this Communique, the added values are calculated at current prices, the growth rates of added values are calculated at comparable prices.

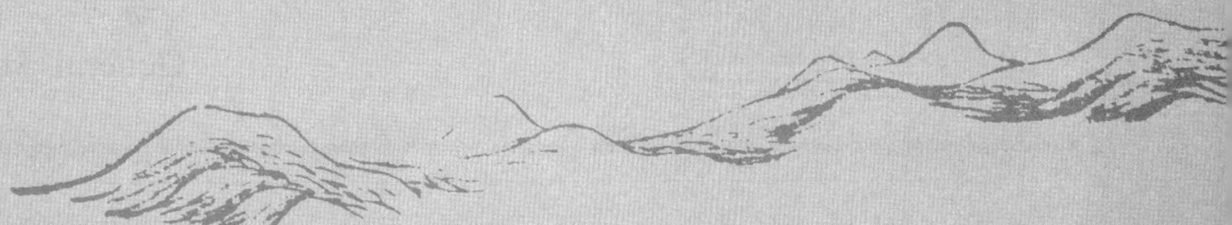

第一篇
CHAPTER-I

综合
GENERAL SURVEY

1 综　　合
General Survey

主要统计指标
Major Statistical Indicators

全市生产总值	Gross Domestic Product	7019.06	亿元	(100 million yuan)
为上年	As Compared with the Preceding Year	110.1	%	(%)
第一产业	Primary Industry	236.77	亿元	(100 million yuan)
为上年	As Compared with the Preceding Year	102.5	%	(%)
第二产业	Secondary Industry	3323.79	亿元	(100 million yuan)
为上年	As Compared with the Preceding Year	109.8	%	(%)
#工业	Industry	2944.0	亿元	(100 million yuan)
为上年	As Compared with the Preceding Year	111.3	%	(%)
第三产业	Tertiary Industry	3458.5	亿元	(100 million yuan)
为上年	As Compared with the Preceding Year	111.0	%	(%)
全市户籍人均生产总值	Per Capita GDP	101370	元	(yuan)
为上年	As Compared with the Preceding Year	109.1	%	(%)
生产总值构成	Composition of Gross Domestic Product	100	%	(%)
第一产业	Primary Industry	3.3	%	(%)
第二产业	Secondary Industry	47.4	%	(%)
#工业	Industry	42.0	%	(%)
第三产业	Tertiary Industry	49.3	%	(%)

1-01 行政区划(2011年末)
Administrative Division(End of 2011)

单位:个　　(unit)

地　区	Region	乡镇 Towns and Townships	#镇 Towns	街道 Subdistrict Offices	村、居委会 Villages and Neighborhood Committees	#村 Villages
全　市	**Whole City**	**109**	**86**	**84**	**3041**	**2073**
市　区	Urban District	29	29	68	1518	670
上城区	Shangcheng	-	-	6	54	-
下城区	Xiacheng	-	-	8	72	-
江干区	Jianggan	4	4	6	158	6
拱墅区	Gongshu	-	-	10	92	-
西湖区	Xihu	2	2	10	196	58
高新(滨江)区	Hi-Tech(Binjiang)	-	-	3	47	7
萧山区	Xiaoshan	17	17	11	571	411
余杭区	Yuhang	6	6	14	328	188
桐庐县	Tonglu	10	6	4	202	183
淳安县	Chun'an	23	11	-	436	425
建德市	Jiande	13	12	3	271	232
富阳市	Fuyang	21	15	4	302	276
临安市	Lin'an	13	13	5	312	287

1－02　土地面积和人口密度(2011 年末)
Land Area and Population Density(End of 2011)

地　　区	Region	土地面积 (平方公里) Land Area (sq. km)	年末总人口 (万人) Population (10000 persons)	人口密度 (人/平方公里) Population Density (person/sq. km)
全　　市	**Whole City**	**16596**	**695.71**	**419**
市　区	Urban District	3068	440.34	1435
上城区	Shangcheng	18	32.79	18217
下城区	Xiacheng	31	40.37	13023
江干区	Jianggan	210	45.28	2156
拱墅区	Gongshu	88	31.4	3568
西湖区	Xihu	263	63.97	2432
高新(滨江)区	Hi－Tech(Binjiang)	73	15.99	2190
萧山区	Xiaoshan	1163	122.87	1056
余杭区	Yuhang	1222	87.67	717
桐庐县	Tonglu	1780	40.47	227
淳安县	Chun'an	4452	45.66	103
建德市	Jiande	2364	51.16	216
富阳市	Fuyang	1808	65.38	362
临安市	Lin'an	3124	52.7	169

1－03 平均每天主要社会经济活动

Selected Indicators on Average Daily Social and Economic Activities

指标 Item	1995	2000	2005	2006	2007	2008	2009	2010	2011
全市生产总值（万元） Gross Domestic Product (10,000 yuan)	20877	37878	80621	94288	112333	130991	139385	162991	192303
工业增加值（万元） Value－Added of Industry (10,000 yuan)	10023	16670	36427	42715	50752	58630	57565	68550	80524
规模以上工业企业利税总额（万元） Total Pre－tax Profits of Industrial Enterprises above Designated Size (10,000 yuan)	1728	4428	12347	15432	20010	21976	24181	33324	36452
农林牧渔业总产值（万元） Gross Output Value of Farming, Forestry, Animal Husbandry and Fishery (10,000 yuan)	2730	4182	6013	6175	6771	7500	7938	8667	9783
固定资产投资（万元） Investment in Fixed Assets (10,000 yuan)	4291	10319	35008	37629	50788	51570	60142	72654	82607
住宅竣工面积（平方米） Floor Space of Residential Buildings Completed (sq. m)	8751	11501	19327	15876	21153	24472	15949	21981	21098
社会消费品零售总额（万元） Total Retail Sales of Consumer Goods (10,000 yuan)	8201	14101	26724	30476	35515	42695	49450	58797	69818
城乡居民储蓄新增额（万元） The Increased Amount of Residents´Savings Deposits (10,000 yuan)	2819	1223	9767	9961	2181	23062	22195	19289	15247
财政收入合计（万元） Total Financial Revenue (10,000 yuan)	1510	3914	14268	17109	21601	24947	27930	34121	40792

注:本表按当年价计算。2003 年起城乡居民储蓄新增额为本外币合并数据。

a) Figures in value terms in this table are calculated at current prices. The increased amount of residents´savings deposits include both RMB and foreign currencies.

1－04 国民经济

Major Indicators of

指　　标		Item	
年末常住人口	（万人）	Long－term Residents（End of 2011）	（10,000 persons）
年末户籍人口	（万人）	Honsehold Registration Population（End of 2011）	（10,000 persons）
#非农业人口	（万人）	Non－agriculture Population	（10,000 persons）
年末从业人员数	（万人）	Total Number of Employed Persons（End of 2011）	（10,000 persons）
全市生产总值	（亿元）	Gross Domestic Product	（100 million yuan）
第一产业	（亿元）	Primary Industry	（100 million yuan）
第二产业	（亿元）	Secondary Industry	（100 million yuan）
第三产业	（亿元）	Tertiary Industry	（100 million yuan）
人均生产总值（户籍）	（元）	Per Capita GDP（Household）	（yuan）
人均生产总值（常住）	（元）	Per Capita GDP（Long－term）	（yuan）
主要农产品产量		Output of Major Farm Products	
粮食	（万吨）	Grain	（10,000 tons）
棉花	（吨）	Cotton	（ton）
油菜籽	（吨）	Rapeseeds	（ton）
茶叶	（吨）	Tea	（ton）
蚕茧	（吨）	Silk－worm Cocoons	（ton）
猪年末存栏	（万头）	Hogs in Stock at Year End	（10,000 heads）
肉类产量	（万吨）	Output of Meat	（10,000 tons）
淡水产品产量	（吨）	Freshwater Aquatic Products	（ton）
全部工业总产值	（亿元）	The Total Output Value of Industrial Enterprises	（100 million yuan）
规模以上工业总产值	（亿元）	The Output Valne of Industrial Enterprises Above Designated Size	（100 million yuan）
规模以上工业企业利税总额	（亿元）	Total Pre－tax Profits of Industrial Enterprises Above Designated Size	（100 million yuan）
全社会交通运输客运量	（万人次）	Total Passenger Traffic	（10,000 person－times）
全社会交通运输货运量	（万吨）	Total Freight Traffic	（10,000 tons）
固定资产投资	（亿元）	Investment in Fixed Assets	（100 million yuan）
社会消费品零售总额	（亿元）	Total Retail Sales of Consumer Goods	（100 million yuan）

注：1. 交通运输客货运输量1990年起为全社会数，1990年以前为交通系统数。
2. 境外旅游者人数1995年开始为全市数，1994年及以前系市区数。
3. 规模以上工业的计算口径，从1997年开始改为全部国有和年销售收入500万元及以上的非国有企业数，1996年以前系乡及乡以上数。

主要指标
National Economy

1980	1985	1990	1995	2000	2005	2006	2007	2008	2009	2010	2011
		583.21		701.7	771.3	789.4	807.0	820.2	833.4	870.54	873.80
515.53	543.05	574.78	597.96	621.58	660.45	666.31	672.35	677.64	683.38	689.12	695.71
128.88	153.46	169.00	191.43	226.99	297.54	309.78	323.75	340.76	354.48	365.24	376.03
293.98	330.37	363.49	422.55	408.11	481.1	512.21	533.09	569.16	597.47	626.33	637.77
40.65	90.49	189.62	762.01	1382.56	2943.84	3443.50	4104.01	4788.97	5087.55	5949.17	7019.06
8.15	15.97	30.94	69.25	103.96	148.21	154.86	163.47	179.83	190.51	208.41	236.77
25.36	52.08	96.17	410.00	709.32	1494.36	1728.39	2045.88	2372.58	2387.12	2844.07	3323.79
7.14	22.44	62.51	282.76	569.28	1301.27	1560.25	1894.66	2236.56	2509.92	2896.69	3458.5
791	1675	3310	12797	22342	44871	51908	61315	70948	74761	86691	101370
					38542	44128	51416	58861	61533	69828	80478
151.74	180	189.56	174.5	153.08	103.5	107.07	106.93	110.16	107.24	100.25	97.81
8007	6704	6693	8038	2112	1038	935	912	957	959	929	828
46621	51849	60683	61446	80436	70733	67395	69501	78058	80081	76676	79815
18880	22742	26429	19824	24810	25551	26939	28207	29623	30204	30500	31385
6165	7980	11085	13240	9308	16339	18384	20389	18987	17870	15637	16127
190.16	166.1	159	147.58	172.16	165.28	152.47	151.94	170.43	178.61	192.53	203.23
9.53	11.16	14.93	19.21	25.24	30.74	29.25	26.68	29.52	30.92	31.79	32.50
14080	30400	47588	63294	91626	147800	157300	175944	182098	196520	208945	212277
					6589.51	8258.30	9846.47	11016.27	10870.32	12810.52	14881.98
61.79	128.59	292.26	1020.03	1543.57	5441.13	6975.46	8351.4	9379.58	9390.73	11081.04	12352.92
13.6	24.81	31.54	63.05	161.61	450.68	576.51	730.5	802.13	882.62	1224.48	1330.48
3905	6724	8119	16620	18607	24124	25810	28026	29084	30116	33772	34778
2070	2488	6522	10347	11459	19909	20924	22569	22550	22372	25915	28831
4.58	14.19	22.92	156.63	376.65	1277.8	1373.45	1583.78	1882.29	2195.17	2651.88	3100.02
20.54	47.81	98.17	299.35	514.68	978.43	1119.19	1308.29	1577.59	1804.93	2146.08	2548.36

a) Since 1990 the data on passenger traffic and freight traffic included non – transportation system, while data for previous years only included transportation system.
b) Since 1995 the data on foreign tourists included whole municipality, while data for previous years only included urban district.
c) The data on pre – tax profits of industrial enterprises included all state – owned enterprises and non – state – owned industrial enterprises with annual sales income of over 5 million yuan, before 1997, refer to enterprises at township and above level.

1－04 续表

指 标		Item	
境外旅游者人数	(万人次)	Number of Foreign Tourists	(10,000 person－times)
财政总收入	(亿元)	Total Financial Revenue	(100 million yuan)
财政支出合计(预算内)	(亿元)	Total Financial Expenditure	(100 million yuan)
金融机构存款余额	(亿元)	Deposits of Financial Institutions	(100 million yuan)
金融机构贷款余额	(亿元)	Loans of Financial Institutions	(100 million yuan)
城乡居民储蓄余额	(亿元)	Residents´Savings Deposit	(100 million yuan)
非私营单位在岗职工工资总额	(亿元)	Total Wages of Fully Employed Staff and Workers in Non－private Units	(100 million yuan)
非私营单位在岗职工平均工资	(元)	Average Wage of Fully Employed Staff and Workers in Non－private Units	(yuan)
市区居民消费价格指数	(以1978年为100)	Consumer Price Index in Urban District	(Year of 1978＝100)
市区商品零售价格指数	(以1978年为100)	Retail Price Index in Urban District	(Year of 1978＝100)
市区居民年人均可支配收入	(元)	Per Capita Annual Disposable Income in Urban District	(yuan)
农村居民年人均纯收入	(元)	Per Capita Annual Net Income in Rural Areas	(yuan)
高等学校在校学生数	(人)	Student Enrollment in Institutions of Higher Education	(person)
中等专业学校在校学生数	(人)	Student Enrollment in Secondary Specialized Schools	(person)
普通中学在校学生数	(人)	Student Enrollment in Secondary Schools	(person)
小学在校学生数	(人)	Student Enrollment in Primary Schools	(person)
卫生机构数	(个)	Number of Health Institutions	(unit)
#医院	(个)	Number of Hospitals	(unit)
卫生技术人员	(人)	Number of Medical Technical Personnel	(person)
#执业(助理)医师	(人)	Number of Certified Doctors(Include Assistant Doctors)	(person)
床位数	(张)	Number of Beds in Health Institutions	(unit)
#医院	(张)	Beds in Hospital	(unit)

注:2002年起医院数据不包括卫生院。

continued

1980	1985	1990	1995	2000	2005	2006	2007	2008	2009	2010	2011
12.5	23.84	38.83	44.13	70.71	151.36	182.02	208.60	221.33	230.40	275.71	306.31
11.85	18.65	25.25	55.13	142.85	520.79	624.49	788.42	910.55	1019.43	1245.43	1488.92
2.17	5.77	11.82	24.91	73.43	238.33	275.48	335.72	419.67	490.40	616.58	747.50
18.1	48.5	133.77	707.97	2088.47	6748.72	7855.55	9310.96	11333.35	14284.21	17084.35	18396.57
17.34	58.01	162.27	567.2	1686.64	5545.3	6603.86	8430.68	10069.05	13113.30	15078.73	16573.74
4.04	15.96	69.75	342.34	788.56	2191.66	2555.24	2634.83	3476.59	4286.92	4990.97	5547.48
6.79	13.01	27.79	89.05	126.75	297.02	381.17	495.48	641.64	754.91	933.06	1122.28
777	1266	2382	7156	14257	31069	32791	36496	40193	43947	48772	54408
109.24	140.21	246.68	503.06	611.07	623.07	630.55	652.62	684.60	675.00	701.33	734.99
110.28	142.61	256.45	476.99	504.42	470.47	471.41	486.02	515.18	507.97	526.76	549.94
521	1026	1985	6301	9668	16601	19027	21689	24104	26864	30035	34065
250	624	1171	3012	4894	7655	8515	9549	10692	11822	13186	15245
23545	36996	39866	63124	122386	351918	373563	392770	409559	429774	434811	446721
9453	16527	23564	42784	45238	20344	12540	8927	5514	4016	3999	4100
247734	244399	199940	257071	342533	362257	359704	361191	364758	359956	352997	340634
560244	414839	460514	513988	485679	458942	459529	456152	452143	445132	453897	465289
1381	1582	1738	1712	1599	2196	2570	2607	2544	2687	2819	2958
425	404	440	414	396	127	134	138	141	144	151	167
21110	25593	30990	34245	35487	42353	45375	49780	52379	56270	61117	65869
8311	11503	14483	16465	16317	17833	18831	20701	21223	22753	24345	25773
16317	19637	24121	26684	27166	33251	33972	36928	38114	40226	42828	45291
13478	15010	18879	21360	23303	25907	27186	29987	31416	33094	33611	39363

a) From 2002, figures of hospitals exclude health centers.

1－05 主要年份全市生产总值及发展指数(1978 年＝100)

Gross Domestic Product and its Indices in Main Years(Year of 1978＝100)

单位:万元 (10000 yuan)

年 份 Year	全市生产总值(当年价格) Gross Domestic Product (Current Price)	第一产业 Primary Industry	第二产业 Secondary Industry	第三产业 Tertiary Industry	人均生产总值(元)(按户籍) Per Capita GDP (yuan)	全市生产总值指数(%) Indices of Gross Domestic product(%) (1978＝100)	第一产业 Primary Industry	第二产业 Secondary Industry	第三产业 Tertiary Industry
1978	284046	63372	169344	51330	565	100.00	100.00	100.00	100.00
1979	335285	83852	194132	57301	659	113.33	114.23	114.00	110.01
1980	406508	81524	253545	71439	791	135.65	105.63	151.06	130.71
1981	468206	90955	287632	89619	904	154.04	108.74	172.17	162.30
1982	501854	108769	294725	98360	957	165.12	129.80	177.73	176.31
1983	558947	101106	334413	123428	1054	183.63	115.62	203.10	219.86
1984	694690	126443	405535	162712	1298	225.25	140.10	245.38	283.68
1985	904897	159684	520853	224360	1675	268.85	139.90	300.80	352.81
1986	1053589	177589	601277	274723	1917	299.88	145.01	335.28	409.85
1987	1260162	204366	718892	336904	2276	338.38	148.69	382.23	471.62
1988	1525427	256838	855305	413284	2717	363.26	145.46	419.82	497.15
1989	1662945	282746	896736	483463	2928	352.06	145.10	396.51	508.97
1990	1896216	309404	961673	625139	3310	372.37	154.40	422.20	528.01
1991	2279545	334024	1131088	814433	3952	439.77	161.12	492.38	669.52
1992	2900690	349033	1487838	1063819	4996	540.48	161.61	637.53	814.80
1993	4247094	419364	2264440	1563290	7263	703.16	171.15	878.66	1004.65
1994	5855239	575131	3143430	2136678	9924	888.09	185.01	1161.59	1225.67
1995	7620055	692510	4100008	2827537	12797	1064.82	198.15	1434.56	1445.06
1996	9066133	839985	4776225	3449923	15095	1203.25	208.85	1644.01	1621.36
1997	10363299	913611	5415017	4034671	17113	1360.88	223.05	1852.80	1861.32
1998	11348899	960558	5879589	4508752	18611	1513.30	244.02	2071.43	2060.48
1999	12252795	975821	6307510	4969464	19961	1667.66	257.44	2280.64	2287.13
2000	13825616	1039641	7093233	5692742	22342	1867.78	272.11	2565.72	2563.87
2001	15680138	1114569	7935809	6629760	25074	2095.65	292.25	2891.60	2884.40
2002	17818302	1146388	9018225	7653689	28150	2372.28	304.23	3276.18	3308.41
2003	20997744	1265890	10757812	8974042	32819	2732.87	322.48	3885.55	3725.27
2004	25431796	1322341	13182254	10927201	39293	3142.80	338.93	4534.44	4257.98
2005	29438430	1482145	14943581	13012704	44871	3551.36	350.45	5037.76	4956.29
2006	34434972	1548594	17283905	15602473	51908	4059.54	364.71	5672.80	5820.31
2007	41040117	1634719	20458811	18946588	61315	4651.74	372.78	6483.45	6761.14
2008	47889748	1798300	23725807	22365641	70948	5165.17	386.73	7062.80	7705.13
2009	50875529	1905093	23871200	25099237	74761	5680.15	398.74	7521.81	8799.61
2010	59491687	2084144	28440693	28966850	86691	6361.77	408.71	8462.04	9881.96
2011	70190579	2367708	33237887	34584984	101370	7004.31	418.93	9291.32	10968.98

注:1. 2008 年为经济普查正式数。

2. 2005－2007 已按经济普查数调整。

a) The data of 2008 were numbers of 2008 economic cencus.

b) The data of 2005 to 2007 had been adjusted auording to 2008 economic cencus.

1-06 主要年份市区生产总值及发展指数(1978年=100)

Gross Domestic Product and its Indices of Urban District in Main Years(Year of 1978=100)

单位:万元 (10000 yuan)

年份 Year	生产总值(当年价格) Gross Domestic Product (Current Price)	第一产业 Primary Industry	第二产业 Secondary Industry	第三产业 Tertiary Industry	人均生产总值(元)(按户籍) Per Capita GDP (yuan)	生产总值指数(%) Indices of Gross Domestic product(%) (1978=100)	第一产业 Primary Industry	第二产业 Secondary Industry	第三产业 Tertiary Industry
1978	141995	5215	106663	30117	1389	100.00	100.00	100.00	100.00
1979	167206	6527	126517	34162	1555	116.40	109.40	118.10	111.60
1980	208220	5943	159161	43116	1863	145.30	94.00	150.90	133.90
1981	229243	6165	171946	51132	2005	159.90	90.30	163.90	157.20
1982	248297	7327	183284	57686	2125	173.70	107.30	176.00	175.60
1983	282171	5938	200334	75899	2369	197.90	83.10	193.80	229.50
1984	353781	8469	244445	100867	2919	245.40	114.90	235.50	298.40
1985	448574	11233	293579	143762	3633	289.90	120.70	270.10	382.20
1986	513639	12245	324585	176809	4042	317.30	122.60	287.70	445.10
1987	605234	15408	370668	219158	4724	353.20	137.10	313.80	517.40
1988	708474	19602	425319	263553	5441	370.80	136.00	332.70	534.00
1989	772208	23869	435847	312492	5848	347.00	146.70	296.70	545.20
1990	896496	23919	470844	401733	6722	366.50	147.60	314.60	573.60
1991	1096628	25767	547949	522912	8158	426.00	151.40	356.30	691.10
1992	1413278	27611	712697	672969	10420	535.30	153.10	447.40	877.80
1993	2086571	36208	1052187	998176	15196	687.60	157.70	583.70	1117.40
1994	2788314	48257	1395127	1344931	19945	870.90	172.30	779.60	1335.30
1995	3697794	57784	1866784	1773226	25969	1041.60	183.50	945.70	1574.30
1996	4727377	110881	2356408	2260088	28552	1194.90	194.70	1103.60	1769.50
1997	5414265	130062	2630349	2653853	32227	1354.90	214.20	1230.30	2052.60
1998	5905726	134320	2786159	2985247	34620	1482.50	230.70	1337.20	2266.10
1999	6317335	145242	2915614	3256479	36394	1599.30	254.50	1431.10	2467.80
2000	7111586	145715	3278310	3687561	40127	1785.50	255.50	1596.70	2763.90
2001	12260891	582492	6026353	5652046	32607	2017.20	275.70	1805.30	3126.00
2002	14042278	605433	6901224	6535621	36640	2300.80	290.00	2038.60	3607.40
2003	16647332	665083	8343138	7639111	42675	2664.80	302.20	2448.40	4058.30
2004	20362738	664676	10368453	9329609	51241	3077.40	313.10	2873.90	4630.50
2005	23495459	732463	11582930	11180067	57934	3461.24	318.17	3141.49	5406.57
2006	27483121	755663	13254773	13472684	66731	3955.94	320.48	3493.88	6399.62
2007	32738842	773208	15546960	16418675	78541	4525.33	322.73	3948.39	7455.84
2008	38139834	830741	17926048	19383045	90400	5018.47	324.83	4266.45	8505.21
2009	40698687	874987	18120921	21702778	95342	5539.47	332.99	4563.27	9686.26
2010	47407788	941591	21452228	25013969	109708	6204.21	337.31	5124.56	10867.99
2011	55898574	1054368	24984624	29859582	127745	6824.63	343.72	5601.14	12052.60

注:1. 2008年为经济普查正式数。
2. 2005-2007已按经济普查数调整。
3. 从2001年起市区数据包括萧山区和余杭区。
a) The data of 2008 were numbers of 2008 economic census.
b) The data of 2005 to 2007 had been adjusted according to 2008 economic census.
c) Data in this table include Xiaoshan and Yuhang district since 2001.

1-07 主要年份全市生产总值指数(上年=100)

Indices of Gross Domestic Product in Main Years (Preceding Year = 100)

年 份 Year	生产总值 Gross Domestic Product	第一产业 Primary Industry	第二产业 Secondary Industry	第三产业 Tertiary Industry	人均生产总值 (按户籍) Per Capita GDP (Household registered)
1978	120.2	119.1	123.7	111.6	119.0
1979	113.3	114.2	114.0	110.0	112.1
1980	119.7	92.5	132.5	118.8	118.4
1981	113.6	102.9	114.0	124.2	112.6
1982	107.2	119.4	103.2	108.6	105.9
1983	111.2	89.1	114.3	124.7	109.9
1984	122.7	121.2	120.8	129.0	121.6
1985	119.4	99.9	122.6	124.4	118.2
1986	111.5	103.7	111.5	116.2	110.3
1987	112.8	102.5	114.0	115.1	111.3
1988	107.4	97.8	109.8	105.4	105.8
1989	96.9	99.8	94.4	102.4	95.8
1990	105.8	106.4	106.5	103.7	104.9
1991	118.1	104.4	116.6	126.8	117.3
1992	122.9	100.3	129.5	121.7	122.1
1993	130.1	105.9	137.8	123.3	129.1
1994	126.3	108.1	132.2	122.0	125.2
1995	119.9	107.1	123.5	117.9	118.8
1996	113.0	105.4	114.6	112.2	112.0
1997	113.1	106.8	112.7	114.8	112.1
1998	111.2	109.4	111.8	110.7	110.5
1999	110.2	105.5	110.1	111.0	109.4
2000	112.0	105.7	112.5	112.1	111.1
2001	112.2	107.4	112.7	112.5	111.1
2002	113.2	104.1	113.3	114.7	111.8
2003	115.2	106.0	118.6	112.6	114.0
2004	115.0	105.1	116.7	114.3	113.7
2005	113.0	103.4	111.1	116.4	111.5
2006	114.3	104.1	112.6	117.4	113.0
2007	114.6	102.2	114.3	116.2	113.6
2008	111.0	103.7	108.9	114.0	110.1
2009	110.0	103.1	106.5	114.2	109.1
2010	112.0	102.5	112.5	112.3	111.1
2011	110.1	102.5	109.8	111.0	109.1

注:1. 本表按可比价格计算。

2. 2005-2008 已按经济普查数调整。

a) The indices in this table are calculated at comparable prices.

b) The data of 2005 to 2008 had been adjusted according to 2008 economic census.

1-08 主要年份市区生产总值指数(上年=100)

Indices of Gross Domestic Product of Urban District in Main Years(Preceding Year=100)

年 份 Year	生产总值 Gross Domestic Product	第一产业 Primary Industry	第二产业 Secondary Industry	第三产业 Tertiary Industry	人均生产总值 (按户籍) Per Capita GDP (Household registered)
1978	120.1	118.8	122.3	113.6	118.0
1979	116.4	109.4	118.1	111.6	111.4
1980	124.8	85.9	127.8	120.0	119.7
1981	110.1	96.1	108.6	117.4	107.6
1982	108.6	118.8	107.4	111.7	106.3
1983	113.9	77.5	110.1	130.7	111.7
1984	124.0	138.2	121.5	130.0	121.8
1985	118.2	105.0	114.7	128.1	116.0
1986	109.4	101.6	106.5	116.7	107.4
1987	111.3	111.8	109.1	116.0	109.4
1988	105.0	99.2	106.0	103.2	103.3
1989	93.6	107.9	89.2	102.1	92.2
1990	105.6	100.6	106.0	105.2	104.6
1991	116.2	102.6	113.3	120.5	115.3
1992	125.7	101.1	125.6	127.0	124.5
1993	128.5	103.0	130.5	127.3	126.9
1994	126.6	109.3	133.6	119.5	124.4
1995	119.6	106.5	121.3	117.9	117.4
1996	114.7	106.1	116.7	112.4	105.3
1997	113.4	110.0	111.5	116.0	104.7
1998	109.4	107.7	108.7	110.4	107.8
1999	107.9	110.3	107.0	108.9	106.0
2000	111.6	100.4	111.6	112.0	109.3
2001	113.0	107.9	113.1	113.1	111.2
2002	114.1	105.2	112.9	115.4	111.9
2003	115.8	104.2	120.1	112.5	113.8
2004	115.5	103.6	117.4	114.1	113.4
2005	112.5	101.6	109.3	116.8	110.2
2006	114.3	100.7	111.2	118.4	112.5
2007	114.4	100.7	113.0	116.5	113.0
2008	110.9	100.7	108.1	114.1	109.5
2009	110.4	102.5	107.0	113.9	109.1
2010	112.0	101.3	112.3	112.2	110.7
2011	110.0	101.9	109.3	110.9	108.6

注:1. 本表按可比价格计算。
2. 2005-2008 已按经济普查数调整。

a) The indices in this table are calculated at comparable prices.

b) The data of 2005 to 2008 had been adjusted according to 2008 economic census.

1－09 全市生产
Composition of

单位:万元

行　　业	Sector	全 Whole 2011	全 Whole 为上年(%) As Compared with the Preceding Year(%)
全市生产总值	Gross Domestic Product	70190579	110.1
第一产业	Primary Industry	2367708	102.5
第二产业	Secondary Industry	33237887	109.8
工业	Industry	29439962	111.3
建筑业	Construction	3797925	98.6
第三产业	Tertiary Industry	34584984	111.0
交通运输、仓储及邮政业	Transportation,Storage and Post	1895390	109.3
批发和零售业	Wholesale & Retail Trade	6420660	113.6
住宿和餐饮业	Lodging and Catering	1195547	113.8
金融业	Banking and Insurance	7443188	112.8
房地产业	Real Estate	4344338	96.1
科学研究、技术服务和地质勘查业	Scientific Research,Technical Service and Geological Prospecting	1425830	115.4
居民服务和其他服务业	Service for the Residents and Other	612636	111.6
教育	Education	2025386	107.9
卫生、社会保障和社会福利业	Health Care,Sports & Social Welfare	1101967	112.6
文化、体育和娱乐业	Culture,Sports and Entertainment	563396	119.5
公共管理和社会组织	Public Management and Social Organizations	2308848	110.8

注:本表绝对数按当年价格计算,为上年(%)按可比价格计算。

总值构成(2011 年)

Gross Domestic Product(2011)

(10000 yuan)

市 City		其 中:市 区 Urban District			
比 重 (%) Proportion(%)		2011	为上年(%) As Compared with the Preceding Year(%)	比 重 (%) Proportion(%)	
2011	2010			2011	2010
100.0	100.0	55898574	110.0	100.0	100.0
3.3	3.5	1054368	101.9	1.9	2.0
47.4	47.8	24984624	109.3	44.7	45.2
42.0	42.1	21914726	111.1	39.2	39.3
5.4	5.7	3069898	97.5	5.5	5.9
49.3	48.7	29859582	110.9	53.4	52.8
2.7	2.7	1444460	107.4	2.6	2.6
9.1	8.6	5489146	111.8	9.8	9.4
1.7	1.7	985421	112.1	1.8	1.8
10.6	10.2	6671519	113.6	11.9	11.4
6.2	7.4	3671182	96.6	6.6	7.8
2.0	2.0	1372866	115.2	2.5	2.4
0.9	0.9	453389	107.1	0.8	0.8
2.9	3.1	1635331	107.7	2.9	3.1
1.6	1.6	943643	113.8	1.7	1.7
0.8	0.7	520542	121.6	0.9	0.8
3.3	3.4	1838289	109.5	3.3	3.5

a) Absolute figures in this table are calculated at current prices, while indices are calculated at comparable price.

1-10 分县(市)生产总值(2011年)

Gross Domestic Product by Region(2011)

单位:万元 (10000 yuan)

地区	Region	生产总值总计 Gross Domestic Product	第一产业 Primary Industry	第二产业 Secondary Industry	工业 Industry	建筑业 Construction	第三产业 Tertiary Industry	户籍人口人均GDP(元) Household Registered Per Capita GDP (yuan)	常住人口人均GDP(元) Long-term Residents Per Capita GDP (yuan)
全市	**Whole City**	**70190579**	**2367708**	**33237887**	**29439962**	**3797925**	**34584984**	**101370**	**80478**
市区	Urban District	55898574	1054368	24984624	21914726	3069898	29859582	127745	89330
萧山区	Xiaoshan	14459187	528775	8869836	8252210	617626	5060576	118106	95439
余杭区	Yuhang	7387153	436754	3879080	3476411	402669	3071319	85022	62960
桐庐县	Tonglu	2335219	183348	1419879	1279339	140540	731992	57858	57348
淳安县	Chun'an	1401746	248773	603912	465851	138061	549061	30779	41515
建德市	Jiande	2240123	238574	1270115	1169530	100585	731434	43846	51879
富阳市	Fuyang	4910986	331636	2972275	2778628	193647	1607075	75320	68260
临安市	Lin'an	3403931	311009	1987082	1831888	155194	1105840	64661	59922

注:1.本表按当年价格计算。

a) Data in this table are calculated at current prices.

1－11　主要指标占全省比重(2011年)

Proportion of Main Indicators in Whole Province(2011)

指　标 Item		全　省 Zhejiang Province	杭州市 Hangzhou City	杭州市占全省(%) Proportion of Hangzhou in Zhejiang(%)
年末常住人口 Long－term Residents(End of 2011)	(万人) (10000 persons)	5463	873.8	16.0
年末户籍人口 Household Registration Population(End of 2011)	(万人) (10000 persons)	4781.31	695.71	14.6
#非农业人口 Non－agriculture Population	(万人) (10000 persons)	1501.88	376.03	25.0
年末从业人员数 Total Number of Employed Persons	(万人) (10000 persons)	3674.1	637.77	17.4
生产总值 Gross Domestic Product	(亿元) (100 million yuan)	32000.1	7019.06	21.9
第一产业 Primary Industry	(亿元) (100 million yuan)	1580.57	236.77	15.0
第二产业 Secondary Industry	(亿元) (100 million yuan)	16404.18	3323.79	20.3
第三产业 Tertiary Industry	(亿元) (100 million yuan)	14015.35	3458.5	24.7
常住人均生产总值 Per Capita GDP of Long－term Residents	(元) (yuan)	58665	80478	－
农林牧渔业总产值 Gross Output Value of Farming, Forestry, Animal Husbandry and Fishery	(亿元) (100 million yuan)	2534.9	357.07	14.1
主要农产品产量 Output of Major Farm Products				
粮食 Grain	(万吨) (10000 tons)	781.6	97.8	12.5
棉花 Cotton	(万吨) (10000 tons)	3.24	0.08	2.5
蚕茧 Silk－worm Cocoons	(万吨) (10000 tons)	6.53	1.61	24.7
生猪年末存栏 Hogs in Stock at Year End	(万头) (10000 heads)	1281.93	203.23	15.9
猪牛羊肉产量 Output of Pork, Beef & Mutton	(万吨) (10000 tons)	138.82	57.92	41.7
淡水产品总产量 Freshwater Aquatic products	(万吨) (10000 tons)	104.83	21.26	20.3

1－11 续表1 continued 1

指　标 Item		全　省 Zhejiang Province	杭州市 Hangzhou City	杭州市占全省（%） Proportion of Hangzhou in Zhejiang（%）
规模以上工业企业利税总额 Total Pre－tax Profits of Industrial Enterprises above Designed Size	（亿元） （100 million yuan）	3929.97	1311.74	33.4
主要工业产品产量 Output of Major Industrial Products				
发电量 Electricity	（亿千瓦时） （100 million kwh）	2774.2	182.75	6.6
氢氧化钠（烧碱）（折100%） Caustic Soda（100% discount）	（万吨） （10000 tons）	126.72	20.31	16.0
碳酸钠（纯碱） Soda Ash	（万吨） （10000 tons）	24.36	24.36	100.0
合成氨 Synthetic Ammonia	（万吨） （10000 tons）	47.25	15.18	32.1
水泥 Cement	（万吨） （10000 tons）	12122.29	2030.59	16.8
平板玻璃 Plate Glass	（万重量箱） （10000 weight cases）	3995.69	476.62	11.9
钢材 Steels	（万吨） （10000 tons）	3135.31	964.88	30.8
化学纤维 Chemical Fiber	（万吨） （10000 tons）	1505.54	533.16	35.4
纱 Yarn	（万吨） （10000 tons）	198.77	56.58	28.5
自行车 Bicycles	（万辆） （10000 units）	1534.95	647.93	42.2
彩色电视机 Colour TV Sets	（万台） （10000 units）	497.3	11.34	2.3
电冰箱 Household Refrigerator	（万台） （10000 units）	626.79	104.75	16.7
洗衣机 Washing Machine	（万台） （10000 units）	1775.07	364.69	20.5
全社会交通运输客运量 Total Passenger Traffic	（万人次） （10000 person－times）	231900	34778	15.0
全社会交通运输货运量 Total Freight Traffic	（万吨） （10000 tons）	185677	28831	15.5

1－11 续表2 continued 2

指 标 Item		全 省 Zhejiang Province	杭州市 Hangzhou City	杭州市占全省(%) Proportion of Hangzhou in Zhejiang(%)
固定资产投资 Investment in Fixed Assets	(亿元) (100 million yuan)	14077.25	3100.02	22.1
社会消费品零售总额 Total Retail Sales of Consumer Goods	(亿元) (100 million yuan)	11930.6	2548.36	21.4
出口额 Total Exports	(亿美元) (100 million USD)	2163.6	415.21	19.2
实际利用外资 Foreign Capital Actually Used	(亿美元) (100 million USD)	153.98	47.22	30.7
境外旅游者人数 Number of International Tourists	(万人次) (10000 person－times)	773.69	306.31	39.6
财政总收入 Total Financial Revenue	(亿元) (100 million yuan)	5925	1488.92	25.1
地方财政预算内收入 Financial Revenue	(亿元) (100 million yuan)	3150.8	785.15	24.9
地方财政预算内支出 Financial Expenditure	(亿元) (100 million yuan)	3842.74	747.50	19.5
金融机构存款余额(本外币) Deposits of Financial Institutions	(亿元) (100 million yuan)	60893.14	18396.57	30.2
金融机构贷款余额(本外币) Loans of Financial Institutions	(亿元) (100 million yuan)	53239.34	16573.74	31.1
城乡居民储蓄存款余额 Residents´Savings Deposits	(亿元) (100 million yuan)	23945.23	5547.48	23.2
非私营单位在岗职工平均工资 Average Wage of Fully Employed Staff and Workers of Non－private Units	(元) (yuan)	46660	54408	－
城镇居民人均可支配收入 Per Capita Annual Disposable Income in Urban District	(元) (yuan)	30971	34065	－
农民人均纯收入 Per Capita Annual Net Income in Rural Areas	(元) (yuan)	13071	15245	－
高等学校在校学生数 Number of Institutions of Higher Education	(万人) (10000 persons)	95.9	44.67	46.6
中等专业学校在校学生数 Number of Secondary Specialized Schools	(万人) (10000 persons)	11.46	0.41	3.6
普通中学在校学生数 Number of Secondary Schools	(万人) (10000 persons)	244.5	34.06	13.9
小学在校学生数 Number of Primary Schools	(万人) (10000 persons)	344.1	46.53	13.5

1-12 国民经济主要指标人均水平(按户籍)

Major Per Capita Indicators of National Economy(Household registered)

指　　标 Item	1995	2000	2005	2006	2007	2008	2009	2010	2011
全市生产总值 (元) Gross Domestic Product (yuan)	12797	22342	44871	51908	61315	70948	74761	86691	101370
规模以上工业总产值 (元) Gross Industrial Output Value above Designatted Size (yuan)	17131	24943	82936	105150	124773	138958	137995	161310	176632
农林牧渔业总产值 (元) Gross Output Value of Farming, Forestry, Animal Husbandry and Fishery (yuan)	1673	2467	3345	3398	3693	4056	4258	4610	5165
社会消费品零售总额 (元) Total Retail Sales of Consumer Goods (yuan)	5027	8317	14869	16768	19368	23087	26523	31273	36804
财政总收入 (元) Financial Revenue (yuan)	926	2308	7938	9414	11780	13490	14980	18148	21503
#地方财政预算内收入 (元) Financial Revenue of Local Government (yuan)	387	1118	3818	4543	5851	6746	7653	9783	11339
地方财政预算内支出 (元) Financial Expenditure (yuan)	418	1187	3633	4119	5016	6217	7026	8985	10796
城镇居民可支配收入 (元) Annual Disposable Income in Urban District (yuan)	6301	9668	16601	19027	21689	24104	26864	30035	34065
城镇居民消费性支出 (元) Annual Living Expenditure in Urban District (yuan)	5559	7790	13438	14472	14896	16719	18595	20219	22642
农民纯收入 (元) Annual Net Income in Rural Area (yuan)	3012	4894	7655	8515	9546	10692	11822	13186	15245
农民消费性支出 (元) Annual Living Expenditure in Rural Area (yuan)	2373	3393	6004	6674	7568	8446	9065	10267	12125

1－13　企业家信心指数(2011 年)
Expectation Indices of Entrepreneurs(2011)

单位:点　　(point)

指　标	Item	第一季度 1st. Quarter	第二季度 2nd. Quarter	第三季度 3rd. Quarter	第四季度 4th. Quarter
全市	**Total**	**129.37**	**122.71**	**116.64**	**112.20**
按行业分	**Grouped by Sector**				
工业	Industry	136.10	128.41	118.44	117.30
建筑业	Construction	135.84	112.09	110.50	102.54
交通运输、仓储及邮电通信业	Transportation, Storage and Post	111.65	122.00	108.21	108.21
批发零售贸易业	Wholesale and Retail Trade	127.57	116.73	118.48	99.14
房地产业	Real Estate	86.76	70.38	74.10	67.44
社会服务业	Social Services	119.33	135.89	128.57	132.20
信息传输、计算机服务和软件业	Information Transmission, Computer Service and Software	141.66	154.11	155.83	147.51
住宿和餐饮业	Lodging and Catering	126.56	132.59	132.01	123.04
按经济类型分	**Grouped by Status of Registration**				
国有企业	State－owned	126.02	119.11	125.72	115.83
集体企业	Collective－owned	133.33	155.56	142.73	111.11
有限责任公司	Limited－liability Companies	124.62	115.85	114.72	103.35
股份有限公司	Share Holding Ltd. Companies	142.88	137.40	120.42	122.42
港、澳、台投资企业	Enterprises With Investment from Hong Kong, Macao and Taiwan	116.17	107.05	104.09	97.49
外商投资企业	Enterprises With Foreign Investment	146.09	140.70	133.53	139.84
按企业规模分	**Grouped by Size of Enterprises**				
大型企业	Large	138.40	139.32	126.96	116.15
中型企业	Medium	133.02	124.64	119.63	114.95
小型企业	Small	114.63	108.64	108.07	100.63

1-14 企业景气指数(2011 年)
Expectation Indices of Enterprises(2011)

单位:点 (point)

指标	Item	第一季度 1st. Quarter	第二季度 2nd. Quarter	第三季度 3rd. Quarter	第四季度 4th. Quarter
全市	**Total**	**127.97**	**129.88**	**125.17**	**120.72**
按行业分	**Grouped by Sector**				
工业	Industry	126.12	128.33	119.73	115.89
建筑业	Construction	115.96	124.88	114.14	132.65
交通运输、仓储及邮电通信业	Transportation, Storage and Post	128.89	128.89	132.34	101.31
批发零售贸易业	Wholesale and Retail Trade	145.10	137.54	147.30	134.80
房地产业	Real Estate	107.61	108.70	108.74	86.81
社会服务业	Social Services	135.42	139.09	138.65	145.10
信息传输、计算机服务和软件业	Information Transmission, Computer Service and Software	155.42	155.03	153.33	162.61
住宿和餐饮业	Lodging and Catering	126.56	144.49	139.73	133.38
按经济类型分	**Grouped by Status of Registration**				
国有企业	State - owned	115.70	126.78	121.77	128.90
集体企业	Collective - owned	100.00	111.11	111.11	100.00
有限责任公司	Limited - liability Companies	124.92	128.66	126.19	115.93
股份有限公司	Share Holding Ltd. Companies	155.33	159.39	143.64	146.54
港、澳、台投资企业	Enterprises With Investment from Hong Kong, Macao and Taiwan	122.06	113.93	119.23	97.64
外商投资企业	Enterprises With Foreign Investment	136.75	147.08	135.02	123.45
按企业规模分	**Grouped by Size of Enterprises**				
大型企业	Large	149.02	159.55	148.39	139.97
中型企业	Medium	127.83	128.91	123.36	118.22
小型企业	Small	115.24	114.81	117.39	113.13

1－15 市区分月气象概况(2011 年)

Monthly Meteorological Conditions in Urban District(2011)

月 份	Month	平均气温(度) Average Temperature(℃)	日照时数(小时) Sunshine Hours(hours)	降雨天数(天) Rainfall Days (day)	降水量(毫米) Precipitation(mm.)
全 年	**Annual Total**	**17.2**	**1496.1**	**134**	**1359.9**
1 月	January	1.4	95.3	12	68
2 月	February	6.7	106.6	5	19.6
3 月	March	10	148.8	9	43.8
4 月	April	17.3	173.4	9	55.4
5 月	May	22.2	172.5	8	71.1
6 月	June	24.9	77.9	20	541.4
7 月	July	30.2	185.2	12	129.9
8 月	August	28.5	143.2	20	222.4
9 月	September	24.5	110.7	8	60.4
10 月	October	18.6	85.0	11	51.5
11 月	November	15.9	95.3	13	55.8
12 月	December	6.3	102.2	7	40.6

1－16 气　象
Meteorological

指　标		Item		市　区 Urban District	#萧山区 Xiaoshan
一、气　温		The Atmospheric Temperature			
全年平均气温	（度）	Annual Average Temperature	（℃）	17.2	17.3
极端最高气温	（度）	The Highest Temperature of the Year	（℃）	38.4	38.8
出现日期	（日/月）	Date	（d/m）	26/7	30/7
极端最低气温	（度）	The Lowest Temperature of the Year	（℃）	－5	－5.8
出现日期	（日/月）	Date	（d/m）	17/1	16/1
二、降　雨		Rainfall			
本年降雨日数	（日）	Total Rainy Days	（day）	134	138
全年降雨总量	（毫米）	Annual Rainfall	（millimeters）	1359.9	1355.1
最长连续降雨日数	（日）	Longest Consecutive Days of Rain	（day）	11	11
最长连续降雨总量	（毫米）	Rainfall	（millimeters）	321.9	290.3
最长连续降雨起止日期	（日/月）	Start/End	（d/m）	9－19/6	9－19/6
日最大降雨量	（毫米）	Maximum Daily Rainfall	（millimeters）	64	65.8
出现日期	（日/月）	Date	（d/m）	31/7	19/6
三、全年日照总时数	**（小时）**	**Total Sunshine Hours**	**（hours）**	**1496.1**	**1781.9**
四、霜　雪		Frost & Snow			
全年降霜日数	（日）	Annual Frost Days	（day）	40	49
初霜日期	（日/月）	Start Date	（d/m）	3/12	3/12
终霜日期	（日/月）	End Date	（d/m）	30/3	30/3

概　　况(2011 年)
Conditions by Region(2011)

桐庐县 Tonglu	淳安县 Chun'an	建德市 Jiande	富阳市 Fuyang	临安市 Lin'an
16.7	17.1	16.7	16.8	16
38	36.8	38.8	38.6	37.7
2 天/7	24/7	31/7	30/7	26/7
-5.9	-4.6	-4.7	-6.1	-7.7
16/1	16/1	16/1	17/1	17/1
137	130	143	137	130
1463.7	1407.5	1489.6	1310.6	1385.7
11	11	12	11	11
381.8	409.6	410.2	323.2	339.2
9-20/6	9-19/6	9-20/6	9-19/6	9-19/6
105.6	114.2	135.7	68.7	76.6
15/6	15/6	15/6	11/5	14/6
1522.9	**1814.4**	**1775.9**	**1674**	**1755.7**
35	31	42	38	45
10/12	10/12	4/12	3/12	3/12
9/3	9/3	9/3	2/3	8/3

主要统计指标解释

生产总值(GDP) 指一个国家(或地区)所有常住单位在一定时期内生产活动的最终成果。生产总值有三种表现形态,即价值形态、收入形态和产品形态。从价值形态看,它是所有常住单位在一定时期内生产的全部货物和服务价值超过同期中间投入的全部非固定资产货物和服务价值的差额,即所有常住单位的增加值之和;从收入形态看,它是所有常住单位在一定时期内创造并分配给常住单位和非常住单位的初次收入分配之和;从产品形态看,它是所有常住单位在一定时期内最终使用的货物和服务价值与货物和服务净出口价值之和。在实际核算中,生产总值有三种计算方法,即生产法、收入法和支出法。三种方法分别从不同的方面反映生产总值及其构成。

三次产业 是根据社会生产活动历史发展的顺序对产业结构的划分,产品直接取自自然界的部门称为第一产业,对初级产品进行再加工的部门称为第二产业,为生产和消费提供各种服务的部门称为第三产业。它是世界上较为通用的产业结构分类,但各国的划分不尽一致。我国的三次产业划分是:

第一产业:农业(包括种植业、林业、牧业、渔业和农林牧渔服务业)。

第二产业:工业(包括采矿业,制造业,电力、燃气及水的生产和供应业)和建筑业。

第三产业:除第一、第二产业以外的其他各业。由于第三产业包括的行业多、范围广,根据我国的实际情况,第三产业可分为两大部分:一是流通部门,二是服务部门。具体又分为四个层次:

第一层次:流通部门,包括交通运输、仓储及邮电通信业,批发和零售贸易、餐饮业。

第二层次:为生产和生活服务的部门,包括金融、保险业,地质勘查业、水利管理业,房地产业,社会服务业,农、林、牧、渔服务业,交通运输辅助业,综合技术服务业等。

第三层次:为提高科学文化水平和居民素质服务的部门,包括教育、文化艺术及广播电影电视业,卫生、体育和社会福利业,科学研究等。

第四层次:为社会公共需要服务的部门,包括国家机关、政党机关和社会团体以及军队、警察等。

降水量 从天空降落到地面的液态或固态(经融化后)降水,未经蒸发、渗透、流失而在水平面上积聚的深度。降水量以毫米为单位。

空气的温度(简称气温) 表示空气冷热程度的物理量。

日照时数 太阳在一地实际照射地面的时数。

Explanatory Notes on Main Statistical Indicators

Gross Domestic Product (GDP) refers to the final products of all resident units in a country (or a region) during a certain period of time. Gross domestic product is expressed in three different forms, i. e. value, income, and products respectively. The form of value refers to the total value of all products and services produced by all resident units during a certain period of time minus total value of intermediate input of materials and services of the nature of non – fixed assets or the summation of the value – added of all resident units; the form of income includes all the income created by all resident units and distributed primarily to all resident and non – resident units; the form of products refers to the value of all final goods and services for final use by all resident units plus the value of net exports of goods and services during a given period of time. In the practice of national accounting, gross domestic product is calculated with three approaches, i. e. production approach, income approach, and expenditure approach, which reflect gross domestic product and its composition from different aspects.

Three Industries Industry structure has been classified according to the historical sequence of development. Primary industry refers to extraction of natural resources; secondary industry involves processing of primary products; and tertiary industry provides services of various kinds for production and consumption. The above classification is universal although it varies to someextent from country to country. Industry in China comprises:

Primary industry: agriculture (including farming, forestry, animal husbandry and fishery and services for agriculture sector)

Secondary industry: industry (including mining and quarrying, manufacturing, production and supply of electricity, water and gas) and construction.

Tertiary industry: all other industries not included in primary of secondary industry.

Due to the fact that tertiary industry involves in a large variety of industries in China, it is divided into two sectors: circulation sector and service sector and further into four levels:

The first level: circulation sector, including transportation, storage, postal and telecommunications, wholesale and retail trade and catering trade.

The second level: service sector providing services for production and consumption, including banking, insurance, geological survey, water conservancy management, real estates, service for residents, service for agriculture, forestry, animal husbandry, fishery, subsidiary services for transportation and communications, comprehensive technical services, etc.

The third level: service sector for upgrading scientific, educational and cultural level of the people, including education, culture and arts, broadcasting, movies, television, public health, sports, social welfare and scientific research, etc.

The fourth level: sector providing services for public needs, including government agencies, political parties, social organizations, military and police service.

Precipitation refers to the depth of rainfall onto the ground (as well as liquefied from solid forms) from above the air prior to its vaporization, seepage, running off.

It is calculated in the unit of millimeter (mm).

Air Temperature refers to the physical quantity reflecting the extent of coldness and hotness of the air.

Duration of sunshine refers to the real time for the ground to receive sunshine at a certain place.

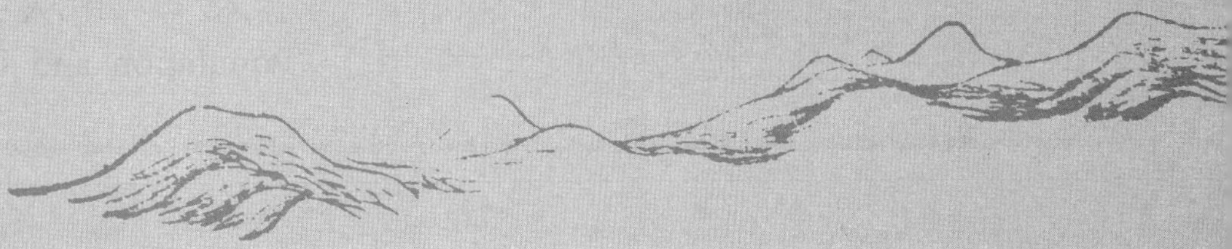

第 二 篇
CHAPTER-2

人口和从业人员
POPULATION AND EMPLOYMENT

2 人口和从业人员
Population and Employment

主要统计指标
Major Statistical Indicators

年末总户数	Total Households(year-end)	218.26	万户	(10, 000 Subscribers)
为上年	As Compared with the Preceding Year	100.8	%	(%)
年末总人口	Total Population(year-end)	695.71	万人	(10, 000 persons)
为上年	As Compared with the Preceding Year	101.0	%	(%)
#男性	Male	349.09	万人	(10, 000 persons)
为上年	As Compared with the Preceding Year	100.7	%	(%)
#非农业人口	Non-agriculture Population	376.03	万人	(10, 000 persons)
为上年	As Compared with the Preceding Year	103.0	%	(%)
年末市区总人口	Population of Urban District(year-end)	440.34	万人	(10, 000 persons)
为上年	As Compared with the Preceding Year	101.3	%	(%)
#男性	Male	219.86	万人	(10, 000 persons)
为上年	As Compared with the Preceding Year	101.0	%	(%)
#非农业人口	Non-agriculture Population	317.63	万人	(10, 000 persons)
为上年	As Compared with the Preceding Year	103.3	%	(%)
人口自然增长率	Natural Growth Rate	4.64	‰	(‰)
年末从业人员	Number of Employed Persons(year-end)	637.77	万人	(10, 000 persons)
为上年	As Compared with the Preceding Year	101.8	%	(%)

2－01 历次普查常住人口情况

Long－term Residents in the Past Population Census

单位:万人 (10000 person)

地 区 Region		第一次人口普查 1953.7.1 the First Population Census (1953.7.1)	第二次人口普查 1964.7.1 the Second Population Census (1964.7.1)	第三次人口普查 1982.7.1 the Third Population Census (1982.7.1)	第四次人口普查 1990.7.1 the Fourth Population Census (1991.7.1)	第五次人口普查 2000.11.1 the Fifth Population Census (2000.11.1)	第六次人口普查 2010.11.1 the Sixth Population Census (2010.11.1)
杭州市	**Hangzhou**	**301.13**	**421.90**	**526.05**	**583.21**	**687.87**	**870.04**
杭州市区	Urban District	172.26	243.65	305.77	346.76	450.23	624.20
上城区	Shangcheng	－	－	－	21.10	33.51	34.46
下城区	Xiacheng	－	－	－	25.66	41.24	52.61
江干区	Jianggan	－	－	－	36.12	56.54	99.88
拱墅区	Gongshu	－	－	－	29.34	42.93	55.19
西湖区	Xihu	－	－	－	35.40	59.33	82.00
高新(滨江)区	Hi－Tech(Binjiang)	－	－	－	－	11.59	31.90
萧山区	Xiaoshan	56.32	82.34	106.11	113.06	123.33	151.13
余杭区	Yuhang	52.28	64.96	80.50	86.08	81.77	117.03
桐庐县	Tonglu	19.73	26.20	34.83	37.66	37.81	40.64
淳安县	Chun'an	27.49	38.66	42.03	43.55	38.23	33.68
建德市	Jiande	26.42	38.15	43.64	47.63	47.31	43.08
富阳市	Fuyang	29.22	39.66	54.13	58.07	62.86	71.77
临安市	Lin'an	26.01	35.57	45.65	49.55	51.42	56.67

2-02 主要年份全市总户数与总人口数
Households and Population in Main Years

年份 Year	总户数（万户） Total Households (10000 households)	总人口数（万人） Total Population (10000 persons)	#非农业人口（万人） Non-agriculture Population (10000 persons)	按性别分 By Sex 男（万人） Male (10000 persons)	女（万人） Female (10000 persons)
1978	117.89	505.55	116.06	260.74	244.81
1979	116.61	511.83	124.60	263.97	247.86
1980	119.11	515.53	128.88	266.02	249.51
1981	125.96	520.73	134.56	268.69	252.04
1982	131.53	528.06	139.94	272.72	255.34
1983	135.55	533.06	143.34	275.64	257.41
1984	139.24	537.49	147.46	278.04	259.45
1985	145.23	543.05	153.46	281.11	261.94
1986	151.59	549.53	157.19	284.57	264.96
1987	157.66	557.63	161.12	288.70	268.93
1988	164.41	565.04	164.87	292.21	272.83
1989	169.09	570.98	167.28	295.15	275.83
1990	171.94	574.78	169.00	297.02	277.76
1991	174.78	578.73	171.25	298.85	279.88
1992	177.68	582.40	174.03	300.63	281.77
1993	179.17	587.10	179.11	303.03	284.07
1994	180.65	592.93	186.50	306.00	286.93
1995	182.55	597.96	191.43	308.25	289.71
1996	184.33	603.22	196.68	310.76	292.46
1997	186.28	607.96	204.39	313.02	294.94
1998	187.80	611.64	210.52	314.69	296.95
1999	191.60	616.05	219.05	316.63	299.42
2000	193.48	621.58	227.00	319.09	302.49
2001	195.56	629.14	237.77	322.78	306.36
2002	198.27	636.81	252.02	326.62	310.19
2003	201.12	642.78	263.67	329.04	313.74
2004	204.52	651.68	282.58	332.62	319.06
2005	207.42	660.45	297.54	336.12	324.33
2006	209.91	666.31	309.78	338.23	328.08
2007	211.99	672.35	323.75	340.50	331.85
2008	213.74	677.64	340.76	342.45	335.19
2009	215.28	683.38	354.48	344.51	338.87
2010	216.51	689.12	365.24	346.56	342.56
2011	218.26	695.71	376.03	349.09	346.62

注:按公安户籍人口统计。

a) Figures in this table are based on the household registered statistics which published by Public Security Bureau.

2-03 主要年份市区总户数与总人口数

Urban District Households and Population in Main Years

年份 Year	总户数 (万户) Total Households (10000 households)	总人口数 (万人) Total Population (10000 persons)	#非农业人口(万人) Non-agriculture Population (10000 persons)	按性别分 By Sex 男(万人) Male (10000 persons)	按性别分 By Sex 女(万人) Female (10000 persons)
1978	25.52	104.53	78.73	53.95	50.58
1979	26.23	110.50	85.05	57.09	53.41
1980	27.23	113.08	87.93	58.56	54.52
1981	29.88	115.59	90.53	59.96	55.63
1982	31.24	118.05	92.72	61.28	56.77
1983	32.69	120.13	94.94	62.43	57.70
1984	34.07	122.29	97.34	63.63	58.66
1985	35.36	124.67	100.01	64.96	59.71
1986	37.02	127.07	102.59	66.29	60.78
1987	38.70	129.16	104.09	67.38	61.78
1988	40.05	131.26	107.30	68.46	62.80
1989	41.19	132.84	108.88	69.28	63.56
1990	42.26	133.89	109.97	69.75	64.14
1991	42.98	134.97	111.20	70.33	64.64
1992	43.63	136.30	112.70	71.08	65.22
1993	44.55	138.33	115.13	72.22	66.11
1994	45.04	141.27	118.48	73.82	67.45
1995	46.06	143.52	121.38	74.91	68.61
1996	52.39	166.73	128.76	87.15	79.58
1997	53.14	169.29	131.76	88.53	80.76
1998	53.92	171.89	134.62	89.86	82.03
1999	54.64	175.27	139.29	91.65	83.62
2000	55.34	179.18	143.69	93.64	85.54
2001	115.81	379.49	193.26	194.59	184.90
2002	117.11	387.01	205.98	198.47	188.54
2003	119.01	393.19	216.13	201.14	192.05
2004	120.56	401.59	233.08	204.43	197.16
2005	122.02	409.52	245.56	207.70	201.82
2006	123.31	414.18	256.42	209.45	204.73
2007	124.40	419.50	269.30	211.59	207.91
2008	125.56	424.30	285.11	213.54	210.76
2009	126.92	429.44	297.83	215.56	213.88
2010	128.43	434.82	307.52	217.65	217.16
2011	130.14	440.34	317.63	219.86	220.48

注:从2001年起市区数据包括萧山区和余杭区。

a) Figures in this table include Xiaoshan and Yuhang district since 2001.

2-04 分地区总户数与总人口数(2011年末)
Households and Population by Region(End of 2011)

地 区 Region	总户数 (万户) Total Households (10000 households)	总人口数 (万人) Total Population (10000 persons)	#非农业人口(万人) Non-agriculture Population (10000 persons)	按性别分 By Sex 男(万人) Male (10000 persons)	女(万人) Female (10000 persons)
全 市 Whole City	**218.26**	**695.71**	**376.03**	**349.09**	**346.62**
市 区 Urban District	130.14	440.34	317.63	219.86	220.48
上城区 Shangcheng	11.52	32.79	32.79	16.48	16.31
下城区 Xiacheng	12.70	40.37	40.37	20.44	19.93
江干区 Jianggan	12.10	45.28	43.89	22.65	22.63
拱墅区 Gongshu	10.73	31.40	31.40	15.91	15.49
西湖区 Xihu	16.88	63.97	57.30	32.78	31.19
高新(滨江)区 Hi-Tech(Binjiang)	4.28	15.99	14.85	8.11	7.88
萧山区 Xiaoshan	37.62	122.87	50.64	60.42	62.45
余杭区 Yuhang	24.31	87.67	46.39	43.07	44.60
桐庐县 Tonglu	14.97	40.47	12.46	20.36	20.11
淳安县 Chun'an	14.92	45.66	7.92	23.31	22.35
建德市 Jiande	17.22	51.16	13.01	26.15	25.01
富阳市 Fuyang	22.07	65.38	13.98	33.06	32.32
临安市 Lin'an	18.94	52.70	11.03	26.35	26.35

2-05 分地区户籍人口年龄构成(2011 年末)

Age Structure of Household Registered Population by Region(End of 2011)

地　区 Region	18 岁以下 under 18 years old		18-35 岁 18～35 years old		35-60 岁 35～60 years old		60 岁以上 over 60 years old	
	人数(万人) Number of people (10000 person)	占总人口% of the total population	人数(万人) Number of people (10000 person)	占总人口% of the total population	人数(万人) Number of people (10000 person)	占总人口% of the total population	人数(万人) Number of people (10000 person)	占总人口% of the total population
全　市 Whole City	**105.26**	**15.1**	**177.55**	**25.5**	**289.18**	**41.6**	**123.72**	**17.8**
市　区 Urban District	65.53	14.9	117.81	26.8	177.00	40.2	79.99	18.2
上城区 Shangcheng	3.28	10.0	8.29	25.3	13.20	40.3	8.02	24.5
下城区 Xiacheng	4.62	11.4	12.34	30.6	15.06	37.3	8.36	20.7
江干区 Jianggan	6.60	14.6	15.09	33.3	16.30	36.0	7.28	16.1
拱墅区 Gongshu	3.91	12.5	8.19	26.1	12.67	40.4	6.62	21.1
西湖区 Xihu	9.40	14.7	22.76	35.6	22.55	35.3	9.26	14.5
高新(滨江)区 Hi-Tech(Binjiang)	2.95	18.4	5.26	32.9	5.71	35.7	2.07	12.9
萧山区 Xiaoshan	20.95	17.1	26.28	21.4	52.82	43.0	22.82	18.6
余杭区 Yuhang	13.82	15.8	19.60	22.4	38.69	44.1	15.56	17.7
桐庐县 Tonglu	6.24	15.4	9.49	23.4	17.56	43.4	7.18	17.7
淳安县 Chun'an	7.24	15.9	10.45	22.9	20.47	44.8	7.49	16.4
建德市 Jiande	7.70	15.1	12.05	23.6	22.12	43.2	9.29	18.2
富阳市 Fuyang	11.12	17.0	15.33	23.4	28.34	43.3	10.59	16.2
临安市 Lin'an	7.42	14.1	12.42	23.6	23.68	44.9	9.17	17.4

2-06 主要年份全市人口自然变动情况
Natural Changes of Population in Main Years

年份 Year	出生 Birth		死亡 Death		自然增长 Natural Growth	
	人数(人) Birth Population (person)	出生率(‰) Birth Rate(‰)	人数(人) Death Population (person)	死亡率(‰) Death Rate(‰)	人数(人) Natural Growth Population (person)	自然增长率(‰) Natural Growth Rate(‰)
1978	73550	14.63	29928	2.95	43622	8.68
1979	71442	14.04	29500	5.80	41942	8.24
1980	52145	10.15	30727	5.98	21418	4.17
1981	73015	14.09	31352	6.05	41663	8.04
1982	82910	15.81	30805	5.87	52105	9.94
1983	69940	13.18	33598	6.33	36342	6.85
1984	60091	11.23	33070	6.18	27021	5.05
1985	66757	12.36	33715	6.24	33042	6.12
1986	84702	15.50	33576	6.15	51126	9.35
1987	94127	17.00	33238	6.00	60889	11.00
1988	85472	15.23	35356	6.30	50116	8.93
1989	81048	14.27	34031	5.99	47017	8.28
1990	76579	13.37	34977	6.11	41602	7.26
1991	66144	11.47	33534	5.81	32610	5.66
1992	61708	10.63	34681	5.97	27027	4.66
1993	62465	10.68	34127	5.84	28338	4.84
1994	63580	10.78	35099	5.95	28481	4.83
1995	62586	10.51	36186	6.08	26400	4.43
1996	63680	10.60	25417	5.90	28263	4.70
1997	58471	9.65	34663	5.72	23808	3.93
1998	53951	8.85	38302	6.28	15649	2.57
1999	59085	9.63	36866	6.01	22219	3.62
2000	62300	10.07	40218	6.50	22082	3.57
2001	52088	8.33	33827	5.41	18261	2.92
2002	53064	8.38	35867	5.67	17197	2.72
2003	51420	8.04	36662	5.73	14758	2.31
2004	59940	9.26	34078	5.27	25862	3.99
2005	57233	8.72	35417	5.39	21816	3.33
2006	57790	8.71	38892	5.86	18898	2.85
2007	60296	9.01	37833	5.65	22463	3.36
2008	61332	9.09	42648	6.32	18684	2.77
2009	62441	9.18	39159	5.76	23282	3.42
2010	69606	10.14	46193	6.73	23413	3.41
2011	70337	10.16	38225	5.52	32112	4.64

注:本表按公安部门统计。

a) Figures in this table are based on the Public Security Bureau.

2-07 主要年份市区人口自然变动情况
Natural Changes of Urban Population in Main Years

年 份 Year	出 生 Birth		死 亡 Death		自然增长 Natural Growth	
	人数(人) Birth Population (person)	出生率(‰) Birth Rate(‰)	人数(人) Death Population (person)	死亡率(‰) Death Rate(‰)	人数(人) Natural Growth Population (person)	自然增长率(‰) Natural Growth Rate(‰)
1978	11923	11.56	6449	6.25	5474	5.31
1979	13184	12.26	5808	5.40	7376	6.86
1980	9708	8.68	6511	5.82	3197	2.86
1981	14938	13.06	6599	5.77	8339	7.29
1982	18092	15.49	6494	5.56	11598	9.93
1983	17107	14.36	6949	5.84	10158	8.52
1984	16257	13.41	6892	5.69	9365	7.72
1985	15824	12.81	7403	6.84	8421	6.82
1986	17120	13.60	6865	5.45	10255	8.15
1987	18701	14.60	7070	5.52	11631	9.08
1988	18503	14.21	7503	5.76	11000	8.45
1989	15868	12.02	6985	5.29	8883	6.73
1990	14085	10.56	7490	5.62	6595	4.94
1991	10195	7.58	7025	5.22	3170	2.36
1992	9994	7.37	7259	5.35	2735	2.02
1993	10099	7.35	7196	5.24	2903	2.11
1994	9918	7.09	7082	5.06	2836	2.03
1995	9806	6.89	7367	5.17	2439	1.72
1996	12098	7.80	8221	5.30	3877	2.50
1997	12304	7.32	8630	5.13	3674	2.19
1998	11714	6.87	9060	5.31	2654	1.56
1999	13694	7.89	8148	4.69	5546	3.20
2000	15058	8.50	10996	6.20	4062	2.30
2001	30902	8.22	19439	5.17	11463	3.05
2002	33156	8.65	19922	5.20	13234	3.45
2003	29019	7.44	21176	5.43	7843	2.01
2004	34858	8.77	19445	4.89	15413	3.88
2005	34056	8.39	21310	5.25	12746	3.14
2006	33260	8.08	21156	5.14	12104	2.94
2007	37029	8.88	20051	4.81	16978	4.07
2008	38703	9.17	21428	5.08	17275	4.09
2009	40293	9.44	22178	5.20	18115	4.24
2010	47052	10.89	25404	5.88	21648	5.01
2011	47256	10.80	22140	5.06	25116	5.74

注:从2001年起市区数据包括萧山区和余杭区。
a) Figures in this table include Xiaoshan and Yuhang district since 2001.

2-08 分地区人口自然变动情况(2011 年末)
Natural Changes of Population by Region(End of 2011)

地区 Region	出生 Birth		死亡 Death		自然增长 Natural Growth	
	人数(人) Birth Population (person)	出生率(‰) Birth Rate(‰)	人数(人) Death Population (person)	死亡率(‰) Death Rate(‰)	人数(人) Natural Growth Population (person)	自然增长率(‰) Natural Growth Rate(‰)
全市 Whole City	**70337**	**10.16**	**38225**	**5.52**	**32112**	**4.64**
市区 Urban District	47256	10.80	22140	5.06	25116	5.74
上城区 Shangcheng	2695	8.23	2065	6.31	630	1.92
下城区 Xiacheng	4124	10.25	1859	4.62	2265	5.63
江干区 Jianggan	5858	13.02	1731	3.85	4127	9.17
拱墅区 Gongshu	3565	11.41	1733	5.55	1832	5.86
西湖区 Xihu	7417	11.69	2081	3.28	5336	8.41
高新(滨江)区 Hi-Tech(Binjiang)	2469	15.83	561	3.60	1908	12.24
萧山区 Xiaoshan	11192	9.14	6935	5.66	4257	3.48
余杭区 Yuhang	9936	11.44	5175	5.96	4761	5.48
桐庐县 Tonglu	3462	8.58	2719	6.74	743	1.84
淳安县 Chun'an	3973	8.72	3121	6.85	852	1.87
建德市 Jiande	4400	8.61	3452	6.76	948	1.86
富阳市 Fuyang	6274	9.62	3898	5.98	2376	3.64
临安市 Lin'an	4972	9.45	2895	5.50	2077	3.95

2－09　分地区人口机械变动情况(2011 年)

Mechanical Changes of Population by Region(2011)

单位:人　　(person)

地　　区 Region	本年迁入人数 Number of the Persons Moved in(person)		本年迁出人数 Number of the Persons Moved Out(person)		本年净迁入人数 Net Persons Moved in
	省　内 From Zhejiang Province	省　外 From Other Provinces	省　内 To Zhejiang Province	省　外 To Other Provinces	
全　市 Whole City	**42622**	**56813**	**42205**	**21640**	**35590**
市　区 Urban District	29696	47082	26818	18829	31131
上城区 Shangcheng	1739	2478	493	813	2911
下城区 Xiacheng	3057	4255	2642	2088	2582
江干区 Jianggan	6122	9846	9326	5540	1102
拱墅区 Gongshu	2661	1989	2172	660	1818
西湖区 Xihu	7265	12179	7184	6728	5532
高新(滨江)区 Hi－Tech(Binjiang)	2288	2958	2516	750	1980
萧山区 Xiaoshan	2286	4676	1194	1186	4582
余杭区 Yuhang	4278	8701	1291	1064	10624
桐庐县 Tonglu	1317	1702	1080	341	1598
淳安县 Chun'an	2854	1977	2862	355	1614
建德市 Jiande	3197	1765	3795	527	640
富阳市 Fuyang	3531	2139	3463	772	1435
临安市 Lin'an	2027	2148	4187	816	－828

2－10 计划生育情况(2011 年)
Situations of Birth Control(2011)

单位:%　　　　(%)

地区 Region		综合避孕率 Contraception Rate	计划生育率 Rate of Birth Under Control	独生子女领证率 The Only－child Certification Rate
全　市	**Whole City**	**86.75**	**97.90**	**41.10**
市　区	Urban District	85.13	98.69	47.27
上城区	Shangcheng	81.13	98.76	62.15
下城区	Xiacheng	80.53	98.79	52.66
江干区	Jianggan	87.01	99.02	58.20
拱墅区	Gongshu	82.98	98.90	51.72
西湖区	Xihu	86.13	98.66	37.36
高新(滨江)区	Hi－Tech(Binjiang)	83.97	99.13	35.61
萧山区	Xiaoshan	85.94	98.30	41.56
余杭区	Yuhang	86.63	98.76	51.35
桐庐县	Tonglu	89.19	97.28	31.25
淳安县	Chun'an	91.93	95.21	30.71
建德市	Jiande	89.21	95.80	29.18
富阳市	Fuyang	89.41	96.40	31.77
临安市	Lin'an	87.00	97.06	33.77

2－11 婚姻登记情况
Marriage Registration Situations

地区 Region	2011 准予登记结婚对数 Marriages Legally Registered (couples)	2011 #再婚人数 Re－married (person)	2011 离婚对数 Divorces (couples)	2010 准予登记结婚对数 Marriages Legally Registered (couples)	2010 #再婚人数 Re－married (person)	2010 离婚对数 Divorces (couples)
全 市 Whole City	**75952**	**20104**	**14939**	**70046**	**17988**	**14912**
市 区 Urban District	51556	11614	9195	47045	11126	9303
萧山区 Xiaoshan	9327	2742	1779	9660	2780	1837
余杭区 Yuhang	9035	2309	1631	8125	1585	1685
桐庐县 Tonglu	4098	1421	1054	3426	1482	1067
淳安县 Chun'an	4310	1230	808	3946	1099	808
建德市 Jiande	4819	1547	1169	5849	1053	996
富阳市 Fuyang	5955	2236	1482	5463	1608	1403
临安市 Lin'an	5214	2056	1231	4317	1620	1335

2-12 全市非私营单位
Number of Employed

单位:人

地区、行业	Region, Sector	年末单位从业人员 Employed Persons in Urban Units (year-end)	#女性 Female	在岗职工 Fully Employed Staff & Workers	劳务派遣人员 Labor Dispatch Personnel
全市总计	**Total**	**2643042**	**853186**	**2144463**	**360145**
其中:企业	Enterprises	2234318	670209	1795399	330612
事业	Institutions	285647	147030	237632	24585
机关	Agencies & Organizations	98522	23464	89618	4711
民间非营利组织	Non-profit Organizations	11639	7301	10106	118
其他	Other	12916	5182	11708	119
市区总计	**Urban District**	**2310319**	**734928**	**1858431**	**326915**
其中:企业	Enterprises	1987616	586852	1585230	301252
事业	Institutions	227493	119238	187473	21024
机关	Agencies & Organizations	73453	17930	66524	4449
民间非营利组织	Non-profit Organizations	9924	6202	8491	113
其他	Other	11833	4706	10713	77
上城区	Shangcheng District	191953	81495	140067	35632
下城区	Xiacheng District	224009	87852	178427	24791
江干区	Jianggan District	191019	39213	141393	20949
拱墅区	Gongshu District	184084	46270	124281	48555
西湖区	Xihu District	398143	113125	281091	89777
高新(滨江)区	Hi-Tech(Binjiang) District	180657	57169	156823	20727
萧山区	Xiaoshan District	521542	164622	497685	15702
余杭区	Yuhang District	197035	74213	178420	12875
桐庐县	Tonglu County	47924	20143	42922	2542
淳安县	Chun'an County	36052	12830	30801	3991
建德市	Jiande City	44950	16466	40395	1467
富阳市	Fuyang City	116266	40273	90412	21173
临安市	Lin'an City	87531	28546	81502	4057

从业人员数(2011 年)

Persons in Non - private Units(2011)

(person)

其他从业人员 Other Employed Persons	单位平均从业人数 Annual Average Number of Employed Persons in Urban Unit	在岗职工 Fully Employed Staff & Workers	劳务派遣人员 Labor Dispatch Personnel	其他从业人员 Other Employed Persons
138434	**2609817**	**2062732**	**354549**	**192536**
108307	2207404	1718023	326255	163126
23430	280924	234838	23494	22592
4193	97394	88526	4572	4296
1415	11425	9904	113	1408
1089	12670	11441	115	1114
124973	**2281976**	**1778925**	**324597**	**178454**
101134	1964670	1509213	300143	155314
18996	223385	185147	19977	18261
2480	72583	65787	4298	2498
1320	9731	8312	106	1313
1043	11607	10466	73	1068
16254	189122	138286	35209	15627
20791	236689	175302	26224	35163
28677	197118	145677	20110	31331
11248	177721	122394	43099	12228
27275	378628	255841	90135	32652
3107	175643	151599	19814	4230
8155	508739	474415	15995	18329
5740	196569	177676	13284	5609
2460	47871	42766	2618	2487
1260	35621	29933	4111	1577
3088	45372	40923	1378	3071
4681	111166	89066	17330	4770
1972	87811	81119	4515	2177

单位:人　　　　　　　　　　　　　　2－12　续表

地区、行业	Region,Sector	年末单位从业人员 Employed Persons in Urban Units (year－end)	#女性 Female	在岗职工 Fully Employed Staff & Workers	劳务派遣人员 Labor Dispatch Personnel
按国民经济行业分组	**Grouped by Sector**				
农、林、牧、渔业	Farming,Forestry,Animal Husbandry & Fishery	1609	421	1560	–
采矿业	Mining & Quarrying	2354	434	2209	134
制造业	Manufacturing	790783	314269	705202	75979
电力、煤气及水的生产和供应业	Production & Supply of Electricity,Gas & Water	22296	5158	18685	3365
建筑业	Construction	633677	33076	415352	156980
交通运输、仓储和邮政业	Transportation,Storage,Post & Telecommunications	92882	23134	75760	15263
信息传输、计算机服务和软件业	Information Transmission,Computer Services and Software	74038	29336	62675	9759
批发与零售业	Wholesale & Retail Trade	167165	83757	132710	29106
住宿和餐饮业	Lodging and Catering	100349	57275	92696	3014
金融业	Banking and Insurance	80182	42581	65245	7459
房地产业	Real Estate	66312	23632	59105	3809
租赁与商务服务业	Renting and Business Service	84966	20723	70474	11704
科学研究、技术服务与地质勘查业	Scientific Research,Technical Service and Geological Prospecting	92621	25499	78838	6261
水利、环境和公共设施管理业	Water Conservancy,Environment and Public Utility	45145	15837	30258	9421
居民服务和其他服务业	Service for the Residents and Other	8306	2957	6421	1502
教育	Education	152668	81625	130154	11624
卫生、社会保障和社会福利业	Health Care,Sports & Social Welfare	85724	52659	70777	6690
文化、体育与娱乐业	Culture,Sports and Entertainment	20850	10027	16143	2685
公共管理与社会组织	Public Management and Social Organizations	121115	30786	110199	5390

continued (person)

其他从业人员 Other Employed Persons	单位平均从业人数 Annual Average Number of Employed Persons in Urban Unit	在岗职工 Fully Employed Staff & Workers	劳务派遣人员 Labor Dispatch Personnel	其他从业人员 Other Employed Persons
49	1571	1527	–	44
11	2374	2211	151	12
9602	792649	704051	78690	9908
246	22052	18500	3324	228
61345	635754	373834	151625	110295
1859	90880	74683	14449	1748
1604	71172	60132	9434	1606
5349	162319	128619	28745	4955
4639	87426	73980	2925	10521
7478	77507	62714	7487	7306
3398	64933	57867	3719	3347
2788	83491	69234	11829	2428
7522	89243	76236	5820	7187
5466	46019	29979	9690	6350
383	8218	6305	1500	413
10890	150705	129147	10925	10633
8257	83034	68890	6215	7929
2022	20637	16097	2549	1991
5526	119833	108726	5472	5635

2－13 全市国有单位

Number of Employed Persons

单位:人

地区、行业	Region, Sector	年末单位从业人员 Employed Persons in Urban Units (year－end)	#女性 Female	在岗职工 Fully Employed Staff & Workers	劳务派遣人员 Labor Dispatch Personnel
总　计	**Total**	**569459**	**216504**	**471838**	**62337**
按隶属关系分	**Grouped by Subordination**				
中央属	Central	99402	27209	74821	22160
省　属	Provincial	152793	60927	123957	16427
市　属	City	89496	33757	74304	10456
县及县以下	County and Lower Levels	220748	91633	192654	12634
其　他	Others	7020	2978	6102	660
按企业、事业、机关分	**Grouped by Enterprises, Institutions & Agencies**				
企业	Enterprises	202988	56576	159379	33710
事业	Institutions	265071	134916	220280	23850
机关	Agencies & Organizations	98522	23464	89618	4711
民间非营利组织	Non－profit Organizations	2109	1275	1886	16
其他	Others	769	273	675	50
按国民经济行业分组	**Grouped by Sector**				
农、林、牧、渔业	Farming, Forestry, Animal Husbandry & Fishery	678	116	656	－
采矿业	Mining & Quarrying	105	7	105	－
制造业	Manufacturing	20197	4547	18764	647
电力、煤气及水的生产和供应业	Production & Supply of Electricity, Gas & Water	12836	2879	9739	3064
建筑业	Construction	11617	1039	7010	1469
交通运输、仓储和邮政业	Transportation, Storage, Post & Telecommunications	47246	11501	39579	6823
信息传输、计算机服务和软件业	Information Transmission, Computer Services and Software	8952	4264	5801	3135
批发与零售业	Wholesale & Retail Trade	9680	3826	8042	1477
住宿和餐饮业	Lodging and Catering	9967	5195	8049	1584
金融业	Banking and Insurance	14429	7546	11025	1227
房地产业	Real Estate	5869	1941	5054	596
租赁与商务服务业	Renting and Business Service	37098	5009	27025	9202
科学研究、技术服务与地质勘查业	Scientific Research, Technical Service and Geological Prospecting	37669	11570	32351	2812
水利、环境和公共设施管理业	Water Conservancy, Environment and Public Utility	20063	8288	13435	4100
居民服务和其他服务业	Service for the Residents and Other	4269	1655	2808	1251
教育	Education	130958	68088	111589	10897
卫生、社会保障和社会福利业	Health Care, Sports & Social Welfare	71202	44276	58464	6120
文化、体育与娱乐业	Culture, Sports and Entertainment	16732	7992	12311	2559
公共管理与社会组织	Public Management and Social Organizations	109892	26765	100031	5374

从业人员数(2011 年)
in State – owned Units(2011)

(person)

其他从业人员 Other Employed Persons	单位平均从业人数 Annual Average Number of Employed Persons in Urban Unit	在岗职工 Fully Employed Staff & Workers	劳务派遣人员 Labor Dispatch Personnel	其他从业人员 Other Employed Persons
35284	**564681**	**468067**	**60798**	**35816**
2421	99180	74671	22142	2367
12409	150367	122704	15513	12150
4736	90117	74176	10006	5935
15460	218126	190484	12542	15100
258	6891	6032	595	264
9899	203715	159190	33343	11182
20941	260646	217776	22819	20051
4193	97394	88526	4572	4296
207	2162	1919	16	227
44	764	656	48	60
22	680	658	–	22
–	105	105	–	–
786	20444	19034	605	805
33	12597	9520	3039	38
3138	14375	8162	1572	4641
844	46937	39568	6523	846
16	8876	5766	3095	15
161	9537	7938	1435	164
334	10067	8232	1480	355
2177	13902	10701	1151	2050
219	5812	5032	566	214
871	36792	26526	9571	695
2506	36849	31780	2580	2489
2528	20042	13391	4144	2507
210	4251	2807	1234	210
8472	129042	110801	10250	7991
6618	69067	57072	5678	6317
1862	16604	12323	2417	1864
4487	108702	98651	5458	4593

2－14　全市集体单位

Number of Employed Persons

单位:人

地区、行业	Region, Sector	年末单位从业人员 Employed Persons in Urban Units (year－end)	#女性 Female	在岗职工 Fully Employed Staff & Workers	劳务派遣人员 Labor Dispatch Personnel
总　　计	**Total**	**52863**	**19178**	**47149**	**2232**
按企业、事业分	**Grouped by Enterprises, Institutions & Agencies**				
企业	Enterprises	36312	9600	33141	1647
事业	Institutions	15578	9106	13285	578
机关	Agencies & Organizations	–	–	–	–
民间非营利组织	Non－profit Organizations	464	303	264	7
其他	Others	509	169	459	–
按国民经济行业分组	**Grouped by Sector**				
农、林、牧、渔业	Farming, Forestry, Animal Husbandry & Fishery	104	35	104	–
采矿业	Mining & Quarrying	535	65	534	–
制造业	Manufacturing	4401	1900	4034	224
电力、煤气及水的生产和供应业	Production & Supply of Electricity, Gas & Water	180	54	178	–
建筑业	Construction	2157	447	1357	423
交通运输、仓储和邮政业	Transportation, Storage, Post & Telecommunications	6819	754	6535	203
信息传输、计算机服务和软件业	Information Transmission, Computer Services and Software	366	203	270	44
批发与零售业	Wholesale & Retail Trade	1883	670	1772	35
住宿和餐饮业	Lodging and Catering	2538	1443	2355	102
金融业	Banking and Insurance	–	–	–	–
房地产业	Real Estate	1428	461	1093	177
租赁与商务服务业	Renting and Business Service	13953	2576	13491	42
科学研究、技术服务与地质勘查业	Scientific Research, Technical Service and Geological Prospecting	1350	452	1006	253
水利、环境和公共设施管理业	Water Conservancy, Environment and Public Utility	2603	1350	1995	89
居民服务和其他服务业	Service for the Residents and Other	558	202	523	3
教育	Education	5931	3939	5036	280
卫生、社会保障和社会福利业	Health Care, Sports & Social Welfare	7761	4500	6627	351
文化、体育与娱乐业	Culture, Sports and Entertainment	115	75	106	6
公共管理与社会组织	Public Management and Social Organizations	181	52	133	–

从业人员数(2011 年)
in Collective - owned Units(2011)

(person)

其他从业人员 Other Employed Persons	单位平均从业人数 Annual Average Number of Employed Persons in Urban Unit	在岗职工 Fully Employed Staff & Workers	劳务派遣人员 Labor Dispatch Personnel	其他从业人员 Other Employed Persons
3482	**52389**	**46861**	**2026**	**3502**
1524	36250	33229	1472	1549
1715	15320	13040	548	1732
–	–	–	–	–
193	429	252	6	171
50	390	340	–	50
–	104	104	–	–
1	551	549	–	2
143	4582	4209	213	160
2	184	182	–	2
377	2374	1680	326	368
81	6707	6369	261	77
52	375	273	44	58
76	1917	1799	39	79
81	2589	2410	102	77
–	–	–	–	–
158	1425	1099	166	160
420	13512	13052	38	422
91	1258	996	176	86
519	2564	1958	85	521
32	566	516	3	47
615	5870	4999	237	634
783	7517	6430	329	758
3	110	100	7	3
48	184	136	–	48

2-15 全市其他非私营单位
Number of Employed Persons

单位:人

地区、行业	Region, Sector	年末单位从业人员 Employed Persons in Urban Units (year-end)	#女性 Female	在岗职工 Fully Employed Staff & Workers	劳务派遣人员 Labor Dispatch Personnel
总　计	**Total**	**2020720**	**617504**	**1625476**	**295576**
按登记注册类型分组	**Grouped by Registration**				
1. 内资	Domestic Funded	1446474	357837	1125687	231435
2. 港澳台投资经济	Funded by Entrepreneurs from Hong Kong, Macao & Taiwan	231413	106137	204852	23182
3. 外商投资经济	Foreign Funded	342833	153530	294937	40959
按企业、事业分	**Grouped by Enterprises, Institutions**				
企业	Enterprises	1995018	604033	1602879	295255
事业	Institutions	4998	3008	4067	157
民间非营利组织	Non-profit Organizations	9066	5723	7956	95
其他	Others	11638	4740	10574	69
按国民经济行业分组	**Grouped by Sector**				
农、林、牧、渔业	Farming, Forestry, Animal Husbandry & Fishery	827	270	800	-
采矿业	Mining & Quarrying	1714	362	1570	134
制造业	Manufacturing	766185	307822	682404	75108
电力、煤气及水的生产和供应业	Production & Supply of Electricity, Gas & Water	9280	2225	8768	301
建筑业	Construction	619903	31590	406985	155088
交通运输、仓储和邮政业	Transportation, Storage, Post & Telecommunications	38817	10879	29646	8237
信息传输、计算机服务和软件业	Information Transmission, Computer Services and Software	64720	24869	56604	6580
批发与零售业	Wholesale & Retail Trade	155602	79261	122896	27594
住宿和餐饮业	Lodging and Catering	87844	50637	82292	1328
金融业	Banking and Insurance	65753	35035	54220	6232
房地产业	Real Estate	59015	21230	52958	3036
租赁与商务服务业	Renting and Business Service	33915	13138	29958	2460
科学研究、技术服务与地质勘查业	Scientific Research, Technical Service and Geological Prospecting	53602	13477	45481	3196
水利、环境和公共设施管理业	Water Conservancy, Environment and Public Utility	22479	6199	14828	5232
居民服务和其他服务业	Service for the Residents and Other	3479	1100	3090	248
教育	Education	15779	9598	13529	447
卫生、社会保障和社会福利业	Health Care, Sports & Social Welfare	6761	3883	5686	219
文化、体育与娱乐业	Culture, Sports and Entertainment	4003	1960	3726	120
公共管理与社会组织	Public Management and Social Organizations	11042	3969	10035	16

从业人员数(2011 年)

in Other Non - private Units (2011)

(person)

其他从业人员 Other Employed Persons	单位平均从业人数 Annual Average Number of Employed Persons in Urban Unit	在岗职工 Fully Employed Staff & Workers	劳务派遣人员 Labor Dispatch Personnel	其他从业人员 Other Employed Persons
99668	**1992747**	**1547804**	**291725**	**153218**
89352	1429544	1067839	224824	136881
3379	230515	203677	23320	3518
6937	332688	276288	43581	12819
96884	1967439	1525604	291440	150395
774	4958	4022	127	809
1015	8834	7733	91	1010
995	11516	10445	67	1004
27	787	765	–	22
10	1718	1557	151	10
8673	767623	680808	77872	8943
211	9271	8798	285	188
57830	619005	363992	149727	105286
934	37236	28746	7665	825
1536	61921	54093	6295	1533
5112	150865	118882	27271	4712
4224	74770	63338	1343	10089
5301	63605	52013	6336	5256
3021	57696	51736	2987	2973
1497	33187	29656	2220	1311
4925	51136	43460	3064	4612
2419	23413	14630	5461	3322
141	3401	2982	263	156
1803	15793	13347	438	2008
856	6450	5388	208	854
157	3923	3674	125	124
991	10947	9939	14	994

2-16 按三次产业分从业人员人数

Number of Employed Persons by Three Industries

单位:万人 (10000 persons)

指标名称	Item	2011年末 (End of 2011)	2010年末 (End of 2010)
全市总计	**Total**	**637.77**	**626.33**
第一产业	Primary Industry	72.21	75.70
第二产业	Secondary Industry	289.12	286.26
第三产业	Tertiary Industry	276.44	264.37
市　区	**Urban District**	**469.90**	**455.07**
第一产业	Primary Industry	24.55	25.59
第二产业	Secondary Industry	223.00	215.80
第三产业	Tertiary Industry	222.35	213.68

主要统计指标解释

人口数 指一定时点、一定地区范围内的有生命的个人的总和。

年度统计的年末人口数是指每年 12 月 31 日 24 时的人口数。

出生率(又称粗出生率) 指一定时期内(通常为一年)平均每千人所出生的人数的比率,一般用千分率表示。计算公式:

$$出生率 = \frac{年出生人数}{年平均人数} \times 1000‰$$

出生人数是指活产婴儿,即胎儿脱离母体时(不管怀孕月数),有过呼吸或其他生命现象。

年平均人数是年初、年底人口数的平均数,也可用年中人口数代替。

死亡率(又称粗死亡率) 指一定时期内(通常为一年)一定地区的死亡人数与同期平均人数(或期中人数)之比,一般用千分率表示。计算公式:

$$死亡率 = \frac{年死亡人数}{年平均人数} \times 1000‰$$

人口自然增长率 指一定时期内(通常为一年)人口自然增加数(出生人数减死亡人数)与该时期内平均人数(或期中人数)之比,一般用千分率表示。计算公式:

$$人口自然增长率 = \frac{本年出生人数 - 本年死亡人数}{年平均人数} \times 1000‰$$

人口自然增长率 = 人口出生率 - 人口死亡率

从业人员 指从事一定社会劳动并取得劳动报酬或经营收入人员,包括各级机关企事业单位从业人员、个体户主、个体从业人员、农村从业人员及其他未包括的从业人员(包括宗教职业者、现役军人等)。

单位从业人员 是指在各级国家机关、政党机关、社会团体及企业、事业单位中工作,并取得劳动报酬的全部人员。包括在岗职工、再就业的离退休人员、民办教师、在各单位中工作的外方人员和港、澳、台方人员以及聘用的外单位下岗职工、兼职人员、从事第二职业人员、使用的劳务派遣人员和服务外包人员。各单位的从业人员反映了实际参加生产或工作的全部劳动力。

在岗职工 指在本单位工作并由单位支付劳动报酬的人员,以及在本单位有工作岗位,但由于学习、病伤产假等原因暂未工作,仍由单位支付劳动报酬的人,包括本单位临时性用工并支付劳动报酬的人员。

Explanatory Notes on Main Statistical Indicators

Total Population refers to the total number of people alive at a certain point of time within a given area. The annual statistics on total population is taken at midnight, the 31st of December .

Birth Rate (or Crude Birth Rate) refers to the ratio of the number of births to the average population during a certain period of time (usually a year) ,which is often expressed in ‰. The following formula is used:

$$\text{Birth Rate} = \frac{\text{Number of Births}}{\text{Average Number of Population}} \times 1000‰$$

Number of births refers to live births, i. e. the births when babies had showed any vital phenomena regardless of the length of pregnancy.

Annual Average Number of Population is the average of the number of population at the beginning of the year and that at the end of the year. Sometimes it is substituted for with the mid – year population.

Death Rate (or Crude Death Rate) refers to the ratio of the number of deaths to the average population (or mid – year population) during a certain period of time (usually a year) ,which is often expressed in ‰. The following formula is used:

$$\text{Death Rate} = \frac{\text{Number of Deaths}}{\text{Annual Average Number of Population}} \times 1000‰$$

Natural Growth Rate of Population refers to the ratio of natural increase in population (number of births minus number of deaths) in a certain period of time (usually a year) to the average population(or mid – year population) of the same period, which is often expressed in ‰. The following formulas are applied:

$$\text{Natural Growth Rate of Population} = \frac{\text{Number of Births} - \text{Number of Deaths}}{\text{Average Number of Population}} \times 1000‰$$

Natural Growth Rate of Population = Birth Rate – Death Rate

Employed Persons refer to persons who are engaged in social labour and receive remuneration payment or earn business income, including all employees of government, enterprises and institutions, self – employed workers, employed persons in the rural areas and other employed workers(including religious professionals, servicemen, etc.).

Persons Employed in Various Units refer to all the persons who are working in government agencies of various levels, political and party organizations, social organizations, enterprises, institutions, and receiving wages or other forms of payment. Including fully employed staff and works, re – employed retirees, teachers in schools run by the local people, foreigners and Chinese compatriots from Hong Kong, Macao, and Taiwan working in various units, part – time employees, employees of other units working temporarily, employees holding the second job, dispatch personnels and outsourcing staff. Persons Employed in various units reflect the actual total labor force which are engaged in the production or work.

Fully Employed Staff and Workers refer to persons who work in, and receive wages from their working units, as well as persons who have their work posts, but are temporarily absent from work for reasons of study or on sick, injury or maternal leave and still receive wages from their working units. including persons who are engaged in temporary employment and receive remuneration payment.

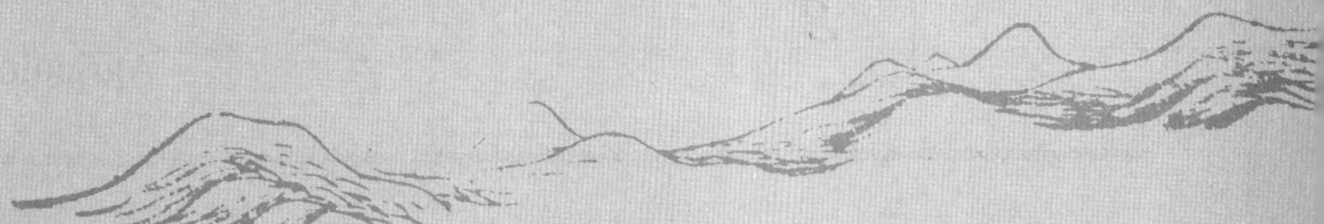

第三篇
CHAPTER-3

农业
AGRICULTURE

3 农　　业 Agriculture

主要统计指标
Major Statistical Indicators

农村机械总动力	Total Power of Agricultural Machinery	336.75	万千瓦	(10, 000 kw)
为上年	As Compared with the Preceding Year	101.7	%	(%)
农村经济总收入	Total Rural Economic Income	15001.35	亿元	(100 million yuan)
为上年	As Compared with the Preceding Year	115.6	%	(%)
农村从业人员数	Total Employees in rural areas	262.10	万人	(10, 000 persons)
为上年	As Compared with the Preceding Year	100.1	%	(%)
农林牧渔业总产值	Gross Output Value of Farming,Forestry,Animal Husbandry and Fishery	357.07	亿元	(100 million yuan)
为上年	As Compared with the Preceding Year	112.9	%	(%)
粮食总产量	Total Output of Grain Crops	97.81	万吨	(10, 000 tons)
为上年	As Compared with the Preceding Year	97.6	%	(%)
肉类产量	Total Output of Meat	32.50	万吨	(10, 000 tons)
为上年	As Compared with the Preceding Year	102.2	%	(%)

3－01　农村基本情况
Basic Situations of Rural Areas

指　　标	Item	1995	2000	2005	2006	2007	2008	2009	2010	2011
农村基层组织	**Rural Grassroots Units**									
乡镇政府（个）	Number of Township & Town Governments (unit)	230	234	149	141	136	136	130	128	109
#镇政府（个）	Number of Town Governments (unit)	134	140	110	108	105	105	99	97	86
村民委员会（个）	Number of Villagers´Committees (unit)	4681	4616	3681	3660	2501	2120	2113	2098	2081
村民小组（万个）	Villager Group (10000 units)	3.61	3.53	3.43	3.43	3.40	3.29	3.24	3.26	3.27
农村户数、人口、从业人员	**Rural Households, Population & Labor Force**									
农村常住户数（万户）	Resident Households in Rural Areas (10000 households)	121.23	118.11	139.85	137.01	136.89	131.87	131.46	131.82	132.94
农村常住人口数（万人）	Resident Population in Rural Areas (10000 persons)	402.77	395.00	447.36	444.27	443.49	433.39	429.13	431.34	434.23
农村从业人员数（万人）	Labor Force in Rural Areas (10000 persons)	257.70	247.11	267.05	266.68	266.32	260.16	259.32	261.77	262.10
按性别分	Grouped by Sex									
男性（万人）	Male (10000 persons)	137.57	130.37	141.43	140.75	140.03	137.16	136.86	138.18	137.33
女性（万人）	Female (10000 persons)	120.13	116.74	125.62	125.93	126.29	123.00	122.46	123.59	124.77
按行业分	Grouped by Sector									
农林牧渔业（万人）	Farming, Forestry, Animal Husbandry & Fishery (10000 persons)	136.65	116.05	88.82	83.99	79.96	78.08	75.79	73.24	69.39
工　　业（万人）	Industry (10000 persons)	63.40	59.27	85.50	88.65	93.58	89.91	90.75	93.70	97.00
建　筑　业（万人）	Construction (10000 persons)	12.04	13.02	16.51	16.98	17.66	17.70	18.10	18.68	19.55
交通运输、仓储业及邮电通讯业（万人）	Transportation, Storage, Post & Telecommunications (10000 persons)	8.67	9.29	11.22	11.64	11.66	11.65	11.52	11.48	-
批发、零售贸易、餐饮业（万人）	Wholesale, Retail Trade & Catering Services (10000 persons)	7.28	10.62	18.03	18.74	19.57	19.58	20.10	20.76	-
其它非农行业（万人）	Other Non－agricultural Trades (10000 persons)	29.66	38.86	46.97	46.68	43.89	43.24	43.06	43.91	76.16
#外出临时工、合同工（万人）	Contract or Temporary Workers Going Outside (10000 persons)	15.40	22.01	23.89	23.55	22.57	24.05	23.08	24.21	-
在农村从业人员中：外出（万人）	Among the Total Rural Labor Force: Going Outside (10000 persons)	19.14	35.73	43.22	44.12	47.26	-	-	-	-
#出省的（万人）	Going to Other Provinces (10000 persons)	2.06	4.47	5.66	5.08	5.62	-	-	-	-

注：2002年起农村住户数、农村人口包括农村居委会户数、人口和农村外来户户数、人口。

a) From 2002, rural households and population in rural areas includes the natives and from the outside.

3－02 分地区

Basic Situations of

指　标	Item	全　市 Whole City	市　区 Urban District	#江干区 Jianggan	#拱墅区 Gongshu
农村基层组织	**Rural Grassroots Units**				
乡镇政府　（个）	Number of Township & Town Governments　(unit)	109	29	4	–
#镇政府　（个）	Number of Town Governments　(unit)	86	29	4	–
农村街道办事处　（个）	Sub－district office in Rural Areas　(unit)	49	33	–	3
村民委员会　（个）	Number of Villagers′Committees　(unit)	2081	672	6	–
村民小组　（万个）	Villagers′Group　(10000 unit)	3.27	1.19	0.01	–
农村户数、人口、从业人员	**Rural Households, Population & Labor Force**				
农村常住户数　（万户）	Resident Households in Rural Areas　(10000 households)	132.94	64.98	1.77	0.35
农村常住人口数　（万人）	Resident Population in Rural Areas　(10000 persons)	434.23	226.46	7.37	1.31
农村从业人员数　（万人）	Practitioners in Rural Areas　(10000 persons)	262.10	131.74	3.69	0.67
农村基础设施水平	**Public Facilities in Rural Areas**				
自来水受益村数　（个）	Number of Villages with Access to Tap Water　(unit)	2081	672	6	–
通汽车村数　（个）	Number of Villages with Highways　(unit)	2081	672	6	–
通电话村数　（个）	Number of Villages with Telephone Communication　(unit)	2081	672	6	–

农村基本情况(2011 年)

Rural Areas by Region(2011)

#西湖区 Xihu	#高新(滨江)区 Hi-Tech(Binjiang)	#萧山区 Xiaoshan	#余杭区 Yuhang	桐庐县 Tonglu	淳安县 Chun'an	建德市 Jiande	富阳市 Fuyan	临安市 Lin'an
2	-	17	6	10	23	13	21	13
2	-	17	6	6	11	12	15	13
2	3	11	13	4	-	3	4	5
49	9	411	188	183	425	232	282	287
0.07	0.01	0.72	0.37	0.26	0.40	0.46	0.47	0.49
4.31	2.77	36.60	18.90	10.70	12.09	12.59	16.85	15.73
16.30	10.17	118.03	72.72	31.33	37.04	40.09	53.27	46.04
8.74	5.66	67.85	44.78	20.32	24.23	23.94	33.48	28.39
49	9	411	188	183	425	232	282	287
49	9	411	188	183	425	232	282	287
49	9	411	188	183	425	232	282	287

3－03 分地区

Rural Labor Force

单位:万人

指　　标	Item	全　市 Whole City	市　区 Urban District	#江干区 Jianggan	#拱墅区 Gongshu
总　　计	**Total**	**262.10**	**131.74**	**3.69**	**0.67**
#女	Female	124.77	63.91	1.78	0.31
农、林、牧、渔业	Farming, Forestry, Animal Husbandry & Fishery	69.39	23.6	0.62	0.01
#农业	Farming	52.35	18.7	0.61	0.01
牧业	Animal Husbandry	7.04	1.37	–	–
工　业	Industry	97.00	59.58	1.28	0.34
建筑业	Construction	19.55	11.55	0.19	0.03
交通运输、仓储业及邮电通讯业	Transportation, Storage, Post & Telecommunications				
批发、零售贸易、餐饮业	Wholesale, Retail Trade & Catering Services				
其它非农行业	Other Non－agricultural Trades	76.16	37.01	1.60	0.29
#外出临时工、合同工	Contract or Temporary Workers Going Outside				

农村从业人员(2011 年)

by Region(2011)

(10000 persons)

#西湖区 Xihu	#高新(滨江)区 Hi-Tech(Binjiang)	#萧山区 Xiaoshan	#余杭区 Yuhang	桐庐县 Tonglu	淳安县 Chun'an	建德市 Jiande	富阳市 Fuyan	临安市 Lin'an
8.74	**5.66**	**67.85**	**44.78**	**20.32**	**24.23**	**23.94**	**33.48**	**28.39**
4.19	2.79	33.41	21.24	9.91	10.9	10.99	15.51	13.55
2.13	0.28	12.02	8.37	6.27	11.38	9.87	10.43	7.84
1.52	0.24	9.66	6.49	5.12	7.83	8.22	8.45	4.03
0.07	0.01	0.86	0.43	0.60	2.25	0.97	0.91	0.94
1.77	2.56	32.64	20.99	7.61	1.63	5.70	12.24	10.24
0.86	0.58	6.92	2.97	1.51	1.17	1.90	2.05	1.37
3.98	2.24	16.27	12.45	4.93	10.05	6.47	8.76	8.94

3－04 主要年份农林牧渔业总产值

Gross Output Value of Farming, Forestry, Animal Husbandry and Fishery in Main Years

单位:万元 (10000 yuan)

年份 Year	农林牧渔业总产值 Gross Output Value	#农业产值 Farming	#种植业产值 Planting	林业产值 Forestry	牧业产值 Animal Husbandry	渔业产值 Fishery
1978	85922	67365	64378	3430	14474	653
1979	115649	84727	81989	4629	25216	1077
1980	112377	79006	76059	7262	25015	1094
1981	120792	87354	81659	8309	23799	1330
1982	150606	107566	103346	8912	31801	2327
1983	148878	103685	96272	9800	32693	2700
1984	177029	122567	115286	14769	35922	3771
1985	212961	136893	126026	19095	50110	6863
1986	238285	150803	138254	19990	58197	9295
1987	281326	173080	155960	26427	70129	11690
1988	358500	208838	187648	31434	101013	17215
1989	386805	225969	201389	27857	113952	19027
1990	421045	260031	233055	26962	113424	20628
1991	463578	284275	254834	37763	117458	24082
1992	497915	300828	256833	35589	133867	27631
1993	600760	365124	300736	47476	154766	33394
1994	812473	496392	415366	58627	217217	40237
1995	996440	620057	526328	81321	244054	51008
1996	1173294	740202	617573	95740	271652	65700
1997	1287650	797812	665172	114510	294153	81175
1998	1367578	845106	701850	121197	289085	112190
1999	1414737	876685	737406	126000	293495	118557
2000	1526530	903322	754311	136848	331563	154797
2001	1649978	965005	816884	149264	362303	173406
2002	1685036	932995	886285	162227	391844	197970
2003	1890129	991556	949138	182595	417798	232599
2004	1982683	1010947	972594	206787	457619	234080
2005	2194799	1136559	1103981	233039	495900	270810
2006	2253822	1224822	1191816	267748	490448	206082
2007	2471427	1308047	1279758	294707	585536	222601
2008	2737605	1408124	1374083	320212	636633	309270
2009	2897371	1497362	1462791	362317	642892	325626
2010	3163392	1698775	1673470	329278	705596	349011
2011	3570744	1907895	1882876	348535	836532	389985

注:本表按当年价格计算;从 2003 年起农林牧渔总产值包括农林牧渔业服务业产值(下同)。

a) Data in this table are calculated at current prices. From 2003, Gross Output Value includes the value of service for the farming, forestry, animal husbandry and fishery sector.

3-05 主要年份农林牧渔业总产值构成

Composition of Gross Output Value of Farming, Forestry, Animal Husbandry and Fishery in Main Years

单位:%　　(%)

年份 Year	农林牧渔业总产值 Gross Output Value	#农业产值 Farming	#种植业产值 Planting	林业产值 Forestry	牧业产值 Animal Husbandry	渔业产值 Fishery
1978	100.0	78.4	74.9	4.0	16.8	0.8
1979	100.0	73.3	70.9	4.0	21.8	0.9
1980	100.0	70.3	67.7	6.5	22.2	1.0
1981	100.0	72.3	67.6	6.9	19.7	1.1
1982	100.0	71.4	68.6	5.9	21.1	1.6
1983	100.0	69.6	64.7	6.6	22.0	1.8
1984	100.0	69.2	65.1	8.3	20.3	2.2
1985	100.0	64.3	59.2	9.0	23.5	3.2
1986	100.0	63.3	58.0	8.4	24.4	3.9
1987	100.0	61.5	55.4	9.4	24.9	4.2
1988	100.0	58.2	52.3	8.8	28.2	4.8
1989	100.0	58.4	52.1	7.2	29.5	4.9
1990	100.0	61.8	55.4	6.4	26.9	4.9
1991	100.0	61.3	55.0	8.2	25.3	5.2
1992	100.0	60.4	51.6	7.2	26.9	5.5
1993	100.0	60.8	50.1	7.9	25.8	5.5
1994	100.0	61.1	51.1	7.2	26.7	5.0
1995	100.0	62.2	52.8	8.2	24.5	5.1
1996	100.0	63.1	52.6	8.2	23.1	5.6
1997	100.0	62.0	51.7	8.9	22.8	6.3
1998	100.0	61.8	51.3	8.9	21.1	8.2
1999	100.0	62.0	52.1	8.9	20.7	8.4
2000	100.0	59.2	49.4	9.0	21.7	10.1
2001	100.0	58.5	52.2	9.0	22.0	10.5
2002	100.0	55.4	52.6	9.6	23.3	11.7
2003	100.0	52.5	50.2	9.7	22.1	12.3
2004	100.0	51.0	49.1	10.4	23.1	11.8
2005	100.0	51.8	50.3	10.6	22.6	12.3
2006	100.0	54.3	52.9	11.9	21.8	9.1
2007	100.0	52.9	51.8	11.9	23.7	9.0
2008	100.0	51.4	50.2	11.7	23.3	11.3
2009	100.0	51.7	50.5	12.5	22.2	11.2
2010	100.0	53.7	52.9	10.4	22.3	11.0
2011	100.0	53.4	52.7	9.8	23.4	10.9

注:本表按当年价格计算。
a) Figures in value terms in this table are calculated at current prices.

3-06 主要年份农林牧渔业分项产值

Gross Output Value of Farming, Forestry, Animal Husbandry and Fishery by Branch in Main Years

单位:万元 (10000 yuan)

指　标	Item	1995	2000	2005	2006	2007	2008	2009	2010	2011
农林牧渔业总产值(现价)	**Gross Output Value (Current Price)**	**996440**	**1526530**	**2194799**	**2253822**	**2471427**	**2737605**	**2897371**	**3163392**	**3570744**
#一、农业产值	**Farming**	**620057**	**903322**	**1136559**	**1224822**	**1308047**	**1408124**	**1497362**	**1698775**	**1907895**
1.种植业产值	Planting	526328	754311	1103981	1191816	1279758	1374083	1462791	1673470	1882876
粮食	Grain	262321	208546	178981	187293	194032	217705	217895	215990	230246
油料	Oil-bearing Crops	19675	19583	21608	20111	22987	28809	30796	31137	35245
棉花	Cotton	11829	2205	1146	1012	1058	1126	1155	1255	1155
麻类	Fiber Crops	3863	384	176	115	97	55	30	42	21
甘蔗	Sugarcane	14274	23815	19075	17028	18697	18942	20074	18756	20067
烟叶	Tobacco	1	5	7	2	3	1	1	1	2
药材类	Crude Drugs	1725	6005	15800	20428	23901	23432	35546	42927	50530
蔬菜	Vegetables	151614	303583	357734	382697	415720	447147	454890	535623	607469
茶、桑、果	Tea, Mulberry & Fruits	48599	106727	254379	285994	306954	330717	360120	484261	565641
其他	Others	12427	83458	255075	277136	296309	306149	342284	343478	372500
2.其他农业产值	Other Farming	93729	149011	32578	33006	28289	34041	34571	25305	25019
二、林业产值	**Forestry**	**81321**	**136848**	**233039**	**267748**	**294707**	**320212**	**362317**	**329278**	**348535**
人造林木生长	Artificial Forestry	11286	18226	23140	22474	22376	24053	26310	27964	23828
林产品	Forest Products	45123	89914	168348	185455	203082	225872	260694	184740	197815
竹木采伐	Lumbering	24912	28708	41551	59819	69249	70287	75313	82063	90806
采集野生植物	Wild Plant collected								34511	36086
三、牧业产值	**Animal Husbandry**	**244054**	**331563**	**495900**	**490448**	**585536**	**636633**	**642892**	**705596**	**836532**
牲畜	Livestock Raising	143879	175732	292025	283198	366339	390789	387278	430193	534840
家禽饲养	Poultry Raising	35302	65548	68631	50444	61077	72229	72167	70201	69653
活的畜禽产品	Livestock Products	37197	44098	68143	62467	76374	94738	97739	109625	124024
捕猎野兽野禽	Hunting Wild Beast and Wild Fowl	491	2102	2856	3050	3222	3620	4058	4455	4698
其他动物饲养	Other Animals Raising	27185	44083	64245	91289	78524	75257	81650	91122	103317
四、渔业产值	**Fishery**	**51008**	**154797**	**270810**	**206082**	**222601**	**309270**	**325626**	**349011**	**389985**

注:从2010年开始,茶、桑、果中包含坚果类产值,种植业中的“采集野生植物”产值归入到林业里。

a) Since 2010, the output value of nuts was included in Tea, Mulberry & Fruits. The output value of "Collecting wild plants" was included in Forestry.

3-07 主要年份农林牧渔业分项产值构成

Composition of Gross Output Value of Farming, Forestry, Animal Husbandry and Fishery by Branch in Main Years

单位:%　　(%)

指　标	Item	1995	2000	2005	2006	2007	2008	2009	2010	2011
农林牧渔业总产值(现价)	**Gross Output Value (Current Price)**	**100**	**100**	**100**	**100**	**100**	**100**	**100**	**100**	**100**
#一、农业产值	**Farming**	**62.2**	**59.2**	**51.8**	**54.3**	**52.9**	**51.4**	**51.7**	**53.7**	**53.4**
1.种植业产值	Planting	52.8	49.4	50.3	52.9	51.8	50.2	50.5	52.9	52.7
粮食	Grain	26.3	13.7	8.2	8.3	7.9	8.0	7.5	6.8	6.4
油料	Oil Plants	2.0	1.3	1.0	0.9	0.9	1.1	1.1	1.0	1.0
棉花	Cotton	1.2	0.1	0.1	-	-	-	-	-	-
麻类	Fiber Crops	0.4	-	-	-	-	-	-	-	-
甘蔗	Sugarcane	1.4	1.6	0.9	0.8	0.8	0.7	0.7	0.6	0.6
烟叶	Tobacco	-	-	-	-	-	-	-	-	-
药材类	Crude Drugs	0.2	0.4	0.7	0.9	1.0	0.9	1.2	1.4	1.4
蔬菜	Vegetables	15.2	19.9	16.3	17.0	16.8	16.3	15.7	16.9	17.0
茶、桑、果	Tea, Mulberry & Fruits	4.9	7.0	11.6	12.7	12.4	12.1	12.4	15.3	15.8
其他	Others	1.2	5.4	11.5	12.3	12.0	11.1	11.9	10.9	10.5
2.其他农业产值	Other Farming	9.4	9.8	1.5	1.4	1.1	1.2	1.2	0.8	0.7
二、林业产值	**Forestry**	**8.2**	**9.0**	**10.6**	**11.9**	**11.9**	**11.7**	**12.5**	**10.4**	**9.8**
人造林木生长	Artificial Forestry	1.2	1.2	1.1	1.0	0.9	0.9	0.9	0.9	0.7
林产品	Forest Products	4.5	5.9	7.6	8.2	8.2	8.2	9.0	5.8	5.5
竹木采伐	Lumbering	2.5	1.9	1.9	2.7	2.8	2.6	2.6	2.6	2.5
采集野生植物	Wild Plant collected								1.1	1.1
三、牧业产值	**Animal Husbandry**	**24.5**	**21.7**	**22.6**	**21.8**	**23.7**	**23.3**	**22.2**	**22.3**	**23.4**
牲畜	Livestock Raising	14.4	11.5	13.3	12.6	14.8	14.3	13.4	13.6	15.0
家禽饲养	Poultry Raising	3.6	4.3	3.1	2.2	2.5	2.6	2.5	2.2	2.0
活的畜禽产品	Livestock Products	3.7	2.9	3.2	2.8	3.1	3.5	3.4	3.5	3.5
捕猎野兽野禽	Hunting Wild Beast and Wild Fowl	-	0.1	0.1	0.1	0.1	0.1	0.1	0.1	0.1
其他动物饲养	Other Animals Raising	2.8	2.9	2.9	4.1	3.2	2.8	2.8	2.9	2.8
四、渔业产值	**Fishery**	**5.1**	**10.1**	**12.3**	**9.1**	**9.0**	**11.3**	**11.2**	**11.0**	**10.9**

3－08 分地区农林牧

Gross Output Value of Farming, Forestry,

单位：万元

指　　标	Item	全　市 Whole City	市　区 Urban District	#江干区 Jianggan	#拱墅区 Gongshu
合　　计	**Gross Output Value**	**3570744**	**1653578**	**13548**	**3110**
#一、农业产值	**Farming**	**1907895**	**855127**	**10750**	**3047**
（一）种植业产值	Planting	1882876	853194	10735	3047
#副产品产值	By－products	11312	4908		
1. 粮食作物	Grain	230246	106713		
谷　　物	Cereal	166260	82900		
豆　　类	Beans	32351	14792		
薯　　类	Tubers	31635	9021		
2. 油　　料	Oil Plants	35245	9950		
3. 棉　　花	Cotton	1155	675		
4. 麻　　类	Fiber Crops	21	9		
5. 甘　　蔗	Sugarcane	20067	15022		
6. 烟　　叶	Tobacco	2			
7. 药 材 类	Crude Drugs	50530	707		
8. 蔬　　菜	Vegetables	607469	327700	9844	51
9. 茶、桑、果	Tea, Mulberry & Fruits	565641	124196	226	
10. 其　　他	Others	372500	268222	665	2996
（二）其他农业产值	Other Farming	25019	1933	15	
二、林业产值	**Forestry**	**348535**	**72726**	**17**	**8**
1. 人造林木生长	Artificial Forestry	23828	6215	17	8
2. 林产品	Forest Products	197815	39975		
3. 村及村以下竹木采伐	Lumbering	90806	23538		
4. 采集野生植物	Wild Plant collected	36086	2998		
三、牧业产值	**Animal Husbandry**	**836532**	**373911**	**1383**	**1**
1. 牲畜	Livestock	534840	291379	1365	
2. 家禽饲养	Poultry Raising	69653	39667		1
3. 活的畜禽产品	Livestock Products	124024	28659		
4. 捕猎野兽野禽	Hunting Wild Beast and Wild Fowl	4698	610		
5. 其他动物饲养	Other Animals Raising	103317	13596	18	
四、渔业产值	**Fishery**	**389985**	**289903**	**1301**	**54**

注：本表按当年价格计算。

渔业总产值(2011 年)

Animal Husbandry and Fishery by Region(2011)

(10000 yuan)

#西湖区 Xihu	#高新(滨江)区 Hi-Tech(Binjiang)	#萧山区 Xiaoshan	#余杭区 Yuhang	桐庐县 Tonglu	淳安县 Chun'an	建德市 Jiande	富阳市 Fuyang	临安市 Lin'an
63424	**28191**	**842222**	**677352**	**269324**	**352436**	**377410**	**468740**	**449256**
25935	**22025**	**458648**	**321832**	**162235**	**225184**	**203320**	**259403**	**202626**
25691	22025	458614	320192	162139	224465	193334	248536	201208
192	15	2895	1788	923	1268	1203	1668	1342
3485	317	45827	56633	30019	17242	21365	30210	24697
2464	284	35052	44649	18510	10245	15756	22897	15952
430	23	9469	4870	6348	2176	2800	3670	2565
591	10	1306	7114	5161	4821	2809	3643	6180
60		5845	4039	7244	4193	4908	5570	3380
		498	177		147	330		3
		5	4		12			
268	190	12305	2259	1581	1080	1011	1366	7
					2			
128		39	540	4290	23923	10680	5848	5082
8160	8844	186023	110407	42940	62576	49953	90874	33426
6302	1366	28445	79925	61562	104658	96793	68636	109796
7288	11308	179627	66208	14503	10632	8294	46032	24817
244		34	1640	96	719	9986	10867	1418
596	**17**	**10610**	**61408**	**23180**	**34257**	**16396**	**67519**	**134457**
575	17	1136	4392	341	6543	1004	6284	3441
21		6881	33073	14099	9855	5468	40876	87542
		2407	21131	4478	9120	7643	9836	36191
		186	2812	4262	8739	2281	10523	7283
3824	**1978**	**251800**	**107087**	**58734**	**64711**	**129492**	**110864**	**98820**
2417	1882	215260	69224	29249	31561	39221	72769	70661
424	66	19645	19493	3262	960	8620	14432	2712
332	15	5624	16119		3137	77549	8481	6198
		324	286	932	133	374	2361	288
651	15	10947	1965	25291	28920	3728	12821	18961
32349	**4171**	**93270**	**153825**	**20331**	**25099**	**19802**	**27889**	**6961**

a) Data in this table are calculated at current prices.

3－09 农林牧渔业

Value－Added and Commodity Output Value of Farming,

单位:万元

指　　标	Item	全　市 Whole City	市　区 Urban District	#江干区 Jianggan	#拱墅区 Gongshu
一、总产值	**Gross Output Value**	**3570744**	**1653578**	**13548**	**3110**
#农业产值	Farming	1907895	855127	10750	3047
林业产值	Forestry	348535	72726	17	8
牧业产值	Animal Husbandry	836532	373911	1383	1
渔业产值	Fishery	389985	289903	1301	54
二、中间消耗	**Intermediate Consume**	**1203036**	**599210**	**4955**	**1106**
1. 物质消耗	Material Consume	899075	431452	3526	736
2. 劳务支出	Labor Services Expense	303961	167758	1429	370
#农业中间消耗	Agriculture Consume	521375	233300	4083	1085
林业中间消耗	Forestry Consume	71474	22097	2	3
牧业中间消耗	Animal Husbandry Consume	415079	193945	321	–
渔业中间消耗	Fishery Consume	136529	107515	501	18
三、增加值	**The Value－Added**	**2367708**	**1054368**	**8593**	**2004**
1. 生产法	1. Production Approach				
#农业增加值	Farming	1386520	621827	6667	1962
林业增加值	Forestry	277061	50629	15	5
牧业增加值	Husbandry	421453	179966	1062	1
渔业增加值	Fishery	253456	182388	800	36
2. 收入法	2. Income Approach				
#固定资产折旧	Depreciation of Fixed Assets	108519	54817	2801	185
劳动者报酬	Compensation of Laborers	2375762	1040664	5792	1819

注:本表按当年价格计算。

产值及增加值（2011 年）

Forestry, Animal Husbandry and Fishery (2011)

（10000 yuan）

#西湖区 Xihu	#高新(滨江)区 Hi-Tech(Binjiang)	#萧山区 Xiaoshan	#余杭区 Yuhang	桐庐县 Tonglu	淳安县 Chun'an	建德市 Jiande	富阳市 Fuyang	临安市 Lin'an
63424	**28191**	**842222**	**677352**	**269324**	**352436**	**377410**	**468740**	**449256**
25935	22025	458648	321832	162235	225184	203320	259403	202626
596	17	10610	61408	23180	34257	16396	67519	134457
3824	1978	251800	107087	58734	64711	129492	110864	98820
32349	4171	93270	153825	20331	25099	19802	27889	6961
20896	**9955**	**313447**	**240598**	**85976**	**103663**	**138836**	**137104**	**138247**
15566	5415	224521	175935	57446	76135	116786	108124	109132
5330	4540	88926	64663	28530	27528	22050	28980	29115
8994	6808	125505	83643	47799	53927	56956	69825	59568
75	7	6007	15976	3951	8492	2923	7038	26973
1760	717	125032	62746	25352	30799	67504	52160	45319
9618	2423	38287	54993	5744	8947	5653	6243	2427
42528	**18236**	**528775**	**436754**	**183348**	**248773**	**238574**	**331636**	**311009**
16941	15217	333143	238189	114436	171257	146364	189578	143058
521	10	4603	45432	19229	25765	13473	60481	107484
2064	1261	126768	44341	33382	33912	61988	58704	53501
22731	1748	54983	98832	14587	16152	14149	21646	4534
2962	1605	25280	20306	11312	4995	14566	7822	15007
39566	16631	510970	450086	181887	250056	275216	324015	303924

a) Data in this table are calculated at current prices.

3－10 主要农作物播种面积及产量
Sown Areas and Yield of Major Farm Crops

指 标	Item	2011			2010		
		播种面积（千公顷）Sown Area（1000 hectares）	总产量（吨）Total Output（ton）	公顷产量（公斤）Yield per Hectare（kg/hectare）	播种面积（千公顷）Sown Area（1000 hectares）	总产量（吨）Total Output（ton）	公顷产量（公斤）Yield per Hectare（kg/hectare）
农作物总计	**Total Farm Crops**	**373.42**	**－**	**－**	**381.83**	**－**	**－**
一、粮食作物合计	**Grain Crops**	**167.82**	**978057**	**5828**	**174.65**	**1002517**	**5740**
#春粮	#Spring Grain	25.06	94634	3777	26.15	95934	3669
秋粮	Autumn Grain	140.78	871528	6191	146.43	893895	6105
（一）谷 物	Cereals	111.37	754321	6773	118.49	792057	6685
1.稻谷	Rice	75.16	590857	7861	80.78	626331	7753
①早稻及早中稻	Early Rice & Semi－late Rice	1.96	11834	6035	2.08	11997	5765
②晚稻及迟中稻	Late Rice & Semi－late Rice	73.2	579023	7910	78.71	614334	7806
#单季稻	#Single－crop Rice	71.21	563974	7920	76.36	597765	7828
2.小麦	Wheat	15.31	62617	4090	16.41	65237	3976
3.大麦	Barley	0.43	1627	3749	0.51	1759	3449
4.玉米	Corn	19.18	93904	4896	19.39	93216	4807
5.其他谷物	Other Cereals	1.29	5316	4127	1.4	5514	3950
（二）豆 类	Beans	34.04	101318	2977	34.45	93164	2704
1.大豆	Soybeans	25.11	75535	3008	25.63	68389	2668
2.蚕（豌）豆	Broad Beans	4.55	12233	2687	4.63	12331	2663
3.杂豆	Other Beans	4.38	13550	3096	4.19	12444	2971
（三）薯 类	Tubers	22.41	122418	5464	21.71	117296	5403

3－10 续表 continued

指 标	Item	2011			2010		
		播种面积（千公顷）Sown Area（1000 hectares）	总产量（吨）Total Output（ton）	公顷产量（公斤）Yield per Hectare（kg/hectare）	播种面积（千公顷）Sown Area（1000 hectares）	总产量（吨）Total Output（ton）	公顷产量（公斤）Yield per Hectare（kg/hectare）
二、油料合计	**Oil Plants**	**42.07**	**90179**	**2143**	**43.08**	**86556**	**2009**
1. 油菜籽	Rapeseeds	37.99	79815	2101	39.09	76676	1962
2. 花生	Peanuts	2.79	8401	3013	2.73	8052	2948
3. 芝麻	Sesame	1.29	1963	1522	1.26	1828	1445
三、棉花（皮棉）	**Cotton**	**0.61**	**828**	**1360**	**0.66**	**929**	**1412**
四、麻类合计	**Fiber Cropers**	**0.01**	**58**	**4833**	**0.04**	**125**	**3571**
五、甘蔗	**Sugar Crops**	**2.28**	**140965**	**61854**	**2.48**	**149231**	**60125**
六、烟叶	**Tobacco**	**–**	**2**	**2000**	**–**	**1**	**333**
七、药材类	**Crude Drugs**	**4.13**	**24424**	**5920**	**4.07**	**23306**	**5731**
八、蔬菜	**Vegetables**	**97.2**	**3164609**	**32559**	**98.06**	**3124381**	**31862**
九、果用瓜	**Melon as Fruit**	**12.47**	**426334**	**34186**	**12.77**	**421277**	**32992**
#1. 西瓜	Watermelon	9.67	358537	37066	10.04	354309	35297
2. 草莓	Strawberry	0.84	26905	32183	0.83	26434	31887
十、花卉园艺	**Flower Gardening**	**33.44**	**–**	**–**	**31.94**	**–**	**–**
十一、其他作物	**Others**	**13.39**	**–**	**–**	**14.08**	**–**	**–**
#绿肥	Green Manure	2.14	–	–	1.99	–	–

3-11 分地区粮食

Sown Areas and Yield of

指标		Item		全市 Whole City	市区 Urban District	#江干区 Jianggan	#拱墅区 Gongshu	#西湖区 Xihu	#高新(滨江)区 Hi-Tech (Binjiang)
一、粮食播种面积总计	**(公顷)**	**Sown Area of Grain Crops**	**(hectare)**	**167819**	**73031**	**–**	**–**	**2475**	**225**
春粮	(公顷)	Spring Grain	(hectare)	25057	13100	–	–	171	87
早稻	(公顷)	Early Rice	(hectare)	1961	1094	–	–	–	–
晚稻	(公顷)	Late Rice	(hectare)	73201	37286	–	–	1308	98
薯类	(公顷)	Tubers	(hectare)	22406	3414	–	–	236	–
玉米	(公顷)	Corn	(hectare)	19179	4330	–	–	260	20
大豆	(公顷)	Soybeans	(hectare)	25111	13262	–	–	300	19
杂豆	(公顷)	Other Beans	(hectare)	4376	1331	–	–	163	1
其他谷物	(公顷)	Other Cereals	(hectare)	1288	257	–	–	88	–
二、粮食总产量	**(吨)**	**Yield of Grain Crops**	**(ton)**	**978057**	**447641**	**–**	**–**	**17698**	**1235**
春粮	(吨)	Spring Grain	(ton)	94634	56889	–	–	468	289
早稻	(吨)	Early Rice	(ton)	11834	6929	–	–	–	–
晚稻	(吨)	Late Rice	(ton)	579023	299122	–	–	11153	786
薯类	(吨)	Tubers	(ton)	122418	21162	–	–	2722	–
玉米	(吨)	Corn	(ton)	93904	22310	–	–	1605	85
大豆	(吨)	Soybeans	(ton)	75535	39536	–	–	869	43
杂豆	(吨)	Other Beans	(ton)	13550	4484	–	–	449	4
其他谷物	(吨)	Other Cereals	(ton)	5316	1169	–	–	590	–
三、粮食平均每公顷产量	**(公斤)**	**Yield of Grain Crops per Hectare**	**(kg)**	**5828**	**6129**	**–**	**–**	**7148**	**5489**
春粮	(公斤)	Spring Grain	(kg)	3777	4343	–	–	2737	3306
早稻	(公斤)	Early Rice	(kg)	6035	6334	–	–	–	–
晚稻	(公斤)	Late Rice	(kg)	7910	8022	–	–	8527	8020
薯类	(公斤)	Tubers	(kg)	5464	6199	–	–	11534	–
玉米	(公斤)	Corn	(kg)	4896	5152	–	–	6173	4250
大豆	(公斤)	Soybeans	(kg)	3008	2981	–	–	2897	2263

备注:春粮包括薯类中的马铃薯。

播种面积及产量(2011年)
Grain Crops by Region(2011)

#萧山区 Xiaoshan	#余杭区 Yuhang	桐庐县 Tonglu	淳安县 Chun'an	建德市 Jiande	富阳市 Fuyang	临安市 Lin'an
43061	**26844**	**16247**	**22119**	**17871**	**23277**	**15274**
9560	3182	2050	1910	2581	3041	2375
133	894	36	–	758	73	–
18741	16880	6740	3650	7942	11273	6310
1078	2100	2946	6712	2793	3587	2954
2571	1479	1987	5927	1867	2767	2301
10684	2259	2335	4042	1958	2049	1465
442	725	591	478	342	981	653
75	94	265	187	188	282	109
241747	**184836**	**95778**	**93915**	**100994**	**149448**	**90281**
45079	10678	5801	5352	8174	10442	7976
821	5832	227	–	4255	423	–
145435	140274	52059	26753	61353	89698	50038
6643	11769	18055	29103	13096	23265	17737
12495	8125	9883	26043	9263	15562	10843
30343	8281	8933	8386	5921	7875	4884
1473	2558	1888	880	721	3689	1888
305	274	1179	445	684	1395	444
5625	**6885**	**5897**	**4246**	**5651**	**6420**	**5911**
4715	3354	2830	2802	3166	3434	3358
6158	6523	6306	–	5611	5795	–
7760	8310	7724	7330	7725	7957	7930
6162	5604	6128	4335	4689	6486	6004
4860	5494	4974	4394	4963	5624	4712
2840	3666	3826	2075	3022	3843	3334

a) Spring grain includes patato in tubers.

3－12 油、菜、茶、

Statistics on Rapeseeds, Vegetables, Tea,

指标	Item	全市 Whole City	市区 Urban District	#江干区 Jianggan	#拱墅区 Gongshu	#西湖区 Xihu	#高新(滨江)区 Hi－Tech (Binjiang)
一、油菜籽	Rapeseeds						
播种面积 （公顷）	Sown Area (hectare)	37994	8674	－	－	121	－
每公顷产量 （公斤）	Yield per Hectare (kg)	2101	2247	－	－	2074	－
总产量 （吨）	Total Output (ton)	79815	19494	－	－	251	－
二、蔬菜	Vegetables						
播种面积 （公顷）	Sown Area (hectare)	97196	58586	1896	15	2570	966
总产量 （吨）	Total Output (ton)	3164609	1833883	49219	260	51161	44298
三、茶叶	Tea						
（一）茶园面积 （公顷）	Tea Garden Area (hectare)	33174	6230	29	－	908	57
（二）总产量 （吨）	Output of Tea (ton)	31385	11604	11	－	515	36
春　茶 （吨）	Spring Tea (ton)	19829	6278	11	－	207	18
夏　茶 （吨）	Summer Tea (ton)	5867	2921	－	－	85	8
秋　茶 （吨）	Autumn Tea (ton)	5689	2405	－	－	223	10
四、桑蚕	Silkworm Cocoons & Mulberry						
（一）桑园总面积 （公顷）	Mulberry Garden Area (hectare)	15259	1460	1	－	－	－
（二）蚕茧总产量 （吨）	Output of Silkworm Cocoons (ton)	16127	352	9	－	－	－
春　茧 （吨）	Spring Silkworm Cocoons (ton)	7568	285	6	－	－	－
夏　茧 （吨）	Summer Silkworm Cocoons (ton)	1296	13	－	－	－	－
秋　茧 （吨）	Autumn Silkworm Cocoons (ton)	7263	54	3	－	－	－

蚕、果生产情况（2011 年）

Silkworm Cocoons and Fruits Production（2011）

#萧山区 Xiaoshan	#余杭区 Yuhang	桐庐县 Tonglu	淳安县 Chun'an	建德市 Jiande	富阳市 Fuyang	临安市 Lin'an
4678	3862	6350	7038	5636	7467	2829
2410	2058	1945	1877	1851	2383	2309
11275	7948	12352	13213	10433	17792	6531
28644	23608	6140	8783	7348	10321	6018
1113908	552033	205756	316098	209298	454370	145204
1287	3606	3509	12801	3607	3593	3434
891	9949	1835	7132	3153	5659	2002
741	5214	1290	4610	2541	3488	1622
54	2751	245	766	503	1303	129
96	1984	300	1756	109	868	251
98	1361	1982	7292	1292	1093	2140
6	337	3662	6376	874	2046	2817
6	273	1969	2548	484	894	1388
–	13	82	856	50	275	20
–	51	1611	2972	340	877	1409

3－12　续表

指标	Item	全市 Whole City	市区 Urban District	#江干区 Jianggan	#拱墅区 Gongshu	#西湖区 Xihu	#高新(滨江)区 Hi－Tech (Binjiang)
五、水果生产	**Fruits**						
(一)果园面积合计(公顷)	Area of Orchards (hectare)	27637	5522	–	–	82	99
柑桔园 (公顷)	Citrus (hectare)	9594	106	–	–	13	8
梨　园 (公顷)	Pears (hectare)	4010	1189	–	–	16	35
桃　园 (公顷)	Peaches (hectare)	3268	635	–	–	7	1
杨梅园 (公顷)	Red Bayberry (hectare)	2863	1001	–	–	7	49
枇杷园 (公顷)	Loquat (hectare)	2210	763	–	–	–	–
柿子园 (公顷)	Persimmons (hectare)	866	114	–	–	3	–
葡萄园 (公顷)	Grapes (hectare)	747	223	–	–	34	3
其他果园 (公顷)	Others (hectare)	4079	1491	–	–	2	3
(二)水果总产量 (吨)	Yield of Fruits (ton)	803122	234253	–	–	2627	3426
柑　桔 (吨)	Citrus (ton)	164100	1123	–	–	298	90
梨　头 (吨)	Pears (ton)	62531	14807	–	–	384	690
桃　子 (吨)	Peaches (ton)	65788	11237	–	–	140	12
杨　梅 (吨)	Red Bayberry (ton)	13583	4200	–	–	18	12
枇　杷 (吨)	Loquat (ton)	12950	5856	–	–	–	–
柿　子 (吨)	Persimmons (ton)	9109	1148	–	–	55	–
葡　萄 (吨)	Grapes (ton)	12968	3763	–	–	924	12
果用瓜 (吨)	Melon as Fruit (ton)	426334	185180	–	–	761	2508
其他水果 (吨)	Others (ton)	35759	6939	–	–	47	102

注:水果产量包括果用瓜和草莓产量。

continued

#萧山区 Xiaoshan	#余杭区 Yuhang	桐庐县 Tonglu	淳安县 Chun'an	建德市 Jiande	富阳市 Fuyang	临安市 Lin'an
2493	2848	3065	8679	6158	2602	1611
31	54	548	4709	3863	253	115
230	908	1152	543	293	552	281
208	419	470	755	315	782	311
730	215	341	404	523	404	190
1	762	126	745	491	76	9
84	27	47	436	145	95	29
106	80	118	51	25	200	130
1103	383	263	1036	503	240	546
130407	96453	92250	116903	172306	141130	46280
403	332	7272	61011	89353	4757	584
2330	11403	18593	4344	5791	14736	4260
2228	8857	8427	5823	3669	30444	6188
3171	999	1265	1068	1198	4502	1350
15	5841	356	3847	2051	720	120
628	465	519	3334	1192	2766	150
1672	1155	1247	596	230	5985	1147
114708	65863	52384	26816	63561	73201	25192
5252	1538	2187	10064	5261	4019	7289

a) Yield of fruits including melon as fruit and yield of strawberry.

3－13 分地区畜牧业
Statistics on Animal

指 标		Item		全市 Whole City	市区 Urban District	#江干区 Jianggan	#拱墅区 Gongshu
一、生猪饲养		**Hogs**					
生猪年末存栏	(万头)	Being Raised at Year－end	(10000 heads)	203.23	111.97	0.16	–
#能繁殖的母猪	(万头)	#Reproducible	(10000 heads)	17.3	11.51	0.06	–
年内肥猪出栏	(万头)	Slaughtered Hogs of the Year	(10000 heads)	342.35	185.69	0.37	–
全年饲养量	(万头)	Number of Hogs Raised in the year	(10000 heads)	545.58	297.66	0.53	–
二、牛		**Cattle & Buffaloes**					
牛年末存栏	(头)	Being Raised at Year－end	(head)	21129	8306	–	–
#良种及改良种乳牛	(头)	#Improved Milk Cows	(head)	10851	7559	–	–
牛年内出栏	(头)	Slaughtered Cattle & Buffaloes of the Year	(head)	9563	1114	–	–
三、羊		**Sheep & Goats**					
羊年末存栏	(万只)	Being Raised at Year－end	(10000 heads)	17.68	10.33	3.5	–
羊年内出栏	(万只)	Slaughtered Sheep & Goats of the Year	(10000 heads)	23.46	12.13	2.15	–
四、家禽		**Poultry**					
家禽年末存栏	(万只)	Being Raised at Year－end	(10000 heads)	2039.4	731.8	–	–
家禽年内出栏	(万只)	Slaughtered Poultry of the Year	(10000 heads)	4296.84	2466.95	–	0.41
五、兔		**Rabbits**					
兔年末存栏	(万只)	Being Raised at Year－end	(10000 heads)	24.81	6.1	–	–
兔年内出栏	(万只)	Slaughtered Rabbits of the Year	(10000 heads)	67.32	8.56	–	–
六、年末养蜂箱数	**(箱)**	**Beehives**	**(case)**	**168720**	**31013**	**–**	**–**
七、畜禽产品产量		**Output of Livestock Products**					
1. 肉类产量	(吨)	Output of Meat	(ton)	324952	174792	981	2
#猪　肉	(吨)	Pork	(ton)	252672	135187	272	–

渔业生产(2011 年)

Husbanday and Fishery by Region(2011)

#西湖区 Xihu	#高新(滨江)区 Hi-Tech(Binjiang)	#萧山区 Xiaoshan	#余杭区 Yuhang	桐庐县 Tonglu	淳安县 Chun'an	建德市 Jiande	富阳市 Fuyang	临安市 Lin'an
2.04	0.47	95.99	12.74	12.91	17.67	20.28	19.8	20.6
0.03	0.03	10.2	1.13	0.73	0.77	1.91	0.97	1.41
1.99	0.98	147.14	34.43	22.99	21.98	23.35	48.94	39.4
4.03	1.45	243.13	47.17	35.9	39.65	43.63	68.74	60
14	–	2265	712	2407	2039	1776	3528	3073
–	–	2008	236	–	–	204	1411	1677
12	–	113	359	1289	947	847	2822	2544
0.06	–	2.45	4.28	1.47	0.25	1.03	2.99	1.61
0.09	–	3.86	6	1.94	0.29	0.68	6.45	1.97
18.02	1.18	381.68	329.84	92.91	43.05	874.88	203.35	93.41
30.89	3.92	1212.47	1217.16	149.17	54.63	546.92	922.24	156.93
–	–	1.22	4.88	3.8	0.32	3.14	1.77	9.68
–	–	2.7	5.86	7.49	0.36	5.37	7.99	37.55
100	**–**	**28193**	**2720**	**69618**	**21585**	**10238**	**26321**	**9945**
1733	884	121975	48518	20104	18027	26080	52071	33878
1298	819	102996	29259	16878	16985	17309	36705	29608

3－13　续表

指　标	Item	全市 Whole City	市区 Urban District	#江干区 Jianggan	#拱墅区 Gongshu	#西湖区 Xihu	#高新(滨江)区 Hi－Tech (Binjiang)
牛　肉　（吨）	Beef　（ton）	1528	224	－	－	2	－
羊　肉　（吨）	Mutton　（ton）	4531	2647	709	－	14	－
兔　肉　（吨）	Rabbit Meat　（ton）	1392	187	－	－	－	－
禽　肉　（吨）	Poultry Meat　（ton）	64327	36547	－	2	419	65
2.禽蛋产量　（吨）	Poultry Eggs　（ton）	159400	31380	－	－	737	21
3.蜂蜜产量　（吨）	Honey　（ton）	21185	2173	－	－	3	13
4.蜂皇浆产量　（公斤）	Honey Tonic　（kg）	565310	98294	－	－	300	345
5.牛奶产量　（吨）	Milk　（ton）	42202	27922	－	－	－	－
6.兔毛产量　（吨）	Rabbit Wool　（ton）	56	16	－	－	－	－
八、渔业生产	**Fishery**						
（一）淡水产品产量总计（吨）	Total Output of Freshwater Aquatic Products　（ton）	212277	162492	580	41	29822	2139
其中：养殖产量（吨）	Artificially Cultured　（ton）	194361	151333	500	41	21715	1289
1.鱼　类　（吨）	Fish　（ton）	112700	77142	290	40	15701	754
#鲫　鱼　（吨）	#Crucians　（ton）	12487	6407	70	30	2719	270
鳊　鱼　（吨）	Breams　（ton）	6279	2781	15	－	900	40
黑　鱼　（吨）	Snake Heads　（ton）	19098	19034	－	－	1093	20
2.虾蟹类　（吨）	Shrimps, Prawns & Crabs　（ton）	45476	44309	30	－	1289	495
3.贝　类　（吨）	Shellfish　（ton）	1211	104	－	－	104	－
4.其　他　（吨）	Others　（ton）	34974	29778	180	1	4621	40
#甲　鱼　（吨）	Turtles　（ton）	32501	28488	－	1	4215	38
（二）淡水养殖面积合计（公顷）	Freshwater Aquiculture Area　（hectare）	60911	12196	140	17	2467	244

continued

#萧山区 Xiaoshan	#余杭区 Yuhang	桐庐县 Tonglu	淳安县 Chun'an	建德市 Jiande	富阳市 Fuyang	临安市 Lin'an
21	81	232	140	126	417	389
733	1186	342	44	113	966	419
39	148	357	7	108	120	613
18186	17844	2169	847	8354	13840	2570
3933	26639	6068	3977	101676	10557	5742
1623	534	8135	2284	398	7056	1139
95710	1939	337481	26878	13325	54202	35130
7672	450	–	–	481	8259	5540
3	13	–	–	–	–	40
64112	63792	7333	14559	12933	10449	4511
63462	62380	6981	12079	10155	9829	3984
18763	41208	3111	11928	8962	7953	3604
206	3051	717	1112	1267	2201	783
–	1815	69	860	1532	822	215
7477	10439	–	–	–	56	8
39090	1845	134	–	170	834	29
–	–	–	–	868	239	–
5609	19327	3736	151	155	803	351
19074	5160	3115	151	73	383	291
3895	4797	1440	41040	2010	1503	2722

3－14　分地区林业
Statistics on Forestry

指　标		Item		全市 Whole City	市区 Urban District
一、营林情况		**Afforestation**			
1. 当年造林面积	（公顷）	Afforested Areas	（hectare）	5573	634
#用材林	（公顷）	#Timber Forest	（hectare）	916	－
经济林	（公顷）	Economic Forest	（hectare）	1350	－
2. 迹地更新面积	（公顷）	Area of Forest Updating	（hectare）	2718	33
3. 封山育林面积	（公顷）	Area of Afforestation in Enclosed Mountain	（hectare）	83234	35922
4. 零星（四旁）植树	（万株）	Planting Trees	（10000 plant）	517.66	323.66
5. 幼林抚育作业面积	（公顷）	Area of Seedling Cultivated	（hectare）	6983	1291
6. 成林抚育面积	（公顷）	Area of Grown Forest Cultivated	（hectare）	27567	17367
二、林产品产量		**Output of Forest Products**			
1. 油桐籽	（吨）	Tung－oil Seeds	（ton）	－	－
2. 油茶籽	（吨）	Tea－oil Seeds	（ton）	9447	－
3. 竹笋干	（吨）	Dried Bamboo Shoots	（ton）	41125	10552
4. 核　桃	（吨）	Walnuts	（ton）	19286	50
5. 板　栗	（吨）	Chestnuts	（ton）	12414	987
三、竹木采伐量		**Lumbering**			
1. 木　材	（万立方米）	Timber Cut	（10000 cu. m）	33.07	1.37
2. 竹　材	（万支）	Bamboo Cut	（10000 pieces）	2278	895

生产(2011年)
by Region(2011)

#萧山区 Xiaoshan	#余杭区 Yuhang	桐庐县 Tonglu	淳安县 Chun'an	建德市 Jiande	富阳市 Fuyang	临安市 Lin'an
394	108	718	1540	607	1600	474
–	–	195	140	239	133	209
–	–	76	392	167	560	155
1	32	362	312	798	520	693
13339	21247	39755	4250	1794	1133	380
35	282.46	49	78	15	31	21
	1291	906	2133	1300	20	1333
	17367	–	3533	3667	1333	1667
–	–	–	–	–	–	–
–	–	1500	6803	1034	–	110
1650	8902	400	4387	786	1500	23500
–	50	1080	5020	36	100	13000
759	228	2800	3867	2532	1843	385
0.39	0.69	4.04	9.58	7.55	2.33	8.2
139	755	173	405	69	286	450

3－15 分地区灌溉和水利
Irrigation and Water Conservancy

指　　标		Item		全　市 Whole City
一、水库		Reservoirs		
已建成水库个数	（个）	Number of Completed Reservoirs	(unit)	627
总库容	（立方米）	Total reservoir capacity	(Cubic meters)	2361631
二、灌溉面积		Irrigated Area		
1. 有效灌溉面积(农田面积)	（千公顷）	Irrigable Land	(1000 hectares)	165.244
2. 旱涝保收面积	（千公顷）	Area of Stable Yields Despite Drought or Excessive Rain	(1000 hectares)	134.361
3. 机电排灌面积	（千公顷）	Electrical Irrigation Area	(1000 hectares)	116.774
三、机电井		Motor－pumped Well		
已配套机电井	（眼）	Motor－pumped Well System	(unit)	122
装机容量	（千瓦）	Installed Capacity	(kw)	480

设施情况(2011 年)
Facilities by Region(2011)

市　区 Urban District	#江干区 Jianggan	#拱墅区 Gongshu	#西湖区 Xihu	#高新(滨江)区 Hi－Tech (Binjiang)	#萧山区 Xiaoshan	#余杭区 Yuhang	桐庐县 Tonglu	淳安县 Chun'an	建德市 Jiande	富阳市 Fuyang	临安市 Lin'an
45	–	1	2	–	14	28	93	65	138	142	144
4781	–	10. 2	84	–	465	4222	113735	15334	2169878	8071	49832
90. 154	0. 75	0. 11	2. 724	0. 45	53. 61	32. 51	11. 95	9. 1	14. 85	21. 22	17. 97
79. 399	0. 75	–	2. 139	0. 45	44. 88	31. 18	9. 257	7. 435	11. 61	14. 54	12. 12
87. 604	0. 75	–	2. 724	0. 45	53. 08	30. 6	5. 14	1. 98	4. 67	14. 3	3. 08
122						122					
480						480					

3－16 分地区主要农

Possession of Major Agricultural

指　　标		Item		全　　市 Whole City	
				2011 年	为上年(%) As Compared with the Preceding Year(%)
一、农业机械总动力	**(千瓦)**	**Total Power of Agricultural Machinery**	**(kw)**	**3367473.49**	**101.7**
耕作机械动力	(千瓦)	Cultivation Machinery	(kw)	218534.25	104.8
收获机械动力	(千瓦)	Harvest Machinery	(kw)	274956.76	96.7
植保机械动力	(千瓦)	Plant Protection Machinery	(kw)	39244.1	118.9
排灌机械动力	(千瓦)	Drainage & Irrigation Machinery	(kw)	415857.36	98.8
农副产品加工机械动力	(千瓦)	Processing Machinery of Agricultural Products	(kw)	187751.66	102.4
运输机械动力	(千瓦)	Transport Machinery	(kw)	911659.5	99.1
渔业机械动力	(千瓦)	Fishery Machinery	(kw)	113932.6	104.7
其他机械动力	(千瓦)	Other Machinery	(kw)	1205537.26	105
二、主要农机具		**Agricultural Machinery and Machinery For Processing Farm Products**			
大中型拖拉机	(台)	Large & Medium Tractors	(unit)	908	106.1
机引农具	(台)	Mechanized Farm Implement	(unit)	1809	116.8
农用小型拖拉机	(台)	Mini－tractors	(unit)	16149	101.5
联合收获机	(台)	Combine Harvesters	(unit)	1005	103.4
机动割晒机	(台)	Motorized Harvesters	(unit)	8	53.3
机动脱粒机	(台)	Motorized Thresher	(unit)	172542	95.4
谷物烘干机	(台)	Cereal Dryer	(unit)	174	185.1
机动喷雾(粉)器	(架)	Motorized Sprayer	(unit)	27135	134.7
农用水泵	(台)	Water Pump for Agricultural Use	(unit)	143048	96.9
节水喷灌机械	(套)	Saving Water and Sprinkling Machinery	(set)	5790	153.2
粮食加工机械	(台)	Grain Processing Machinery	(unit)	21844	110.7
棉花加工机械	(台)	Cotton Processing Machinery	(unit)	243	100.4
油料加工机械	(台)	Oil Processing Machinery	(unit)	1611	99.5
农用运输机械	(台)	Vehicles for Agricultural Use	(unit)	40048	97
淡水机动渔船	(艘)	Motorized Fishing Boats	(unit)	2079	103.4

机具年末拥有量(2011年)
Machinery at the Year - end by Region(2011)

市区 Urban District	#萧山区 Xiaoshan	#余杭区 Yuhang	桐庐县 Tonglu	淳安县 Chun'an	建德市 Jiande	富阳市 Fuyang	临安市 Lin'an
1652265.1	**776862**	**508434**	**255364**	**283071.39**	**285382**	**441336**	**450055**
105973.5	52939	48663	16429	14169.75	20930	30470	30562
124121	43293	79315	38663	7080.76	31472	55566	18054
7189	3961	2954	1463	2236.1	4349	3128	20879
193723	82625	88031	36215	19727.36	51822	56336	58034
56766	33603	16923	11681	53321.66	21838	14260	29885
402334.8	263902	124981	93563	54449.7	73283	134382	153647
96378.3	73736	10796	999	12345.3	1906	1851	453
665779.5	222803	136771	56351	119740.76	79782	145343	138541
745	555	187	21	3	7	122	10
1682	1304	378	17	2	19	74	15
6242	1975	3863	1612	1511	2059	2490	2235
620	450	147	77	8	55	227	18
4	–	4	–	1	–	2	1
79982	24051	55570	25895	3148	20359	31643	11515
107	58	49	10	9	20	17	11
5003	2764	1664	622	1348	1709	1536	16917
40006	16634	19530	15261	4096	22818	15143	45724
552	152	381	41	472	2720	6	1999
2914	1627	1146	1365	8970	1823	1016	5756
87	70	17	32	57	14	47	6
226	157	48	245	626	256	88	170
17042	10566	5645	4147	2125	3201	7582	5951
416	141	88	23	1331	231	50	28

3－17 农业机械作业和
Agricultural Mechanization and

指　标		Item		全　市 Whole City 2011 年	为上年(%) As Compared with the Preceding Year(%)
一、农业机械作业		**Agricultural Mechanization**			
当年机械收割面积	(千公顷)	Harvest Area by Tractors	(1000 hectares)	93.74	90.3
二、农村用电量	**(万千瓦时)**	**Electricity Consumed in Rural Area**	**(10000 kwh)**	**1129507**	**103.3**
三、农业化肥用量		**Consumption of Chemical Fertilizer**			
(一)按实物量计算	(吨)	Physical Quantity Consumption	(ton)	557540	94.4
1.氮　肥	(吨)	Nitrogenous Fertilizer	(ton)	251045	92.5
2.磷　肥	(吨)	Phosphate Fertilizer	(ton)	87225	94.5
3.钾　肥	(吨)	Potash Fertilizer	(ton)	43246	95.2
4.复合肥	(吨)	Compound Fertilizer	(ton)	176024	97.2
(二)按折纯法计算	(吨)	Pure Consumption	(ton)	109714	95.3
1.氮　肥	(吨)	Nitrogenous Fertilizer	(ton)	54127	92.6
2.磷　肥	(吨)	Phosphate Fertilizer	(ton)	12604	97.0
3.钾　肥	(吨)	Potash Fertilizer	(ton)	8271	95.7
4.复合肥	(吨)	Compound Fertilizer	(ton)	34712	99.1
四、农用塑料薄膜使用量	**(吨)**	**Use of Plastic Film**	**(ton)**	**9767**	**121.9**
五、农用柴油使用量	**(吨)**	**Consumption of Diesel Oil**	**(ton)**	**29298**	**106.3**
六、农药使用量	**(吨)**	**Consumption of Pesticide**	**(ton)**	**8308**	**95.1**

物资消耗情况(2011 年)
Material Consumption(2011)

市　区 Urban District	#萧山区 Xiaoshan	#余杭区 Yuhang	桐庐县 Tonglu	淳安县 Chun'an	建德市 Jiande	富阳市 Fuyang	临安市 Lin'an
54.34	31.73	19.77	8.63	1.07	9.85	13.87	5.98
555751	**230378**	**218468**	**69158**	**10611**	**20000**	**377455**	**96532**
317427	239793	66736	39477	59482	51223	23506	66425
145187	107208	33517	18422	31751	23352	13310	19023
54632	43612	9602	8622	7013	7284	3046	6628
21086	14733	5548	4377	6528	4466	558	6231
96522	74240	18069	8056	14190	16121	6592	34543
49170	28542	16574	8230	7436	18211	9866	16801
23713	15203	7050	3775	3067	10615	5590	7367
5922	3926	1516	1485	808	2129	1097	1163
3332	1841	1227	1030	408	1622	279	1600
16203	7572	6781	1940	3153	3845	2900	6671
3002	**2188**	**409**	**709**	**3587**	**1748**	**199**	**522**
10940	**8032**	**2587**	**4857**	**1647**	**3992**	**279**	**7583**
3353	**2097**	**1061**	**815**	**706**	**1299**	**960**	**1175**

3-18 农村经济
Rural Economic Income

单位:万元

指　标	Item	全　市 Whole City	
		2011 年	为上年(%) As Compared with the Preceding Year(%)
一、农村经济总收入	**Total Rural Economic Income**	**150013528**	**115.6**
#出售产品收入	Sales Income	99915150	113.0
1.农林牧渔业收入	Income from Farming, Forestry, Animal Husbandry & Fishery	3610896	109.3
①农业收入	Income from Farming	1938035	109.2
#出售种植业产品收入	Income from Planting	1730952	
②林业收入	Income from Forestry	467049	107.3
③牧业收入	Income from Animal Husbandry	783762	112.3
④渔业收入	Income from Fishery	422050	107
2.工业收入	Income from Industry	102751198	111.4
3.建筑业收入	Income from Construction	10151930	130.1
4.运输业收入	Income from Transportation	2773398	127.7
5.商业、饮食业收入	Income from Trade & Catering Services	13240866	129.5
6.服务业收入	Income from Services	14890657	122.6
7.其他收入	Other Income	2594583	131.2
二、农村经济总费用	**Total Rural Economic Expenses**	**133680656**	**115.5**
#生产费用	Production Expenses	120813010	113.3
三、可分配净收入	**Disposable Net Income**	**17431112**	**114.9**
#国家税金	State Taxes		
农民所得收入	Farmers' Earnings	6302542	111.8
每人平均所得(元)	Per Capita Income(yuan)	15587	
为上年(%)	As Compared with the Preceding Year(%)	113	

收入分配(2011 年)
Distribution(2011)

(10000 yuan)

市区 Urban District	#萧山区 Xiaoshan	#余杭区 Yuhang	桐庐县 Tonglu	淳安县 Chun'an	建德市 Jiande	富阳市 Fuyang	临安市 Lin'an
109721778	**58610295**	**20577487**	**5765054**	**2223296**	**4336109**	**18335465**	**9631826**
72218252	46713474	16996432	5287906	1503736	3159455	11003523	6742278
1465363	749555	561692	251614	493218	324247	718998	357456
814294	444440	265720	135887	286262	162480	392393	146719
764303	428692	256117	110006	240224	148595	341007	126817
54350	14944	38958	35041	105473	16024	120822	135340
276912	143182	126161	51487	88746	136651	159458	70508
319808	146989	130853	29199	12737	9093	46325	4889
72003962	48129095	17150483	5119298	1304187	3484259	12968633	7870860
8623409	4231621	547824	80990	95046	70129	847805	434551
1676998	940875	384917	84555	89395	55845	695161	171444
10616532	479071	926288	115020	112421	57703	1877167	462024
13710414	3657938	430665	73208	94187	44156	836341	132351
1625101	422140	575618	40370	34842	299770	391360	203140
98510722	**52521202**	**17925080**	**4866467**	**1930733**	**3832927**	**16285741**	**8254065**
91624150	48405370	16675855	4388086	1675894	3034500	12778596	7311784
11797253	**6581761**	**2858611**	**962185**	**377697**	**601034**	**2185836**	**1507107**
3736355	1763590	1229801	381853	311567	400797	859704	612266
	18323	18179	12356	8291	10291	16607	14357
	110.3	114.4	113.5	115.7	113.2	111.8	113.9

3－19 乡(镇)

Statistics on Towns

乡镇名称 Town		村民委员会(个) Number of Villagers' Committees (unit)	农村常住户数(户) Resident Households in Rural Areas (household)	农村常住人口数(人) Resident Population in Rural Areas (person)	农村从业人员数(人) Labor Force in Rural Areas (person)
江干区	**Jianggan District**				
丁桥镇	Dingqiao	2	487	1933	1188
笕桥镇	Jianqiao	–	5624	23331	11837
彭埠镇	Pengbu	–	5384	22187	10282
九堡镇	Jiubao	4	6183	26237	13584
拱墅区	**Gongshu District**				
康桥街道	Kangqiao Subdistrict	–	1424	5497	2661
半山街道	Banshan Subdistrict	–	745	2977	1998
祥符街道	Xiangfu Subdistrict	–	1345	4572	1991
西湖区	**Xihu District**				
留下街道	Liuxia Subdistrict	2	3348	10310	5308
转塘街道	Zhuantang Subdistrict	16	14443	53721	25679
双浦镇	Shuangpu	27	14661	57126	30457
三墩镇	Sandun	4	10619	41884	25863
高新(滨江)区	**Hi－Tech(Bingjiang) District**				
浦沿街道	Puyan Subdistrict	3	9317	36587	20137
长河街道	Changhe Subdistrict	1	11878	42504	23415
西兴街道	Xixing Subdistrict	5	6463	22584	13070
开发区	**Development Zone**				
下沙街道	Xiasha Subdistrict	–	–	–	–
西湖风景名胜区	**The West Lake Scenic Zone**				
西湖街道	West Lake Subdistrict	9	2825	5610	3442

基本情况(2011 年)
and Townships(2011)

乡镇常用耕地面积(亩) Commonly used cultivated area of township (mu)	粮食播种面积(亩) Sown Area of Grain Crops (mu)	粮食总产量(吨) Yield of Grain Crops (ton)	农业总产值(当年价格)(万元) Gross Output Value of Agriculture (10000 yuan)	财政总收入(万元) Financial Revenue (10000 yuan)	农村经济总收入(万元) Total Income of Rural Economy (10000 yuan)	农民人均年纯收入(元) Per Capita Annual Net Income (yuan)
285	–	–	309	61000	796451	17685
3866	–	–	5050	150114	2738286	20081
3676	–	–	3406	59068	2143161	19131
5044	–	–	4614	48200	1558359	17550
56	–	–	11	38411	4578409	18632
155	–	–	94	51097	1816551	18618
2186	–	–	–	63252	1101183	18494
325	–	–	601	78476	488470	19710
7075	3903	1678	10532	97063	627394	18916
23353	22029	10617	42972	10002	1045756	17679
14442	11204	5403	9983	92139	662646	18643
3720	820	344	6332	40297	1851868	17503
2194	283	123	10782	39991	1757891	18720
3283	2275	817	11077	68353	1537079	17618
–	6380	2049	19337	–	–	20479
–	–	–	6394	9255	70264	18061

3－19　续表1

乡 镇 名 称 Town		村民委员会(个) Number of Villagers' Committees (unit)	农村常住户数 (户) Resident Households in Rural Areas (household)	农村常住人口数 (人) Resident Population in Rural Areas (person)	农村从业人员数 (人) Labor Force in Rural Areas (person)
萧山区	**Xiaoshan District**				
楼塔镇	Louta	12	9092	27489	14542
河上镇	Heshang	15	9902	28735	16851
戴村镇	Daicun	22	10269	35470	23533
浦阳镇	Puyang	18	12881	39166	23976
进化镇	Jinhua	25	14701	51060	30659
临浦镇	Linpu	20	14180	48522	27222
义桥镇	Yiqiao	21	13899	45618	28882
所前镇	Suoqian	19	13525	45491	23288
衙前镇	Yaqian	11	6968	25500	14985
闻堰镇	Wenyan	6	5821	21186	13505
宁围镇	Ningwei	15	18412	54296	25777
新街镇	Xinjie	15	17256	53921	32323
坎山镇	Kanshan	19	15607	53389	31043
瓜沥镇	Guali	23	18738	56368	39836
党山镇	Dangshan	21	14455	45172	28282
益农镇	Yinong	19	14338	44036	27864
靖江街道	Jingjiang Subdistrict	10	10963	31977	19855
南阳街道	Nanyang Subdistrict	13	11922	38630	23744
义蓬街道	Yipeng Subdistrict	22	18898	59326	40136
河庄街道	Hezhuang Subdistrict	20	13891	48947	30042
党湾镇	Dangwan	17	12828	39134	25402
新湾街道	Xinwan Subdistrict	12	8062	28483	13200
城厢街道	Chengxiang Subdistrict	–	12546	45437	10491
北干街道	Beigan Subdistrict	6	16325	55022	17649
蜀山街道	Shushan Subdistrict	8	15449	50672	33856
新塘街道	Xintang Subdistrict	17	20175	72598	39735
前进街道	Qianjin Subdistrict	3	4249	15628	9312
临江街道	Linjiang Subdistrict	2	1188	4160	2660
余杭区	**Yuhang District**				
运河镇	Yunhe	14	9642	38741	24549

continued 1

乡镇常用耕地面积(亩) Commonly used cultivated area of township (mu)	粮食播种面积(亩) Sown Area of Grain Crops (mu)	粮食总产量(吨) Yield of Grain Crops (ton)	农业总产值(当年价格)(万元) Gross Output Value of Agriculture (10000 yuan)	财政总收入(万元) Financial Revenue (10000 yuan)	农村经济总收入(万元) Total Income of Rural Economy (10000 yuan)	农民人均年纯收入(元) Per Capita Annual Net Income (yuan)
12710	11239	4234	12020	23199	324276	13111
13058	13286	5413	11595	26352	1174376	13703
18432	16993	7030	17053	40014	1010793	15392
19636	20358	9568	21324	37279	767561	15800
18626	19885	9676	26735	37154	827646	15768
17954	14155	5797	31405	121116	1691840	15810
21524	20376	9768	27902	57729	1193613	17591
17220	16739	8281	36500	50147	1709087	16971
8528	5179	1857	8807	94595	5476386	22043
4561	2255	824	12283	72905	1191914	19203
25279	6056	2669	44070	485259	15962775	26037
31393	10715	3535	68596	90320	3273543	20268
29305	17316	5365	34458	45587	1387464	18932
31582	37024	13795	33108	146701	3813212	19114
40812	57677	23191	43173	57472	3776884	17429
43119	49852	19172	44990	64943	4111535	18351
21396	30918	11087	24442	43933	832879	20418
25969	28307	11522	32300	47079	1106686	19312
49300	65441	22642	70215	88022	1069498	17845
39276	64390	22399	46825	36157	1023277	19365
34315	56539	21415	40996	37910	1541323	19628
20154	35145	12525	23819	23369	483639	17106
2080	1225	433	2818	186009	571070	17587
3757	400	158	4562	146474	500044	23450
13825	4314	1432	13630	48396	1119809	16252
11352	2308	900	15118	120698	2080781	17225
11494	13205	4552	11248	15823	70027	15165
6244	7600	2630	6319	95708	16500	13977
13979	11148	5077	39047	15857	819759	18380

3－19 续表2

乡镇名称 Town		村民委员会(个) Number of Villagers' Committees (unit)	农村常住户数(户) Resident Households in Rural Areas (household)	农村常住人口数(人) Resident Population in Rural Areas (person)	农村从业人员数(人) Labor Force in Rural Areas (person)
乔司镇	Qiaosi	11	9870	39467	24135
塘栖镇	Tangxi	27	17949	70910	45935
仁和镇	Renhe	18	16113	64865	41403
崇贤镇	Chongxian	11	10583	43003	29147
余杭镇	Yuhang	14	12561	43991	22751
闲林镇	Xianlin	8	5871	23245	13790
仓前镇	Cangqian	9	8039	31498	20817
中泰乡	Zhongtai	10	7931	32090	15947
良渚镇	Liangzhu	23	21373	88276	53968
瓶窑镇	Pingyao	13	11282	40672	25982
径山镇	Jingshan	13	10407	33965	23170
黄湖镇	Huanghu	5	4741	14934	8719
鸬鸟镇	Luniao	6	3710	12299	8035
百丈镇	Baizhang	6	3243	10690	6590
临平街道	Linping Subdistrict	–	2661	10640	6886
南苑街道	Nanyuan Subdistrict	–	7125	30915	18358
星桥街道	Xingqiao Subdistrict	–	7459	26405	9400
五常街道	Wuchang Subdistrict	–	7034	32321	15430
桐庐县	**Tonglu County**				
桐君街道	Tongjun Subdistrict	6	3938	11611	7320
旧县街道	Jiuxian Subdistrict	5	3158	8724	5499
富春江镇	Fuchunjiang	15	6697	19675	10137
江南镇	Jiangnan	20	13636	48829	30012
凤川镇	Fengchuan	8	5687	17628	8467
新合乡	Xinghe	5	1681	4711	3292
横村镇	Hengcun	24	14925	41246	25145
莪山畲族乡	Eshan	7	2938	8902	5583
钟山乡	Zhongshan	11	5792	15997	13214
分水镇	Fenshui	26	17968	49309	30628

continued 2

乡镇常用耕地面积(亩) Commonly used cultivated area of township (mu)	粮食播种面积(亩) Sown Area of Grain Crops (mu)	粮食总产量(吨) Yield of Grain Crops (ton)	农业总产值(当年价格)(万元) Gross Output Value of Agriculture (10000 yuan)	财政总收入(万元) Financial Revenue (10000 yuan)	农村经济总收入(万元) Total Income of Rural Economy (10000 yuan)	农民人均年纯收入(元) Per Capita Annual Net Income (yuan)
18469	7285	1734	29245	60239	1258502	18938
34434	34917	15444	56859	281574	2466136	19800
37777	39852	19108	50205	31772	1144142	17517
17587	14606	6779	25787	27032	1872422	18287
49629	54344	26265	46479	53701	1306136	18519
10458	13108	5483	23169	72586	1555295	19811
28243	42380	19407	29642	65187	599376	18885
19280	16605	7314	20583	35053	466716	18300
49611	40300	20972	45238	166911	2199286	17172
42156	34901	17320	57174	67009	1734764	16971
47772	39203	17976	75016	26030	642787	15922
14188	11580	4690	20343	5198	266785	17050
11665	10485	5154	37320	4727	225899	16908
2216	5880	2252	15163	3905	318092	18531
2682	1636	618	18018	22144	297904	18064
13134	8836	3121	31050	40900	615653	18359
5375	1165	399	11800	16192	482417	19209
5140	1015	284	2955	82696	1033263	24200
5181	6801	2866	11875	25916	45472	11684
7341	8335	3264	5830	7481	201829	14631
13056	20698	9844	24214	33866	543626	13548
25171	22741	9033	14749	18355	786781	12725
12050	12132	5087	14877	3215	213442	12155
4136	3187	1421	3048	411	49697	11213
41957	35500	14211	33165	26944	1103888	14565
6894	9941	3812	8714	1615	101156	10633
17733	20914	6951	12775	21932	165108	11608
29974	33531	13175	55006	27300	840080	12824

3－19 续表3

乡镇名称 Town		村民委员会(个) Number of Villagers' Committees (unit)	农村常住户数(户) Resident Households in Rural Areas (household)	农村常住人口数(人) Resident Population in Rural Areas (person)	农村从业人员数(人) Labor Force in Rural Areas (person)
瑶琳镇	Yaolin	16	10322	31310	22428
百江镇	Baijiang	15	5279	12353	12467
合村乡	Hecun	6	2822	8754	6933
城南街道	Chengnan	19	12111	34237	22118
淳安县	**Chun'an County**				
千岛湖镇	Qiandaohu	22	8353	23308	14820
文昌镇	Wenchang	16	4196	12883	8342
石林镇	Shilin	8	1462	4463	2950
临歧镇	Linqi	17	5819	19483	12891
威坪镇	Weiping	44	14401	42295	27880
姜家镇	Jiangjia	28	8021	24995	16180
梓桐镇	Zitong	19	6085	18610	12288
汾口镇	Fenkou	51	16507	52248	34080
中洲镇	Zhongzhou	19	5841	18982	12345
大墅镇	Dashu	17	4349	13771	9176
枫树岭镇	Fengshuling	28	5834	17562	11430
里商乡	Lishang	16	3353	10714	7080
金峰乡	Jinfeng	11	1767	5248	3392
富文乡	Fuwen	10	2018	6279	4280
左口乡	Zuokou	11	3238	10603	6849
屏门乡	Pingmen	15	3888	11583	7864
瑶山乡	Yaoshan	11	2830	9260	6024
王阜乡	Wangfu	18	6048	17687	11235
宋村乡	Songcun	8	2134	5735	3819
鸠坑乡	Jiukeng	9	2488	7278	4934
浪川乡	Langchuan	19	6128	18132	11985

continued 3

乡镇常用耕地面积(亩) Commonly used cultivated area of township (mu)	粮食播种面积(亩) Sown Area of Grain Crops (mu)	粮食总产量(吨) Yield of Grain Crops (ton)	农业总产值(当年价格)(万元) Gross Output Value of Agriculture (10000 yuan)	财政总收入(万元) Financial Revenue (10000 yuan)	农村经济总收入(万元) Total Income of Rural Economy (10000 yuan)	农民人均年纯收入(元) Per Capita Annual Net Income (yuan)
28275	26974	9980	28891	5305	278699	11431
13884	15738	5108	12896	1122	100878	10326
7754	12190	4509	14057	556	36985	9045
12344	15023	6539	23599	11552	925483	11655
7121	8779	2780	19977	11382	299067	9585
6497	12690	3557	15603	4324	149666	9489
2315	4810	1161	6092	1514	42368	9436
11827	15311	4270	19011	4310	61218	9173
19693	31670	7616	33851	9247	197966	7733
13392	23297	7419	20214	4748	133268	8446
10954	26833	7522	19320	2889	143070	8840
25961	44760	14415	33775	9770	339174	7696
9040	13904	4556	12200	3902	61090	7154
9426	10752	3664	10434	2718	200800	9093
13677	13208	4670	19837	3143	115010	8846
3355	10723	2458	11565	2034	49331	8998
3877	6225	2351	6825	1392	17450	8088
4543	7155	1939	7020	2240	34135	8413
5105	11169	3009	10270	1778	25184	7954
5298	17047	3446	13562	2130	54035	8465
4400	10636	2537	13373	1383	40654	8838
4220	13351	2975	13476	2534	44226	6792
1848	3436	621	5004	1585	14789	6948
1672	5332	1252	7415	1690	36153	7381
10713	17449	5651	14137	2603	80585	8637

3－19 续表4

乡镇名称 Town		村民委员会(个) Number of Villagers´ Committees (unit)	农村常住户数 (户) Resident Households in Rural Areas (household)	农村常住人口数 (人) Resident Population in Rural Areas (person)	农村从业人员数 (人) Labor Force in Rural Areas (person)
界首乡	Jieshou	13	2711	8274	5421
安阳乡	Anyang	15	3391	11007	7055
建德市	**Jiande City**				
新安江街道	Xin´anjiang Subdistrict	4	3845	11941	7671
洋溪街道	Yangxi Subdistrict	5	5598	12501	9339
更楼街道	Genglou Subdistrict	14	8008	23586	12783
莲花镇	Lianhua	6	3135	10523	6636
乾潭镇	Qiantan	24	12527	40529	23133
钦堂乡	Qintang	7	2628	8511	5163
梅城镇	Meicheng	13	8514	27752	14796
杨村桥镇	Yangcunqiao	13	5763	19284	11518
下涯镇	Xiaya	11	7798	25896	14982
大洋镇	Dayang	19	9637	32372	19489
三都镇	Sandu	19	9484	26995	15573
寿昌镇	Shouchang	23	10705	35594	21354
航头镇	Hangtou	18	9675	32478	19115
大慈岩镇	Daciyan	12	6411	19624	11966
大同镇	Datong	34	16285	53624	33846
李家镇	Lijia	10	5859	19642	12031

continued 4

乡镇常用耕地面积(亩) Commonly used cultivated area of township (mu)	粮食播种面积(亩) Sown Area of Grain Crops (mu)	粮食总产量(吨) Yield of Grain Crops (ton)	农业总产值(当年价格)(万元) Gross Output Value of Agriculture (10000 yuan)	财政总收入(万元) Financial Revenue (10000 yuan)	农村经济总收入(万元) Total Income of Rural Economy (10000 yuan)	农民人均年纯收入(元) Per Capita Annual Net Income (yuan)
5593	8621	2054	14109	2015	32643	8321
6814	13578	3701	12977	2260	51414	8641
3403	3431	1217	12052	47843	155268	12412
2966	3482	937	5531	8744	86960	10873
10178	14081	8171	10038	6512	65973	10587
5525	4907	2000	28297	1564	95533	12779
24800	26772	9744	19855	12453	984631	13945
7141	9870	3657	6503	2966	36841	12228
16996	16269	6270	28829	9920	579093	10676
14267	14460	6173	29105	2037	264649	12780
16087	15011	5433	36892	3823	236524	9433
21066	21996	7467	31781	8128	282098	8978
17846	12915	6601	44523	1986	217659	8461
20481	27868	12141	13258	14956	502736	10108
25656	25541	12058	26834	2211	126641	9199
15320	16264	7143	17307	3052	202275	8129
34814	39369	16947	29951	8591	175253	8435
10965	15849	6171	13795	4635	78391	10115

3－19 续表 5

乡镇名称 Town		村民委员会(个) Number of Villagers' Committees (unit)	农村常住户数(户) Resident Households in Rural Areas (household)	农村常住人口数(人) Resident Population in Rural Areas (person)	农村从业人员数(人) Labor Force in Rural Areas (person)
富阳市	**Fuyang City**				
万市镇	Wanshi	15	6594	21543	13698
洞桥镇	Dongqiao	11	5860	18628	11452
胥口镇	Xukou	13	5624	17282	9695
永昌镇	Yongchang	5	3347	10504	6302
渌渚镇	Luzhu	13	5173	16024	10678
新登镇	Xindeng	31	18055	55098	33660
上官乡	Shangguan	5	2711	8238	4641
常绿镇	Changlu	8	4462	13840	9355
大源镇	Dayuan	15	11290	36391	22739
灵桥镇	Lingqiao	13	7248	23923	14152
里山镇	Lishan	5	3068	10187	6214
渔山乡	Yushan	4	3763	12919	8875
场口镇	Changkou	24	13124	40254	25385
龙门镇	Longmen	4	2502	6871	4546
环山乡	Huanshan	7	3716	12032	7539
常安镇	Chang'an	16	7378	24404	15412
湖源乡	Huyuan	10	3288	11190	7754
高桥镇	Gaoqiao	16	9494	30742	20094
受降镇	Shouxiang	6	5948	17949	10903
春建乡	Chunjian	6	2909	8808	5441
新桐乡	Xintong	7	4104	12336	8017

continued 5

乡镇常用耕地面积(亩) Commonly used cultivated area of township (mu)	粮食播种面积(亩) Sown Area of Grain Crops (mu)	粮食总产量(吨) Yield of Grain Crops (ton)	农业总产值(当年价格)(万元) Gross Output Value of Agriculture (10000 yuan)	财政总收入(万元) Financial Revenue (10000 yuan)	农村经济总收入(万元) Total Income of Rural Economy (10000 yuan)	农民人均年纯收入(元) Per Capita Annual Net Income (yuan)
18774	26259	10553	42014	8331	441567	13951
16542	17062	6580	58334	8845	331630	13949
16680	15181	7069	27586	8415	164953	13149
8467	8478	4120	16922	5360	112831	16750
11153	15927	7242	29239	8990	191710	16325
37669	37624	15789	61494	48319	1109690	15130
2593	3475	1448	6188	3319	83412	16827
3917	6336	2679	6902	3575	117567	14045
8610	9531	3835	18825	24617	1641554	21425
8803	9679	4073	13761	48440	499205	18773
3816	6410	2710	6806	4080	340427	16236
4776	7830	3245	9237	3339	187760	16194
25186	27508	11578	31820	15326	321559	12561
4354	5322	2519	5816	3928	52900	13782
5803	6777	2857	5229	13210	799827	15328
13589	15957	6664	16717	6825	281260	11465
8641	6656	2845	11618	7072	40248	11573
18112	25265	11054	52053	40266	2304984	22610
6753	10391	4168	20414	19397	1439782	22603
7550	9310	3642	22808	4355	141486	15889
8759	11498	5418	9424	5184	112068	14055

3－19　续表6

乡 镇 名 称 Town	村民委员会(个) Number of Villagers' Committees (unit)	农村常住户数 (户) Resident Households in Rural Areas (household)	农村常住人口数 (人) Resident Population in Rural Areas (person)	农村从业人员数 (人) Labor Force in Rural Areas (person)
鹿山街道　Lushan Subdistrict	9	7296	21189	13332
富春街道　Fuchun Subdistrict	15	10714	30282	20642
春江街道　Chunjiang Subdistrict	9	7817	27116	16726
东洲街道　Dongzhou Subdistrict	15	12966	44938	27526
临安市　Lin'an City				
玲珑街道　Linlong Subdistrict	16	9481	26218	13622
锦南街道　Jinnan Subdistrict	9	8177	19950	7665
锦城街道　Jincheng Subdistrict	5	12548	33853	12454
锦北街道　Jinbei Subdistrict	12	10333	28474	13292
青山湖街道 Qingshanghu Subdistrict	19	10502	31508	19844
高虹镇　Gaohong	9	7266	22800	16233
太湖源镇　Taihuyuan	20	11706	31971	20887
於潜镇　Yuqian	30	18871	49936	27585
太阳镇　Taiyang	18	9309	24421	16727
潜川镇　Qianchuan	16	8494	21932	15202
昌化镇　Changhua	14	5216	15102	11454
河桥镇　Heqiao	11	5035	14686	11203
湍口镇　Tuankou	13	3816	12817	9080
清凉峰镇　Qingliangfeng	17	10599	29160	19104
岛石镇　Daoshi	16	9074	26133	16875
板桥镇　Banqiao	15	9467	27889	15871
天目山镇　Tianmushan	23	11652	33261	21858
龙岗镇　Longgang	24	6992	22660	14966

continued 6

乡镇常用耕地面积(亩) Commonly used cultivated area of township (mu)	粮食播种面积(亩) Sown Area of Grain Crops (mu)	粮食总产量(吨) Yield of Grain Crops (ton)	农业总产值(当年价格)(万元) Gross Output Value of Agriculture (10000 yuan)	财政总收入(万元) Financial Revenue (10000 yuan)	农村经济总收入(万元) Total Income of Rural Economy (10000 yuan)	农民人均年纯收入(元) Per Capita Annual Net Income (yuan)
13011	12693	5908	23161	42484	541416	19691
17541	20658	8679	21616	87044	3090243	20681
7184	9913	4004	14738	114941	2596947	22077
21704	22074	10128	48009	39754	888265	19502
10507	8897	4007	16514	22815	1289441	15775
4316	4271	1608	5360	7397	73995	13658
5853	5384	2129	10523	26311	912522	16160
6723	7742	3042	23157	12181	498725	14159
14270	13061	5980	27769	140100	1497701	17818
8999	8600	4293	16673	6038	439485	15551
27943	17637	6436	43187	7703	1015230	15983
34955	15362	6091	60842	16518	900000	15043
17672	13924	6167	28536	5414	560449	13459
8952	6913	2305	38277	2371	334306	13728
12673	11250	4413	14828	10220	320000	15058
13043	11294	4734	13572	1918	86261	9828
6804	10282	3199	16001	2316	52200	11935
15784	23253	7403	27866	4203	128036	12806
8968	16190	4940	36084	2285	124287	11649
13113	17474	6794	47317	13894	438010	14334
27466	18890	8605	67788	5297	296550	14478
16564	18700	8143	24795	7190	264557	13068

主要统计指标解释

农林牧渔业总产值 是以货币表现的农、林、牧、渔业全部产品的总量和对农林牧渔生产活动进行的各种支持性服务活动的价值。他反映一定时期内的农林牧渔业生产的总规模和总成果。

农林牧渔业的统计范围是:

(1)农业 包括农作物种植业和其他农业。

农作物种植业 包括谷类、豆类、薯类、棉花、麻类、烟叶、蔬菜、药材、瓜类和其他农作物的种植以及茶园、桑园、果园的生产经营。

其他农业 包括采集野生植物的果实、纤维、树脂、油料以及柴草、野生药材、菌类等。

(2)林业 包括林木的栽培(不包括茶园、桑园和果园的栽培、管理和收获等活动)、林产品的采集和村及村以下合作经济组织和农户的竹木砍伐。

(3)牧业 包括除渔业养殖以外的一切动物饲养和放牧以及野生动物的捕猎和饲养。

(4)渔业 包括水生动物和海藻类植物的养殖和捕捞。

(5)农林牧渔服务业 包括对农林牧渔生产活动进行的各种支持性服务活动。

粮食产量 指全社会的产量,包括国营农场等全民所有制经营、集体统一经营的和农民家庭经营的产量,还包括工矿企业家属办的农场和其他生产单位的产量。粮食除包括稻谷、小麦、大麦、玉米、高粱、谷子及其他杂粮外,还包括薯类和豆类。其产量计算方法,豆类按去豆荚后的干豆计算,薯类按5公斤鲜薯折1公斤粮食计算,其他粮食一律按脱粒后的原粮计算。

猪、牛、羊肉产量 指当年出栏并已屠宰的猪、牛、羊的肉产量,即屠宰后除去头蹄下水后带骨的(即胴体重)重量。

水产品产量 指人工养殖的水产品和天然生长的水产品的捕捞量。包括海水的鱼类、虾蟹类、贝类和藻类以及内陆水域的鱼类、虾蟹类和贝类,不包括淡水生植物。

有效灌溉面积 指具有一定的水源,地块比较平整、灌溉工程或设备已经配套,在一般年景下当年能够进行正常灌溉的耕地面积。

农业机械总动力 指主要用于农、林、牧、渔业的各种动力机械的动力总和。包括耕作机械、排灌机械、收获机械、农用运输机械、植物保护机械、牧业机械、林业机械和其他农业机械[内燃机按引擎马力折成瓦(特)计算,电动机按功率折成瓦(特)计算]。不包括专门用于乡、镇、村、组办工业、基本建设、非农业运输、科学试验和教学等非农业方面的动力机械与作业机械。

农村用电量 指本年度内扣除在农村中的全民所有制工业、交通、基建单位的用电量以后的农村生产上和生活上的全年用电总度数(全年累计数),包括国家电网的供电量,也包括农村自办电站的供电量。

农用化肥施用量 指本年内实际用于农业生产的化肥数量。包括氮肥、磷肥、钾肥及复合肥。化肥施用量要求按折纯量计算数量。折纯量是指氮肥、磷肥、钾肥分别按含氮、含五氧化二磷、含氧化钾的百分之一百成份进行折算后的数量。复合肥按其所含主要成份折算。

Explanatory Notes on Main Statistical Indicators

Gross Output Value of Farming, Forestry, Animal Husbandry and Fishery refers to the total volume of products of farming, forestry, animal husbandry and fishery in value terms and output value of all kinds of service activities that support farming, forestry, animal husbandry and fishery production. It reflects the total scale and total result of agricultural production during a given period of time.

The statistical scopes for Farming, Forestry, Animal Husbandry and Fishery are:

(1) **Farming** include crop cultivation and other farming crop cultivation, include planting of grain, beans, tubers, cotton, oil – bearing crops, sugar crops, fiber crops, tobacco, vegetables, medicinal materials, melons and others, as well as tea, mulberry and fruit plantation.

Other farming include gathering of wild plant fruits, fiber, gum, oil, firewood, wild medicinal materials, fungi and commodity industry run by rural household.

(2) **Forestry** include planting of trees (not including planting, management & harvest of tea, mulberry and fruit plantation), collection of forest products, cutting and felling of bamboo and trees by villages and other cooperative organizations under villages.

(3) **Animal Husbandry** include raising and grazing of any kind of animal and hunting and raising of wild animal, excluding fish breeding.

(4) **Fishery** include cultivation and catches of aquatic animals and seaweed.

(5) **Service Industry for Farming, Forestry, Animal Husbandry and Fishery** refers to all kinds of service activities that support farming, forestry, animal husbandry and fishery production.

Grain Yield refers to the total yield including grains produced by state farms, collective units, industrial enterprises and mines. Grain includes rice, wheat, corn, sorghum, millet and other miscellaneous grains as well as tubers and beans. Output of beans refers to dry beans without pods. The output of tubers was converted into that of grain at the ratio 5:1. Output of all other grains refers to husked grain.

Output of Pork, Beef, and Mutton refers to the meat of slaughtered hogs, cattle, sheep and goats with head, feet and offal taken away.

Output of Aquatic Products refers to catches of both artificially cultured and naturally grown aquatic products, including fish, shrimps, crabs and shellfish in sea and inland water as well as seaweed. Freshwater plants are not included.

Irrigated Area refers to areas that are effectively irrigated, i. e. level land which has water source and complete sets of irrigation facilities to lift and move adequate water for irrigation purpose under normal conditions.

Total Power of Farm Machinery refers to total mechanical power of machinery used in farming, forestry, animal husbandry, and fishery, including ploughing, irrigation and drainage, harvesting, transport, plant protection, stock breeding, forestry and fishery. The power of internal combustion engines is required to convert horsepower into watts and the power of electric motors is required to be converted into watts. Machinery employed for non – agricultural purposes, such as the machines used in township – run and village – run industry, construction, non – agricultural transport, scientific experiments and teaching, is excluded.

Electricity Consumption in Rural Areas refers to the total degree of electricity consumption in rural production and living (annual aggregate) after discounting the ownership by the whole people in the rural areas of industrial, transport and infrastructure unit of electricity consumption, including the national grid power supply, and also including the power supply in rural areas on their own power station.

Consumption of Chemical Fertilizers in Agriculture refers to the quantity of chemical fertilizers applied in agriculture in the year, including nitrogenous fertilizer, phosphate fertilizer, potash fertilizer, and compound fertilizer. The consumption of chemical fertilizers is required in calculation to convert the gross weight into weight into weight containing 100% effective component (e. g. 100% nitrogen content in nitrogenous fertilizer, 100% phosphorous pentoxide contents in phosphate fertilizer, 100% potassium oxide contents in potash fertilizer). Compound fertilizer is converted with its major component.

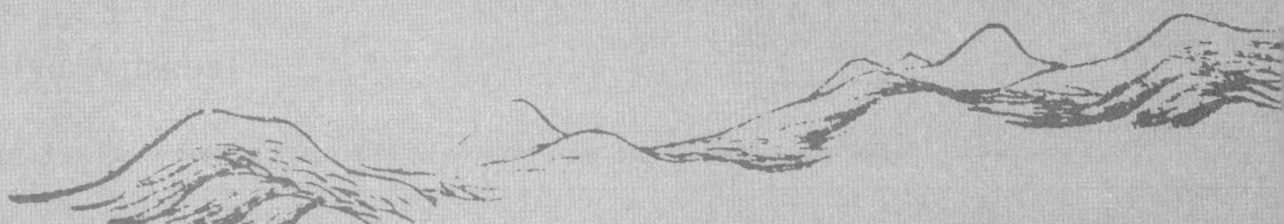

第 四 篇
CHAPTER-4

工业、能源
INDUSTRY AND ENERGY

4 工业、能源
Industry and Energy

主要统计指标
Major Statistical Indicators

规模以上工业企业单位数	Number of Industrial Enterprises above Designated Size	5868	个	(unit)
为上年	As Compared with the Preceding Year	101.3	%	(%)
规模以上工业销售产值	Sales Value of Industrial Enterprises above Designated Size	12181.22	亿元	(100 million yuan)
为上年	As Compared with the Preceding Year	120.2	%	(%)
规模以上工业总产值	Gross Output Value of Industrial Enterprises above Designated Size	12352.92	亿元	(100 million yuan)
为上年	As Compared with the Preceding Year	120.5	%	(%)
轻工业	Light Industry	4866.08	亿元	(100 million yuan)
为上年	As Compared with the Preceding Year	117.9	%	(%)
重工业	Heavy Industry	7486.84	亿元	(100 million yuan)
为上年	As Compared with the Preceding Year	122.3	%	(%)

4－01　主要年份工业企业单位数

Number of Industrial Enterprises in Main Years

单位:个　　(unit)

年　份 Year	合　计 Total	国有经济 State－owned Enterprises	集体经济 Collective－owned Enterprises	其他各种经济类型 Enterprises of Other Types of Ownership
全市　Whole City				
1978	2868	680	2188	－
1980	3519	691	－	－
1985	5800	823	－	－
1990	6183	921	4966	11
1991	6234	933	5219	82
1992	6235	941	5162	132
1995	6744	1086	4722	936
1996	6148	1011	4268	869
1997	4980	760	3250	970
1998	2559	464	815	1280
1999	2474	396	689	1389
2000	2715	282	598	1835
2001	3580	237	252	3091
2002	4015	172	232	3611
2003	4689	144	219	4326
2004	7738	185	192	7361
2005	7359	124	169	7066
2006	7826	110	162	7554
2007	8674	71	131	8472
2008	9907	73	101	9733
2009	10032	71	84	9877
2010	10370	74	68	10228
2011	5868	52	25	5791
市区　Urban District				
1978	787	313	414	－
1980	894	315	579	－
1985	1250	345	859	7
1990	1360	361	971	28
1991	1411	382	990	39
1992	1490	395	1024	71
1995	1998	440	1102	456
1996	2043	458	1109	476
1997	1733	372	951	410
1998	1019	315	315	389
1999	959	255	284	420
2000	1005	182	253	570
2001	2645	195	200	2250
2002	2838	140	178	2520
2003	3230	115	158	2957
2004	5527	156	122	5249
2005	4995	98	104	4793
2006	5195	85	91	5019
2007	5726	54	77	5595
2008	6530	55	64	6411
2009	6477	52	49	6376
2010	6478	51	37	6390
2011	3867	36	10	3821

注:1997 年及以前为乡及以上工业;1998－2010 年为主营业务收入 500 万及以上;2011 年为主营业务收入 2000 万及以上(后同)。

a) Data in 2011 refer to all the industrial enterprises with annual Sales income of over 20 million yuan, data in 1998－2010 refer to all the industrial enterprises with annual sales income of over 5 million yuan, data in 1997and before refer to enterprises at township and above level.

4－02 主要年份

Gross Industrial

单位:万元

年 份 Year	规模以上工业 Industry above Designated Size	# 轻 工 业 Light Industry
全市 Whole City		
1978	429624	–
1980	617910	–
1985	1285888	793766
1990	2922600	1848911
1991	3524900	2201757
1992	4527400	2735168
1995	10200259	5600664
1996	8831167	4606720
1997	9114651	4871887
1998	11099357	5726407
1999	12000796	6129963
2000	15435682	7623300
2001	19195133	9957027
2002	24002972	12435498
2003	32025226	15652463
2004	44865779	19761946
2005	54411271	24059690
2006	69754590	29093450
2007	83514029	35878400
2008	93795792	38735329
2009	93907334	40115956
2010	110810397	45764739
2011	123529249	48660810
市区 Urban District		
1978	304242	–
1980	433623	–
1985	812246	512767
1990	1533000	1026764
1991	1814600	1140394
1992	2291300	1379154
1995	4760900	2507752
1996	4599778	2460319
1997	4997257	2889406
1998	6110192	3068600
1999	6280838	3178286
2000	7804302	3635578
2001	16156245	8377563
2002	20252484	10431428
2003	26945006	13080771
2004	37564968	16361706
2005	44775260	19601053
2006	57255453	23722868
2007	67565456	29452269
2008	74564803	31236743
2009	74059755	32178951
2010	86653885	36440816
2011	97800625	39467105

工业总产值
Output Value in Main Years

(10000 yuan)

重工业 Heavy Industry	国有经济 State - owned	集体经济 Collective - owned	其他经济 Other Types of Ownership
-	334799	94825	-
-	451349	166561	-
492122	726172	546642	13074
1073689	1532900	1300900	88800
1323143	1779400	1601400	144200
1792232	2141000	2084000	302400
4599595	3585284	3999638	2615337
4224447	2905614	3320757	2604796
4242764	3185886	2971634	2957131
5372950	3422316	2824793	4852248
5870833	3164602	2543981	6292213
7812382	1860336	2698406	10876940
9238106	1788783	1911315	15495035
11567474	2147066	2151485	19704421
16372763	2484171	2444002	27097053
25103833	3419970	558890	40886919
30351581	6054280	603438	47753553
40661140	6776754	667615	62310221
47635629	7688908	517878	75307243
55060463	7440679	386111	85969002
53791378	7576482	354714	85976138
65045658	9050510	300262	101459625
74868439	10220511	171901	113136837
-	248534	55708	-
-	335789	97834	-
301998	536498	267613	8135
599899	1067400	416500	49100
674072	1237600	496800	80200
917085	1497400	601200	192700
2753196	2252300	908900	1599700
2139459	2018768	951432	1629578
2609217	2537740	819984	1639533
3041592	2989467	1123013	1997712
3102552	2668519	979070	2633249
4168724	1498595	968509	5337198
7778681	1695132	1792228	12668885
9821056	2036097	2045450	16170937
13864235	2390424	2305431	22249151
21203262	3097656	419720	34047592
25174207	5592419	390555	38792286
33532585	6305071	347788	50602594
38113187	7123810	323842	60117804
43328060	6812616	219140	67533047
41880805	6880470	148937	67030348
50213069	8155395	156026	78342464
58333520	9253445	70299	88476881

4－03 分县(市)工业

Number of Industrial

单位:个

项　目	Item	全　市 Whole City	市区 Urban District	#萧山区 Xiaoshan
规模以上工业合计	**Industrial above Designated Size**	**5868**	**3867**	**1765**
一、按轻重工业分	**Grouped by Light & Heavy Industry**			
轻工业	Light Industry	2961	1942	1049
重工业	Heavy Industry	2907	1925	716
二、按所有制分	**Grouped by Ownership**			
国有企业	State－owned Enterprises	52	36	7
集体企业	Collective－owned Enterprises	25	10	3
股份合作企业	Cooperative Enterprises	9	8	2
联营企业	Joint Ownership Enterprises	3	2	
股份制企业	Share－holding Corporations	4213	2714	1239
外商及港澳台投资企业	Enterprises with Investment from Foreign、Hong Kong、Macao and Taiwan	1252	969	427
其他企业	Other Enterprises	314	128	87
合计中:国有控股企业	Of the Total: Controlling Share Hold Enterprises	172	124	23
三、按企业规模分	**Grouped by Size of Enterprises**			
大型企业	Large	130	114	38
中型企业	Medium－sized	809	619	317
小微企业	Small	4929	3134	1410

企业单位数(2011 年)
Enterprises by Region(2011)

(unit)

#余杭区 Yuhang	桐庐县 Tonglu	淳安县 Chun'an	建德市 Jiande	富阳市 Fuyang	临安市 Lin'an
1049	**347**	**122**	**354**	**663**	**515**
490	218	76	171	322	232
559	129	46	183	341	283
5	3	3	4	2	4
2	3	2	6	1	3
2				1	
1			1		
848	223	94	288	498	396
169	84	9	20	119	51
22	34	14	35	42	61
21	6	6	7	14	15
16	2	1	2	6	5
132	22	11	24	83	50
901	323	110	328	574	460

4－04 分县(市)工业
Gross Industrial

单位:万元

项　目	Item	全　市 Whole City	市　区 Urban District	#萧山区 Xiaoshan
规模以上工业合计	**Industrial above Designated Size**	**123529249**	**97800625**	**47198259**
一、按轻重工业分	**Grouped by Light & Heavy Industry**			
轻工业	Light Industry	48660810	39467105	22154103
重工业	Heavy Industry	74868439	58333520	25044156
二、按所有制分	**Grouped by Ownership**			
国有企业	State－owned Enterprises	10220511	9253445	1203341
集体企业	Collective－owned Enterprises	171901	70299	14719
股份合作企业	Cooperative Enterprises	41517	38487	14117
联营企业	Joint Ownership Enterprises	287034	9239	－
股份制企业	Share－holding Corporations	73327257	54205308	34800536
外商及港澳台投资企业	Enterprises with Investment from Foreign、Hong Kong、Macao and Taiwan	37357379	33332431	10564122
其他企业	Other Enterprises	2123651	891416	601425
合计中:国有控股企业	Of the Total: Controlling Share Hold Enterprises	18190940	16032526	2114281
三、按企业规模分	**Grouped by Size of Enterprises**			
大型企业	Large	43517735	40433793	18749740
中型企业	Medium－sized	33469373	25441927	14212248
小微企业	Small	46542142	31924905	14236271

总产值(2011 年)
Output Value by Region(2011)

(10000 yuan)

#余杭区 Yuhang	桐庐县 Tonglu	淳安县 Chun'an	建德市 Jiande	富阳市 Fuyang	临安市 Lin'an
13082756	**3785100**	**1800052**	**3752064**	**10734317**	**5657091**
4448046	1597388	1346486	1061508	3353635	1834688
8634710	2187712	453566	2690556	7380682	3822403
434129	99961	52783	223027	346051	245245
18484	11891	26355	36004	18673	8679
6297	–	–	–	3030	–
6825	–	–	277795	–	–
9514659	2392302	1485401	2893345	8263830	4087071
2932178	1095094	149871	208560	1897354	674068
170184	185852	85642	113334	205380	642028
754169	170343	64218	330071	948862	644920
2809464	144711	97647	507473	1578851	755261
3592854	1037603	440140	1103797	3277065	2168840
6680438	2602786	1262265	2140793	5878401	2732991

4-05 分县(市)工业
Gross Industrial

单位:万元

项 目	Item	全 市 Whole City	市 区 Urban District	#萧山区 Xiaoshan
规模以上工业合计	**Industrial above Designated Size**	**121812164**	**96531393**	**46567390**
一、按轻重工业分	**Grouped by Light & Heavy Industry**			
轻工业	Light Industry	47747259	38770229	21712530
重工业	Heavy Industry	74064905	57761164	24854860
二、按所有制分	**Grouped by Ownership**			
国有企业	State - owned Enterprises	10188681	9226913	1201700
集体企业	Collective - owned Enterprises	166881	67860	14559
股份合作企业	Cooperative Enterprises	40385	37355	14396
联营企业	Joint Ownership Enterprises	287011	9216	-
股份制企业	Share - holding Corporations	72175310	53405950	34392222
外商及港澳台投资企业	Enterprises with Investment from Foreign、Hong Kong、Macao and Taiwan	36860720	32905351	10352141
其他企业	Other Enterprises	2093177	878749	592372
合计中:国有控股企业	Of the Total:Controlling Share Hold Enterprises	18270164	16122592	2086824
三、按企业规模分	**Grouped by Size of Enterprises**			
大型企业	Large	43231236	40200488	18677798
中型企业	Medium - sized	32884603	24955747	13917720
小微企业	Small	45696326	31375158	13971872

销售产值(2011 年)

Products Sales by Region(2011)

(10000 yuan)

#余杭区 Yuhang	桐庐县 Tonglu	淳安县 Chun'an	建德市 Jiande	富阳市 Fuyang	临安市 Lin'an
12696080	**3740713**	**1770030**	**3686995**	**10527927**	**5555106**
4333895	1579025	1324000	1034143	3251324	1788537
8362185	2161688	446030	2652852	7276603	3766569
433953	99961	52615	223112	344551	241530
17587	12070	26355	36309	15720	8568
5953	–	–	–	3030	–
6802	–	–	277795	–	–
9258531	2366524	1456206	2830355	8105636	4010639
2806027	1080974	149746	207586	1858739	658325
167229	181184	85109	111839	200251	636045
721966	169754	64878	331136	939916	641888
2718125	138114	92852	498971	1545529	755283
3481892	1041119	426945	1094455	3239514	2126823
6496063	2561480	1250234	2093570	5742884	2673000

4－06 全市规模以上工业

Main Economic Indicators of Industrial

单位:万元

项 目	Item	企业单位数（个）Number of Enterprises (unit)	#亏损企业(个) Loss Making Enterprises (unit)	工业总产值（当年价格）Gross Industrial Output Value (current price)	工业销售产值 Value of Industrial Products Sales
总 计	**Total**	**5868**	**749**	**123529249**	**121812164**
按隶属关系分	**Grouped by Subordination**				
中 央 属	Central	26	7	7629546	7587274
省 属	Provincial	52	6	4750846	4748209
市 属	Municipal	3805	517	86501725	85278590
县(市)属	County and below	1985	219	24647132	24198091
按所有制分	**Grouped by Ownership**				
国有企业	State－owned Enterprises	52	11	10220511	10188681
集体企业	Collective－owned Enterprises	25	2	171901	166881
股份合作企业	Cooperative Enterprises	9	2	41517	40385
联营企业	Joint Ownership Enterprises	3	－	287034	287011
股份制企业	Share－holding Corporations	4213	460	73327257	72175310
外商及港澳台投资企业	Enterprises with Investment from Foreign、Hong Kong、Macao and Taiwan	1252	250	37357379	36860720
其他企业	Other Enterprises	314	24	2123651	2093177
按企业规模分	**Grouped by Size of Enterprises**				
大型企业	Large	130	5	43517735	43231236
中型企业	Medium－sized	809	103	33469373	32884603
小微企业	Small	4929	641	46542142	45696326
按轻重工业分	**Grouped by Light & Heavy Industry**				
轻工业	Light Industry	2961	385	48660810	47747259
重工业	Heavy Industry	2907	364	74868439	74064905

注:本表范围为年主营业务收入2000万元及以上工业。

企业主要经济指标(一)
Enterprises Above Designated Size(Ⅰ)

(10000 yuan)

出口交货值 Export delivery value	实收资本 Total Capital Hold	国家资本 State Capital	个人资本 Personal Capital	港澳台资本 Hongkong, Macau and TaiWan Capital	外商资本 Foreign Capital	全部从业人员年平均人数(人) Annual Average Number of Staff and Workers (person)
19337584	**19004018**	**997757**	**5029857**	**2478414**	**3493553**	**1246121**
9261	395754	203530	12822	–	–	15533
142618	762680	273424	2780	96229	74486	30447
15389834	13956957	394810	3560931	2077197	3187237	921961
3795871	3888627	125993	1453325	304988	231830	278180
38710	567663	457140	5558	–	–	32282
29787	25964	–	1049	178	–	2264
–	6335	–	462	–	–	921
–	30600	–	–	–	–	1288
8884254	9993749	412297	4603179	26039	32357	734995
10023241	8190435	128321	284510	2450947	3458493	444649
361592	189272	–	135100	1250	2703	29722
7325199	4476491	430603	570470	944779	934451	313321
5630947	5581392	421024	1229676	702388	1026304	409887
6381439	8946135	146130	3229711	831247	1532799	522913
9667319	8331230	301608	2195738	1287768	1745177	639338
9670266	10672787	696149	2834119	1190646	1748377	606783

a) Data in this table refer to enterprises with annual sales income of over 20 million yuan.

项　目	Item	企业单位数（个）Number of Enterprises (unit)	#亏损企业(个) Loss Making Enterprises (unit)	工业总产值(当年价格) Gross Industrial Output Value (current price)	工业销售产值 Value of Industrial Products Sales
按市、县分	**Grouped by County**				
市　区	Urban District	3867	528	97800625	96531393
#萧山区	Xiaoshan	1765	197	47198259	46567390
余杭区	Yuhang	1049	169	13082756	12696080
桐庐县	Tonglu	347	25	3785100	3740713
淳安县	Chun'an	122	3	1800052	1770030
建德市	Jiande	354	18	3752064	3686995
富阳市	Fuyang	663	90	10734317	10527927
临安市	Lin'an	515	85	5657091	5555106
按国民经济行业分	**Grouped by Economic Sector**				
煤炭开采和洗选业	Coal Mining and Dressing			–	–
黑色金属矿采选业	Ferrous Metals Mining and Dressing	1	–	2643	2476
有色金属矿采选业	Nonferrous Metals Mining and Dressing	7	2	66798	67975
非金属矿采选业	Nonmetal Minerals Mining and Dressing	31	1	184318	182286
农副食品加工业	Agricultural Products Processing	114	4	1058691	1055979
食品制造业	Food Manufacturing	97	16	2035146	2031167
饮料制造业	Beverage Manufacturing	56	7	2156960	2122421
烟草制品业	Tobacco Processing	2	0	2132761	2132366
纺织业	Textile Industry	879	94	10015243	9820130
纺织服装、鞋、帽制造业	Textile Products, Garments, Shoes and Caps Processing	283	60	2369043	2332102
皮革、毛皮、羽毛(绒)及其制品业	Leather, Furs, Down and Related Products	142	21	1790414	1767677
木材加工及木、竹、藤、棕、草制品业	Timber Processing, Bamboo, Cane, Palm Fiber and Straw Products	41	2	265369	265448
家具制造业	Furniture Manufacturing	86	10	1265344	1239247

continued 1 (10000 yuan)

出口交货值 Export delivery value	实收资本 Total Capital Hold	国家资本 State Capital	个人资本 Personal Capital	港澳台资本 Hongkong, Macau and TaiWan Capital	外商资本 Foreign Capital	全部从业人员年平均人数（人） Annual Average Number of Staff and Workers (person)
15541551	15012656	795426	3572834	2173426	3261723	962361
6784597	6132933	153746	1760237	920823	1000266	422970
2462288	2196244	34962	802867	303817	314428	196287
1217715	548110	32135	172653	72872	48271	42894
98745	193594	2886	58512	12666	8915	17665
907322	557208	45221	242034	3728	39762	39907
597898	1798592	98078	703855	120895	111795	103902
974353	893857	24013	279968	94827	23087	79392
–	–	–	–	–	–	
–	500	500	–	–	–	105
–	11048	–	10548	–	–	833
3413	45375	3900	16407	–	35	2806
141650	133977	–	57567	8598	8289	11168
98869	389342	21585	71756	74396	145065	26163
31151	482627	427	30093	53214	174182	18803
4373	69571	63971	4200	1400	–	2415
2456820	1758226	6979	713146	304011	197384	165324
1360613	557314	–	86190	295564	72644	79939
1064374	195990	–	47528	50142	23783	32380
57205	52980	–	26040	2318	1913	4855
631270	301789	–	60562	32030	112108	30323

单位:万元　　4－06　续表2

项　目	Item	企业单位数(个) Number of Enterprises (unit)	#亏损企业(个) Loss Making Enterprises (unit)	工业总产值(当年价格) Gross Industrial Output Value (current price)	工业销售产值 Value of Industrial Products Sales
造纸及纸制品业	Paper Making and Paper Products	349	28	4207409	4088236
印刷业和记录媒介的复制	Printing and Record Media	75	16	607664	594172
文教体育用品制造业	Cultural, Educational and Sports Goods	61	12	464083	458546
石油加工、炼焦及核燃料加工业	Petroleum Processing, Coking and Nuclear Fuel Processing	7	1	548940	546161
化学原料及化学制品制造业	Raw Chemical Materials and Chemical Products	342	36	9905077	9799378
医药制造业	Medical and Pharmaceutical Products	73	9	2151561	2021138
化学纤维制造业	Chemical Fiber	95	14	8382042	8190040
橡胶制品业	Rubber Products	53	11	3323564	3558504
塑料制品业	Plastic Products	259	31	2917156	2887984
非金属矿物制品业	Nonmetal Minerals Products	311	41	4965929	4882294
黑色金属冶炼及压延加工业	Smelting and Processing of Ferrous Metals	80	16	4513855	4460267
有色金属冶炼及压延加工业	Smelting and Processing of Nonferrous Metals	68	14	2501802	2458032
金属制品业	Metals Products	320	46	4543522	4484565
通用设备制造业	Ordinary Machinery	551	49	8806534	8694296
专用设备制造业	For Special Purpose Equipment Manufacturing	203	24	2150828	2097177
交通运输设备制造业	Transport Equipment Manufacturing	226	38	11268459	11181925
电气机械及器材制造业	Electric Equipment and Machinery	500	78	9935263	9716384
通信设备、计算机及其他电子设备制造业	Telecommunications Equipment, Computers and Other Electronic Equipment Manufacturing	235	35	7257685	7086376
仪器仪表及文化、办公用机械制造业	Instruments, Meters, Cultural and Office Machinery	134	14	2360242	2282396
工艺品及其他制造业	Craftworks and Other Manufacturing	97	7	1293730	1252807
废弃资源和废旧材料回收加工业	Waste Resouces and Waste or Old Material Recycled	12	2	532306	536378
电力、热力的生产和供应业	Production and Supply of Electric Power and Hot Water	49	4	6171651	6152370
燃气生产和供应业	Production and Supply of Gas	12	-	1101354	1098829
水的生产和供应业	Production and Supply of Tap Water	17	6	275867	264637

continued 2 (10000 yuan)

出口交货值 Export delivery value	实收资本 Total Capital Hold	国家资本 State Capital	个人资本 Personal Capital	港澳台资本 Hongkong, Macau and TaiWan Capital	外商资本 Foreign Capital	全部从业人员年平均人数（人） Annual Average Number of Staff and Workers (person)
158332	720635	2235	327208	51131	67424	51795
20815	182108	10695	65368	28814	2336	10025
265493	143145	–	19447	28850	81683	12057
293	32830	23580	5338	334	–	1264
1115794	1195631	17955	373925	98234	226967	51403
243339	542062	87223	60968	24676	224633	27445
389252	757784	–	223290	112332	55227	30317
756826	284572	3231	41283	13951	78362	29445
344658	559898	1091	174978	77673	138717	32205
232014	920176	12653	267871	120597	182098	53238
70457	348679	120820	152371	9840	5315	22344
44054	140918	–	63911	9954	10161	6962
531177	605978	14622	261841	49783	83560	47651
1281854	1768268	92763	502248	204176	289126	105159
403176	541232	7580	118213	26697	211203	30123
2270911	887389	37293	159728	124410	114500	72887
2317215	2117323	22466	496150	255996	499765	122271
2374191	1661684	95910	300296	358059	324902	90293
316707	361142	3980	168053	1123	89442	32895
351289	156083	2489	55267	25959	11034	17983
–	27517	–	22560	–	3907	1273
–	505714	221284	35390	27522	32043	15378
–	213570	46458	2616	132	25745	1972
–	330944	76066	7500	6500	–	4622

4－07 全市规模以上工业

Main Economic Indicators of Industrial

单位：万元

项　目	Item	资产总计 Total Assets	流动资产合　计 Total Circulating Funds	应收账款 Receivables	存　货 Stock
总　　计	**Total**	**109686901**	**67097621**	**15547127**	**15304716**
按隶属关系分	**Grouped by Subordination**				
中　央　属	Central	5030719	1942269	169166	936991
省　　属	Provincial	4751397	1988243	219693	408170
市　　属	Municipal	79033075	50291884	11706546	11333414
县(市)属	County and below	20871711	12875226	3451722	2626140
按所有制分	**Grouped by Ownership**				
国有企业	State－owned Enterprises	7823358	3022700	136422	1080788
集体企业	Collective－owned Enterprises	178352	106002	38004	14676
股份合作企业	Cooperative Enterprises	92029	54320	5868	11512
联营企业	Joint Ownership Enterprises	51037	23734	12113	845
股份制企业	Share－holding Corporations	66080015	39792998	8782002	8863385
外商及港澳台投资企业	Enterprises with Investment from Foreign、Hong Kong、Macao and Taiwan	34258305	23285256	6300458	5155928
其他企业	Other Enterprises	1203806	812612	272262	177582
按企业规模分	**Grouped by Size of Enterprises**				
大型企业	Large	36666538	22187891	4704144	5623114
中型企业	Medium－sized	31746176	19462943	4135078	4486845
小微企业	Small	41274188	25446787	6707906	5194757
按轻重工业分	**Grouped by Light & Heavy Industry**				
轻工业	Light Industry	45166581	28182363	5710579	6357687
重工业	Heavy Industry	64520321	38915258	9836549	8947029

企业主要经济指标(二)

Enterprises Above Designated Size(Ⅱ)

(10000 yuan)

产成品 Finished Products	固定资产合计 Fixed Assets	累计折旧 Accumulated Depreciation	本年折旧 Depreciation of the year	负债合计 Total Liabilities	流动负债合计 Total Current Liabilities	非流动负债合计 Total Non-current Liabilities	所有者权益合计 Creditors´Equity
5957291	**27483078**	**15860768**	**2519183**	**64847447**	**55752306**	**9095141**	**44839454**
127959	3770437	2164138	93060	3063616	1126415	1937201	1967103
110867	1671092	1227786	164228	2520894	2084616	436278	2230504
4664330	16805864	10192549	1803390	46601014	41245932	5355082	32432060
1054135	5235685	2276295	458504	12661923	11295343	1366580	8209788
80644	4781399	3075356	205814	4246802	2249614	1997188	3576556
6910	38877	35468	5780	103954	97720	6235	74398
4049	21339	14928	1350	56331	48612	7719	35698
2	18215	2211	1273	16300	16300	-	34737
3694486	14499899	7822347	1458405	40712665	35182521	5530144	25367351
2095754	7816212	4762115	817094	18908849	17385830	1523019	15349456
75445	307138	148344	29466	802547	771709	30838	401259
1880629	7073598	4931290	739623	19920049	16736705	3183345	16746489
1857434	8181210	4533360	842654	19254816	16864183	2390633	12491360
2219229	12228270	6396118	936906	25672582	22151417	3521164	15601606
2469578	11192017	6531471	1127949	25606246	23190167	2416079	19560335
3487713	16291062	9329297	1391233	39241201	32562139	6679062	25279120

单位:万元　　4-07　续表1

项　目	Item	资产总计 Total Assets	流动资产合　计 Total Circulating Funds	应收账款 Receivables	存　货 Stock
按市、县分	**Grouped by County**				
市　区	Urban District	88067057	53945326	12069607	12624481
#萧山区	Xiaoshan	41174069	24905127	4304441	5875753
余杭区	Yuhang	12029274	7637195	1958337	1734029
桐庐县	Tonglu	2696281	1531393	455486	317530
淳安县	Chun'an	998813	529230	153871	110994
建德市	Jiande	3066717	1595667	332879	309889
富阳市	Fuyang	10100171	6492077	1548705	1296652
临安市	Lin'an	4757862	3003928	986580	645171
按国民经济行业分	**Grouped by Economic Sector**				
煤炭开采和洗选业	Coal Mining and Dressing	-	-	-	-
黑色金属矿采选业	Ferrous Metals Mining and Dressing	1163	863	319	55
有色金属矿采选业	Nonferrous Metals Mining and Dressing	82297	43152	1860	7391
非金属矿采选业	Nonmetal Minerals Mining and Dressing	210006	89367	19873	4458
农副食品加工业	Agricultural Products Processing	714339	469734	115985	136008
食品制造业	Food Manufacturing	1776953	1231479	531331	155246
饮料制造业	Beverage Manufacturing	1759025	893005	178765	189849
烟草制品业	Tobacco Processing	1759387	1200613	30024	749247
纺织业	Textile Industry	9457747	5803259	949378	1211670
纺织服装、鞋、帽制造业	Textile Products, Garments, Shoes and Caps Processing	2386361	1563858	262877	369843
皮革、毛皮、羽毛(绒)及其制品业	Leather, Furs, Down and Related Products	1575658	1207359	261569	303219
木材加工及木、竹、藤、棕、草制品业	Timber Processing, Bamboo, Cane, Palm Fiber and Straw Products	235925	147464	35490	33443
家具制造业	Furniture Manufacturing	1165223	829335	160227	183544

continued 1　　　　(10000 yuan)

产成品 Finished Products	固定资产合计 Fixed Assets	累计折旧 Accumulated Depreciation	本年折旧 Depreciation of the year	负债合计 Total Liabilities	流动负债合计 Total Current Liabilities	非流动负债合计 Total Non－current Liabilities	所有者权益合计 Creditors´Equity
4873013	21856325	13311017	2033348	51644400	44044189	7600210	36422658
2242943	9058749	5211613	949820	25961642	22495505	3466137	15212427
788895	3173759	1623815	347658	7342315	6839236	503079	4686959
100475	765111	337852	64888	1664178	1519039	145139	1032102
47161	357745	175938	35261	519961	456144	63817	478852
122587	872404	446958	76567	1731011	1459565	271447	1335705
553435	2452865	1050509	199692	6462487	5661830	800656	3637684
260621	1178629	538494	109427	2825410	2611538	213872	1932453
–	–	–	–	–	–	–	–
55	300	201	50	89	89	–	1074
4124	7786	10441	789	43783	39353	4430	38514
1665	51283	26537	6480	155750	123766	31984	54256
62918	164783	62857	14671	447975	428530	19445	266364
63855	353287	241186	30976	709258	672158	37099	1067696
54534	580446	479647	68749	869979	816644	53335	889046
40417	332179	225087	29889	188265	187724	541	1571122
584529	2554954	1619289	287360	6135653	5706275	429378	3322094
128155	585337	252815	45032	1420120	1375865	44255	966241
78810	207809	109441	19328	1053725	1013338	40387	521933
13041	67160	30465	5424	154740	139541	15199	81186
50252	224370	105925	18448	691514	690993	522	473709

项　目	Item	资产总计 Total Assets	流动资产合　计 Total Circulating Funds	应收账款 Receivables	存　货 Stock
造纸及纸制品业	Paper Making and Paper Products	4396933	2953947	747308	482194
印刷业和记录媒介的复制	Printing and Record Media	830170	459823	119476	85405
文教体育用品制造业	Cultural, Educational and Sports Goods	348911	189598	34167	62159
石油加工、炼焦及核燃料加工业	Petroleum Processing, Coking and Nuclear Fuel Processing	139866	86188	20965	46600
化学原料及化学制品制造业	Raw Chemical Materials and Chemical Products	7268709	4468770	974662	901914
医药制造业	Medical and Pharmaceutical Products	2544158	1615361	494601	434962
化学纤维制造业	Chemical Fiber	6509012	3658098	209714	714189
橡胶制品业	Rubber Products	2056282	1169366	234863	456648
塑料制品业	Plastic Products	2527854	1585541	488063	301843
非金属矿物制品业	Nonmetal Mineral Products	5422445	3431325	1029215	559045
黑色金属冶炼及压延加工业	Smelting and Processing of Ferrous Metals	3962062	2307078	156301	493114
有色金属冶炼及压延加工业	Smelting and Processing of Nonferrous Metals	1032937	793169	79799	300118
金属制品业	Metal Products	3594189	2521184	644263	663740
通用设备制造业	Ordinary Machinery	9183147	6028827	1781649	1523373
专用设备制造业	For Special Purpose Equipment Manufacturing	2378577	1685201	627572	372907
交通运输设备制造业	Transport Equipment Manufacturing	9339296	5020379	968281	1492138
电气机械及器材制造业	Electric Equipment and Machinery	9587935	6430871	2338418	1267977
通信设备、计算机及其他电子设备制造业	Telecommunications Equipment, Computers and Other Electronic Equipment Manufacturing	7158092	5257677	1304530	1153306
仪器仪表及文化、办公用机械制造业	Instruments, Meters, Cultural and Office Machinery	2262399	1606153	507261	338245
工艺品及其他制造业	Craftworks and Other Manufacturing	801987	522986	86595	172499
废弃资源和废旧材料回收加工业	Waste Resouces and Waste or Old Material Recycled	241898	193306	16096	67358
电力、热力的生产和供应业	Production and Supply of Electric Power and Hot Water	4647775	1071828	83702	60369
燃气生产和供应业	Production and Supply of Gas	748595	166150	40734	5492
水的生产和供应业	Production and Supply of Tap Water	1579591	395310	11195	5150

continued 2 (10000 yuan)

产成品 Finished Products	固定资产合计 Fixed Assets	累计折旧 Accumulated Depreciation	本年折旧 Depreciation of the year	负债合计 Total Liabilities	流动负债合计 Total Current Liabilities	非流动负债合计 Total Non－current Liabilities	所有者权益合计 Creditors′Equity
223741	1080939	564694	105051	2990692	2818258	172434	1406240
34182	271198	206568	33432	523519	486285	37234	306651
13571	118411	53583	11129	150001	139469	10533	198910
6221	50985	63699	4972	189698	189698	–	－49832
420561	1769726	915926	186348	4284554	3664954	619599	2984155
194795	654615	274672	41971	1252152	1056390	195762	1292006
359974	1495144	820233	160463	3879314	3311823	567491	2629699
274777	653492	389849	79117	1363953	1193838	170114	692329
145333	637339	356018	76361	1480030	1391027	89003	1047824
335464	1359458	823741	148443	3597152	3276968	320184	1825293
156990	701531	682875	76941	2554107	2361083	193023	1407955
115042	129402	55018	10747	721772	701853	19919	311165
276973	780242	322628	76413	2388451	2174016	214434	1205739
565979	1672992	814397	156377	5163155	4801284	361871	4019992
138909	504602	249775	44972	1305395	1195713	109682	1073182
338935	1252059	742125	139637	6338132	4967023	1371109	3001163
577509	1899015	906427	184050	5464934	4837209	627725	4123002
476314	925166	710885	112065	3146942	2851957	294985	4011150
117791	433499	220261	39149	1151886	1014336	137550	1110513
75668	200540	133218	22490	428604	381766	46839	373383
16555	23257	9946	2580	198249	194623	3626	43649
4854	4443003	2557583	171862	3283386	1110858	2172528	1364389
3910	431330	259226	37572	390649	142394	248255	357946
890	865440	563536	69847	729873	295206	434667	849718

4－08 全市规模以上工业

Main Economic Indicators of Industrial

单位:万元

项 目	Item	主营业务收入 Revenues in Main Business	主营业务成本 Costs in Main Business	主营业务税金及附加 Sales Taxes and Extra Charges in Main Business
总 计	**Total**	**120225671**	**100918462**	**1937162**
按隶属关系分	**Grouped by Subordination**			
中 央 属	Central	4737900	2866334	1434899
省 属	Provincial	4883083	4318814	22255
市 属	Municipal	86737765	73249079	385970
县(市)属	County and Below	23866924	20484236	94038
按所有制分	**Grouped by Ownership**			
国有企业	State－owned Enterprises	7352028	5198171	1446317
集体企业	Collective－owned Enterprises	164383	138642	2522
股份合作企业	Cooperative Enterprises	40862	33645	159
联营企业	Joint Ownership Enterprises	286770	250471	114
股份制企业	Share－holding Corporations	72994302	63672494	292295
外商及港澳台投资企业	Enterprises with Investment from Foreign、Hong Kong、Macao and Taiwan	37325806	29804842	186619
其他企业	Other Enterprises	2061519	1820198	9137
按企业规模分	**Grouped by Size of Enterprises**			
大型企业	Large	43884113	35456573	1523609
中型企业	Medium－sized	33680763	28508625	228683
小微企业	Small	42660795	36953264	184870
按轻重工业分	**Grouped by Light & Heavy Industry**			
轻工业	Light Industry	48686399	39365417	1558615
重工业	Heavy Industry	71539272	61553045	378548

企业主要经济指标(三)
Enterprises Above Designated Size(Ⅲ)

(10000 yuan)

销售费用 Sales Expenses	管理费用 Management Expenses	财务费用 Financial Expenses	利息支出 Interest Expenditure	营业利润 Business Profits	利润总额 Total Profits	利税总额 Total Pre - tax Profits	本年应交增值税 Value Added Tax Payable
3906126	**5082566**	**1693676**	**1910972**	**7595092**	**7955252**	**13304807**	**3389879**
85834	139210	26250	25549	178303	167049	1972977	369409
29026	285610	29866	77363	219185	228741	408017	156859
3258688	3727412	1196467	1373164	5615497	5936887	8527608	2188546
532577	930334	441093	434896	1582107	1622575	2396206	675066
84332	324494	19354	67836	272337	261102	2169065	460287
4773	12329	1538	1384	14356	14854	25598	8204
927	4406	1119	2272	1125	1897	3253	1197
26	1545	1557	1561	36992	37022	38138	1003
1471401	2678413	1284841	1372470	4237734	4432564	6470842	1730540
2305190	1995019	358877	440352	2929767	3106894	4439766	1141014
39477	66359	26391	25097	102781	100918	158145	47636
1913281	1553388	372472	527802	3413687	3564920	6384889	1295564
1069819	1659175	540744	581072	1899376	2010818	3239234	996105
923026	1870003	780461	802097	2282028	2379514	3680684	1098210
2237315	2006955	700170	783083	3139101	3230095	6491697	1696776
1668811	3075611	993506	1127889	4455991	4725157	6813110	1693103

单位:万元　　　　4-08　续表1

项　目	Item	主营业务收　入 Revenues in Main Business	主营业务成　本 Costs in Main Business	主营业务税金及附加 Sales Taxes and Extra Charges in Main Business
按市、县分	**Grouped by County**			
市　区	Urban District	95264020	79435603	1838735
#萧山区	Xiaoshan	46571626	41434316	199433
余杭区	Yuhang	12817263	10985521	53798
桐庐县	Tonglu	3607396	3144419	14393
淳安县	Chun'an	1730722	1469790	11697
建德市	Jiande	3599309	3046918	16847
富阳市	Fuyang	10570169	9210825	33665
临安市	Lin'an	5454055	4610907	21825
按国民经济行业分	**Grouped by Economic Sector**			
煤炭开采和洗选业	Coal Mining and Dressing	-	-	-
黑色金属矿采选业	Ferrous Metals Mining and Dressing	2567	1578	27
有色金属矿采选业	Nonferrous Metals Mining and Dressing	67650	44434	642
非金属矿采选业	Nonmetal Minerals Mining and Dressing	178856	133006	3537
农副食品加工业	Agricultural Products Processing	1067592	931513	3490
食品制造业	Food Manufacturing	2118415	1609957	9143
饮料制造业	Beverage Manufacturing	2770620	2163870	35234
烟草制品业	Tobacco Processing	2118818	424864	1331062
纺织业	Textile Industry	9760047	8700307	46288
纺织服装、鞋、帽制造业	Textile Products, Garments, Shoes and Caps Processing	2324178	1945123	14880
皮革、毛皮、羽毛(绒)及其制品业	Leather, Furs, Down and Related Products	1753323	1543532	8249
木材加工及木、竹、藤、棕、草制品业	Timber Processing, Bamboo, Cane, Palm Fiber and Straw Products	268906	227788	2457
家具制造业	Furniture Manufacturing	1225897	1011240	6622

continued 1 (10000 yuan)

销售费用 Sales Expenses	管理费用 Management Expenses	财务费用 Financial Expenses	利息支出 Interest Expenditure	营业利润 Business Profits	利润总额 Total Profits	利税总额 Total Pre - tax Profits	本年应交增值税 Value Added Tax Payable
3370036	4072801	1240315	1464279	6010778	6330116	10867446	2680824
593579	1273878	858221	960994	2445747	2508769	3686150	974044
462981	651502	191259	193366	550847	595685	988246	337060
58139	119912	41604	41004	260269	261790	407773	131269
69974	69720	13599	13255	112311	122983	179699	44983
84531	149324	50071	49975	290473	315746	431254	98331
173899	374258	271455	266309	584264	582186	888125	268680
149548	296552	76632	76149	336996	342431	530510	165794
–	–	–	–	–	–	–	–
246	438	–	–	277	277	593	289
1928	7063	1661	1601	12919	12840	18175	4693
10135	11767	6460	6544	16622	16058	29861	10262
31732	31281	18097	17768	55515	61629	91146	25803
275309	87302	– 1642	11319	146524	146467	252800	97185
324502	76891	5781	9050	188720	203585	336364	97545
61498	80957	– 7375	– 7554	199905	184512	1787282	271671
119836	300748	211137	225874	429681	454418	724510	223074
73218	144805	49450	43199	106062	108455	204788	81335
34673	58492	40242	40080	70525	74602	147350	63668
10263	13489	6330	6119	11916	13321	24668	8883
55594	52441	18682	19063	86719	88230	136266	41405

单位:万元 4-08 续表2

项 目	Item	主营业务收入 Revenues in Main Business	主营业务成本 Costs in Main Business	主营业务税金及附加 Sales Taxes and Extra Charges in Main Business
造纸及纸制品业	Paper Making and Paper Products	4093248	3518806	16396
印刷业和记录媒介的复制	Printing and Record Media	599630	514056	2574
文教体育用品制造业	Cultural, Educational and Sports Goods	455023	395449	1935
石油加工、炼焦及核燃料加工业	Petroleum Processing, Coking and Nuclear Fuel Processing	549621	480062	97112
化学原料及化学制品制造业	Raw Chemical Materials and Chemical Products	9852054	8077911	26876
医药制造业	Medical and Pharmaceutical Products	2007320	1007356	18142
化学纤维制造业	Chemical Fiber	8378770	7620081	20939
橡胶制品业	Rubber Products	3578126	3243114	12619
塑料制品业	Plastic Products	2850658	2446545	11169
非金属矿物制品业	Nonmetal Mineral Products	4948867	4101688	22961
黑色金属冶炼及压延加工业	Smelting and Processing of Ferrous Metals	4527685	4184880	15032
有色金属冶炼及压延加工业	Smelting and Processing of Nonferrous Metals	2464081	2328266	4328
金属制品业	Metal Products	4487636	4014957	16171
通用设备制造业	Ordinary Machinery	8920544	7369743	34814
专用设备制造业	For Special Purpose Equipment Manufacturing	2123145	1702144	12502
交通运输设备制造业	Transport Equipment Manufacturing	11035264	9937607	51343
电气机械及器材制造业	Electric Equipment and Machinery	9759287	8231781	29059
通信设备、计算机及其他电子设备制造业	Telecommunications Equipment, Computers and Other Electronic Equipment Manufacturing	7223463	5461002	41782
仪器仪表及文化、办公用机械制造业	Instruments, Meters, Cultural and Office Machinery	2250562	1710502	13321
工艺品及其他制造业	Craftworks and Other Manufacturing	1273553	1151952	6161
废弃资源和废旧材料回收加工业	Waste Resouces and Waste or Old Material Recycled	516805	468416	2404
电力、热力的生产和供应业	Production and Supply of Electric Power and Hot Water	3293149	3014180	10983
燃气生产和供应业	Production and Supply of Gas	1113596	984317	5053
水的生产和供应业	Production and Supply of Tap Water	266719	216436	1854

continued 2 (10000 yuan)

销售费用 Sales Expenses	管理费用 Management Expenses	财务费用 Financial Expenses	利息支出 Interest Expenditure	营业利润 Business Profits	利润总额 Total Profits	利税总额 Total Pre - tax Profits	本年应交增值税 Value Added Tax Payable
75660	151468	129238	130643	224581	233060	375659	125499
13662	35832	12299	14250	29294	29584	51081	17572
13434	25433	2842	3380	16881	17047	32957	13877
2741	11542	5697	5849	-47506	-50476	89551	42916
419419	488246	155294	165559	793010	794062	1101968	280814
557839	223268	3094	12138	308373	316898	489719	153506
46438	99330	94301	123405	533559	541835	747738	184804
101269	54402	37746	37792	136631	137028	200521	50824
58601	110128	51716	54043	185364	188175	267834	68354
177631	184995	104646	114114	369228	409725	624699	189001
21153	139296	40897	86449	162252	160171	280630	105415
6696	24384	23998	23786	86660	87387	153663	61938
56080	176325	71965	74477	164505	170966	260621	73345
237758	527333	88876	98704	790318	818084	1097674	243550
56078	150224	29186	29260	195223	201403	263914	49802
157562	305351	197660	241240	447406	484391	642432	106398
381404	564840	146927	150721	481790	490766	729555	209091
337386	543440	29101	44718	889813	1018328	1255969	195184
123046	195152	28894	27013	203250	228989	332823	81491
13253	36340	17392	17537	52210	54460	84858	24212
764	4787	5225	5055	41031	38235	73205	32566
1904	111182	47552	52789	134612	139007	261378	110168
30951	23098	9931	10512	71295	74520	114001	34427
16463	30499	10377	14476	-72	7214	18560	9313

4-09 市区规模以上工业

Main Economic Indicators of Industrial Enterprises

单位:万元

项目	Item	企业单位数(个) Number of Enterprises (unit)	#亏损企业(个) Loss Making Enterprises (unit)	工业总产值(当年价格) Gross Industrial Output Value (current price)	工业销售产值 Value of Industrial Products Sales
总计	**Total**	**3867**	**528**	**97800625**	**96531393**
按隶属关系分	**Grouped by Subordination**				
中央属	Central	20	5	7306728	7266015
省属	Provincial	42	6	3992173	3986789
市属	Municipal	3805	517	86501725	85278590
按所有制分	**Grouped by Ownership**				
国有企业	State - owned Enterprises	36	7	9253445	9226913
集体企业	Collective - owned Enterprises	10	2	70299	67860
股份合作企业	Cooperative Enterprises	8	2	38487	37355
联营企业	Joint Ownership Enterprises	2	-	9239	9216
股份制企业	Share - holding Corporations	2714	310	54205308	53405950
外商及港澳台投资企业	Enterprises with Investment from Foreign、Hong Kong、Macao and Taiwan	969	198	33332431	32905351
其他企业	Other Enterprises	128	9	891415	878748
按企业规模分	**Grouped by Size of Enterprises**				
大型企业	Large	114	5	40433793	40200488
中型企业	Medium - sized	619	84	25441927	24955747
小微企业	Small	3134	439	31924905	31375158
按轻重工业分	**Grouped by Light & Heavy Industry**				
轻工业	Light Industry	1942	274	39467105	38770229
重工业	Heavy Industry	1925	254	58333520	57761164

企业主要经济指标(一)
Above Designated Size in Urban District(Ⅰ)

(10000 yuan)

出口交货值 Export delivery value	实收资本 Total Capital Hold	国家资本 State Capital	个人资本 Personal Capital	港澳台资本 Hongkong, Macau and TaiWan Capital	外商资本 Foreign Capital	全部从业人员年平均人数(人) Annual Average Number of Staff and Workers (person)
15541551	**15012656**	**795426**	**3572834**	**2173426**	**3261723**	**962361**
9261	325444	153720	9822	–	–	13851
142456	730256	246895	2082	96229	74486	26549
15389834	13956957	394810	3560931	2077197	3187237	921961
38710	459248	372944	4958	–	–	26330
21349	14781	–	930	178	–	1247
–	5797	–	462	–	–	876
–	600	–	–	–	–	237
6650170	7211633	305023	3296363	19702	30507	531811
8713458	7226656	117458	193630	2152296	3231185	386623
117864	93942	–	76492	1250	31	15237
6978848	4150153	424352	445494	943780	905882	290623
4550514	4310700	263884	858584	581303	982420	319060
4012190	6551803	107190	2268757	648344	1373422	352678
7244374	6799283	206695	1609562	1150146	1654987	490344
8297177	8213373	588731	1963273	1023281	1606736	472017

单位:万元 4－09 续表1

项 目	Item	企业单位数（个）Number of Enterprises (unit)	#亏损企业(个) Loss Making Enterprises (unit)	工业总产值（当年价格）Gross Industrial Output Value (current price)	工业销售产值 Value of Industrial Products Sales
按国民经济行业分	**Grouped by Economic Sector**				
煤炭开采和洗选业	Coal Mining and Dressing	–	–	–	–
黑色金属矿采选业	Ferrous Metals Mining and Dressing	–	–	–	–
有色金属矿采选业	Nonferrous Metals Mining and Dressing	–	–	–	–
非金属矿采选业	Nonmetal Minerals Mining and Dressing	4	–	40293	40102
农副食品加工业	Agricultural Products Processing	57	3	708264	710392
食品制造业	Food Manufacturing	67	9	1837922	1837327
饮料制造业	Beverage Manufacturing	29	5	1614229	1597947
烟草制品业	Tobacco Processing	2	–	2132761	2132366
纺织业	Textile Industry	651	81	8157832	7995291
纺织服装、鞋、帽制造业	Textile Products, Garments, Shoes and Caps Processing	241	51	2065491	2029890
皮革、毛皮、羽毛(绒)及其制品业	Leather, Furs, Down and Related Products	93	11	1332870	1314634
木材加工及木、竹、藤、棕、草制品业	Timber Processing, Bamboo, Cane, Palm Fiber and Straw Products	21	–	176112	178128
家具制造业	Furniture Manufacturing	64	8	1038328	1015251
造纸及纸制品业	Paper Making and Paper Products	85	7	1327694	1297787
印刷业和记录媒介的复制	Printing and Record Media	64	14	575086	562117
文教体育用品制造业	Cultural, Educational and Sports Goods	31	6	321162	318981
石油加工、炼焦及核燃料加工业	Petroleum Processing, Coking and Nuclear Fuel Processing	5	1	536002	533482

continued 1 (10000 yuan)

出口交货值 Export delivery value	实收资本 Total Capital Hold	国家资本 State Capital	个人资本 Personal Capital	港澳台资本 Hongkong, Macau and TaiWan Capital	外商资本 Foreign Capital	全部从业人员年平均人数（人） Annual Average Number of Staff and Workers (person)
–	–	–	–	–	–	
–	–	–	–	–	–	
–	–	–	–	–	–	
–	1128	–	15	–	–	738
91392	93795	–	37348	7729	7822	8115
46635	341445	21585	49741	62766	145035	22743
10858	346948	427	8028	52384	167169	14844
4373	69571	63971	4200	1400	–	2415
1677871	1590020	560	650273	278398	189405	135786
1206347	500115	–	64497	287656	70288	72987
689219	153649	–	32136	39029	21277	22910
28725	35526	–	19992	1231	673	3053
495174	245267	–	41046	26147	96546	25468
46729	215820	2235	57452	17033	55861	15170
20815	171943	10695	60679	24368	2336	9128
162682	112912	–	12177	15173	81309	8067
293	30418	23580	4338	–	–	1141

项　目	Item	企业单位数(个) Number of Enterprises (unit)	#亏损企业(个) Loss Making Enterprises (unit)	工业总产值(当年价格) Gross Industrial Output Value (current price)	工业销售产值 Value of Industrial Products Sales
化学原料及化学制品制造业	Raw Chemical Materials and Chemical Products	215	20	7698166	7637699
医药制造业	Medical and Pharmaceutical Products	57	7	1949978	1829908
化学纤维制造业	Chemical Fiber	84	11	8223396	8035153
橡胶制品业	Rubber Products	27	7	2793375	3000434
塑料制品业	Plastic Products	183	19	2425920	2413181
非金属矿物制品业	Nonmetal Mineral Products	187	25	3378637	3302523
黑色金属冶炼及压延加工业	Smelting and Processing of Ferrous Metals	57	13	3887568	3845335
有色金属冶炼及压延加工业	Smelting and Processing of Nonferrous Metals	20	6	374164	359914
金属制品业	Metal Products	200	35	3198473	3174513
通用设备制造业	Ordinary Machinery	408	40	6770136	6687665
专用设备制造业	For Special Purpose Equipment Manufacturing	150	19	1794977	1750495
交通运输设备制造业	Transport Equipment Manufacturing	182	34	10882657	10803259
电气机械及器材制造业	Electric Equipment and Machinery	267	49	6086204	5955466
通信设备、计算机及其他电子设备制造业	Telecommunications Equipment, Computers and Other Electronic Equipment Manufacturing	179	26	6702610	6541447
仪器仪表及文化、办公用机械制造业	Instruments, Meters, Cultural and Office Machinery	118	11	2279486	2204134
工艺品及其他制造业	Craftworks and Other Manufacturing	73	7	1142875	1100731
废弃资源和废旧材料回收加工业	Waste Resouces and Waste or Old Material Recycled	2	–	11946	11542
电力、热力的生产和供应业	Production and Supply of Electric Power and Hot Water	25	–	5019197	5009855
燃气生产和供应业	Production and Supply of Gas	10	–	1088015	1085368
水的生产和供应业	Production and Supply of Tap Water	9	3	228806	219075

continued 2 (10000 yuan)

出口交货值 Export delivery value	实收资本 Total Capital Hold	国家资本 State Capital	个人资本 Personal Capital	港澳台资本 Hongkong, Macau and TaiWan Capital	外商资本 Foreign Capital	全部从业人员年平均人数（人） Annual Average Number of Staff and Workers (person)
690641	801948	11262	214993	63712	178708	36374
186931	406370	7223	35698	24676	224196	24094
359748	739575	–	222888	111187	52648	28787
715453	194402	3231	36036	8072	78362	23486
248430	437676	–	125112	65900	120602	25202
205144	610262	458	200247	51890	177457	36032
69655	282373	120820	97442	9286	4715	19379
40920	42039	–	13575	8937	3205	2244
347959	447541	14622	163573	37379	75423	34459
1052115	1474679	92389	418848	194228	277180	83905
370646	460298	3180	92881	17258	204917	24055
2191219	825778	37293	131046	122114	111093	65053
1718407	1587526	22461	302056	247066	457553	77107
2304892	1542326	95910	238066	348398	313278	78595
296724	340794	3980	154540	845	89335	31075
261554	116811	2489	44107	17511	7918	15598
–	4407	–	500	–	3907	131
–	304835	147524	32590	27522	24219	8663
–	199654	40000	2216	132	19287	1778
–	284809	69531	4500	4000	–	3779

4－10　市区规模以上工业

Main Economic Indicators of Industrial

单位:万元

项　目	Item	资产总计 Total Assets	流动资产合计 Total Circulating Funds	应收账款 Receivables	存　货 Stock
总　　计	**Total**	**88067057**	**53945326**	**12069607**	**12624481**
按隶属关系分	**Grouped by Subordination**				
中　央　属	Central	4731330	1770893	158761	903153
省　　属	Provincial	4302653	1882549	204299	387914
市　　属	Municipal	79033075	50291884	11706546	11333414
按所有制分	**Grouped by Ownership**				
国有企业	State－owned Enterprises	7135438	2844314	127493	1045430
集体企业	Collective－owned Enterprises	84828	38011	10527	5493
股份合作企业	Cooperative Enterprises	90838	54132	6486	11443
联营企业	Joint Ownership Enterprises	7375	5851	2071	289
股份制企业	Share－holding Corporations	50045783	30020862	6239188	6878589
外商及港澳台投资企业	Enterprises with Investment from Foreign、Hong Kong、Macao and Taiwan	30065002	20556406	5537625	4612073
其他企业	Other Enterprises	637794	425750	146217	71165
按企业规模分	**Grouped by Size of Enterprises**				
大型企业	Large	34196085	20845165	4328097	5253340
中型企业	Medium－sized	23813173	14964146	3075085	3598346
小微企业	Small	30057800	18136015	4666424	3772794
按轻重工业分	**Grouped by Light & Heavy Industry**				
轻工业	Light Industry	36474523	22762906	4403323	5296468
重工业	Heavy Industry	51592535	31182420	7666284	7328013

企业主要经济指标(二)

Enterprises Above Designated Size in Urban District(Ⅱ)

(10000 yuan)

产成品 Finished Products	固定资产合计 Fixed Assets	累计折旧 Accumulated Depreciation	本年折旧 Depreciation of the year	负债合计 Total Liabilities	流动负债合计 Total Current Liabilities	非流动负债合计 Total Non – current Liabilities	所有者权益合计 Creditors′ Equity
4873013	**21856325**	**13311017**	**2033348**	**51644400**	**44044189**	**7600210**	**36422658**
106419	3666841	2017807	85182	2792913	909052	1883861	1938417
102265	1383620	1100662	144776	2250472	1889205	361268	2052181
4664330	16805864	10192549	1803390	46601014	41245932	5355082	32432060
74587	4318204	2743607	168820	3856128	1988570	1867558	3279310
3473	26148	18048	3459	43213	37202	6011	41616
4049	20494	13402	1241	55774	48115	7659	35065
2	1440	986	219	5223	5223	–	2151
2862474	10545624	6163109	1119891	30995606	26575448	4420158	19050178
1899765	6773915	4282444	723107	16274662	14999146	1275516	13790340
28662	170501	89421	16612	413795	390486	23309	223998
1739129	6522654	4681657	703066	18672985	15664616	3008369	15523100
1518041	5888615	3528320	648294	14604567	12930069	1674499	9208606
1615844	9445056	5101040	681988	18366848	15449505	2917343	11690952
2043840	8875964	5547855	930698	20031914	18149106	1882808	16442608
2829173	12980361	7763163	1102650	31612485	25895084	5717402	19980049

单位:万元 4-10 续表1

项 目	Item	资产总计 Total Assets	流动资产合 计 Total Circulating Funds	应收账款 Receivables	存 货 Stock
按国民经济行业分	**Grouped by Economic Sector**				
煤炭开采和洗选业	Coal Mining and Dressing	–	–	–	–
黑色金属矿采选业	Ferrous Metals Mining and Dressing	–	–	–	–
有色金属矿采选业	Nonferrous Metals Mining and Dressing	–	–	–	–
非金属矿采选业	Nonmetal Minerals Mining and Dressing	28844	13645	4819	863
农副食品加工业	Agricultural Products Processing	526538	350830	79671	111688
食品制造业	Food Manufacturing	1563148	1088841	502538	120302
饮料制造业	Beverage Manufacturing	1283966	701683	149050	134283
烟草制品业	Tobacco Processing	1759387	1200613	30024	749247
纺织业	Textile Industry	8452333	5239619	825576	1052486
纺织服装、鞋、帽制造业	Textile Products, Garments, Shoes and Caps Processing	2052090	1366317	235985	317717
皮革、毛皮、羽毛(绒)及其制品业	Leather, Furs, Down and Related Products	1351158	1071581	217956	264919
木材加工及木、竹、藤、棕、草制品业	Timber Processing, Bamboo, Cane, Palm Fiber and Straw Products	168305	102635	23987	19855
家具制造业	Furniture Manufacturing	979273	699787	131868	155166
造纸及纸制品业	Paper Making and Paper Products	1092758	687026	214803	129582
印刷业和记录媒介的复制	Printing and Record Media	767774	418064	113725	80877
文教体育用品制造业	Cultural, Educational and Sports Goods	265848	139757	22004	51435
石油加工、炼焦及核燃料加工业	Petroleum Processing, Coking and Nuclear Fuel Processing	128269	77323	18019	43252

continued 1 (10000 yuan)

产成品 Finished Products	固定资产合计 Fixed Assets	累计折旧 Accumulated Depreciation	本年折旧 Depreciation of the year	负债合计 Total Liabilities	流动负债合计 Total Current Liabilities	非流动负债合计 Total Non - current Liabilities	所有者权益合计 Creditors´Equity
–	–	–	–	–	–	–	–
–	–	–	–	–	–	–	–
–	–	–	–	–	–	–	–
216	8341	10691	2286	20653	20653	–	8191
51987	115056	48814	11001	335553	319094	16460	190984
52080	309913	222737	27409	590924	557985	32939	972224
38174	408526	392446	48850	588457	580422	8035	695509
40417	332179	225087	29889	188265	187724	541	1571122
528892	2243847	1466634	255564	5491667	5151870	339797	2960666
106270	507326	222872	39713	1234240	1194915	39325	817851
69710	151758	87388	13207	907898	876335	31563	443260
8560	50764	22093	3868	105745	91707	14038	62560
44965	177438	89460	14939	585210	584735	475	394063
43332	290303	187640	33025	645174	585868	59306	447584
32177	255840	190452	31436	481515	457167	24348	286258
9173	99690	40019	8972	103471	93000	10471	162377
5257	48546	62359	4737	183735	183735	–	–55466

项　目	Item	资产总计 Total Assets	流动资产合　计 Total Circulating Funds	应收账款 Receivables	存　货 Stock
化学原料及化学制品制造业	Raw Chemical Materials and Chemical Products	5146804	3236760	668910	701806
医药制造业	Medical and Pharmaceutical Products	1946523	1356431	448553	394916
化学纤维制造业	Chemical Fiber	6421748	3598429	199686	689899
橡胶制品业	Rubber Products	1831151	1056727	191055	438207
塑料制品业	Plastic Products	1989714	1223731	372831	242952
非金属矿物制品业	Nonmetal Mineral Products	3795232	2594780	828447	432959
黑色金属冶炼及压延加工业	Smelting and Processing of Ferrous Metals	3634759	2071642	114049	442157
有色金属冶炼及压延加工业	Smelting and Processing of Nonferrous Metals	206733	123760	33755	37294
金属制品业	Metal Products	2789663	1962631	480260	539629
通用设备制造业	Ordinary Machinery	7542477	5021003	1457056	1236488
专用设备制造业	For Special Purpose Equipment Manufacturing	2030867	1431072	560062	317039
交通运输设备制造业	Transport Equipment Manufacturing	8955760	4785680	893101	1434041
电气机械及器材制造业	Electric Equipment and Machinery	6170976	4149364	1403406	875157
通信设备、计算机及其他电子设备制造业	Telecommunications Equipment, Computers and Other Electronic Equipment Manufacturing	6640699	4917115	1187633	1082323
仪器仪表及文化、办公用机械制造业	Instruments, Meters, Cultural and Office Machinery	2180642	1553167	482483	328302
工艺品及其他制造业	Craftworks and Other Manufacturing	646479	430300	62140	152025
废弃资源和废旧材料回收加工业	Waste Resouces and Waste or Old Material Recycled	18660	13006	2289	2426
电力、热力的生产和供应业	Production and Supply of Electric Power and Hot Water	3635097	780328	65027	38329
燃气生产和供应业	Production and Supply of Gas	725415	159234	39898	5152
水的生产和供应业	Production and Supply of Tap Water	1337970	322448	8941	1709

continued 2 (10000 yuan)

产成品 Finished Products	固定资产合计 Fixed Assets	累计折旧 Accumulated Depreciation	本年折旧 Depreciation of the year	负债合计 Total Liabilities	流动负债合计 Total Current Liabilities	非流动负债合计 Total Non－current Liabilities	所有者权益合计 Creditors´Equity
332374	1338513	687891	146705	3123982	2652864	471118	2022822
180220	393168	236845	34250	968961	917795	51165	977563
350558	1476032	808759	158453	3814309	3246818	567491	2607439
268125	576253	355683	69785	1258781	1110173	148608	572370
114069	548788	322344	68037	1153292	1072906	80386	836421
281431	776562	554345	93669	2589705	2419224	170481	1205527
135976	654676	660602	71821	2337085	2145872	191213	1297673
8200	46751	21257	3842	120693	119638	1055	86041
218589	622992	265438	61553	1855101	1670202	184899	934562
458640	1324830	717242	130771	4229002	3958408	270595	3313475
121973	432889	220693	39154	1101784	996224	105560	929083
325076	1179085	711614	132273	6157974	4796121	1361852	2797786
413649	1169333	600250	121730	3435951	3066248	369703	2735026
442434	811717	663057	103510	2826515	2550928	275587	3814184
114365	412457	210997	37554	1108594	974935	133659	1072048
70446	151184	119336	19254	333704	292426	41278	312775
1688	4526	4739	766	10160	9590	570	8501
–	3788582	2128118	120715	2771823	773826	1997997	863274
3806	418616	254988	36910	384374	140086	244288	341041
189	729843	498129	57701	600106	244696	355409	737864

4－11　市区规模以上工业

Main Economic Indicators of Industrial

单位:万元

项　目	Item	主营业务收　入 Revenues in Main Business	主营业务成　本 Costs in Main Business	主营业务税金及附加 Sales Taxes and Extra Charges in Main Business
总　　计	**Total**	**95264020**	**79435603**	**1838735**
按隶属关系分	**Grouped by Subordination**			
中　央　属	Central	4403406	2507546	1434098
省　　　属	Provincial	4122850	3678979	18666
市　　　属	Municipal	86737765	73249079	385970
按所有制分	**Grouped by Ownership**			
国有企业	State－owned Enterprises	6423076	4379746	1441547
集体企业	Collective－owned Enterprises	67064	55430	995
股份合作企业	Cooperative Enterprises	37833	30916	146
联营企业	Joint Ownership Enterprises	9237	7775	48
股份制企业	Share－holding Corporations	54441081	47747439	220432
外商及港澳台投资企业	Enterprises with Investment from Foreign、Hong Kong、Macao and Taiwan	33417036	26454277	170289
其他企业	Other Enterprises	868693	760021	5277
按企业规模分	**Grouped by Size of Enterprises**			
大型企业	Large	40837977	32726350	1515168
中型企业	Medium－sized	25832309	21881413	194743
小微企业	Small	28593734	24827840	128824
按轻重工业分	**Grouped by Light & Heavy Industry**			
轻工业	Light Industry	39842140	31765663	1516369
重工业	Heavy Industry	55421881	47669940	322366

企业主要经济指标(三)
Enterprises Above Designated Size in Urban District(Ⅲ)

(10000 yuan)

销售费用 Sales Expenses	管理费用 Management Expenses	财务费用 Financial Expenses	利息支出 Interest Expenditure	营业利润 Business Profits	利润总额 Total Profits	利税总额 Total Pre - tax Profits	本年应交增值税 Value Added Tax Payable
3370036	**4072801**	**1240315**	**1464279**	**6010778**	**6330116**	**10867446**	**2680824**
85144	137135	22811	22662	201973	190231	1990368	364594
26204	208255	21038	68453	193308	202998	349470	127685
3258688	3727412	1196467	1373164	5615497	5936887	8527608	2188546
81166	242711	7995	55435	257372	243937	2105872	419246
1956	5384	596	665	3874	4085	6692	1611
927	4299	999	2152	1063	1836	3055	1073
26	878	108	108	453	492	886	346
1055704	1976753	952895	1045150	2977414	3133398	4573135	1204581
2218430	1813326	262890	346556	2722069	2898430	4103285	1033015
11827	29451	14834	14212	48532	47938	74521	20952
1856087	1449605	336395	492650	3263175	3401792	6135363	1217624
908405	1300456	396194	432832	1315471	1410304	2359285	751445
605544	1322740	507726	538798	1432132	1518020	2372797	711755
2021006	1654835	499054	585199	2645640	2715789	5687972	1450769
1349029	2417967	741262	879080	3365138	3614327	5179473	1230055

单位:万元

4-11 续表1

项 目	Item	主营业务收入 Revenues in Main Business	主营业务成本 Costs in Main Business	主营业务税金及附加 Sales Taxes and Extra Charges in Main Business
按国民经济行业分	**Grouped by Economic Sector**			
煤炭开采和洗选业	Coal Mining and Dressing	-	-	-
黑色金属矿采选业	Ferrous Metals Mining and Dressing	-	-	-
有色金属矿采选业	Nonferrous Metals Mining and Dressing	-	-	-
非金属矿采选业	Nonmetal Minerals Mining and Dressing	39435	32422	1311
农副食品加工业	Agricultural Products Processing	728068	631699	2175
食品制造业	Food Manufacturing	1925660	1449534	7394
饮料制造业	Beverage Manufacturing	2295305	1796384	27784
烟草制品业	Tobacco Processing	2118818	424864	1331062
纺织业	Textile Industry	7938631	7081504	37865
纺织服装、鞋、帽制造业	Textile Products, Garments, Shoes and Caps Processing	2028067	1689655	12824
皮革、毛皮、羽毛(绒)及其制品业	Leather, Furs, Down and Related Products	1302114	1151057	6284
木材加工及木、竹、藤、棕、草制品业	Timber Processing, Bamboo, Cane, Palm Fiber and Straw Products	180190	151714	1861
家具制造业	Furniture Manufacturing	1011942	828357	5836
造纸及纸制品业	Paper Making and Paper Products	1326565	1147316	5641
印刷业和记录媒介的复制	Printing and Record Media	568427	488294	2392
文教体育用品制造业	Cultural, Educational and Sports Goods	316432	277383	1306
石油加工、炼焦及核燃料加工业	Petroleum Processing, Coking and Nuclear Fuel Processing	536939	470725	97024

continued 1 (10000 yuan)

销售费用 Sales Expenses	管理费用 Management Expenses	财务费用 Financial Expenses	利息支出 Interest Expenditure	营业利润 Business Profits	利润总额 Total Profits	利税总额 Total Pre - tax Profits	本年应交增值税 Value Added Tax Payable
–	–	–	–	–	–	–	–
–	–	–	–	–	–	–	–
–	–	–	–	–	–	–	–
906	2896	257	223	1642	1559	5235	2366
26913	22349	12648	13116	35041	40363	61440	18691
267437	76055	-5567	7544	133183	131994	231300	91907
261014	61388	1839	4715	158937	165603	274526	81139
61498	80957	-7375	-7554	199905	184512	1787282	271671
95562	249524	184064	200303	329876	350881	569840	180527
68669	131299	44672	37562	87476	89441	175725	73406
23227	44578	35762	36259	43225	46879	102485	48492
8056	9742	3864	3903	6870	8210	14874	4796
47236	44193	13941	14745	77887	79302	120441	35295
37688	48527	24150	25289	72782	79462	124455	39286
13060	33396	11588	13356	27507	27703	47823	16377
8692	18586	1109	2067	10007	10191	21612	10018
1729	10375	5469	5621	-48357	-51324	88146	42445

单位:万元　　4-11　续表2

项　目	Item	主营业务收　入 Revenues in Main Business	主营业务成　本 Costs in Main Business	主营业务税金及附加 Sales Taxes and Extra Charges in Main Business
化学原料及化学制品制造业	Raw Chemical Materials and Chemical Products	7721613	6273860	20305
医药制造业	Medical and Pharmaceutical Products	1818791	866659	17406
化学纤维制造业	Chemical Fiber	8234901	7490712	20395
橡胶制品业	Rubber Products	3013919	2733745	11903
塑料制品业	Plastic Products	2374341	2044054	9413
非金属矿物制品业	Nonmetal Mineral Products	3350349	2884890	13222
黑色金属冶炼及压延加工业	Smelting and Processing of Ferrous Metals	3926634	3648607	12373
有色金属冶炼及压延加工业	Smelting and Processing of Nonferrous Metals	342867	316351	795
金属制品业	Metal Products	3202231	2884108	11516
通用设备制造业	Ordinary Machinery	6906878	5662397	28541
专用设备制造业	For Special Purpose Equipment Manufacturing	1784156	1429042	9836
交通运输设备制造业	Transport Equipment Manufacturing	10681370	9644522	50168
电气机械及器材制造业	Electric Equipment and Machinery	6087026	5042684	20664
通信设备、计算机及其他电子设备制造业	Telecommunications Equipment, Computers and Other Electronic Equipment Manufacturing	6711497	5050442	40037
仪器仪表及文化、办公用机械制造业	Instruments, Meters, Cultural and Office Machinery	2172089	1647896	12734
工艺品及其他制造业	Craftworks and Other Manufacturing	1123563	1022168	5721
废弃资源和废旧材料回收加工业	Waste Resouces and Waste or Old Material Recycled	11542	7975	95
电力、热力的生产和供应业	Production and Supply of Electric Power and Hot Water	2160711	2011444	6161
燃气生产和供应业	Production and Supply of Gas	1100142	972492	5018
水的生产和供应业	Production and Supply of Tap Water	222810	180650	1677

continued 2 (10000 yuan)

销售费用 Sales Expenses	管理费用 Management Expenses	财务费用 Financial Expenses	利息支出 Interest Expenditure	营业利润 Business Profits	利润总额 Total Profits	利税总额 Total Pre - tax Profits	本年应交增值税 Value Added Tax Payable
360940	378736	123287	134439	639999	630756	883747	232553
551104	200787	-709	7724	295826	303472	466256	144205
43551	95090	90717	120201	529046	536797	739034	181683
98647	45845	31566	31793	94809	95303	151576	44369
44619	86189	37141	40747	162358	164971	232248	57762
134043	128425	63735	70552	137389	166043	283281	104008
16599	131825	34279	80929	113837	115998	220513	92135
3019	7324	4503	5129	11871	12214	16597	3588
37002	131766	52591	56457	90547	97412	163759	54693
191520	415608	73253	82671	655295	678944	904793	196101
44307	124769	23802	23768	164960	169639	220759	41087
148432	281527	190890	234228	424201	459723	606427	96237
283965	409278	78428	85432	283105	297203	441847	123692
317146	509504	19016	35977	849031	977885	1199402	180884
120049	188746	27194	25298	198890	224266	324954	78933
10945	31667	14532	14179	41470	43041	71262	22479
126	1090	328	332	1929	1923	2713	696
143	23956	31380	35740	107456	108882	182627	66584
29864	21792	10005	10495	70622	73807	113089	34264
12329	25011	7959	11039	2157	7063	17377	8458

4－12 全市规模以上工业企业

Main Economic Indicators of Industrial Enterprises

单位:万元

项　目	Item	企业单位数（个）Number of Enterprises (unit)	#亏损企业(个) Loss Making Enterprises (unit)	工业总产值(当年价格) Gross Industrial Output Value (current price)	工业销售产值 Value of Industrial Products Sales
按登记注册类型分组	**Grouped by Status of Registration**				
内资企业	Domestic－funded Enterprises	4616	499	86171871	84951444
国有企业	State－owned Enterprises	52	11	10220511	10188681
集体企业	Collective－owned Enterprises	25	2	171901	166881
股份合作企业	Cooperative Enterprises	9	2	41517	40385
联营企业	Joint Ownership Enterprises	3	－	287034	287011
国有联营企业	State Joint Ownership Enterprises			－	－
集体联营企业	Collective Joint Ownership Enterprises	2	－	280209	280209
国有与集体联营企业	Joint State－collective Enterprises			－	－
其他联营企业	Other Joint Ownership Enterprises	1	－	6825	6802
有限责任公司	Limited Liability Corporations	786	91	18918748	18701048
国有独资公司	State－funded Corporations	9	2	229297	221283
其他有限责任公司	Other Limited Liability Corporations	777	89	18689451	18479765
股份有限公司	Share－holding Corporations Ltd.	105	7	8851030	8675933
私营企业	Private Enterprises	3636	386	47681130	46891505
私营独资企业	Private－funded Enterprises	276	21	1936062	1906845
私营合伙企业	Private Partnership Enterprises	38	3	187589	186331
私营有限责任公司	Private Limited Liability Corporations	3267	357	35978194	35264124
私营股份有限公司	Private Share－holding Corporations Ltd.	55	5	9579285	9534205
港、澳、台商投资	Enterprises with Investment from Hong Kong, Macao and Taiwan	565	127	14710963	14413869
内地与港澳台合资经营企业	Joint－venture Enterprises with funds from Hong Kong, Macao and Taiwan	374	68	9137990	8919081
内地与港澳台合作经营企业	Cooperative Enterprises with funds from Hong Kong, Macao and Taiwan	6	1	91465	91290
港澳台商独资经营企业	Enterprises with Sole Investment from Hong Kong, Macao and Taiwan	177	56	4952223	4853596
港澳台商投资股份有限公司	Share－holding Corporations Ltd. with Investment from Hong Kong, Macao and Taiwan	8	2	529284	549903
外商投资企业	Enterprises with Foreign Investment	687	123	22646416	22446851
中外合资经营企业	Joint－venture Enterprises	379	52	12166862	12092381
中外合作经营企业	Cooperation Enterprises	11	1	400186	382747
外商独资经营企业	Enterprises with Sole Foreign Investment	289	68	9374070	9251942
外商投资股份有限公司	Share－holding Corporations Ltd. with Foreign Investment	8	2	705298	719781

主要经济指标按登记注册类型分(2011 年)

Above Designated Size by Status of Registration(2011)

(10000 yuan)

出口交货值 Export delivery value	实收资本 Total Capital Hold	国家资本 State Capital	个人资本 Personal Capital	港澳台资本 Hongkong, Macau and TaiWan Capital	外商资本 Foreign Capital	全部从业人员年平均人数(人) Annual Average Number of Staff and Workers (person)
9314343	10813583	869437	4745348	27467	35060	801472
38710	567663	457140	5558	–	–	32282
29787	25964	–	1049	178	–	2264
–	6335	–	462	–	–	921
–	30600	–	–	–	–	1288
–	–	–	–	–	–	
–	30100	–	–	–	–	1100
–	–	–	–	–	–	
–	500	–	–	–	–	188
1242577	3342729	285142	791176	978	25898	178971
–	170699	40993	–	–	–	5915
1242577	3172030	244148	791176	978	25898	173056
892431	1556643	121138	645080	9256	–	66729
7110838	5283648	6017	3302022	17055	9162	519017
340867	161735	–	113530	1250	2672	25835
20726	27537	–	21570	–	31	3887
4846986	4864803	2637	3097867	15805	6459	452206
1902259	229574	3380	69055	–	–	37089
3732497	3555322	20283	161471	2401244	9614	193903
1845185	1981790	20283	159051	988019	6815	114086
7258	12947	–	407	6128	–	807
1741903	1349354	–	894	1290106	2760	70537
138151	211231	–	1119	116991	40	8473
6290744	4635113	108037	123039	49703	3448879	250746
2945166	1965279	68050	108345	37098	971441	131861
108842	48444	–	877	–	23873	4923
3127780	2469513	–	1000	7905	2387170	105498
108956	151877	39988	12817	4700	66395	8464

单位:万元　　4－12　续表1

项　目	Item	资产总计 Total Assets	流动资产合　计 Total Circulating Funds	应收账款 Receivables	存　货 Stock
按登记注册类型分组	**Grouped by Status of Registration**				
内资企业	Domestic－funded Enterprises	75428596	43812365	9246670	10148788
国有企业	State－owned Enterprises	7823358	3022700	136422	1080788
集体企业	Collective－owned Enterprises	178352	106002	38004	14676
股份合作企业	Cooperative Enterprises	92029	54320	5868	11512
联营企业	Joint Ownership Enterprises	51037	23734	12113	845
国有联营企业	State Joint Ownership Enterprises	－	－	－	－
集体联营企业	Collective Joint Ownership Enterprises	44721	18849	10655	841
国有与集体联营企业	Joint State－collective Enterprises	－	－	－	－
其他联营企业	Other Joint Ownership Enterprises	6316	4885	1458	4
有限责任公司	Limited Liability Corporations	18975224	10848664	2388106	2184702
国有独资公司	State－funded Corporations	795630	287898	10897	14180
其他有限责任公司	Other Limited Liability Corporations	18179595	10560766	2377210	2170522
股份有限公司	Share－holding Corporations Ltd.	11015767	6113881	1275462	1309900
私营企业	Private Enterprises	37292829	23643064	5390695	5546365
私营独资企业	Private－funded Enterprises	1068775	730672	244423	164206
私营合伙企业	Private Partnership Enterprises	135031	81940	27839	13376
私营有限责任公司	Private Limited Liability Corporations	29479792	19312295	4560342	4161821
私营股份有限公司	Private Share－holding Corporations Ltd.	6609232	3518157	558092	1206961
港、澳、台商投资	Enterprises with Investment from Hong Kong, Macao and Taiwan	15845506	10934319	2228188	2136289
内地与港澳台合资经营企业	Joint－venture Enterprises with funds from Hong Kong, Macao and Taiwan	9766040	6407407	1216309	1346734
内地与港澳台合作经营企业	Cooperative Enterprises with funds from Hong Kong, Macao and Taiwan	79285	61673	11222	18815
港澳台商独资经营企业	Enterprises with Sole Investment from Hong Kong, Macao and Taiwan	4935380	3605565	855238	661921
港澳台商投资股份有限公司	Share－holding Corporations Ltd. with Investment from Hong Kong, Macao and Taiwan	1064802	859675	145420	108819
外商投资企业	Enterprises with Foreign Investment	18412799	12350937	4072270	3019639
中外合资经营企业	Joint－venture Enterprises	9938473	6851003	2370237	1660392
中外合作经营企业	Cooperation Enterprises	243647	149467	51926	34891
外商独资经营企业	Enterprises with Sole Foreign Investment	7188834	4579272	1369022	1153248
外商投资股份有限公司	Share－holding Corporations Ltd. with Foreign Investment	1041845	771196	281084	171108

continued 1 (10000 yuan)

产成品 Finished Products	固定资产合计 Fixed Assets	累计折旧 Accumulated Depreciation	本年折旧 Depreciation of the year	负债合计 Total Liabilities	流动负债合计 Total Current Liabilities	非流动负债合计 Total Non－current Liabilities	所有者权益合计 Creditors´Equity
3861537	19666866	11098654	1702089	45938598	38366476	7572122	29489998
80644	4781399	3075356	205814	4246802	2249614	1997188	3576556
6910	38877	35468	5780	103954	97720	6235	74398
4049	21339	14928	1350	56331	48612	7719	35698
2	18215	2211	1273	16300	16300	–	34737
–	–	–	–	–	–	–	–
–	16867	1318	1075	11838	11838	–	32883
–	–	–	–	–	–	–	–
2	1348	894	198	4462	4462	–	1854
973689	5267499	2879958	485186	11834710	9223451	2611259	7140515
6894	390838	406617	33396	419388	133234	286154	376242
966795	4876662	2473341	451790	11415321	9090217	2325105	6764273
568725	2045341	995492	165967	4876173	4150342	725830	6139595
2227517	7494196	4095241	836719	24804329	22580437	2223893	12488500
68468	266147	125652	25097	715759	689874	25885	353016
6976	40991	22692	4369	86788	81835	4953	48243
1894446	6663346	3477141	720842	19584818	18375876	1208942	9894974
257626	523712	469756	86411	4416965	3432852	984113	2192267
867431	3307101	1714016	282854	9083526	8193788	889738	6761981
518308	2192427	1003568	182436	6098569	5412262	686307	3667470
1821	11153	9235	838	42428	41856	572	36857
299989	1015458	630087	94629	2549961	2349387	200574	2385419
47313	88062	71127	4952	392568	390284	2284	672235
1228323	4509111	3048098	534239	9825323	9192042	633281	8587475
702009	2256511	1581745	265009	5986110	5635000	351110	3952363
11066	86179	31888	11757	159109	147262	11848	84538
457757	2030079	1295782	241838	3316234	3064341	251893	3872600
57492	136342	138683	15635	363870	345439	18431	677975

项　目	Item	主营业务收　入 Revenues in Main Business	主营业务成　本 Costs in Main Business	主营业务税金及附加 Sales Taxes and Extra Charges in Main Business
按登记注册类型分组	**Grouped by Status of Registration**			
内资企业	Domestic－funded Enterprises	82899865	71113620	1750544
国有企业	State－owned Enterprises	7352028	5198171	1446317
集体企业	Collective－owned Enterprises	164383	138642	2522
股份合作企业	Cooperative Enterprises	40862	33645	159
联营企业	Joint Ownership Enterprises	286770	250471	114
国有联营企业	State Joint Ownership Enterprises	－	－	－
集体联营企业	Collective Joint Ownership Enterprises	279948	244944	72
国有与集体联营企业	Joint State－collective Enterprises	－	－	－
其他联营企业	Other Joint Ownership Enterprises	6822	5527	42
有限责任公司	Limited Liability Corporations	19476398	16951550	75756
国有独资公司	State－funded Corporations	229576	169291	1434
其他有限责任公司	Other Limited Liability Corporations	19246822	16782259	74322
股份有限公司	Share－holding Corporations Ltd.	9140943	7600739	36505
私营企业	Private Enterprises	46438480	40940403	189172
私营独资企业	Private－funded Enterprises	1877593	1657623	8030
私营合伙企业	Private Partnership Enterprises	183927	162575	1107
私营有限责任公司	Private Limited Liability Corporations	34977808	30602974	149293
私营股份有限公司	Private Share－holding Corporations Ltd.	9399153	8517231	30742
港、澳、台商投资	Enterprises with Investment from Hong Kong, Macao and Taiwan	14603305	11793472	82186
内地与港澳台合资经营企业	Joint－venture Enterprises with funds from Hong Kong, Macao and Taiwan	8983229	7743065	44266
内地与港澳台合作经营企业	Cooperative Enterprises with funds from Hong Kong, Macao and Taiwan	91519	75167	256
港澳台商独资经营企业	Enterprises with Sole Investment from Hong Kong, Macao and Taiwan	4918974	3613037	32597
港澳台商投资股份有限公司	Share－holding Corporations Ltd. with Investment from Hong Kong, Macao and Taiwan	609584	362202	5068
外商投资企业	Enterprises with Foreign Investment	22722501	18011370	104433
中外合资经营企业	Joint－venture Enterprises	12286597	10004581	54708
中外合作经营企业	Cooperation Enterprises	373432	334156	1083
外商独资经营企业	Enterprises with Sole Foreign Investment	9190615	7092977	29372
外商投资股份有限公司	Share－holding Corporations Ltd. with Foreign Investment	871856	579658	19270

continued 2 (10000 yuan)

销售费用 Sales Expenses	管理费用 Management Expenses	财务费用 Financial Expenses	利息支出 Interest Expenditure	营业利润 Business Profits	利润总额 Total Profits	利税总额 Total Pre - tax Profits	本年应交增值税 Value Added Tax Payable
1600936	3087547	1334799	1470620	4665325	4848357	8865041	2248866
84332	324494	19354	67836	272337	261102	2169065	460287
4773	12329	1538	1384	14356	14854	25598	8204
927	4406	1119	2272	1125	1897	3253	1197
26	1545	1557	1561	36992	37022	38138	1003
–	–	–	–	–	–	–	–
26	773	1449	1453	36568	36555	37338	711
–	–	–	–	–	–	–	–
–	772	108	108	424	466	800	292
367472	786224	345501	373589	1202464	1288092	1906305	530414
35593	40024	-2167	821	-10048	1625	12731	9493
331880	746201	347669	372768	1212512	1286467	1893574	520922
280560	429159	66788	79983	838323	893408	1175634	245418
862846	1529389	898943	943995	2299728	2351982	3547048	1002343
35647	58892	23327	22076	96121	94818	145012	41711
3831	7468	3064	3022	6660	6100	13134	5925
741754	1288862	703555	709417	1732297	1766463	2796140	877288
81615	174168	168997	209481	464650	484601	592763	77419
608858	766365	204728	243807	1228161	1352312	1849552	413565
269480	373474	175085	194682	442541	455615	703345	202019
949	4159	678	533	10657	10865	12922	1802
280443	317278	37481	47805	654038	745552	958521	180330
57987	71454	-8516	787	120925	140282	174764	29414
1696332	1228654	154149	196545	1701606	1754582	2590214	727448
801433	569938	117921	127401	845340	878279	1306710	370402
4234	10676	4913	4530	25578	23147	31232	7002
772717	577279	30768	62008	728345	748805	1085699	307173
117948	70759	547	2605	102343	104350	166573	42872

4-13 全市规模以上工业企业

Main Economic Indicators of Industrial

单位:万元

项 目	Item	企业单位数（个）Number of Enterprises (unit)	#亏损企业(个) Loss Making Enterprises (unit)	工业总产值（当年价格）Gross Industrial Output Value (current price)	工业销售产值 Value of Industrial Products Sales
按经济组织类型分组	**Grouped by Type of Ownership**				
独资企业	Solely - owned Enterprises	819	158	26654767	26367946
国有企业	State - owned	52	11	10220511	10188681
集体企业	Collective - owned	25	2	171901	166881
私营独资企业	Private - owned	276	21	1936062	1906845
港澳台商独资经营企业	Enterprises with Sole Investment from Hong Kong, Macao and Taiwan	177	56	4952223	4853596
外商独资经营企业	Enterprises with Sole Foreign Investment	289	68	9374070	9251942
合作、合伙企业	Cooperation and Partnership Enterprises	67	7	1007792	987763
股份合作企业	Share - holding Cooperative	9	2	41517	40385
国有联营企业	State Joint Ownership	-			
集体联营企业	Collective Joint Ownership	2	-	280209	280209
国有与集体联营企业	Joint State - collective Ownership	-			
其他联营企业	Other Joint Ownership	1	-	6825	6802
私营合伙企业	Private Partnership	38	3	187589	186331
内地与港澳台合作经营企业	Cooperative Enterprises with funds from Hong Kong, Macao and Taiwan	6	1	91465	91290
中外合作经营企业	Sino - foreign Cooperation Enterprises	11	1	400186	382747
其他企业	Other Enterprises (Domestic Investment)				
股份有限公司	Share - holding Corporations Ltd.	176	16	19664898	19479822
股份有限公司(内资)	Share - holding Corporations Ltd. (Domestic Investment)	105	7	8851030	8675933
私营股份有限公司	Private Share - holding Corporations Ltd.	55	5	9579285	9534205
港澳台商投资股份有限公司	Share - holding Corporations Ltd. with Investment from Hong Kong, Macao and Taiwan	8	2	529284	549903
外商投资股份有限公司	Share - holding Corporations Ltd. with Foreign Investment	8	2	705298	719781
有限责任公司	Limited Liability Corporations	4806	568	76201793	74976633
国有独资公司	State - owned	9	2	229297	221283
私营有限责任公司	Private	3267	357	35978194	35264124
内地与港澳台合资经营企业	Joint Venture Enterprises with funds from Hong Kong, Macao and Taiwan	374	68	9137990	8919081
中外合资经营企业	Sino - foreign Joint Venture	379	52	12166862	12092381
其他有限责任公司	Others	777	89	18689451	18479765

主要经济指标按经济组织类型分(2011 年)

Enterprises Above Designated Size by the Type of Ownership(2011)

(10000 yuan)

出口交货值 Export delivery value	实收资本 Total Capital Hold	国家资本 State Capital	个人资本 Personal Capital	港澳台资本 Hongkong, Macau and TaiWan Capital	外商资本 Foreign Capital	全部从业人员年平均人数(人) Annual Average Number of Staff and Workers (person)
5279047	4574229	457140	122031	1299439	2392601	236416
38710	567663	457140	5558	–	–	32282
29787	25964	–	1049	178	–	2264
340867	161735	–	113530	1250	2672	25835
1741903	1349354	–	894	1290106	2760	70537
3127780	2469513	–	1000	7905	2387170	105498
136826	125863	–	23317	6128	23904	11826
–	6335	–	462	–	–	921
–	30100	–	–	–	–	1100
–	500	–	–	–	–	188
20726	27537	–	21570	–	31	3887
7258	12947	–	407	6128	–	807
108842	48444	–	877	–	23873	4923
3041798	2149326	164506	728071	130947	66435	120755
892431	1556643	121138	645080	9256	–	66729
1902259	229574	3380	69055	–	–	37089
138151	211231	–	1119	116991	40	8473
108956	151877	39988	12817	4700	66395	8464
10879914	12154600	376111	4156439	1041900	1010614	877124
–	170699	40993	–	–	–	5915
4846986	4864803	2637	3097867	15805	6459	452206
1845185	1981790	20283	159051	988019	6815	114086
2945166	1965279	68050	108345	37098	971441	131861
1242577	3172030	244148	791176	978	25898	173056

单位:万元　　4－13　续表1

项　目	Item	资产总计 Total Assets	流动资产合　计 Total Circulating Funds	应收账款 Receivables	存　货 Stock
按经济组织类型分组	**Grouped by Type of Ownership**				
独资企业	Solely－owned Enterprises	21194698	12044211	2643109	3074839
国有企业	State－owned	7823358	3022700	136422	1080788
集体企业	Collective－owned	178352	106002	38004	14676
私营独资企业	Private－owned	1068775	730672	244423	164206
港澳台商独资经营企业	Enterprises with Sole Investment from Hong Kong, Macao and Taiwan	4935380	3605565	855238	661921
外商独资经营企业	Enterprises with Sole Foreign Investment	7188834	4579272	1369022	1153248
合作、合伙企业	Cooperation and Partnership Enterprises	601029	371132	108967	79439
股份合作企业	Share－holding Cooperative	92029	54320	5868	11512
国有联营企业	State Joint Ownership				
集体联营企业	Collective Joint Ownership	44721	18849	10655	841
国有与集体联营企业	Joint State－collective Ownership				
其他联营企业	Other Joint Ownership	6316	4885	1458	4
私营合伙企业	Private Partnership	135031	81940	27839	13376
内地与港澳台合作经营企业	Cooperative Enterprises with funds from Hong Kong, Macao and Taiwan	79285	61673	11222	18815
中外合作经营企业	Sino－foreign Cooperation Enterprises	243647	149467	51926	34891
其他企业	Other Enterprises (Domestic Investment)				
股份有限公司	Share－holding Corporations Ltd.	19731646	11262909	2260058	2796788
股份有限公司(内资)	Share－holding Corporations Ltd. (Domestic Investment)	11015767	6113881	1275462	1309900
私营股份有限公司	Private Share－holding Corporations Ltd.	6609232	3518157	558092	1206961
港澳台商投资股份有限公司	Share－holding Corporations Ltd. with Investment from Hong Kong, Macao and Taiwan	1064802	859675	145420	108819
外商投资股份有限公司	Share－holding Corporations Ltd. with Foreign Investment	1041845	771196	281084	171108
有限责任公司	Limited Liability Corporations	68159529	43419369	10534994	9353650
国有独资公司	State－owned	795630	287898	10897	14180
私营有限责任公司	Private	29479792	19312295	4560342	4161821
内地与港澳台合资经营企业	Joint Venture Enterprises with funds from Hong Kong, Macao and Taiwan	9766040	6407407	1216309	1346734
中外合资经营企业	Sino－foreign Joint Venture	9938473	6851003	2370237	1660392
其他有限责任公司	Others	18179595	10560766	2377210	2170522

continued 1 (10000 yuan)

产成品 Finished Products	固定资产合计 Fixed Assets	累计折旧 Accumulated Depreciation	本年折旧 Depreciation of the year	负债合计 Total Liabilities	流动负债合计 Total Current Liabilities	非流动负债合计 Total Non－current Liabilities	所有者权益合计 Creditors´Equity
913769	8131960	5162345	573159	10932710	8450936	2481774	10261988
80644	4781399	3075356	205814	4246802	2249614	1997188	3576556
6910	38877	35468	5780	103954	97720	6235	74398
68468	266147	125652	25097	715759	689874	25885	353016
299989	1015458	630087	94629	2549961	2349387	200574	2385419
457757	2030079	1295782	241838	3316234	3064341	251893	3872600
23914	177877	80954	19587	360956	335864	25092	240073
4049	21339	14928	1350	56331	48612	7719	35698
–	16867	1318	1075	11838	11838	–	32883
2	1348	894	198	4462	4462	–	1854
6976	40991	22692	4369	86788	81835	4953	48243
1821	11153	9235	838	42428	41856	572	36857
11066	86179	31888	11757	159109	147262	11848	84538
931156	2793458	1675059	272965	10049575	8318917	1730657	9682072
568725	2045341	995492	165967	4876173	4150342	725830	6139595
257626	523712	469756	86411	4416965	3432852	984113	2192267
47313	88062	71127	4952	392568	390284	2284	672235
57492	136342	138683	15635	363870	345439	18431	677975
4088452	16379784	8942411	1653472	43504207	38646589	4857619	24655322
6894	390838	406617	33396	419388	133234	286154	376242
1894446	6663346	3477141	720842	19584818	18375876	1208942	9894974
518308	2192427	1003568	182436	6098569	5412262	686307	3667470
702009	2256511	1581745	265009	5986110	5635000	351110	3952363
966795	4876662	2473341	451790	11415321	9090217	2325105	6764273

单位:万元　　4-13　续表2

项　目	Item	主营业务收入 Revenues in Main Business	主营业务成本 Costs in Main Business	主营业务税金及附加 Sales Taxes and Extra Charges in Main Business
按经济组织类型分组	**Grouped by Type of Ownership**			
独资企业	Solely - owned Enterprises	23503594	17700449	1518838
国有企业	State - owned	7352028	5198171	1446317
集体企业	Collective - owned	164383	138642	2522
私营独资企业	Private - owned	1877593	1657623	8030
港澳台商独资经营企业	Enterprises with Sole Investment from Hong Kong, Macao and Taiwan	4918974	3613037	32597
外商独资经营企业	Enterprises with Sole Foreign Investment	9190615	7092977	29372
合作、合伙企业	Cooperation and Partnership Enterprises	976510	856013	2718
股份合作企业	Share - holding Cooperative	40862	33645	159
国有联营企业	State Joint Ownership			
集体联营企业	Collective Joint Ownership	279948	244944	72
国有与集体联营企业	Joint State - collective Ownership			
其他联营企业	Other Joint Ownership	6822	5527	42
私营合伙企业	Private Partnership	183927	162575	1107
内地与港澳台合作经营企业	Cooperative Enterprises with funds from Hong Kong, Macao and Taiwan	91519	75167	256
中外合作经营企业	Sino - foreign Cooperation Enterprises	373432	334156	1083
其他企业	Other Enterprises (Domestic Investment)			
股份有限公司	Share - holding Corporations Ltd.	20021536	17059830	91584
股份有限公司(内资)	Share - holding Corporations Ltd. (Domestic Investment)	9140943	7600739	36505
私营股份有限公司	Private Share - holding Corporations Ltd.	9399153	8517231	30742
港澳台商投资股份有限公司	Share - holding Corporations Ltd. with Investment from Hong Kong, Macao and Taiwan	609584	362202	5068
外商投资股份有限公司	Share - holding Corporations Ltd. with Foreign Investment	871856	579658	19270
有限责任公司	Limited Liability Corporations	75724031	65302170	324022
国有独资公司	State - owned	229576	169291	1434
私营有限责任公司	Private	34977808	30602974	149293
内地与港澳台合资经营企业	Joint Venture Enterprises with funds from Hong Kong, Macao and Taiwan	8983229	7743065	44266
中外合资经营企业	Sino - foreign Joint Venture	12286597	10004581	54708
其他有限责任公司	Others	19246822	16782259	74322

continued 2 (10000 yuan)

销售费用 Sales Expenses	管理费用 Management Expenses	财务费用 Financial Expenses	利息支出 Interest Expenditure	营业利润 Business Profits	利润总额 Total Profits	利税总额 Total Pre - tax Profits	本年应交增值税 Value Added Tax Payable
1177912	1290273	112468	201109	1765197	1865131	4383895	997705
84332	324494	19354	67836	272337	261102	2169065	460287
4773	12329	1538	1384	14356	14854	25598	8204
35647	58892	23327	22076	96121	94818	145012	41711
280443	317278	37481	47805	654038	745552	958521	180330
772717	577279	30768	62008	728345	748805	1085699	307173
9966	28254	11331	11918	81013	79031	98679	16929
927	4406	1119	2272	1125	1897	3253	1197
26	773	1449	1453	36568	36555	37338	711
–	772	108	108	424	466	800	292
3831	7468	3064	3022	6660	6100	13134	5925
949	4159	678	533	10657	10865	12922	1802
4234	10676	4913	4530	25578	23147	31232	7002
538110	745541	227816	292857	1526240	1622640	2109733	395124
280560	429159	66788	79983	838323	893408	1175634	245418
81615	174168	168997	209481	464650	484601	592763	77419
57987	71454	-8516	787	120925	140282	174764	29414
117948	70759	547	2605	102343	104350	166573	42872
2180139	3018499	1342062	1405089	4222642	4388449	6712500	1980123
35593	40024	-2167	821	-10048	1625	12731	9493
741754	1288862	703555	709417	1732297	1766463	2796140	877288
269480	373474	175085	194682	442541	455615	703345	202019
801433	569938	117921	127401	845340	878279	1306710	370402
331880	746201	347669	372768	1212512	1286467	1893574	520922

4-14 全市1998-2011年规模以上工业企业主要经济效益指标

Main Economic Indicators of Industrial Enterprises Above Designated Size(1998-2011)

单位:亿元 (100 million yuan)

年份 Year	规模以上工业总产值 Output Value of Industrial Enterprises Above Designated Size	规模以上工业增加值 Added Value of Industrial Enterprises Above Designated Size	资产总计 Total Assets	流动资产合计 Total Current Assets	主营业务收入 Revenne from Principal Business	利润总额 Total Profits	利税总额 Total Profits and Tax
1998	1109.94	274.70	1486.02	732.72	1036.09	38.44	101.36
1999	1200.07	298.90	1620.93	800.60	1132.80	54.47	127.89
2000	1543.57	360.97	1828.35	946.32	1465.49	76.20	161.61
2001	1919.51	444.91	2148.96	1122.07	1828.28	107.56	208.54
2002	2400.30	597.01	2514.19	1313.92	2288.21	145.48	274.98
2003	3202.52	783.51	3258.93	1783.5	3117.46	194.16	359.54
2004	4486.58	1019.47	4118.31	2300.84	4363.27	226.74	427.23
2005	5441.13	1126.54	4781.34	2692.73	5282.8	234.99	450.68
2006	6975.46	1363.17	5564.68	3215.19	6807.64	314.49	576.51
2007	8351.40	1717.65	6573.12	3880.23	8057.03	414.55	730.50
2008	9379.58	1743.20	7506.26	4437.50	8976.46	453.92	802.13
2009	9390.73	1792.00	8405.62	4968.21	9026.32	510.97	882.62
2010	11081.04	2153.83	9937.41	6011.68	10843.24	764.47	1224.48
2011	12352.92	2369.00	10968.69	6709.76	12022.57	795.53	1330.48

4-14 续表 continued

年份 Year	工业增加值率(%) Rate of Industrial Added Valne(%)	资产负债率(%) Rate of Assets and Liabilites	流动资产周转次数(计量单位为次) the Number of Current Assets Turnover	成本费用利润率(%) Profit Rate of Costs	全员劳动生产率(元/人) All-personnel Labor Productivity (Yuan/Ren)	产品销售率(%) Prodnct Sales Rate(%)
1998	24.75	57.02	1.47	3.86	37976	95.91
1999	24.91	55.69	1.46	5.06	44307	98.07
2000	23.39	58.59	1.62	5.49	52713	97.19
2001	23.18	57.20	1.70	6.26	59518	97.40
2002	24.87	56.82	1.82	6.84	76402	97.76
2003	24.47	58.70	1.87	6.69	91284	97.68
2004	22.72	59.80	2.00	5.50	98809	98.10
2005	20.70	60.12	2.06	4.69	105786	98.25
2006	19.54	59.83	2.23	4.87	120289	98.36
2007	20.57	60.43	2.21	5.44	138016	98.17
2008	18.59	60.42	2.10	5.34	152070	98.14
2009	19.08	59.07	1.86	5.86	151002	98.63
2010	19.44	58.34	1.96	7.60	166516	98.83
2011	19.18	59.12	1.91	6.96	190110	98.61

4－15 主要工业产品生产量(2011 年)
Output of Major Industrial Products(2011)

产品名称		Item		全市 Whole City 2011 年	为上年(%) As Compared with the Preceding Year(%)	市区 Urban District
铁矿石原矿量	(万吨)	The volume of iron ore	(10000 tons)	2.57	99.3	-
原油加工量	(万吨)	Crude oil processing volume	(10000 tons)	62.54	83.2	62.54
发电量	(亿千瓦小时)	Electricity	(100 million kwh)	185.01	106.0	127.38
罐头	(万吨)	Canned Food	(10000 tons)	5.54	74.5	0.66
乳制品	(吨)	Dairy Products	(ton)	185008	133.7	175689
啤酒	(千升)	Beer	(1000 litres)	930634	99.9	722791
软饮料	(万吨)	Soft Drinks	(10000 tons)	718.81	136.6	480.05
精制茶	(吨)	Tea	(ton)	49379.82	121.3	3050.90
卷烟	(亿支)	Cigarettes	(100 million)	512.69	104.3	512.69
方便面	(吨)	Instant Noodle	(ton)	235497	78.8	235497
化学纤维	(吨)	Chemical Fiber	(ton)	5331634	112.9	5181009
其中:合成纤维	(吨)	Synthetic Fibre	(ton)	5188011	113.8	5037386
纱	(万吨)	Yarn	(10000 tons)	56.58	109.5	48.72
布	(万米)	Cloth	(10000 m)	397221	112.1	332182
印染布	(万米)	Printed Fabric	(10000 m)	513781	102.3	494686
蚕丝及交织机织物(含蚕丝≥50%)	(万米)	Silk and Woven Fabrics (Containing Greater than or Equal 50% silk)	(10000 m)	4977.11	89.0	4158.51
服装	(万件)	Garment	(10000 units)	50092.19	96.8	43272.62

4－15　续表1　continued 1

产品名称		Item		全市 Whole City 2011年	为上年(%) As Compared with the Preceding Year(%)	市区 Urban District
皮革鞋靴	（万双）	Leather Footwear	(10000 units)	1379.31	109.5	424.40
家具	（万件）	Furniture	(10000 units)	3932.64	95.1	3620.90
塑料制品	（吨）	Plastic Membrane	(ton)	1733353	111.8	1421142
机制纸及纸板	（万吨）	Machine Made Paper and Paperboard	(10000 tons)	705.75	112.4	24.99
焦炭	（万吨）	Coke	(10000 tons)	52.91	101.3	52.91
盐酸(含量31%以上)	（吨）	Mariatic Acid(above 31% percent)	(ton)	137392	140.5	137392
氢氧化钠(烧碱)(折100%)	（吨）	Caustic Soda	(ton)	203056	145.0	203056
碳酸钠(纯碱)	（吨）	Soda ash	(ton)	243630	204.4	243630
初级形态的塑料(塑料树脂及共聚物)	（吨）	Plastics in Primary Form(Plastic Resins and Copolymers)	(ton)	277814.94	135.4	216130.54
合成氨	（吨）	Synthetic Ammonia	(ton)	151816	169.0	128334
农用氮、磷、钾化学肥料总计(折纯)	（吨）	Chemical Fertilizer	(ton)	81689	179.5	70255
化学农药原药(折有效成分100%)	（吨）	Chemical Pesticide	(ton)	125622.34	100.3	24404.10
涂料(油漆)	（吨）	Paint	(ton)	152883.04	121.4	112850.60
合成洗涤剂	（吨）	Synthetic Detergent	(ton)	118572.50	97.1	96554.50
化学药品原药(化学原料药)	（吨）	Original Drug Chemicals	(ton)	9290.36	109.9	7804.89
中成药	（吨）	Traditional Chinese Medicine	(ton)	7444.84	114.1	7079.45
橡胶轮胎外胎(轮胎外胎)	（万条）	Rubber Tires	(10000 units)	4780.67	112.6	4486.81
水泥	（万吨）	Cement	(10000 tons)	2030.59	105.5	913.41

4－15　续表2　continued 2

产品名称	Item	全市 Whole City 2011 年	为上年(%) As Compared with the Preceding Year(%)	市区 Urban District
平板玻璃　（万重量箱）	Plate Glass　(10000 weight cases)	476.62	108.9	476.62
粗钢　（万吨）	Crude Steel　(10000 tons)	370.18	104.4	370.18
生铁　（万吨）	Pig Iron　(10000 tons)	293.97	109.9	293.97
铁合金　（万吨）	Iron Alloy　(10000 tons)	9.25	108.9	1.13
钢材　（万吨）	Steel Products　(10000 tons)	964.88	110.2	839.69
精炼铜(电解铜)　（吨）	Refined Copper　(ton)	164970	110.6	13262
工业锅炉　（蒸发量吨）	Industry Boiler　(ton)	10776.98	106.4	10776.98
金属切削机床　（台）	Metal－cutting Machine Tools　(unit)	49682	102.9	39963
金属成形机床(锻压设备)　（台）	Metal Forming Machine(Forge Equipment)　(Tai)	20280	87.8	17042
泵(液体泵)　（万台）	Pump　(10000 sets)	57.17	113.1	55.69
滚动轴承(轴承)　（万套）	Bearings　(10000 units)	29294.90	122.3	27898.90
汽车　（辆）	Motor Vehicles　(unit)	10613	305.2	10613
叉车　（台）	Forklift　(unit)	78745	116.4	6600
两轮自行车(自行车)　（万辆）	Bicycles　(10000 units)	647.93	102.9	644.42

4－15　续表3　continued 3

产品名称		Item		全市 Whole City 2011年	为上年(%) As Compared with the Preceding Year(%)	市区 Urban District
交流电动机	（万千瓦）	AC Motor	（10000 kw）	31.42	80.1	21.94
钢绞线	（吨）	Strand	（ton）	58149.03	126.2	57920.66
通信及电子网络用电缆	（万对千米）	Communication Cable	（10000 km）	470.25	63.2	28.86
光缆(光纤通讯电缆)	（万芯千米）	Electric Power Cable	（10000 km）	2386.99	156.6	96.20
家用电冰箱	（万台）	Household Refrigerators	（10000 units）	104.75	97.3	104.75
家用洗衣机	（万台）	Household Washing Machines	（10000 units）	364.69	111.0	364.69
吸排油烟机	（万台）	Smoke Absorbers	（10000 units）	122.89	105.4	122.89
移动通信手持机(手机)	（万部）	Mobile Telephone Sets	（10000 units）	942.57	83.8	942.57
电工仪器仪表	（万台）	Electric Instrument and Apparatus	（10000 units）	3437.43	133.8	2935.10
工业自动调节仪表与控制系统	（万台）	Industrial Automatic Adjustment Meter and Control System	（10000 units）	188.87	124.0	188.86
电光源(灯泡)	（亿只）	Light Bulbs	（100 million units）	15.61	91.2	2.42
彩色电视机	（万部）	Color－Television Sets	（10000 units）	11.34	52.6	11.34
微型计算机设备	（万台）	Micro－computer Equipment	（10000 units）	154.87	98.6	154.87

4－16　单位 GDP 能耗降低情况(2011 年)
Increase or Decrease of Energy Consumption Per Unit of GDP(2011)

地　区	Region	单位 GDP 能耗(吨标准煤/万元) Energy Consumption Per Unit of GDP (tons of SCE/10000 yuan)		单位 GDP 电耗(千瓦时/万元) Electricity Consumption Per Unit of GDP (kwh/10000 yuan)		单位工业增加值能耗降低率 Decrease Rate of Energy Consumption Per Unit of Industriul Value－Added (±%)
		2011 年	降低率 Decrease Rate (±%)	2011 年	降低率 Decrease Rate (±%)	
杭州市	Hangzhou	0.58	4.42	878	－0.12	7.14
#上城区	Shangcheng					17.76
下城区	Xiacheng					11.26
江干区	Jianggan					17.69
拱墅区	Gongshu					6.21
西湖区	Xihu					6.30
高新(滨江)区	Hi－Tech(Binjiang)					5.63
下沙经济技术开发区	HEDA					9.83
萧山区	Xiaoshan	0.75	4.52	1330	－0.19	4.86
余杭区	Yuhang	0.57	4.11	962	－0.46	7.13
桐庐县	Tonglu	0.58	5.03	714	－0.48	10.80
淳安县	Chun'an	0.36	1.02	609	－2.90	8.08
建德市	Jiande	1.09	4.54	1231	－2.37	8.09
富阳市	Fuyang	1.13	4.63	1404	0.88	6.81
临安市	Lin'an	0.57	4.01	910	1.44	7.19

注:1. 江干区不含杭州经济技术开发区。

2. 本表单位 GDP 能源、单位 GDP 电耗指标中的 GDP,采用 2010 年价格计算。

a) HEDA is not included in Jianggan district in this table.

b) The GDP in this table was calculated at 2010 prices.

4－17 全市工业企业主要能源

Energy Consumption of Industrial

行 业 Sector	原煤(吨) Raw Coal(Ton)	洗精煤(吨) Washing Coal(Ton)	焦炭(吨) Coke(Ton)	汽油(吨) Gasoline(Ton)	煤油(吨) Kerosene(Ton)
总 计 Total	**13627578**	**773752**	**1464248**	**51827**	**1450**
煤炭开采和洗选业 Coal Mining and Dressing	–	–	–	–	–
黑色金属矿采选业 Ferrous Metals Mining and Dressing	–	–	–	–	–
有色金属矿采选业 Nonferrous Minerals Mining and Dressing	–	–	–	7	–
非金属矿采选业 Nonmetal Minerals Mining and Dressing	29292	–	–	27	–
农副食品加工业 Agricultural Products Processing	29298	–	–	301	–
食品制造业 Food Manufacturing	29350	–	–	879	–
饮料制造业 Beverage Manufacturing	22484	–	–	722	–
烟草制品业 Tobacco Processing	–	–	–	44	–
纺织业 Textile Processing	1163464	–	–	5871	44
纺织服装、鞋、帽制造业 Textile Products, Garments, Shoes and Caps Processing	8310	93	–	2163	1
皮革、毛皮、羽毛(绒)及其制品业 Leather, Furs, Down and Related Products	48303	–	–	774	–
木材加工及木、竹、藤、棕、草制品业 Timber Processing, Bamboo, Cane, Plam Fiber and Straw Products	211	–	–	141	–
家具制造业 Furniture Manufacturing	2806	34	744	859	–
造纸及纸制品业 Paper Making and Paper Products	427874	–	–	1215	2
印刷业和记录媒介的复制 Printing	735	–	–	1035	–
文教体育用品制造业 Cultural, Educational and Sports Goods	642	–	–	398	–
石油加工、炼焦及核燃料加工业 Petroleum Processing, Coking and Nuclear Fuel Processing	1707	–	–	86	–

消费量按行业分(2011 年)
Enterprises by Sector(2011)

柴油(吨) Diesel oil(Ton)	燃料油(吨) Fuel Oil(Ton)	液化石油气(吨) Liquefied Petroleum Gas(Ton)	天然气(万立方米) Natural Gas (10000 cu. m)	其他石油制品(吨) Other Petroleum Products(Ton)	热力(百万千焦) Heat(Million kilo - joule)	电力(万千瓦时) Electricity (10000 kwh)
186630	**67662**	**18579**	**165047**	**223223**	**84078771**	**3323933**
–	–	–	–	–	–	–
–	–	–	–	–	–	260
14	–	–	–	–	–	1859
7107	–	–	–	35	–	10608
1496	–	34	1	65	80845	13088
2355	107	1184	776	–	1342432	20597
2988	3472	4	136	–	2107012	57736
6067	–	–	–	–	134296	5519
5162	665	652	1027	188	22282298	473322
2306	–	24	10	–	625929	21549
573	–	–	–	–	92084	12691
314	–	–	–	–	–	6485
2807	1047	–	428	–	93742	11316
3491	–	–	205	–	30463240	285942
1158	–	48	205	–	12536	12331
654	–	180	105	4	128540	8153
316	8142	–	–	187229	–	5445

4－17 续表

行业 Sector	原煤(吨) Raw Coal(Ton)	洗精煤(吨) Washing Coal(Ton)	焦炭(吨) Coke(Ton)	汽油(吨) Gasoline(Ton)	煤油(吨) Kerosene(Ton)
化学原料及化学制品制造业 Raw Chemical Materials and Chemical Products	1049156	–	210	4031	71
医药制造业 Medical and Pharmaceutical Products	53124	–	–	729	–
化学纤维制造业 Chemical Fiber	237232	–	–	917	–
橡胶制品业 Rubber Products	290588	–	–	2133	3
塑料制品业 Plastic Products	22131	–	–	1477	1
非金属矿物制品业 Nonmetal Minerals Products	2598155	–	25	3253	–
黑色金属冶炼及压延加工业 Smelting and Processing of Ferrous Metals	581326	773625	1425035	589	–
有色金属冶炼及压延加工业 Smelting and Processing of Nonferrous Metals	29736	–	19599	266	1
金属制品业 Metal Products	31192	–	67	2383	41
通用设备制造业 Ordinary Machinery	64347	–	14331	5339	724
专用设备制造业 Special Purpose Equipment	18680	–	657	1733	1
交通运输设备制造业 Transportation Equtpment	8745	–	865	3448	556
电气机械及器材制造业 Electric Equipment and Machinery	10474	–	82	3435	2
通信设备、计算机及其他电子设备制造业 Telecommunications Equipment, Computers and Other Electronic Equipment	4164	–	263	2721	–
仪器仪表及文化、办公用机械制造业 Instruments, Meters, Cultural and Office Machinery	2545	–	–	1534	1
工艺品及其他制造业 Craftworks and Other Manufacturing	455	–	–	847	1
废弃资源和废旧材料回收加工业 Waste Resouces and Waste or Old Material Recycled	125	–	2369	38	–
电力、热力的生产和供应业 Production and Supply of Electric Power and Hot Water	6860927	–	–	1850	–
燃气生产和供应业 Production and Supply of Gas	–	–	–	268	–
水的生产和供应业 Production and Supply of Tap Water	–	–	–	317	–

continued

柴油(吨) Diesel oil(Ton)	燃料油(吨) Fuel Oil(Ton)	液化石油气(吨) Liquefied Petroleum Gas(Ton)	天然气(万立方米) Natural Gas (10000 cu. m)	其他石油制品(吨) Other Petroleum Products(Ton)	热力(百万千焦) Heat(Million kilo - joule)	电力(万千瓦时) Electricity (10000 kwh)
10973	7108	10	1247	32414	8916466	308510
2266	–	28	1417	45	539926	33411
1399	15892	72	848	437	9080031	329041
1292	–	–	1000	14	3218320	92856
2396	1995	1410	91	246	444876	87965
84849	11084	2184	12676	–	379938	260473
4589	1128	518	2387	–	1336992	358722
1073	11031	155	626	4	44207	40633
5942	3598	120	2513	225	405714	78775
13292	878	1255	1229	1175	180104	123353
1438	–	669	151	77	60535	26087
6001	–	522	674	1019	135176	82006
6533	–	8994	530	18	296402	125742
2505	110	429	128	–	423351	74495
994	–	5	188	13	5911	14716
1176	–	70	80	10	56383	12191
333	1402	–	–	–	–	4857
2157	3	–	136346	6	1191484	268386
392	–	–	21	–	–	555
220	–	13	3	–	–	54261

4-18 电力消费量(2011年)
Electricity Consumption(2011)

单位:万千瓦时 (10000 kwh)

项　目	Item	2011年	为上年(%) As Compared with the Preceding Year(%)
总　计	**Total**	**5752848**	**110.2**
#线路损失电量	#Losses in Transmission	128642	71.0
农林牧渔业	Farming, Forestry, Animal Husbandry and Fishery Conservancy	47270	110.3
工业	Industry	3995998	109.7
轻工业	Light Industry	1947397	110.4
重工业	Heavy Industry	2048600	109.1
#采矿业	#Mining and Quarrying	42470	10.2
制造业	Manufacturing Industry	3658525	111.8
电力、燃气及水的生产和供应业	Produotion and supply of electricity, gas & water	295003	89.0
建筑业	Construction	111677	119.1
交通运输、仓储及邮政业	Transportation, Storage, Post & Telecommunications	62334	112.9
信息传输、计算机服务和软件业	Information Transmission, Computer Services and Software	83727	125.2
商业、住宿和餐饮业	Commerce, Catering and lodging	272357	112.1
金融、房地产、商务及居民服务业	Finance, Real Estate Commerce and Service for the Residents	193876	115.9
公共管理和社会组织	Public Management and Social Organizations	292556	107.3
城乡居民生活用电	Residential Consumption	693054	109.2
城市	Cities	425055	109.3
#乡村	#Rural Areas	267999	109.1

4－19　2001－2011年水资源量和总用水量

Total Water Resources and Water Consumption(2001－2011)

单位:亿立方米　　(100 million Cubic Meters)

		全市 Whole City	市区 Urban District	桐庐 Tonglu	淳安 Chan'an	建德 Jiangde	富阳 Fuyang	临安 Lin'an
2001年	水资源量 Water Resources	156.37	18.87	14.28	41.14	18.54	14.23	26.76
	用水量 Water Consumption	40.29	28.05	2.01	1.03	2.11	4.17	2.92
2002年	水资源量 Water Resources	213	30.21	24.3	65.46	31.59	23.54	37.9
	用水量 Water Consumption	39.92	27.51	2.01	1.05	2.18	4.35	2.82
2003年	水资源量 Water Resources	102.65	9.31	10.32	41.43	15.57	8.13	17.9
	用水量 Water Consumption	44.72	29.13	1.98	1.38	2.3	7.12	2.81
2004年	水资源量 Water Resources	85.28	12.04	10.35	27.82	11.34	9.15	14.58
	用水量 Water Consumption	48.9	32.89	2.21	1.09	2.35	7.17	3.19
2005年	水资源量 Water Resources	90.65	14.32	9.46	26.66	10.36	10.31	19.54
	用水量 Water Consumption	49.58	32.95	2.25	1.24	2.38	7.16	3.61
2006年	水资源量 Water Resources	109.8	15.14	11.7	38.42	13.41	10.36	20.75
	用水量 Water Consumption	48.73	31.39	2.39	1.42	2.68	7.13	3.72
2007年	水资源量 Water Resources	104.13	20.28	10.12	29.88	11.72	11.76	20.36
	用水量 Water Consumption	49.56	32.57	2.53	1.53	3.09	6.45	3.39
2008年	水资源量 Water Resources	154.38	24.58	14.95	49.22	18.52	14.2	32.92
	用水量 Water Consumption	56.7	39.57	2.9	1.32	2.69	6.49	3.7
2009年	水资源量 Water Resources	141.5	23.38	16.67	37.46	15.63	16.33	32.03
	用水量 Water Consumption	54.28	39.24	2.52	1.46	2.81	5.18	3.07
2010年	水资源量 Water Resources	190.4	29.58	19.03	63.61	30.36	17.92	29.91
	用水量 Water Consumption	54.95	39.00	2.79	1.61	2.88	4.80	3.87
2011年	水资源量 Water Resources	136.7	20.21	15.81	41	19.11	13.43	27.13
	用水量 Water Consumption	57.71	40.4	2.98	1.37	2.92	5.83	4.21

主要统计指标解释

工业总产值 是以货币表现的工业企业在报告期内生产的已出售或可供出售工业产品总量,它反映一定时间内工业生产的总规模和总水平,它包括:在本企业内不再进行加工,经检验、包装入库(规定不需包装的产品除外)的成品价值,对外加工费收入,自制半成品,在产品期末初差额价值。工业总产值采用"工厂法"计算,即以工业企业作为一个整体,按企业工业生产活动的最终成果来计算,企业内部不允许重复计算,不能把企业内部各个车间(分厂)生产的成果相加。

工业销售产值 是以货币表现的工业企业在一定时期内销售的本企业生产的工业产品总量。包括已销售的成品、半成品价值,对外提供的工业性作业和对本单位基本建设部门、生活福利部门等提供的产品和工业性作业及自制设备的价值。已销售的成品、半成品不论是本期生产的、还是上期生产的,只要是本期销售出去的均包括在内。对外提供的工业性作业是指企业按合同对外提供的工业性劳务。企业为本单位基本建设部门、生活福利部门等提供的产品和工业性作业及自制设备也应视同销售,这部分也作为销售统计。工业销售产值的计算范围、计算价格和计算方法与工业总产值一致,但两者计算的基础不同;工业销售产值计算的基础是产品销售总量,工业总产值计算的基础是工业产品生产总量。

工业增加值 是指工业行业在报告期内以货币表现的工业生产活动的最终成果。

固定资产原价 固定资产原值指企业在建造、购置、安装、改建、扩建、技术改造某项固定资产时所支出的全部货币总额。它一般包括买价、包装费、运杂费和安装费等。

固定资产净值 是指固定资产原价减去历年已提折旧额后的净额。

利税总额 指企业利润总额、产品销售税金及附加和应交增值税之和。

主营业务收入 指企业销售产品的销售收入和提供劳务等主要经营业务取得的收入总额。

主营业务成本 指企业销售产品和提供劳务等主要经营业务的实际成本。

主营业务税金及附加 指企业销售产品和提供工业性劳务等主要经营业务应负担的城市维护建设税、消费税、资源税和教育费附加。

主营业务利润 指企业销售产品和提供工业性劳务等主要经营业务收入和除其成本、费用、税金后的利润。

利润总额 指企业实现的利润。

应交增值税 指企业在报告期内应交纳的增值税额。

总资产 指企业拥有或控制的全部资产。包括流动资产、长期投资、固定资产、无形及递延资产、其他长期资产、递延税项等,即为企业资产负债表的资产总计项。

(1)流动资产指企业可以在一年内或者超过一年的一个生产周期内变现或耗用的资产合计。包括现金及各种存款、短期投资、应收及预付款项、存货等。

(2)固定资产指企业固定资产净值、固定资产清理、在建工程、待处理固定资产损失所占用的资金合计。

(3)无形资产指企业长期使用而没有实物形态的资产。包括专利权、非专利技术、商标权、著作权、土地使用权、商誉等。

总负债 指企业承担并需要偿还的全部债务。包括流动负债和长期负债、递延税项等,即为企业资产负债表的负债合计项。

(1)流动负债指企业在一年内或者超过一年的一个营业周期内需要偿还的债务合计,其中包括短期借款、应付及预收款项、应付工资、应交税金和应交利润等。

(2)长期负债指企业在一年以上或者超过一年的一个生产周期以上需要偿还的债务合计,其中包括长期借款、应付债务、长期应付款项等。

所有者权益 指企业投资人对企业净资产的所有权。企业净资产等于企业全部资产减去全部负债后的余额。其中包括投资者对企业的最初投入,以及资本公积金、盈余公积金和未分配利润,对股份制企业即为股东权益。

Explanatory Notes on Main Statistical Indicators

Gross Industrial Output Value is the total volume of industrial products sold or available for sale in value terms which reflects the total achievements and overall scale of industrial production during a given period. It includes the value of the finished products, which are not to be further processed in the enterprises and have been inspected, packed and put in storage, the value of industrial services rendered to other units, and the changes in the value of the semi – finished products and products in process between the beginning and closing of the period. The gross industrial output value is calculated with "factory method". No double calculations are to be made within the same enterprise. However, double counting does occur among different enterprises.

Industrial Sales Output Value is the total volume of industrial products sold in value term of an industrial enterprise during a given period. It includes the value of finished products, semi – finished products, industrial operations rendered to other units, products industrial operations & self – made equipment provided to the basic construction department, welfare department, etc. of the enterprise. For finished products & semi – finished products, whether produced in this calculation period or the previous one, if they are sold in this calculation period, they should be included. Industrial operations are industrial services rendered to other units according to contracts. Products, industrial operations & self – made equipment provided to basic construction department, welfare department, etc. of the enterprise should be regarded as act of sale, and included in sales statistics.

The scope , price and method of calculation of industrial sales output value are the same as those for gross industrial output value. But the calculation bases are different: the base for sales output value is the total volume of products sold; the base for gross industrial output value is total volume of production of industrial products.

Value – added of Industry refers to the final results of industrial production of the industrial trade in money terms during the reference period.

Original Value of Fixed Assets refers to the original value of all assets owned by industrial enterprises, calculated at the cost paid at the time of purchase, installation, reconstruction, expansion, and technical innovation and transformation of the said assets, which includes expenses on purchase, package, transportation, and installation, etc.

Net Value of Fixed Assets is obtained by deducting depreciation over years from the original value of fixed assets.

Total Pre – tax Profits refers to the sum of sales tax and extra charges adding total profits.

Sales Revenue of Industrial Products refers to the revenue from the sales of products by industrial enterprises and the revenue from services provided and etc.

Sales Cost of Industrial Products refers to the actual cost of products of industrial enterprises and industrial services provided, etc.

Tax and Extra Charges on Sales of Products refer to the tax on city maintenance and construction, consumption tax, resources tax and extra charges for education , which should be borne by the enterprises in selling products and providing industrial services.

Sales Profit of Products refers to the profit gained by the enterprises by deducting cost, charges and taxes from the business income of the enterprises obtained in selling products and providing industrial services.

Total Profits refer to the profits gained by the enterprises.

Value – added Tax Payable refers to the amount of the value added tax which should be paid by the enterprises in the reporting period.

Total Assets refer to all assets which are owned or controlled by enterprises, including circulating assets, long term investment, fixed assets, intangible assets and deferred assets, other long term assets, and deferred taxes, etc. The summation of above items is equal to total assets shown in the balance sheets of the enterprises.

(1) Circulating assets (working capital) refer to assets which can be cashed in or spent or consumed in an operating cycle of one year or over one year, including cash, all kinds of deposits, short term investment, receivables, advance payment, stock, etc.

(2) Fixed assets refer to the net value of fixed assets, clearance of fixed assets, project under construction, fixed assets losses in suspense. These are corporations' fund holdings.

(3) Intangible assets refer to assets without material form used by enterprises over a lone time, such as patents, non – patent technologies, trade marks, copyright, land use right, business reputation, etc.

Total Liabilities refer to the debts that enterprises are responsible for repayment, including liquid liabilities, long – term liabilities and deferred taxes, etc. Total liabilities correspond to the summation item of liabilities shown in the balance sheets of the enterprises.

(1) Liquid liabilities (also called quick liabilities or immediate liabilities) refer to enterprises' total debt payable within an operating cycle of one year or over one year, including short term loans, payables and advance payments, wages payable, taxes payable and profit payable, etc.

(2) Long term liabilities refers to total debt payable within an operating cycle of one year or over one year, including long – term loans, payable liabilities, long – term payables, etc.

Creditors' Equity refers to investors' ownership of net assets of the enterprise. It is equal to the total assets of the enterprise minus its total liabilities, including the primary input from investors, capital accumulation fund, surplus accumulation fund and undistributed profit. It is the shareholder's equity in share – holding companies.

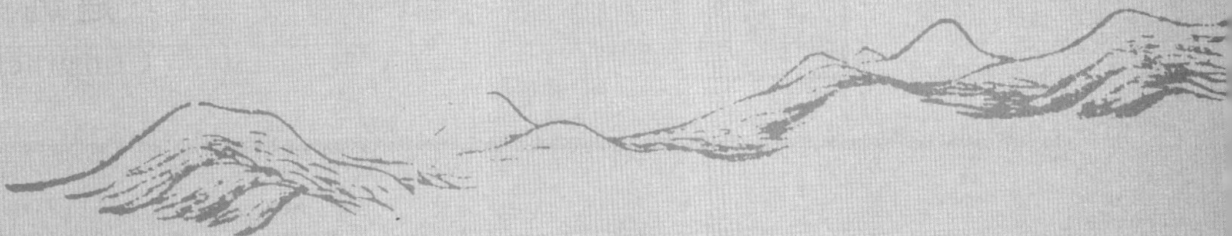

第五篇 CHAPTER-5

建筑业 CONSTRUCTION

5

建筑业
Construction

主要统计指标
Major Statistical Indicators

建筑业总产值	Gross Output Value of Construction	3032.50	亿元	(100 million yuan)
为上年	As Compared with the Preceding Year	113.8	%	(%)
房屋建筑施工面积	Floor Space of Buildings Under Construction	26104	万平方米	(10, 000 sq.m)
为上年	As Compared with the Preceding Year	115.2	%	(%)
房屋建筑竣工面积	Floor Space of Buildings Completed	8556	万平方米	(10, 000 sq.m)
为上年	As Compared with the Preceding Year	104.1	%	(%)

5－01 建筑业总产值(2011年)

Gross Output Value of Construction(2011)

单位:万元 (10000 yuan)

地 区 Region		建筑企业单位数(个) Number of Construction Enterprises (unit)	建筑业总产值 Gross Output Value of Construction	其中: 建筑工程产值 Output Value of Construction Projects	安装工程产值 Output value of Installation Projects	其他产值 Other Output Values
全 市	**Total**	**1373**	**30324975**	**26308977**	**2801907**	**1214091**
市 区	Urban District	1105	27894652	24189301	2602835	1102516
上城区	Shangcheng	88	2096099	1499363	526812	69924
下城区	Xiacheng	96	1498440	1325286	165435	7719
江干区	Jianggan	136	2305195	2080411	213847	10937
拱墅区	Gongshu	154	1988805	1510057	417940	60808
西湖区	Xihu	165	6319594	5600715	480078	238801
高新(滨江)区	Hi－Tech (Binjiang)	44	2409403	2295848	22225	92330
萧山区	Xiaoshan	274	9306340	8065887	622576	617877
余杭区	Yuhang	136	1523958	1376761	142974	4223
桐庐县	Tonglu	46	379043	327576	40561	10906
淳安县	Chun'an	36	248096	222036	13201	12859
建德市	Jiande	36	176718	143404	22904	10410
富阳市	Fuyang	97	1035854	890810	84708	60336
临安市	Lin'an	53	590612	535851	37698	17063

5-02 各种分组总专包

Financial Conditions

单位:万元

指标名称	Item	二、年末资产 Asset and Liabilities 流动资产合计 Circulating Funds	固定资产合计 Fixed Assets	资产合计 Total Assets
总 计	**Total**	**16267419**	**2199708**	**20503443**
其中:特、一、二级企业	of Which: Special Grade, First Grade, Second Grade	14093411	1777441	17692626
其中:国有及国有控股企业	of Which: State-owned and State Holding Enterprises	2455324	293873	3052243
一、按登记注册类型分组	**Grouped by Registration Status**			
内资企业	Domestic Funded	16070463	2171906	20266607
国有企业	State-owned	604924	83226	710782
集体企业	Collective-owned	47196	2256	50120
股份合作企业	Share-holding Cooperative Enterprises	32	90	122
联营企业	Joint Venture			
有限责任公司	Limited Liability Corporations	6405543	720137	8101568
股份有限公司	Share-holding Corporations Ltd.	1499594	176935	1893903
私营企业	Private Enterprises	7513175	1189262	9510112
港、澳、台商投资企业	Funded from Hong Kong, Macao and Taiwan	173245	25004	209386
外商投资企业	Foreign Funded	23711	2797	27450
二、按国民经济行业分组	**Grouped by Sector**			
房屋和土木工程建筑业	Housing and Civil Engineering Construction	14408199	1967718	18267159
建筑安装业	Installation of Lines, Pipelines and Equipment	843760	108880	1032449
建筑装饰业	Fitting and Decoration of Buildings	759403	81694	891132
其他建筑业	Others Construction	256057	41415	312703

企业财务汇总表(2011 年)

of Construction Enterprises(2011)

(10000 yuan)

负债 at Year - end				
流动负债合计 Liquid Liabilities	负债合计 Total Liabilities	所有者权益合计 Owners´Equity	其中:实收资本 of Which: Paid - in Capitals	其中:国家资本 of Which: State Capital
13311213	**13868500**	**6634943**	**3888171**	**153611**
11779054	12309914	5382712	2963202	139396
2244344	2426034	626209	412646	145647
13122356	13678581	6588026	3859869	153611
532091	534108	176674	103931	60836
34229	34514	15606	6021	-
52	52	71	116	-
5575942	5892485	2209083	1152179	92775
1400872	1428478	465424	207459	-
5579171	5788944	3721168	2390165	-
173815	174867	34519	20890	-
15043	15052	12399	7412	-
11861202	12395285	5871874	3363724	121967
673523	688770	343680	241540	24776
571026	578826	312306	215132	3768
205462	205620	107083	67777	3100

指标名称	Item	三、损益 Expenditure, Income 工程结算收入 Revenue of Project Settlement Accounts	工程结算成本 Costs of Project Settlement Accounts
总　计	**Total**	**27003350**	**24442021**
其中:特、一、二级企业	of Which: Special Grade, First Grade, Second Grade	24171217	22034680
其中:国有及国有控股企业	of Which: State－owned and State Holding Enterprises	4123596	3760079
一、按登记注册类型分组	**Grouped by Registration Status**		
内资企业	Domestic Funded	26786234	24253021
国有企业	State－owned	1066338	930996
集体企业	Collective－owned	33228	25762
股份合作企业	Share－holding Cooperative Enterprises	23	8
联营企业	Joint Venture		
有限责任公司	Limited Liability Corporations	11573422	10611848
股份有限公司	Share－holding Corporations Ltd.	2236958	2027653
私营企业	Private Enterprises	11876263	10656754
港、澳、台商投资企业	Funded from Hong Kong, Macao and Taiwan	171806	149491
外商投资企业	Foreign Funded	45311	39508
二、按国民经济行业分组	**Grouped by Sector**		
房屋和土木工程建筑业	Housing and Civil Engineering Construction	24041910	21855049
建筑安装业	Installation of Lines, Pipelines and Equipment	1259776	1067594
建筑装饰业	Fitting and Decoration of Buildings	1243748	1106527
其他建筑业	Others Construction	457917	412852

continued (10000 yuan)

及分配 and Distribution					
工程结算税金及附加 Taxes and Extra Charges Project Settlement Accounts	销售费用 Sales Expenses	管理费用 Management Expenditure	财务费用 Financial Expenditure	利润总额 Total Profits	应交所得税 Income Taxes Payable
837860	**68746**	**720238**	**256538**	**731358**	**148696**
749995	42656	563213	228249	596670	118390
126393	6360	156453	7761	88920	20312
835349	65456	710384	252084	721409	147127
29732	5030	79224	2464	23428	4772
1125	227	4755	205	1249	340
1	–	21	–	–6	1
368317	12377	250672	97554	260275	57488
63263	9390	76733	17754	53376	8743
372911	38432	298979	134107	383086	75783
1693	2719	7879	4070	7752	1177
819	570	1975	384	2198	392
749703	46788	568250	234298	640054	129617
36258	16639	86963	7552	44887	8221
37171	3781	52139	11551	33700	7852
14728	1537	12886	3138	12718	3006

5-03 建筑业企业生产情况

Statistics on Production of Construction Enterprises

指标名称	Item	2006	2007	2008	2009	2010	2011
一、建筑业合同情况	**Contract of Construction**						
签订的合同额 （万元）	Total Value of Contracts （10000 yuan）	20010853	24696898	30088537	36623552	46427916	55290611
上年结转合同额 （万元）	Value from Contracts Signed in 2010 （10000 yuan）	7548539	9290912	11210961	14824477	17396267	22189586
本年新签合同额 （万元）	Value from New Contracts Signed in 2011 （10000 yuan）	12462314	15405986	18877576	21799075	29031649	33101025
二、承包工程完成情况	**Completion of Contracted Projects**						
直接从建设单位承揽工程完成的产值 （万元）	Complete Output Value of Projects Contacted Directly from Investors （10000 yuan）	12662433	14853868	17871119	20791153	26259274	29993008
自行完成施工产值 （万元）	Own－completed Output Value （10000 yuan）	12326935	14495495	17427692	20424041	25689110	29339695
分包出去工程的产值 （万元）	Output Value of Out－sourced Projects （10000 yuan）	335498	358373	443427	367112	570163	653313
从建设单位以外承揽工程完成的产值 （万元）	Completed Output Value of Projects Contacted from Non－investors （10000 yuan）	345587	349254	576832	677632	949202	985280
建筑业总产值 （万元）	Gross Output Value （10000 yuan）	12672522	14844749	18004524	21101673	26638312	30324975
其中：装饰装修产值 （万元）	of Which：Output Value of Fitting and Decoration of Buildings （10000 yuan）	882969	1149597	1404589	1641467	2177414	2556382
其中：在外省完成的产值（万元）	of Which：Completed Output Value outside of Zhejiang Province （10000 yuan）	2686936	3489987	4971040	5828938	8882553	10267000
按构成分	by Structure						
建筑工程产值 （万元）	Output Value of Construction Projects （10000 yuan）	10749915	12768968	15351303	18280567	23307310	26308977
安装工程产值 （万元）	Output value of Installation Projects （10000 yuan）	1497416	1729043	2083405	2193971	2557314	2801907
其他产值 （万元）	Other Output Values （10000 yuan）	425191	346738	569816	627135	773688	1214091
竣工产值 （万元）	Output Value of Buildings Completed （10000 yuan）	8828029	9344723	10976179	12919145	16373795	16286512
房屋建筑施工面积 （万平方米）	Floor Space of Buildings Under Construction （10000 sq. m）	13612.35	15108.93	16059.15	19433.82	22650.40	26104.43
其中：本年新开工面积 （万平方米）	of Which：Beginning Projects in this Year （10000 sq. m）	7165.20	7516.70	7281.49	7839.32	11063.95	12024.02
其中：实行投标承包面积 （万平方米）	of Which：Floor Space of Biding System （10000 sq. m）	12421.93	13865.27	14725.56	18133.40	19792.30	23648.69
其中：本年新开工 （万平方米）	of Which：Beginning Projects in this Year （10000 sq. m）	6695.82	7064.70	6646.09	7390.40	9705.96	11256.35
房屋建筑竣工面积 （万平方米）	Floor space of Buildings Completed （10000 sq. m）	5030.65	5380.57	5799.98	6610.35	8219.87	8556.11
三、年末自有施工机械设备	**Machinery and Equipment Owned（year－end）**						
年末自有施工机械设备净值 （万元）	Net Value of Machinery and Equipment Owned （10000 yuan）	439174	462157	559442	683528	798573	825813
年末自有施工机械设备总台数 （台）	Number of Machinery and Equipment Owned （set）	144384	148722	157385	178586	205574	204139
年末自有施工机械设备总功率 （千瓦）	Total Power of Machinery and Equipment Owned （10000 kw）	1845585	1958612	2435575	2748357	3261216	3611172
四、从业人员情况	**Number of Employed Persons**						
计算劳动生产率的平均人数 （人）	Average Employed Persons Overall Labor Productivity （person）	695674	775498	863862	966098	1149924	
年末从业人员数 （人）	Employed Persons（year－end） （person）	671610	758171	801246	923046	1117287	

主要统计指标解释

建筑业总产值　建筑业总产值是以货币表现的建筑业企业在一定时期内生产的建筑业产品和服务的总和。建筑业总产值包括建筑工程产值、安装工程产值和其他产值三部分内容。

房屋建筑施工面积　指报告期内施过工的全部房屋建筑面积,它包括本期新开工的面积、上期跨入本期继续施工的房屋面积、上期停缓建在本期恢复施工的房屋面积、本期竣工的房屋面积以及本期施工后又停缓建的房屋面积。

房屋建筑竣工面积　指在报告期内房屋建筑按照设计要求已全部完工,达到了使用条件,经检查验收鉴定合格的房屋建筑面积。

工程结算收入(主营业务收入)　指本企业承包工程实现的工程价款结算收入以及向发包单位收取的除工程价款以外按规定列作营业收入的各种款项,如临时设施费、劳动保险费、施工机构调迁费等以及向发包单位收取的各种索赔款。

工程结算成本(主营业务成本)　指在报告期内与发包单位办理工程价款结算的已完工程实际成本。

Explanatory Notes on Main Statistical Indicators

Gross Output Value of Construction refers to total of construction products and services, expressed in money terms, produced or rendered by construction and installation enterprises during a given period of time. It includes: output value of construction projects, output value of installation projects and other output values.

Floor Space of Buildings Under Construction refers to floor space of buildings under construction during the reference period, including the floor space of buildings for which construction has newly started; buildings for which construction has started earlier and is continuing during the reference period; and buildings for which construction has been suspended earlier but has restarted during the reference period; buildings completed during the reference period; and buildings under construction but construction has subsequently been during the reference period.

Floor Space of Buildings Completed refers to the floor space of buildings that are completed in the reference period in accordance with the requirements of the design, up to the standard for being put into use, and having been checked and accepted by departments concerned as qualified ones.

Income from Settlement of Projects refers to the income received by the construction enterprise from the contracted project through settlement procedures, and other charges to the contractor as operational costs in addition to the value of the project, such as temporary facility fee, labor insurance premium, moving cost of construction equipment, as well as various types of claims to the contractor.

Project Settlement Costs refers to the contracting process works price of the actual settlement costs of projects have been completed during the reporting period.

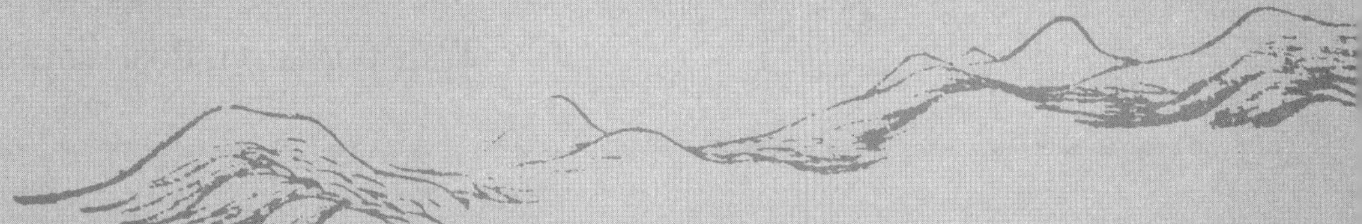

第 六 篇
CHAPTER-6

交通运输、邮电

TRANSPORTATION,POST AND TELECOMMUNICATIONS

6 交通运输、邮电
Transportation, Post and Telecommunications

主要统计指标
Major Statistical Indicators

客运量	Passenger Traffic	34778	万人次	(10, 000 person-times)
为上年	As Compared with the Preceding Year	103.0	%	(%)
货运量	Freight Traffic	28831	万吨	(10, 000 tons)
为上年	As Compared with the Preceding Year	123.7	%	(%)
邮电业务收入	Business Income of Post & Telecommunication Service	157.36	亿元	(100 million yuan)
为上年	As Compared with the Preceding Year	109.2	%	(%)
年末固定电话用户数	Number of Local Telephone Subscribers(year-end)	353.76	万户	(10, 000 subscribers)
为上年	As Compared with the Preceding Year	96.0	%	(%)
年末移动电话用户数	Number of Mobile Telephone Subscribers(year-end)	1218.11	万户	(10, 000 subscribers)
为上年	As Compared with the Preceding Year	114.7	%	(%)

6-01 全市主要年份客运量

Total Passenger Traffic in Main Years

单位:万人次　　　　(10,000 person - times)

年　份 Year	合　计 Total	铁　路 Railways	公　路 Highways	水　路 Waterways	民　航 Civil Aviation
1978	2878	485	-	-	3
1979	3122	560	1829	729	4
1980	3905	672	2358	870	5
1981	4484	769	2857	850	8
1982	5263	813	3377	1064	9
1983	5451	878	3530	1035	8
1984	6056	983	3912	1151	10
1985	6724	1004	4595	1111	14
1986	6765	1034	4768	941	22
1987	6905	1127	4852	896	30
1988	6593	1237	4445	877	34
1989	7493	1182	5488	801	22
1990	8119	1056	6350	691	22
1991	10701	1062	8876	710	53
1992	13358	1083	11538	670	67
1993	13070	1139	11403	454	74
1994	13373	1230	11669	390	84
1995	16620	1242	14921	339	118
1996	16714	1112	15184	273	145
1997	17034	1040	15623	260	111
1998	17395	1120	15925	235	115
1999	17882	1168	16369	235	110
2000	18607	1202	17102	179	124
2001	20342	1342	18707	148	145
2002	21089	1574	19213	108	194
2003	21348	1534	19510	89	215
2004	22833	1908	20372	237	316
2005	24124	2011	21431	304	378
2006	25810	2124	22961	267	458
2007	28026	2255	24836	306	629
2008	29084	2498	25630	277	679
2009	30116	2494	26454	372	796
2010	33772	2741	29671	456	904
2011	34778	2962	30305	595	916

注:客运量全市数自1990年起为全社会数,1990年以前为交通系统数。

a) Since 1990 the data in this table include non - transportation system, while data for previous years only included transportation system.

6-02 全市主要年份货运量

Total Freight Traffic in Main Years

单位:万吨 (10000 tons)

年　份 Year	合　计 Total	铁　路 Railways	公　路 Highways	水　路 Waterways	民　航 Civil Aviation
1978	1706	418	633	655	–
1979	1983	440	771	772	–
1980	2070	444	762	864	–
1981	1972	449	886	637	–
1982	2261	485	795	981	–
1983	2299	488	838	973	–
1984	2385	510	888	987	–
1985	2488	524	890	1074	–
1986	2558	551	874	1133	–
1987	2515	574	899	1041	1
1988	2416	555	823	1037	1
1989	7377	539	5095	1743	–
1990	6522	449	4479	1594	–
1991	7017	451	4891	1675	–
1992	8434	534	6063	1836	1
1993	9082	580	6353	2148	1
1994	8962	491	6563	1907	1
1995	10347	482	7021	2842	2
1996	10962	445	7735	2780	2
1997	11015	406	7932	2676	1
1998	11329	418	8196	2713	2
1999	11684	403	8037	3241	3
2000	11459	417	7865	3173	4
2001	12443	452	8588	3398	5
2002	14347	446	10391	3504	6
2003	16815	438	12118	4253	6
2004	18895	480	13117	5289	9
2005	19909	525	13539	5833	12
2006	20924	569	14588	5754	13
2007	22569	573	16484	5500	12
2008	22550	483	16822	5232	13
2009	22372	427	16536	5396	13
2010	25915	379	19148	6371	17
2011	28831	331	21755	6727	18

注:货运量全市数自1990年起为全社会数,1990年以前为交通系统数。

a) Since 1990 the data in this table include non-transportation system, while data for previous years only included transportation system.

6－03 全社会客货运输量(2011 年)
Total Passenger and Freight Traffic(2011)

项 目	Item	全市 Whole City	为上年(%) As Compared with the Preceding Year(%)
一、客运量合计(万人次)	**Passenger Traffic(10000 person－times)**	**34778**	**103.0**
铁路客运量	Passenger Railways	2962	108.1
民航客运量	Passenger Civil Aviation	916	101.3
公路客运量	Passenger Highways	30305	102.1
水路客运量	Passenger Waterways	595	130.5
二、旅客周转量合计(万人公里)	**Total Passenger－kilometers(10000 passenger－km)**	**1529548**	**107.5**
公路旅客周转量	Passenger－kilometers Highways	1522055	107.5
水路旅客周转量	Passenger－kilometers Waterways	7492.57	120.4
三、货运量合计(万吨)	**Total Freight Traffic(10000 tons)**	**28831**	**111.3**
铁路货运量	Freight Railways	331	87.3
民航货运量	Freight Civil Aviation	18	105.9
公路货运量	Freight Highways	21755	113.6
水路货运量	Freight Waterways	6727	105.6
四、货运周转量合计(万吨公里)	**Total Freight Ton－kilometers(10000 ton－km)**	**4178684**	**111.9**
公路货物周转量	Freight Ton－kilometers Highways	2451057	113.8
水路货物周转量	Freight Ton－kilometers Waterways	1727627	109.4

6－04 分地区交通
Traffic and Transport

项　目		Item		全市 Whole City	市区 Urban District
铁路旅客运量	（万人）	Passenger Railways	(10,000 Persons)	2962	2962
铁路货物运量	（万吨）	Freight Railways	(10,000 tons)	331	274
公路客运量(全社会)	（万人）	Passenger Highways(Whole Society)	(10,000 Persons)	30305	19226
公路货运量(全社会)	（万吨）	Freight Highway(Whole Society)	(10,000 tons)	21755	16560
民用航空货邮运量	（万吨）	Freight Civil Aviation	(10,000 tons)	－	－
民用航空客运量	（万人）	Passenger Civil Aviation	(10,000 Persons)	916	916
水运客运量(全社会)	（万人）	Passenger Waterways(Whole Society)	(10,000 Persons)	595	302
水运货运量(全社会)	（万吨）	Freight Waterways(Whole Society)	(10,000 tons)	6727	5914
民用汽车拥有量	（辆）	Possession of Civil Vehicles	(Unit)	1495503	1265674
其中:私人汽车拥有量	（辆）	in which:Possession of Private Vehicles	(Unit)	1162925	972285

运输情况
Situation by Region

萧山区 Xiaoshan	余杭区 Yuhang	桐庐县 Tonglu	淳安县 Chun'an	建德市 Jiande	富阳市 Fuyang	临安市 Lin'an
669	63	–	–	–	–	–
41	40	–	58	–	–	–
7139	5557	2436	922	2028	2998	2695
5651	1641	702	473	961	1320	1739
–	–	–	–	–	–	–
916	–	–	–	–	–	–
17	–	15	228	17	–	34
1256	3373	94	25	183	447	64
273081	174976	37661	15735	28566	78869	68998
218052	142945	31173	12812	22594	66326	57735

6-05 社会机动车辆年末拥有量(2011年)

Total Number of Motor Vehicles End of the Year(2011)

单位:辆 (unit)

项　目	Item	全市 Whole City	为上年(%) As Compared with the Preceding Year(%)	市区 Urban District
总计	**Total**	**2078150**	**113.4**	**821376**
民用汽车拥有量	**Possession of Civilian Vehicles**	**1495503**	**120.3**	**817617**
#私人汽车	Private Vehicles	1162925	123.4	611288
载客汽车	**Passenger Vehicles**	**1313307**	**121.9**	**731175**
大型载客汽车	Large	15458	171.5	10558
中型载客汽车	Medium	18620	103.1	9815
小型载客汽车	Small	1244142	123.3	697911
微型载客汽车	Minicar	35087	103.1	12891
载货汽车	**Trucks**	**171039**	**110.0**	**81081**
重型载货汽车	Heavy	27989	122.4	15874
中型载货汽车	Light-heavy	27534	100.5	14886
轻型载货汽车	Light	114592	110.4	50097
微型载货汽车	Mini	924	123.0	224
其他汽车	**Else**	**11157**	**105.7**	**5361**
摩托车	**Motorcycles**	**576907**	**101.3**	**639**
普通摩托车	Genera Motorcycles	515411	101.1	517
轻便摩托车	Light Motorcycles	61496	103.2	122

6－06 邮政、电信主要指标(2011 年)
Post and Telecommunications(2011)

项 目		Item		全市 Whole City	为上年(%) As Compared with the Preceding Year(%)	市区 Urban District
邮电业务总收入	(万元)	Total Business Income of Post & Telecommunications Service	(10,000 yuan)	1573563	109.2	－
函件	(万件)	Number of Letters	(10,000 pcs)	21144	105.5	19229
包件	(万件)	Number of Parcels	(10,000 pcs)	83.7	84.9	72.2
汇票	(万张)	Number of Bill of Exchange	(10,000 pcs)	303.1	97.7	256.8
订销报刊累计量	(万份)	Number of Newspapers & Magazines Circulation	(10,000 copies)	27577	103.0	21954
集邮	(万枚)	Philutely	(10,000 pcs)	2309.3	102.8	2147
邮储期末余额	(万元)	Balance of Postal Deposits	(10,000 yuan)	1786160	114.2	1363287
年末固定电话用户数	(万户)	Number of Local Telephone Subscribers (year－end)	(10,000 subscribers)	353.76	96.0	282.04
年末移动电话用户数	(万户)	Number of Subscribers of Mobile Telephone(year－end)	(10,000 subscribers)	1218.11	114.7	1008.59
年末宽带业务户数	(万户)	Number of Wide Band Subscribers	(10,000 subscribers)	241.14	110.7	200.46

主要统计指标解释

货(客)运量　指在一定时期内,各种运输工具实际运送的货物(旅客)数量。是反映运输业为国民经济和人民生活服务的数量指标,也是制定和检查运输生产计划、研究运输发展规模和速度的重要指标。货运按吨计算,客运按人计算。货物不论运输距离长短、货物类别,均按实际重量统计。旅客不论行程远近或票价多少,均按一人一次作为客运量统计;半价票、小孩票也按一人统计。

货物(旅客)周转量　指在一定时期内,由各种运输工具运送的货物(旅客)数量与其相应运输距离的乘积之总和。是反映运输业生产总成果的重要指标,也是编制和检查运输生产计划,计算运输效率、劳动生产率以及核算运输单位成本的主要基础资料。通常以吨公里和人公里为计算单位。计算货物周转量通常按发出站与到达站之间的最短距离,也就是计费距离计算。

移动电话用户　指在邮电部门登记,通过移动电话交换机进入移动电话网,占有移动电话号码的电话用户。用户数量以实际办理登记手续进入邮电部门移动电话网的户数进行计算,一部或一台移动电话统计为一户。

Explanatory Notes on Main Statistical Indicators

Freight(passenger) Traffic refers to the volume of freight (passenger) transported with various means. Freight transport is calculated in tons and passenger traffic is calculated in the number of persons. Despite the type of freight and traveling distance, the freight transport is calculated in the actual weight of the goods: and despite the traveling distance and ticket price, the passenger traffic is calculated by the principle that one person can be counted only once in one travel. The passenger who travel with a half – price ticket or a child ticket is also calculated as one person. The freight (passenger) traffic provides a quantitative measure to show how the transport industry serves the national economy and people, and is also an important indicator for plan the transport industry and for studying the development scale and speed of the transport industry.

Freight Ton – kilometers(Passenger – kilometers) refers to the sum of the products of the volume of transported cargo (passengers) multiplying by the transport distance, usually using ton – kilometer and passenger – kilometer as units for measurement . Normally, the shortest distance between the departure station and the destination station (i. e. , the payable distance) is the basis to calculate the freight ton – kilometers. This is an important indicator to show the total results of the transport industry, to prepare and examine the transport plan and to measure the efficiency, the labour productivity and the unit cost of transport.

Mobile Telephone Subscribers refer to the persons who own mobile telephone number connected with the mobile telephone communication network and registered by post and telecommunications organization. The number of subscribers is calculated only when the subscribers who have gone through all the register formalities and entered into the mobile telephone network. One mobile telephone is treated as a subscriber.

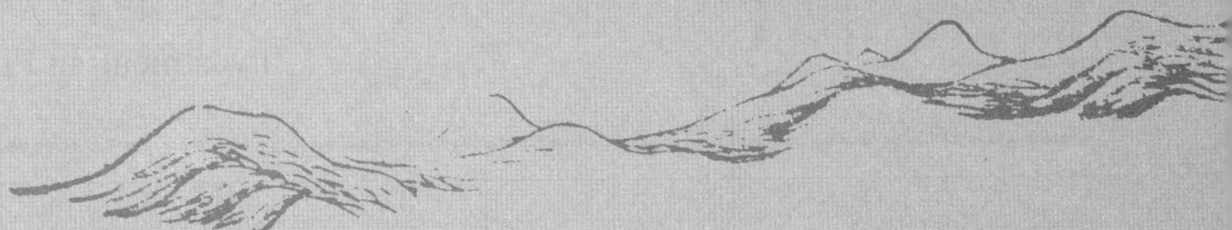

第七篇
CHAPTER-7

固定资产投资
INVESTMENT IN FIXED ASSETS

7 固定资产投资
Investment in Fixed Assets

主要统计指标
Major Statistical Indicators

全市固定资产投资	Investment in Fixed Assets	3100.02	亿元	(100 million yuan)
为上年	As Compared with the Preceding Year	116.9	%	(%)
第一产业	Primary Industry	7.69	亿元	(100 million yuan)
为上年	As Compared with the Preceding Year	183.3	%	(%)
第二产业	Secondary Industry	748.68	亿元	(100 million yuan)
为上年	As Compared with the Preceding Year	108.9	%	(%)
第三产业	Tertiary Industry	2343.65	亿元	(100 million yuan)
为上年	As Compared with the Preceding Year	119.6	%	(%)

7-01 主要年份全市全社会固定资产投资总额

Total Investment in Fixed Assets in Main Years

单位:万元 (10000 yuan)

年份 Year	合计 Total	基本建设 Capital Construction	更新改造 Innovation	房地产开发 Real Estate Development	其他投资 Others	农村集体 Rural collective - owned Units	农村私人投资 Rural Individuals
1978	48307	23941	5316		765	10242	8043
1979	55828	25008	8327		1072	11380	10041
1980	70936	33257	9190		3305	12645	12539
1981	79791	23772	21423		6343	14050	14203
1982	97895	32518	25596		8009	15611	16161
1983	102413	35269	22181		1056	13350	20757
1984	148601	52313	27269		13662	25922	2945
1985	229746	85718	33219		22952	48611	39246
1986	284936	95102	52701		34595	48352	54223
1987	350033	93113	70399		34304	61848	87669
1988	370954	80939	77481		47547	55456	109531
1989	345548	87320	72994		41817	42340	101077
1990	366296	99805	73933	20409	35067	38442	98640
1991	418845	96589	92103	25247	41757	64433	98716
1992	654537	119216	136850	41886	86204	140783	129618
1993	1310914	273991	204412	218006	128973	342267	143265
1994	1620301	397651	205109	320532	136145	358581	202283
1995	2323355	541890	279388	527985	217017	453746	303329
1996	2611772	688794	254507	572749	302283	453720	339719
1997	3033904	906554	323091	572686	335681	538980	355912
1998	3636607	1240740	492814	666244	281942	590911	363956
1999	4354770	1535925	625617	848441	223626	711076	410085
2000	5154923	1704012	770229	1015347	276885	997463	390987
2001	6309723	1938875	996305	1409132	290617	1308500	366294
2002	7697578	2424601	1011054	1982517	205194	1758436	315776
2003	10067440	3260181	945777	2588452	375214	2577280	320536
2004	12022243			3285409			
2005	13866833			4105706			
2006	14607422			4426534			
2007	16841298			5187904			
2008	19805018			6154060			
2009	22916543			7046752			
2010	27531348			9561970			
2011	31000218			13027234			

注:2006 年起全市固定资产投资口径不含 50 万元以下农村非农户投资,2011 年起固定资产投资由计划总投资 500 万元以上项目投资及房地产开发投资构成(下同)。

a) From 2006, the data of investment of non - farmers in village bellow 500000 yuan are excluded in the investment in fixed assets. Since 2011, the Investment in Fixed Assets was composed by investment projects which each of them over 5 million yuan and Investment in real estate. The same as in the following tables.

7-02 主要年份市区全社会固定资产投资总额

Total Investment in Fixed Assets of Urban District in Main Years

单位:万元 (10000 yuan)

年份 Year	合计 Total	基本建设 Capital Construction	更新改造 Innovation	房地产开发 Real Estate Development	其他投资 Others	农村集体 Rural collective-owned Units	农村私人投资 Rural Individuals
1978	22468	16451	3403		557	1087	970
1979	26793	18085	5499		820	1207	1182
1980	35925	24385	6904		1850	1342	1444
1981	41729	19478	15248		3744	1491	1768
1982	52541	26703	17174		4878	1657	2129
1983	57191	29654	15431		4616	3220	4270
1984	88074	45993	20494		6133	8242	7212
1985	125927	70527	22495		10579	14776	7550
1986	154417	81678	36880		17252	6788	11819
1987	163067	80067	46885		13163	8636	14316
1988	159599	63482	46636		22657	9633	17191
1989	150113	65322	44310		20422	7972	12087
1990	170878	79792	48131	12750	12470	6045	11690
1991	176914	66724	56497	16509	14664	12096	10424
1992	231616	62271	84548	29784	22568	20070	12375
1993	499373	140113	119235	115116	37049	70355	17505
1994	717285	227983	129824	189357	46645	100385	23091
1995	1148688	339016	162799	375816	129480	105247	36330
1996	1485008	523573	165631	439245	140633	148576	67350
1997	1821969	731925	245759	445316	176948	147506	74515
1998	2260918	939373	407351	538499	124538	166389	84768
1999	2672757	1195699	466289	636705	98869	193173	82022
2000	3009630	1233350	515716	737950	214280	216928	91406
2001	5381284	1768151	868561	1255605	25330	996347	237290
2002	6388204	2168121	811362	1724128	196471	1301262	186860
2003	7971044	2814796	725643	2176433	334528	1746610	173034
2004	9648206			3088508			
2005	10787387			3485810			
2006	11169155			3653393			
2007	13150724			4298687			
2008	15634404			5269947			
2009	18172403			6261562			
2010	21827468			8486495			
2011	25202394			11409566			

注:2001 年起市区数据含萧山、余杭区。

a) Since 2001, data in the table include Xiaoshan district and Yuhang district.

7-03 主要年份全市固定资产投资按三次产业分

Investment in Fixed Assets Grouped by Three Industries in Main Years

单位:万元 (10000 yuan)

年 份 Year	绝对数(万元) Absolute Figure(10000 yuan)				比重(以投资总额为100) Proportion(%)		
	合 计 Total	第一产业 Primary Industry	第二产业 Secondary Industry	第三产业 Tertiary Industry	第一产业 Primary Industry	第二产业 Secondary Industry	第三产业 Tertiary Industry
1978	23941	2174	14455	7312	9.1	60.4	30.5
1979	34407	2454	19927	12026	7.1	57.9	35.0
1980	45752	1608	26211	17933	3.5	57.3	39.2
1981	51538	850	29176	21512	1.6	56.6	41.8
1982	66123	1352	37648	27123	2.0	57.0	41.0
1983	68306	1297	37823	29186	1.9	55.4	42.7
1984	93244	2831	46619	43794	3.0	50.0	47.0
1985	141889	3207	71608	67074	2.3	50.5	47.2
1986	182398	2265	94394	85739	1.2	51.8	47.0
1987	200516	2994	106600	90922	1.5	53.2	45.3
1988	205967	4746	118736	82485	2.3	57.6	40.1
1989	202131	3038	117651	81442	1.5	58.2	40.3
1990	229214	2181	126263	100770	1.0	55.1	43.9
1991	255696	3204	132303	120189	1.3	51.7	47.0
1992	384136	4424	206659	173053	1.2	53.8	45.0
1993	825382	5650	346416	473316	0.7	42.0	57.3
1994	1059437	3905	354672	700860	0.4	33.5	66.1
1995	1566280	5821	534687	1025772	0.4	34.1	65.5
1996	1819333	3100	640273	1175960	0.2	35.2	64.6
1997	2139012	1712	595966	1541334	-	27.9	72.1
1998	2681740	4053	706948	1970739	0.2	26.4	73.4
1999	3233609	23546	764309	2445754	0.7	23.6	75.7
2000	3766473	774	844334	2921365	0.2	22.4	77.4
2001	4634929	595	953494	3680840	-	20.6	79.4
2002	5623366	6514	1104212	4512640	0.1	19.6	80.3
2003	8952090	10489	3208885	5732716	0.1	35.9	64.0
2004	11081993	15992	4369015	6696986	0.1	39.4	60.5
2005	12777972	13982	4451936	8312054	0.1	34.8	65.1
2006	13734482	17892	4651420	9065170	0.1	33.9	66.0
2007	15837775	23278	5286340	10528157	0.1	33.4	66.5
2008	18822936	30810	5705736	13086390	0.2	30.3	69.5
2009	21951706	31335	6115482	15804889	0.1	27.9	72.0
2010	26518839	41959	6875840	19601040	0.2	25.9	73.9
2011	31000218	76931	7486832	23436455	0.2	24.2	75.6

注:2002年以前为全部城镇及以上投资,不包括农村集体及私人投资。从2003年开始为全部限额以上投资口径。

a) Before year 2002, data in this table refer to urban investments and the rural investments are excluded. From 2003, refer to investment of super - scale projects.

7-04 主要年份全市固定资产投资房屋建筑面积及造价
Floor Space of Buildings and Their Cost in Main Years

年份 Year	施工面积(万平方米) Floor Space of Buildings Under Construction (10000sq. m)	#住宅 Residential Buildings	竣工面积(万平方米) Floor Space of Buildings Completed (10000 sq. m)	#住宅 Residential Buildings	竣工房屋价值(万元) Value of Buildings Completed (10000 yuan)	#住宅 Residential Buildings	每平方米造价(元) Cost Per Square (yuan)	#住宅 Residential Buildings
1978			101.95	39.58	8869	2810	87	71
1979			150.26	68.01	13223	4965	88	73
1980	456.54		202.58	104.44	19448	8564	96	82
1981	507.94		232.25	120.35	26709	12396	115	103
1982	554.89	258.09	281.63	148.66	34095	16470	121	111
1983	531.79	244.36	247.07	125.86	33938	15494	137	123
1984	620.71	293.21	267.85	138.71	42740	18398	160	133
1985	741.47	333.72	327.75	157.85	56561	22825	173	145
1986	674.58	278.19	338.19	160.19	50561	27338	238	170
1987	544.64	149.07	254.73	73.16	68801	14944	270	204
1988	526.70	156.92	230.21	75.44	68407	17820	297	236
1989	420.81	116.12	202.15	64.15	69750	18200	345	284
1990	472.59	209.50	236.44	112.77	93557	34266	396	304
1991	459.00	205.41	226.84	92.72	93158	28599	411	308
1992	604.85	301.21	262.11	114.97	116169	39834	452	350
1993	958.91	533.01	380.29	199.96	224251	105107	589	525
1994	1069.68	613.62	460.20	274.19	375211	212705	815	776
1995	1320.68	737.79	524.58	319.41	491705	274314	937	859
1996	1399.70	758.00	582.70	354.50	688569	370485	1182	1045
1997	1363.80	660.70	642.10	338.00	871361	449235	1357	1329
1998	1456.02	743.59	515.16	271.91	709730	390624	1378	1437
1999	1681.71	956.15	709.10	411.44	1119141	641717	1578	1560
2000	1721.58	949.32	744.42	419.80	1207767	709044	1622	1689
2001	2318.95	1251.92	830.05	402.46	1310380	679449	1579	1688
2002	2713.02	1586.28	890.05	492.95	1623662	956643	1820	1941
2003	4392.79	2083.58	1618.01	651.58	2732763	1353422	1689	2077
2004	5731.48	2909.03	1865.83	717.46	2791115	1313596	1496	1831
2005	6671.39	3628.34	1856.34	801.34	3265491	1865538	1759	2328
2006	7260.08	3747.6	1737.51	706.13	2900836	1580689	1670	2239
2007	7942.07	4040.54	1849.24	858.99	3750264	2329184	2028	2712
2008	9471.42	4160.27	2057.86	846.34	4113211	2171525	1999	2566
2009	10308.45	4441.84	2009.90	700.63	3626421	1684092	1804	2404
2010	12971.81	5534.10	2695.90	902.57	5274936	2285285	1957	2532
2011	15982.64	6442.52	3108.57	991.72	6209320	2498468	1997	2519

注:2002 年以前为全部城镇及以上投资,不包括农村集体及私人投资。从 2003 年开始为全部限额以上投资口径。

a) Before year 2002, data in this table refer to urban investments and the rural investments are excluded. From 2003, refer to investment of super-scale projects.

7-05 主要年份市区固定资产投资房屋建筑面积及造价

Urban District Floor Space of Buildings and Their Cost in Main Years

年 份 Year	施工面积 (万平方米) Floor Space of Buildings Under Construction (10000 sq. m)	#住 宅 Residential Buildings	竣工面积 (万平方米) Floor Space of Buildings Completed (10000sq. m)	#住 宅 Residential Buildings	竣工房屋价值(万元) Value of Buildings Completed (10000 yuan)	#住 宅 Residential Buildings	每平方米造价(元) Cost Per Square (yuan)	#住 宅 Residential Buildings
1978			71.56	29.06	6941	2237	97	77
1979			109.23	53.37	10267	4056	94	76
1980			137.11	76.73	14396	6752	105	88
1981			163.36	90.12	20093	9643	123	107
1982	378.88	172.11	189.92	100.07	25200	11980	133	120
1983	376.32	169.17	157.14	81.68	24029	11045	153	135
1984	465.27	221.72	191.13	104.55	33863	14658	177	140
1985	532.66	258.19	219.79	114.26	40344	17489	184	153
1986	465.75	203.22	219.33	116.70	58619	21149	267	181
1987	336.85	86.05	150.59	41.72	46530	9513	309	228
1988	315.80	90.98	117.71	37.63	38501	10117	330	269
1989	253.41	56.39	99.86	28.89	38680	9087	387	315
1990	301.82	128.50	137.88	62.47	60551	20361	439	326
1991	265.61	118.99	114.19	42.31	53819	12892	471	305
1992	329.16	190.55	115.59	57.36	55758	19706	483	344
1993	500.08	266.80	175.22	104.83	101528	53540	579	511
1994	618.91	352.16	212.06	123.74	182730	102924	862	832
1995	821.03	463.98	244.94	152.10	250073	139666	1021	918
1996	969.10	538.50	350.10	229.00	437239	274244	1249	1196
1997	1017.30	485.20	442.00	232.70	675762	357624	1529	1537
1998	1055.24	541.41	321.17	184.18	516400	317402	1608	1723
1999	1204.30	656.07	489.23	294.85	908844	533675	1858	1810
2000	1176.29	617.80	497.64	269.94	916212	528385	1841	1957
2001	2053.02	1085.30	698.29	325.64	1193818	615802	1710	1891
2002	2330.97	1335.78	744.48	404.35	1483862	869969	1993	2152
2003	3637.82	1699.61	1325.48	516.33	2395039	1174735	1807	2275
2004	4740.42	2453.87	1389.30	528.26	2257386	1068708	1625	2023
2005	5533.58	3039.08	1478.07	661.56	2804402	1626514	1897	2459
2006	5898.15	3114.45	1327.37	580.22	2365342	1357671	1782	2340
2007	6496.01	3357.18	1355.43	674.97	3063585	1992874	2260	2953
2008	7812.71	3466.88	1537.69	668.13	3372465	1827426	2193	2735
2009	8558.17	3807.67	1398.49	537.39	2725150	1321357	1949	2459
2010	10738.49	4759.75	1983.33	732.55	4255543	1927150	2146	2631
2011	13259.13	5451.45	2091.12	797.96	4736356	2122126	2265	2659

注:2002 年以前为全部城镇及以上投资,不包括农村集体及私人投资。从 2003 年开始为全部限额以上投资口径。

a) Before year 2002, data in this table refer to urban investments and the rural investments are excluded. From 2003, refer to investment of super - scale projects.

7－06 分县(市)固定资产
Investment in Fixed Assets

单位:万元

指　　标	Item	全　市 Total 2011年	上　年 Preceding Year	为上年(%) As Compared with the Preceding Year(%)	市　区 Urban District 2011年
全市固定资产投资额	**Investment in Fixed Assets**	**31000218**	**26518839**	**116.9**	**25202394**
#住宅	#Residential Buildings	9178550	7838596	117.1	7798852
#工业投资	Industrial Investment	7474806	6855587	109.0	4801419
#基础设施投资	Infrastructural Investment	6437025	6452236	99.8	5451654
一、按投资、房地产分	**Grouped by Sector**				
投资项目完成额	Investment Projects	17972984	16956869	106.0	13792828
房地产开发完成额	Real Estate	13027234	9561970	136.2	11409566
二、按登记注册类型分	**Grouped by Status of Registration**				
内资	Domestic－funded	28168629	23940232	117.7	22800705
国有	State－owned	7966283	7940680	100.3	6974267
集体	Collective－owned	500484	516448	96.9	398013
股份合作	Cooperative	62434	24938	250.4	60224
国有与集体联营	Joint State－collective Ownership	2310	3045	75.9	－
国有独资公司	State－owned Corporations	826668	603038	137.1	600796
其他有限责任公司	Other Limited Liability Corporations	12446014	9846163	126.4	10570492
股份有限公司	Share－holding Corporations Ltd.	780910	695742	112.2	505960
私营	Private	5490617	4154997	132.1	3611378
其他	Other	92909	155181	59.9	79575
港、澳、台商投资	Investment from Hong Kong, Macao and Taiwan	1640823	1324916	123.8	1359405
外商投资	Foreign Investment	1164342	1236253	94.2	1038839
个体经营	Individual	26424	17438	151.5	3445

投资完成额（2011 年）
by Region（2011）

（10000 yuan）

上　年 Preceding Year	为上年(%) As Compared with the Preceding Year(%)	#萧山区 Xiaoshan	#余杭区 Yuhang	桐庐县 Tonglu	淳安县 Chun'an	建德市 Jiande	富阳市 Fuyang	临安市 Lin'an
21437496	**117.6**	**5190805**	**4134743**	**1158682**	**794383**	**796301**	**1913712**	**1134746**
6872400	113.5	648933	1416588	300584	243013	88590	445523	301988
4293707	111.8	2220882	1057441	506967	235765	405656	901892	623107
5438685	100.2	1353203	842021	135271	154635	117489	401918	176058
12951001	106.5	4174032	2514452	804450	500997	671213	1413015	790481
8486495	134.4	1016773	1620291	354232	293386	125088	500697	344265
19316267	118.0	4529982	3805216	1074879	747333	784908	1626658	1134146
6953730	100.3	1372084	922036	92499	197989	244239	260523	196766
420874	94.6	93609	75474	64269	–	–	34514	3688
24938	241.5	1200	12134	–	–	–	2210	–
–	–	–	–	–	910	–	1400	–
446729	134.5	206586	232480	57660	25599	–	137084	5529
8364921	126.4	1734698	1350523	276530	325511	150812	462737	659932
492945	102.6	138383	67516	18429	20109	29882	116933	89597
2545259	141.9	925578	1139682	557999	177215	355013	610378	178634
66871	119.0	57844	5371	7493	–	4962	879	–
1039898	130.7	388973	191475	69763	14075	3575	194005	–
1081331	96.1	268405	138052	12184	32975	1576	78168	600
–	–	3445	–	1856	–	6242	14881	–

单位:万元　　7－06　续表

指　　标	Item	全　市 Total			市　区 Urban District
		2011 年	上　年 Preceding Year	为上年(%) As Compared with the Preceding Year(%)	2011 年
三、按行业分	**Grouped by Sector**				
农林牧渔业	Farming, Forestry, Animal Husbandry and Fishery	76931	41959	183.3	36112
采矿业	Mining & Quarrying	55990	48177	116.2	875
制造业	Manufacturing	6609003	6124928	107.9	4153964
电力、燃气及水的生产和供应业	Production and Supply of Electricity, Gas and Water	809813	682482	118.7	646580
建筑业	Construction	12026	20253	59.4	10993
交通运输、仓储及邮政业	Transportation, Storage, Post & Telecommunications	2193350	2415265	90.8	1946348
信息传输、计算机服务和软件业	Information Transmission, Computer Services and Software	250459	291493	85.9	250392
批发和零售业	Wholesale & Retail Trade	742992	700713	106.0	655909
住宿和餐饮业	Lodging and Catering	441608	412265	107.1	296190
金融业	Banking and Insurance	26466	4449	594.9	24256
房地产业	Real Estate	15684043	11872598	132.1	13797596
租赁和商务服务业	Renting and Business Service	304285	437254	69.6	271713
科学研究、技术服务和地质勘查业	Scientific Research, Technical Service and Geological Prospecting	188421	94091	200.3	187741
水利、环境和公共设施管理业	Water Conservancy, Environment and Public Utility	2529677	2593603	97.5	2080590
居民服务和其他服务业	Service for the Residents and Other	15236	19362	78.7	7336
教育	Education	382672	339381	112.8	288583
卫生、社会保障和社会福利业	Health Care, Sports & Social Welfare	237048	188622	125.7	189341
文化、体育和娱乐业	Culture, Sports and Entertainment	289770	163703	177.0	254354
公共管理和社会组织	Public Management and Social Organizations	150428	68241	220.4	103521

continued (10000 yuan)

上　年 Preceding Year	为上年(%) As Compared with the Preceding Year(%)	#萧山区 Xiaoshan	#余杭区 Yuhang	桐庐县 Tonglu	淳安县 Chun'an	建德市 Jiande	富阳市 Fuyang	临安市 Lin'an
12988	278.0	31341	4771	490	–	12672	22365	5292
8012	10.9	875	–	8673	9286	12755	15856	8545
3723042	111.6	2121512	982502	468745	210796	374639	832872	567987
562653	114.9	98495	74939	29549	15683	18262	53164	46575
20253	54.3	–	8564	1033	–	–	–	–
2024617	96.1	511219	352150	28197	33986	41579	81452	61788
288767	86.7	6898	33508	–	–	–	67	–
643860	101.9	43265	174589	23917	4113	12330	34374	12349
255085	116.1	65608	36636	75438	26494	16485	9500	17501
4449	545.2	3500	2326	–	–	–	2210	–
10603157	130.1	1346134	1960532	425074	325383	232053	557822	346115
391108	69.5	75374	20448	8476	22837	1259	–	–
94091	199.5	27881	65622	–	–	–	680	–
2178374	95.5	637677	285474	63906	76772	38354	215055	55000
14015	52.3	1707	720	835	–	6166	–	899
279940	103.1	66993	92130	9854	20782	17980	37472	8001
159491	118.7	58504	20519	7069	17022	2389	19686	1541
138424	183.7	50627	12118	4659	22979	467	4158	3153
35170	294.3	43195	7195	2767	8250	8911	26979	–

7－07 分县(市)限额以上工业

Super－Scale Investment

单位:万元

指标	Item	全市 Total 2011年	全市 Total 上年 Preceding Year	全市 Total 为上年(%) As Compared with the Preceding Year(%)	市区 Urban District 2011年
总计	**Total**	**7474806**	**6855587**	**109.0**	**4801419**
一、按登记注册类型分	**Total Investment**				
内资	Domestic－funded	6095787	5463470	111.6	3679674
国有	State－owned	946005	788307	120.0	798654
集体	Collective－owned	49759	47580	104.6	33973
股份合作	Cooperative	4504	7317	61.6	4504
国有独资公司	State－funded Corporations	125540	74408	168.7	119971
其他有限责任公司	Other Limited Liability Corporations	2173063	1983722	109.5	1326098
股份有限公司	Share－holding Corporations Ltd.	456613	396983	115.0	253735
私营	Private	2330557	2126400	109.6	1139677
其他	Other	9746	38753	25.1	3062
港、澳、台商投资	Investment from Hong Kong, Macao and Taiwan	659070	699889	94.2	506653
外商投资	Foreign Investment	707083	678392	104.2	613488
个体经营	Individual	12866	13836	93.0	1604
二、按行业分	**Grouped by Sector**				
采矿业	Mining & Quarrying	55990	48177	116.2	875
制造业	Manufacturing	6609003	6124928	107.9	4153964
农副食品加工业	Agricultural Products Processing	96102	81431	118.0	60396
食品制造业	Food Manufacturing	92303	66420	139.0	64459
饮料制造业	Beverage Manufacturing	116459	97377	119.6	21695
烟草制品业	Tobacco Processing	211016	96754	218.1	211016
纺织业	Textile Processing	625828	621674	100.7	459572
纺织服装、鞋、帽制造业	Textile Products, Garments, Shoes and Caps Processing	109084	80001	136.4	79779

投资完成额(2011 年)

in Industrial Sector by Region(2011)

(10000 yuan)

上 年 Preceding Year	为上年(%) As Compared with the Preceding Year(%)	#萧山区 Xiaoshan	#余杭区 Yuhang	桐庐县 Tonglu	淳安县 Chun'an	建德市 Jiande	富阳市 Fuyang	临安市 Lin'an
4293707	**111.8**	**2220882**	**1057441**	**506967**	**235765**	**405656**	**901892**	**623107**
3197971	115.1	1685318	878498	462513	223709	398316	709068	622507
705006	113.3	56139	46056	18358	8788	30571	22084	67550
20140	168.7	10102	14562	4829	–	–	10384	573
7317	61.6	–	4504	–	–	–	–	–
63558	188.8	37385	34788	1253	1020	–	3296	–
1101069	120.4	925647	164087	100221	96621	111358	124037	414728
229582	110.5	110165	64821	16909	19509	29882	85272	51306
1061976	107.3	543719	548779	318178	97771	222586	463995	88350
9323	32.8	2161	901	2765	–	3919	–	–
506815	100.0	324576	68823	35214	6189	3575	107439	–
588921	104.2	209384	110120	7384	5867	1576	78168	600
–	–	1604	–	1856	–	2189	7217	–
8012	10.9	875	–	8673	9286	12755	15856	8545
3723042	111.6	2121512	982502	468745	210796	374639	832872	567987
46596	129.6	16017	44213	5125	13943	5540	1697	9401
48945	131.7	17081	6226	12435	10201	200	–	5008
9686	224.0	3649	3409	15936	37757	39783	–	1288
96754	218.1	–	–	–	–	–	–	–
471008	97.6	384330	66133	51738	49778	24012	23313	17415
60705	131.4	39852	21945	9356	929	1815	13197	4008

单位:万元 7-07 续表

指标	Item	全市 Total			市区 Urban District
		2011 年	上年 Preceding Year	为上年(%) As Compared with the Preceding Year(%)	2011 年
皮革、毛皮、羽毛(绒)及其制造业	Leather, Furs, Down and Related Products	40091	51096	78.5	23974
木材加工及木、竹、藤、棕、草制品业	Timber Processing, Bamboo, Cane, Palm Fiber and Straw Products	42594	25461	167.3	23414
家具制造业	Furniture Manufacturing	59179	67055	88.3	32408
造纸及纸制品业	Paper Making and Paper Products	278291	293914	94.7	50206
印刷业和记录媒介的复制	Printing and Record Media	61994	85694	72.3	33386
文教体育用品制造业	Cultural, Educational and Sports Goods	62936	75046	83.9	26619
石油加工、炼焦及核燃料加工业	Petroleum and Nuclear Fuel Processing	5400	3531	152.9	4580
化学原料及化学制品制造业	Raw Chemical Material and Chemical Products	422532	339126	124.6	299331
医药制造业	Medical and Pharmaceutical Products	250069	194954	128.3	115870
化学纤维制造业	Chemical Fiber	163069	127883	127.5	159152
橡胶制造业	Rubber Products	191811	160395	119.6	143170
塑料制品业	Plastic Products	255622	195727	130.6	179793
非金属矿物制品业	Nonmetal Mineral Products	281796	293948	95.9	148855
黑色金属冶炼及压延加工业	Smelting and Pressing of Ferrous Metals	89647	90710	98.8	57538
有色金属冶炼及压延加工业	Smelting and Pressing of Nonferrous Metal	136344	119646	114.0	53096
金属制品业	Metal Products	387403	326856	118.5	205622
通用设备制造业	Ordinary Machinery	644814	536877	120.1	412486
专业设备制造业	Special Purpose Equipment	241173	199812	120.7	167091
交通运输设备制造业	Transportation Equipment	579934	742097	78.1	429985
电气机械及器材制造业	Electric Equipment and Machinery	559766	688746	81.3	293071
通信设备、计算机及其他电子设备制造业	Telecommunications Equipment, Computers and Other Electronic Equipment	313330	264010	118.7	206623
仪器仪表及文化、办公用机械制造业	Instruments, Meters, Cultural and Office Machinery	99756	54134	184.3	87588
工艺品及其他制造业	Craftworks and Other Manufacturing	165067	122714	134.5	102869
废弃资源和废旧材料回收加工业	Scrap Recycle and Processing	25593	21839	117.2	320
电力、燃气及水的生产和供应业	Production and Supply of Electricity, Gas and Water	809813	682482	118.7	646580

continued (10000 yuan)

上 年 Preceding Year	为上年(%) As Compared with the Preceding Year(%)	#萧山区 Xiaoshan	#余杭区 Yuhang	桐庐县 Tonglu	淳安县 Chun'an	建德市 Jiande	富阳市 Fuyang	临安市 Lin'an
30874	77.7	21081	2893	569	–	10500	3260	1788
13618	171.9	17026	6388	5954	3327	3348	–	6551
40453	80.1	13649	13259	12793	3117	5520	4450	891
58262	86.2	20578	26799	12132	–	4700	179931	31322
55770	59.9	12146	12644	14608	–	970	10822	2208
29787	89.4	14636	2985	16338	620	2920	12566	3873
2896	158.1	510	1500	820	–	–	–	–
154960	193.2	266865	22369	19546	3255	62683	4810	32907
78911	146.8	6081	27103	11619	6708	5339	89317	21216
126673	125.6	154327	4825	–	–	1018	–	2899
103916	137.8	4772	4742	2811	525	41864	3441	–
143573	125.2	50407	81264	11974	4272	9433	48194	1956
143332	103.9	79868	63191	25932	8238	37786	31856	29129
66563	86.4	40134	16270	3761	–	6825	18317	3206
39787	133.5	45291	6684	13144	–	460	64065	5579
177360	115.9	112172	70898	43797	2726	34579	77316	23363
334220	123.4	258933	133606	75434	8358	21297	64166	63073
167172	100.0	65766	68131	36703	6694	7213	15483	7989
520519	82.6	340513	54488	16725	8852	10960	42256	71156
367532	79.7	59867	121770	40782	17560	13457	72388	122508
215913	95.7	27461	35637	–	15303	96	5413	85895
41753	209.8	4631	31299	928	4550	2280	4410	–
75004	137.2	43869	31511	7785	4083	8601	33443	8286
500	64.0	–	320	–	–	11440	8761	5072
562653	114.9	98495	74939	29549	15683	18262	53164	46575

7－08 分县(市)房地产开发

Real Estate Development

指标	Item	全市 Total 2011年	上年 Preceding Year	为上年(%) As Compared with the Preceding Year(%)	市区 Urban District 2011年
房地产开发投资额 (万元)	**Investment in Real Estate Development (10000 yuan)**	**13027234**	**9561970**	**136.2**	**11409566**
住宅 (万元)	Residential Buildings (10000 yuan)	8065711	6762737	119.3	6784838
办公楼 (万元)	Office Buildings (10000 yuan)	1283983	808391	158.8	1252071
商业营业用房 (万元)	Buildings for Commercial Business (10000 yuan)	1462838	692440	211.3	1304844
其他 (万元)	Others (10000 yuan)	2214702	1298402	170.6	2067813
房屋建筑面积	**Floor space of Buildings**				
施工面积 (万平方米)	Under Construction (10000 sq. m)	7698.26	6227.05	123.6	6529.14
其中:住宅 (万平方米)	#Residential Buildings (10000 sq. m)	4868.47	4249.18	114.6	4010.67
新开工面积(万平方米)	Beginning to Construction Floor Space (10000 sq. m)	2484.00	1929.08	128.8	2040.63
其中:住宅 (万平方米)	#Residential Buildings (10000 sq. m)	1437.74	1267.43	113.4	1126.69
竣工面积 (万平方米)	Construction Completed (10000 sq. m)	1223.86	1100.18	111.2	986.51
其中:住宅 (万平方米)	#Residential Buildings (10000 sq. m)	840.89	802.29	104.8	658.41
商品房销售情况	**Selling of Buildings**				
销售金额 (万元)	Total Sales of Buildings (10000 yuan)	9749038	13967706	69.8	8296122
其中:住宅 (万元)	#Residential Buildings (10000 yuan)	7616738	11372940	67.0	6378732
现房销售额(万元)	Selling of Completed Buildings (10000 yuan)	1163072	1054803	110.3	945850
其中:住宅 (万元)	#Residential Buildings (10000 yuan)	756589	458537	165.0	598201
期房销售金额(万元)	Selling of Futures Buildings (10000 yuan)	8585966	12912903	66.5	7350272
其中:住宅 (万元)	#Residential Buildings (10000 yuan)	6860149	10914403	62.9	5780531
销售面积 (万平方米)	Floor Space of Buildings Sold (10000 sq. m)	734.01	988.34	74.3	567.68
其中:住宅 (万平方米)	#Residential Buildings (10000 sq. m)	597.73	797.59	74.9	451.43
现房销售面积(万平方米)	Floor Space of Completed Buildings Sold (10000 sq. m)	102.99	118.34	87.0	76.69
其中:住宅 (万平方米)	#Residential Buildings (10000 sq. m)	70.27	64.47	109.0	50.80
期房销售面积(万平方米)	Floor Space of Futures Buildings Sold (10000 sq. m)	631.01	870.00	72.5	490.99
其中:住宅 (万平方米)	#Residential Buildings (10000 sq. m)	527.45	733.12	71.9	400.63

投资情况(2011 年)

by Region(2011)

上 年 Preceding Year	为上年(%) As Compared with the Preceding Year(%)	#萧山区 Xiaoshan	#余杭区 Yuhang	桐庐县 Tonglu	淳安县 Chun'an	建德市 Jiande	富阳市 Fuyang	临安市 Lin'an
8486495	**134.4**	**1016773**	**1620291**	**354232**	**293386**	**125088**	**500697**	**344265**
5929013	114.4	577483	1294696	274579	225762	87420	391124	301988
789234	158.6	172957	45299	14469	1399	3482	12426	136
579908	225.0	90585	71588	47370	37828	14119	45603	13074
1188340	174.0	175748	208708	17814	28397	20067	51544	29067
5342.90	122.2	921.32	1725.95	271.12	184.81	112.77	320.62	279.80
3571.80	112.3	511.49	1333.21	211.32	113.60	91.02	214.94	226.92
1562.10	130.6	313.49	495.08	115.08	64.67	43.40	128.45	91.77
979.39	115.0	137.30	356.32	86.35	46.74	33.24	67.52	77.20
915.28	107.8	104.49	234.46	43.72	38.11	25.63	73.38	56.50
661.53	99.5	76.05	185.82	34.66	21.63	21.57	59.95	44.68
12220188	67.9	980729	1698794	276550	154353	192002	427254	402757
9814582	65.0	823685	1567854	224885	135834	166692	360904	349691
862126	109.7	77103	81774	15484	19878	85616	45322	50922
329562	181.5	23556	52278	11538	16991	81346	34608	13905
11358062	64.7	903626	1617020	261066	134475	106386	381932	351835
9485020	60.9	800129	1515576	213347	118843	85346	326296	335786
758.93	74.8	90.29	153.81	40.51	14.71	24.43	34.96	51.71
593.05	76.1	75.36	139.89	36.59	13.24	21.73	28.34	46.40
82.59	92.9	17.80	13.60	2.26	1.64	8.81	5.88	7.71
39.37	129.0	10.40	9.16	1.60	1.34	8.35	4.53	3.65
676.33	72.6	72.48	140.21	38.26	13.07	15.62	29.08	44.00
553.67	72.4	64.96	130.73	34.98	11.90	13.37	23.81	42.75

7-09 分县(市)限额以上农村
Super-Scale Rural Investment

单位:万元

指标	Item	全市 Total			市区 Urban District
		2011年	上年 Preceding Year	为上年(%) As Compared with the Preceding Year(%)	2011年
本年完成投资额	**Total Investment of the Year**	**6032860**	**5157149**	**117.0**	**3896496**
按行业分	**Grouped by Sector**				
农林牧渔业	Farming, Forestry, Animal Husbandry and Fishery	65222	41959	155.4	24403
采矿业	Mining & Quarrying	48499	46887	103.4	875
制造业	Manufacturing	3694493	3345482	110.4	2141483
电力、燃气及水的生产和供应业	Production and Supply of Electricity, Gas and Water	248310	219132	113.3	164559
建筑业	Construction	1033	5586	18.5	-
交通运输、仓储及邮政业	Transportation, Storage, Post & Telecommunications	600642	273556	219.6	502575
信息传输、计算机服务和软件业	Information Transmission, Computer Services and Software	4691	11857	39.6	4691
批发和零售业	Wholesale & Retail Trade	93310	62175	150.1	88745
住宿和餐饮业	Lodging and Catering	68428	68104	100.5	32042
金融业	Banking and Insurance	2326	1300	178.9	2326
房地产业	Real Estate	558366	418392	133.5	429009
租赁和商务服务业	Renting and Busyness Service	45344	26523	171.0	39357
科学研究、技术服务和地质勘查业	Scientific Research, Technical Service and Geological Prospecting	12095	19876	60.9	11415
水利、环境和公共设施管理业	Water Conservancy, Environment and Public Utility	411347	470097	87.5	302818
居民服务和其他服务业	Service for the Residents and Other Service Sector	8787	8581	102.4	1722
教育	Education	94280	99146	95.1	91202
卫生、社会保障和社会福利业	Health Care, Sports & Social Welfare	33757	5048	668.7	27571
文化、体育和娱乐业	Culture, Sports and Entertainment	19224	19998	96.1	13567
公共管理和社会组织	Public Management and Social Organizations	22706	13450	168.8	18136
房屋建筑施工面积(万平方米)	**Floor Space of Buildings Under Construction (10000sq. m)**	**2753.19**	**2063.45**	**133.4**	**1923.60**
其中:住宅	Residential Buildings	275.94	211.41	130.5	170.73
房屋建筑竣工面积(万平方米)	**Floor Space of Buildings Completed (10000sq. m)**	**907.03**	**669.47**	**135.5**	**464.74**
其中:住宅	Residential Buildings	44.04	13.66	322.4	34.02

固定资产投资完成额(2011 年)
by Region(2011)

(10000 yuan)

上 年 Preceding Year	为上年(%) As Compared with the Preceding Year(%)	#萧山区 Xiaoshan	#余杭区 Yuhang	桐庐县 Tonglu	淳安县 Chun'an	建德市 Jiande	富阳市 Fuyang	临安市 Lin'an
3029808	**128.6**	**2356958**	**1410339**	**441508**	**87058**	**409311**	**777378**	**421109**
12988	187.9	19632	4771	490	–	12672	22365	5292
8012	10.9	875		8673	9286	7855	15856	5954
1740658	123.0	1540640	600843	293794	59347	276763	611372	311734
137982	119.3	36263	40313	17015	10951	15906	29148	10731
5586	–	–	–	1033	–	–	–	–
194772	258.0	186757	315818	21984	4747	20036	4050	47250
9491	49.4	–	4691	–	–	–	–	–
49057	180.9	24003	49574	1230	–	–	961	2374
40829	78.5	25992	6050	11937	–	2625	5330	16494
1300	178.9	–	2326	–	–	–	–	–
327703	130.9	243383	168078	44119	499	39274	43615	1850
21689	181.5	26729	12628	4728	–	1259	–	–
19876	57.4	1015	10400	–	–	–	680	–
345943	87.5	184777	118041	23543	1230	23107	42218	18431
3970	43.4	1002	720	–	–	6166	–	899
94897	96.1	29536	61666	1116	–	770	1092	100
5048	546.2	19071	–	4420	–	1075	691	–
1300	1043.6	3190	10377	4659	998	–	–	–
3088	587.3	14093	4043	2767	–	1803	–	–
1350.75	**142.4**	**9721807**	**9133687**	**1832452**	**256571**	**1603256**	**3387246**	**1216338**
145.25	117.5	850718	515086	193930	9309	23080	825739	–
375.61	**123.7**	**2912215**	**1735155**	**804365**	**92287**	**906596**	**1558069**	**1061575**
9.87	344.7	340222	–	30700	9309	23080	37101	–

7－10 房屋建筑面积及造价(2011 年)
Floor Space of Buildings and Their Cost(2011)

指标	Item	施工面积(万平方米) Floor Space of Buildings Under Construction (10000 sq. m)	竣工面积(万平方米) Floor Space of Buildings Completed (10000 sq. m)	竣工房屋的价值(万元) Value of Buildings Completed (10000 yuan)	每平方米造价(元) Cost Per Square Meter (yuan)
全市	**Total**				
房屋建筑面积合计	**Floor Space of Buildings**	**15982.64**	**3108.57**	**6209320**	**1997**
#住宅	#Residential Buildings	6442.52	991.72	2498468	2519
房地产开发	Real Estate Development	7698.26	1222.86	3512365	2872
#住宅	#Residential Buildings	4868.47	840.89	2217033	2637
市区	**Urban District**				
房屋建筑面积合计	**Floor Space of Buildings**	**13259.13**	**2091.12**	**4736356**	**2265**
#住宅	#Residential Buildings	5451.45	797.96	2122126	2659
房地产开发	Real Estate Development	6529.14	986.51	3012709	3054
#住宅	#Residential Buildings	4010.67	658.41	1854772	2817
#萧山区	**Xiaoshan**				
房屋建筑面积合计	**Total Floor Space of Buildings**	**2638.63**	**522.68**	**779145**	**1491**
#住宅	#Residential Buildings	654.24	121.25	239721	1977
房地产开发	Real Estate Development	921.32	104.49	249918	2392
#住宅	#Residential Buildings	511.49	76.05	180666	2376
余杭区	**Yuhang**				
房屋建筑面积合计	**Total Floor Space of Buildings**	**3419.45**	**512.84**	**960896**	**1874**
#住宅	#Residential Buildings	1541.18	190.06	517992	2725
房地产开发	Real Estate Development	1725.95	234.46	627706	2677
#住宅	#Residential Buildings	1333.21	185.82	505825	2722

7－10 续表 continued

指 标	Item	施工面积（万平方米）Floor Space of Buildings Under Construction（10000 sq. m）	竣工面积（万平方米）Floor Space of Buildings Completed（10000 sq. m）	竣工房屋的价值（万元）Value of Buildings Completed（10000 yuan）	每平方米造价（元）Cost Per Square Meter（yuan）
桐庐县	**Tonglu**				
房屋建筑面积合计	**Total Floor Space of Buildings**	**636.84**	**197.81**	**274844**	**1389**
#住宅	#Residential Buildings	235.63	37.73	51477	1364
房地产开发	Real Estate Development	271.12	43.72	59507	1361
#住宅	#Residential Buildings	211.32	34.65	48908	1411
淳安县	**Chun'an**				
房屋建筑面积合计	**Total Floor Space of Buildings**	**298.54**	**58.33**	**142772**	**2448**
#住宅	#Residential Buildings	125.03	22.56	52386	2322
房地产开发	Real Estate Development	184.81	38.12	116941	3068
#住宅	#Residential Buildings	113.60	21.63	51597	2385
建德市	**Jiande**				
房屋建筑面积合计	**Total Floor Space of Buildings**	**358.77**	**146.96**	**170161**	**1158**
#住宅	#Residential Buildings	93.32	23.87	48489	2031
房地产开发	Real Estate Development	112.77	25.63	54509	2127
#住宅	#Residential Buildings	91.02	21.57	46036	2134
富阳市	**Fuyang**				
房屋建筑面积合计	**Total Floor Space of Buildings**	**882.31**	**342.61**	**472277**	**1378**
#住宅	#Residential Buildings	310.17	64.92	125189	1928
房地产开发	Real Estate Development	320.62	73.38	143684	1958
#住宅	#Residential Buildings	214.94	59.95	116919	1950
临安市	**Lin'an**				
房屋建筑面积合计	**Total Floor Space of Buildings**	**547.05**	**271.74**	**412910**	**1520**
#住宅	#Residential Buildings	226.92	44.68	98801	2211
房地产开发	Real Estate Development	279.80	56.50	125015	2213
#住宅	#Residential Buildings	226.92	44.68	98801	2211

7-11 固定资产投资新增生产能力(或效益)(2011年)

The New Productive Capacity or Facilities Created by Investment in Fixed Assets(2011)

指标	Item	全市 Total	市区 Urban District
水泥 (万吨/年)	Cement (10000tons/year)	140	–
塑料树脂及共聚物 (吨/年)	Plastic Resins and Copolymers (tons/year)	217720	210120
化学纤维 (万吨/年)	Chemical Fiber (10000tons/year)	35.49	32.20
其中:合成纤维 (万吨/年)	Of Which:Synthetic fiber (10000tons/year)	32.0	32.0
棉纺锭 (锭)	Cotton Spindles (spindles)	82496	82496
火力发电 (万千瓦)	Thermal Power Generation (10000kilowatt)	0.9	–
水力发电 (万千瓦)	Hydroelectric Power Generation (10000kilowatt)	1.24	0.6
输电线路长度(11万伏及以上) (千米)	Length of Electricity Transmission Line (110000volts and above) (km)	140.5	140.5
新建公路 (公里)	New Highway (km)	29.64	28.52
改建公路 (公里)	Revamped Highway (km)	101.82	22.21
城市污水处理能力 (万吨/每日)	Urban Sewage Treatment Capacity (10000tons/day)	7.35	1.65

主要统计指标解释

固定资产投资完成额　固定资产投资完成额是以货币表现的建造和购置固定资产的工作量以及与此有关的费用的总称。它是反映固定资产投资规模、速度、比例关系和使用方向的综合性指标。

房地产开发投资　包括各种经济类型的房地产开发公司、商品房建设公司及其他房地产开发单位统一开发的包括统代建、拆迁还建的住宅、厂房、仓库、饭店、宾馆、度假村、写字楼、办公楼等房屋建筑物和配套的服务设施、土地开发工程,如道路、给水、排水、供电、供热、通讯、平整场地等基础设施工程的投资。包括非房地产企业实际从事房地产开发或经济活动,不包括单纯的土地交易活动。

施工和竣工房屋建筑面积　房屋建筑面积是从房屋外墙线算起的各层平面面积的总和,包括房屋结构(如柱、墙)占用的面积和地下室面积。多层建筑按各自然层面积总和计算,包括房屋内的楼隔层,突出墙面的眺望间、门斗、有柱雨罩的面积。不包括突出墙面结构的构件、艺术装饰等所占的面积,如台阶等。凹阳台、挑阳台按其水平投影面积一半计算建筑面积。

房屋新开工面积　指在报告期内新开工建设的房屋面积。不包括上期跨入报告期继续施工的房屋面积和上期停缓建而在本期恢复施工的房屋面积。房屋的开工应以房屋正式开始破土刨槽(地基处理或打永久桩)的日期为准。

商品房销售面积　指报告期内出售商品房屋的合同总面积(即双方签署的正式买卖合同中所确定的建筑面积)。由现房销售建筑面积和期房销售建筑面积两部分组成。

(1)现房销售面积:是指在报告期内正式签订买卖合同、已经竣工达到入住条件的商品房屋建筑面积。包括以一次性付款方式和分期付款方式销售的现房建筑面积。

(2)期房销售面积:是指在报告期内正式签订买卖合同、正在建设尚未竣工交付使用的商品房屋建筑面积。包括以一次性付款方式和分期付款方式销售的商品房屋建筑面积。期房销售建筑面积竣工后不再转为现房销售建筑面积。

新增固定资产　指通过投资活动所形成的新的固定资产价值。包括已经建成投入生产或交付使用的工程价值和达到固定资产标准的设备、工具、器具的价值及有关应摊入的费用。它是以价值形式表示的固定资产投资成果的综合性指标,可以综合反映不同时期、不同部门、不同地区的固定资产投资成果。

Explanatory Notes on Main Statistical Indicators

Total Investment in Fixed Assets refer to the volume of activities in construction and purchases of fixed assets in monetary terms and other relative expenses. It is a comprehensive indicator which shows the size, pace, proportional relations and use orientation of investment in fixed assets.

Investment in Real Estate Development include the investment by the real estate development companies, commercial buildings construction companies and other real estate development units of various types of ownership in the construction of house buildings, such as residential buildings, factory buildings, warehouses, hotels, guesthouses, holiday supply, water drainage, power supply, heating, telecommunications, land leveling and other projects of infrastructure, it excludes the activities in simple land transaction.

Floor space of Building Under Construction and Completed refer to total floor space in each story of buildings calculate from the outside line of building walls, including the space occupied by construction like pillars or walls and basements. The floor space of multi - story building includes the total floor space of each story, including area occupied by separating walls, watching rooms, door - ways, and pillars, but excluding protruding wall structures, artistic decoration, etc. (for example, flight of steps). The space of balcony is counted by half of the projection area.

Beginning to Construction Floor Space of Building refer to the area space which constructed in report period, not including the floor whose construction lasted to report period and which stopped in the last period to continue construction in the report period. And the beginning of construction of floor space should base on the date of breaking the earth(disposal the basement or piling).

Selling of the Commercial Building refer to the total area that sold by contract(which reflected in the contract), which include completed and future buildings.

(1) Floor Space of Completed Building: refer to the area which formal contract has been signed and which has been completed and reached the condition of living, including payment in one time and installment payment.

(2) Floor Space of Future Building: refer to the area which signed by formal contract and under constructing, including payment in one time and installment payment. Which can not be turned into completed building's sale when they completed.

Newly Increased Fixed Assets refer to the newly increased value of fixed assets through investment, including the value of projects completed and put into production, the value of equipment, tools, and vessels considered as fixed assets, as well as the relevant expenses as investment in fixed assets. This is a comprehensive indicator of investment in fixed assets, reflecting the achievements of investment in fixed assets in different periods, different sectors, and different regions.

第八篇
CHAPTER-8

国内商业
DOMESTIC TRADE

8 国内商业
Domestic Trade

主要统计指标
Major Statistical Indicators

社会消费品零售总额	Total Retail Sales of Consumer Goods	2548.36	亿元	(100 million yuan)
为上年	As Compared with the Preceding Year	118.7	%	(%)
批发和零售贸易业	Wholesale and Retail Trade	2274.84	亿元	(100 million yuan)
为上年	As Compared with the Preceding Year	118.6	%	(%)
住宿和餐饮业	Lodging and Catering	273.52	亿元	(100 million yuan)
为上年	As Compared with the Preceding Year	119.5	%	(%)

8－01　主要年份社会消费品零售总额
Total Retail Sale of Consumer Goods in Main Years

单位:万元　　　　(10,000 yuan)

年　份 Year	全　市 Total	市　区 Urban District	县(市)合计 All Counties
1978	119509	73653	45856
1979	150462	93342	57120
1980	205381	128440	76941
1981	236188	148152	88036
1982	251068	154582	96486
1983	273664	169508	104156
1984	343722	215901	127821
1985	478117	308901	169216
1986	557963	360479	197484
1987	657838	426745	231093
1988	866373	557374	308999
1989	927019	600816	326203
1990	981713	650278	331435
1991	1155476	777559	377917
1992	1408525	928586	479939
1993	1901509	1300037	601472
1994	2616477	1733572	882905
1995	2993250	1930140	1063110
1996	3478156	2310619	1167537
1997	3815537	2537537	1278000
1998	4178013	2794171	1383842
1999	4574924	3053983	1520941
2000	5146789	3436536	1710253
2001	5790138	4993078	797060
2002	6606548	5701707	904841
2003	7425760	6401970	1023790
2004	8554476	7385662	1168814
2005	9784275	8440559	1343716
2006	11191900	9630210	1561690
2007	13082930	11247539	1835391
2008	15775872	13542665	2233207
2009	18049303	15498990	2550313
2010	21460790	18432319	3028471
2011	25483599	21877831	3605768

注:1. 从 2001 年起市区数据包括萧山区和余杭区。
2. 2010 年零售额口径范围有调整,增幅按同口径计算。

a) Data of urban district include Xiaoshan and Yuhang district since 2001.

b) The statistical coverage of total retail sale in 2010 has been adjusted, but the increase was calculated at the same statistical coverage.

8－02 主要年份分县(市)
Total Retail Sale of Consumer Goods

单位:万元

年 份 Year	全 市 Whole City		市 区 Urban District		
	合 计 Total	为上年(%) As Compared with the Preceding Year(%)	合 计 Total	为上年(%) As Compared with the Preceding Year(%)	#萧山区 Xiaoshan
1978	119509	112.5	73653	115.8	12985
1979	150462	125.9	93342	127.2	16270
1980	205381	136.5	128440	138.1	22292
1981	236188	115.0	148152	115.6	25297
1982	251068	106.3	154582	103.3	29007
1983	273664	109.0	169508	110.1	32136
1984	343722	125.6	215901	128.4	41210
1985	478117	139.1	308901	145.2	51879
1986	557963	116.7	360479	116.8	61421
1987	657838	117.9	426745	118.6	73159
1988	866373	131.7	557374	130.1	101227
1989	927019	107.0	600816	108.3	103419
1990	981713	105.9	650278	109.5	111757
1991	1155476	117.7	777559	120.4	123753
1992	1408525	121.9	928586	118.3	153254
1993	1901509	135.0	1300037	134.4	195472
1994	2616477	137.6	1733572	132.2	299072
1995	2993250	114.4	1930140	118.2	339447
1996	3478156	116.2	2310619	120.9	390364
1997	3815537	109.7	2537537	109.9	431742
1998	4178013	109.5	2794171	110.5	470599
1999	4574924	109.5	3053983	109.3	520482
2000	5146789	112.5	3436536	112.8	602198
2001	5790138	113.6	4993078	113.9	690721
2002	6606548	114.1	5701707	114.2	795711
2003	7425760	112.4	6401970	112.3	929390
2004	8554476	115.2	7385662	115.4	1069728
2005	9784275	114.4	8440559	114.3	1234568
2006	11191900	114.4	9630210	114.1	1462157
2007	13082930	116.9	11247539	116.8	1721511
2008	15775872	120.6	13542665	120.4	2059811
2009	18049303	114.4	15498990	114.4	2376949
2010	21460790	119.9	18432319	120.1	2839433
2011	25483599	118.7	21877831	118.7	3369839

注:1. 从2001年起市区数据包括萧山区和余杭区。
2. 2010年零售额口径范围有调整,增幅按同口径计算。

社会消费品零售总额
by Region in Main Years

(10000 yuan)

#余杭区 Yuhang	桐庐县 Tonglu	淳安县 Chun'an	建德市 Jiande	富阳市 Fuyang	临安市 Lin'an
11472	3536	3507	4390	5209	4757
14439	4283	4274	5300	6435	6119
19917	5501	5225	7119	8661	8226
22172	6456	6201	7970	10226	9714
23435	7101	6663	8562	11016	10702
23496	7694	7168	9380	12307	11975
29292	9235	8331	10770	14972	14011
39798	11826	11081	14687	21013	18932
47499	13217	12525	15832	23400	23590
53005	17394	14449	18076	27939	27071
64653	24390	18944	23545	42601	33639
74044	23029	19014	23138	48836	34723
69360	23141	18764	23820	45364	39229
84399	26350	20950	25107	52807	44551
110075	34110	23983	30770	74865	52882
149128	44909	28038	40237	76162	67526
212955	69025	34179	54562	101829	111283
255972	93736	42143	70570	127592	133650
266467	104234	51794	77620	146348	130710
294446	114032	58994	83837	163324	131625
321241	123154	67136	93169	171654	136889
352723	135223	74293	103417	185730	149073
397166	148745	81054	115062	198917	167111
446812	166892	90133	128754	223782	187499
508919	188087	101581	144849	254887	215437
584748	209153	114990	163244	289297	247106
674799	237598	130974	185772	331534	282936
778848	272394	149456	212138	382960	326768
906960	317484	173272	247425	450365	373144
1064956	371057	201769	288873	526750	446942
1302135	451356	244069	350854	643169	543759
1499377	516037	278356	400157	734925	620838
1767194	608722	328351	484678	871296	735424
2100841	724257	391658	575700	1038410	875743

a) Data of urban district include Xiaoshan and Yuhang district since 2001.

b) The statistical coverage of total retail sale in 2010 has been adjusted, but the increase was calculated at the same statistical coverage.

8－03 社会消费品
Total Retail Sale of

单位:万元

地 区	Region	合 计 Total
全 市	**Total**	**25483599**
市 区	Urban District	21877831
上城区	Shangcheng	2158554
下城区	Xiacheng	5381404
江干区	Jianggan	2234478
拱墅区	Gongshu	2788662
西湖区	Xihu	2796442
高新(滨江)区	Hi－Tech(Binjiang)	477476
萧山区	Xiaoshan	3369839
余杭区	Yuhang	2100841
桐庐县	Tonglu	724257
淳安县	Chun′an	391658
建德市	Jiande	575700
富阳市	Fuyang	1038410
临安市	Lin′an	875743

零售总额(2011 年)
Consumer Goods(2011)

(10000 yuan)

按销售分 By Location		按行业分 By sector	
城镇零售额 City	乡村零售额 County	批发和零售贸易业 Wholesale and Retail Trades	住宿和餐饮业 Hotels and Catering Services
24325079	**1158520**	**22748441**	**2735158**
21877831	–	19673512	2204319
2158554	–	1820960	337594
5381404	–	5053879	327526
2234478	–	2059805	174672
2788662	–	2670081	118581
2796442	–	2517434	279009
477476	–	445945	31531
3369839	–	2863686	506154
2100841	–	1860180	240660
448308	275949	615472	108786
224830	166827	313360	78297
515707	59994	488890	86810
722223	316187	898866	139544
536180	339564	758341	117402

8-04 全市限额以上批发零售贸易企业商品销售总额按登记注册类型分(2011年)

Sales of Wholesale and Retail Trade Above Designated Size by Status of Registration(2011)

单位:万元 (10000 yuan)

项　目	Item	法人企业(个) Number of Enterprises (unit)	销售总额 Total Sales	批发额 Wholesale	零售额 Retail
总　计	**Total**	**3392**	**126634702**	**109143711**	**17490991**
1. 内资企业	**Domestic - funded Enterprises**	**3312**	**120922569**	**105951928**	**14970640**
国有企业	State - owned Enterprises	75	7979303	7569279	410024
集体企业	Collective - owned Enterprises	26	854715	763148	91567
股份合作企业	Cooperative Enterprises	5	22032	17875	4157
联营企业	Joint Ownership Enterprises	13	275039	186623	88416
国有联营企业	State Joint Ownership Enterprises	2	35255	9070	26185
集体联营企业	Collective Joint Ownership Enterprises	2	34195	34195	-
国有与集体联营企业	Joint State - collective Enterprises	8	68673	6442	62231
其他联营企业	Other Joint Ownership Enterprises	1	136916	136916	-
有限责任公司	Limited Liability Corporations	879	51166442	43029913	8136529
国有独资公司	State - funded Corporations	10	2634124	2610183	23942
其他有限责任公司	Other Limited Liability Corporations	869	48532318	40419730	8112588
股份有限公司	Share - holding Corporations Ltd.	93	14961877	11592352	3369526
私营企业	Private Enterprises	2210	45600753	42748714	2852038
私营独资企业	Private - funded Enterprises	59	786907	671444	115463
私营合伙企业	Private Partnership Enterprises	6	61651	58401	3250
私营有限责任公司	Private Limited Liability Corporations	2099	43989257	41367793	2621464
私营股份有限公司	Private Share - holding Corporations Ltd.	46	762938	651077	111861
其他企业	Other Enterprises	11	62408	44025	18383
2. 港、澳、台商投资企业	**Enterprises With Investment from Hong Kong, Macao and Taiwan**	**31**	**1318124**	**532499**	**785624**
合资经营企业(港或澳、台资)	Joint - venture Enterprises(With Funds from Hong Kong, Macao and Taiwan)	11	335049	152246	182802
合作经营企业(港或澳、台资)	Coorperative Enterprises (With Funds from Hong Kong, Macao and Taiwan)	1	68185	-	68185
港、澳、台商独资经营企业	Enterprises With Sole Investment from Hong Kong, Macao and Taiwan	18	907882	380253	527629
港、澳、台商投资股份有限公司	Share - holding Corporations Ltd. With Investment from Hong Kong, Macao and Taiwan	1	7007	-	7007
3. 外商投资企业	**Enterprises With Foreign Investment**	**49**	**4394010**	**2659283**	**1734727**
中外合资经营企业	Joint - venture Enterprises	14	2952920	2433028	519892
中外合作经营企业	Cooperation Enterprises	1	6830	-	6830
外资企业	Enterprises With Sole Foreign Investment	34	1434260	226256	1208005
外商投资股份有限公司	Share - holding Corporations Ltd. With Foreign Investment	-	-	-	-

8-05 全市限额以上批发零售贸易企业商品销售总额按国民经济行业分(2011年)

Sales of Wholesale and Retail Trade Above Designated Size by Sector(2011)

单位:万元 (10000 yuan)

项目	Item	法人企业(个) Number of Enterprises (unit)	销售总额 Total Sales	批发额 Wholesale	零售额 Retail
总计	**Total**	**3392**	**126634702**	**109143711**	**17490991**
一、批发业	**Wholesale**	**2670**	**111484691**	**107316406**	**4168285**
农畜产品批发业	Wholesale of Farm and Animal Products	33	867661	861992	5669
食品、饮料及烟草制品批发	Wholesale of Food, Beverages and Tobaccos	139	8083839	8035635	48204
纺织、服装及日用品批发	Wholesale of Textile Products, Garments, Shoes and Caps	482	11573729	11486682	87047
文化、体育用品及器材批发	Wholesale of Cultural and Sports Goods	67	1510172	1498067	12105
医药及医疗器材批发	Wholesale of Medicines and Medical Appliances	91	4729625	2899104	1830521
矿产品、建材及化工产品批发	Wholesale of Mineral Products, Building and Chemical Materials	1300	69093119	67232361	1860758
机械设备、五金交电及电子产品批发	Wholesale of Machinery, Hardware and Electronic Products	471	13325506	13001526	323980
其中:汽车、摩托车及零配件批发	Wholesale of Automobiles, Motorcycle and Parts	65	3310897	3212301	98595
其他批发	Other	82	2262897	2262897	-
二、零售业	**Retail Trade**	**722**	**15150012**	**1827305**	**13322706**
综合零售	Comprehensive Retail Trade	93	4076079	611329	3464751
食品、饮料及烟草制品专门零售	Specialism Retail of Food, Beverages and Tobaccos	23	120244	14739	105505
纺织、服装及日用品专门零售	Specialism Retail of Textile Products, Garments, Shoes and Caps	52	338859	35243	303615
文化、体育用品及器材专门零售	Specialism Retail of Cultural and Sports Goods	39	442414	124017	318397
医药及医疗器材专门零售	Specialism Retail of Medicines and Medical Appliances	46	345406	23833	321572
汽车、摩托车、燃料及零配件专门零售	Specialism Retail of Automobiles, Motorcycle, Fuels and Parts	356	8419996	797489	7622507
其中:汽车零售	Specialism Retail of Automobiles	225	7011121	612481	6398640
家用电器及电子产品专门零售	Specialism Retail of Household Electric Applianes, and Electronic Products	79	1126191	151148	975043
五金家具及室内装修材料专门零售	Specialism Retail of Hardware and Upholstery Materials	20	108346	22245	86101
无店铺及其他零售	Other Retail Trade	14	172478	47262	125215

8－06 全市限额以上批发零售贸易企业

Main Financial Indicators of Enterprises Above Designated Size in

单位:万元

项　目	Item	法人企业数(个) Number of Enterprises (unit)	年末资产负债 Assets and Liabilities 流动资产合计 Circulating Funds	# 存货 Inventory	固定资产原价 Orginal Value of Fixed Assets
批发零售贸易业企业合计	**Total**	**3392**	**40856187**	**6309927**	**3340107**
1. 内资企业	**Domestic－funded Enterprises**	**3312**	**39043628**	**5927213**	**2925713**
国有企业	State－owned Enterprises	75	2320294	439747	222807
集体企业	Collective－owned Enterprises	26	551875	71327	31103
股份合作企业	Cooperative Enterprises	5	4558	1286	2114
联营企业	Joint Ownership Enterprises	13	82006	12367	5275
国有联营企业	State Joint Ownership Enterprises	2	8021	189	710
集体联营企业	Collective Joint Enterprises	2	33164	4131	302
国有与集体联营企业	Joint State－collective Enterprises	8	5024	607	2328
其他联营企业	Other Joint Ownership Enterprises	1	35797	7441	1934
有限责任公司	Limited Liability Corporations	879	15860933	2629544	1169949
国有独资公司	State－funded Corporations	10	501954	169693	41499
其他有限责任公司	Other Limited Liability Corporations	869	15358980	2459851	1128450
股份有限公司	Share－holding Corporations Ltd.	93	4673152	982955	549049
私营企业	Private Enterprises	2210	15538112	1786331	942834
私营独资企业	Private－funded Enterprises	59	342910	36498	16050
私营合伙企业	Private Partnership Enterprises	6	13742	872	3117
私营有限责任公司	Private Limited Liability Corporations	2099	14618227	1684587	905327
私营股份有限公司	Private Share－holding Corporations Ltd.	46	563232	64374	18340
其他企业	Other Enterprises	11	12699	3657	2582
2. 港、澳、台商投资企业	**Enterprises With Investment from Hong Kong, Macao and Taiwan**	**31**	**363483**	**78429**	**85432**
合资经营企业(港或澳、台资)	Joint－venture Enterprises (With Funds from Hong Kong, Macao and Taiwan)	11	92816	20451	27903
合作经营企业(港或澳、台资)	Coorperative Enterprises (With Funds from Hong Kong, Macao and Taiwan)	1	18171	886	12385
港、澳、台商独资经营企业	Enterprises With Sole Investment from Hong Kong, Macao and Taiwan	18	250922	56553	44080
港、澳、台商投资股份有限公司	Share－holding Corporations Ltd. With Investment from Hong Kong, Macao and Taiwan	1	1574	539	1064
3. 外商投资企业	**Enterprises With Foreign Investment**	**49**	**1449076**	**304285**	**328962**
中外合资经营企业	Joint－venture Enterprises	14	542575	206548	197530
中外合作经营企业	Cooperation Enterprises	1	3982	796	7276
外资企业	Enterprises With Sole Foreign Investment	34	902519	96941	124156
外商投资股份有限公司	Share－holding Corporations Ltd. With Foreign Investment	－	－	－	－

财务状况按登记注册类型分(2011 年)
Wholesale and Retail Sale Trade by Status of Registration(2011)

(10000 yuan)

累计折旧 Accumulated Depreciation	#本年折旧 Depreciation	资产总计 Total Assets	负债合计 Total Liabilities	所有者权益合计 Creditors' Equity	实收资本 Capital Hold	#国家资本 State Capital
1094815	**200133**	**52543988**	**40261716**	**12282272**	**7117123**	**1108774**
977479	**174513**	**50085801**	**38480718**	**11605083**	**6592386**	**1069644**
89515	13496	3181411	1658283	1523128	452013	443083
13226	1301	719606	529264	190342	104702	–
715	22	8088	5672	2416	826	–
2253	351	87503	49792	37711	14638	1564
310	80	8453	4533	3920	1217	1094
287	11	35400	30801	4599	3500	–
1164	139	6413	3976	2436	1266	470
493	121	37238	10483	26755	8656	–
384235	64322	20112767	15813483	4299284	2245798	209260
13204	1370	621207	467496	153711	30501	27921
371031	62952	19491561	15345987	4145574	2215297	181339
187137	24674	7273987	5161714	2112273	1047374	414987
299623	70209	18685770	15250914	3434856	2724340	750
5719	1315	389895	356359	33537	56629	–
440	177	16725	13768	2957	3100	–
286194	67045	17690580	14377883	3312697	2596465	750
7270	1673	588569	502904	85665	68146	–
775	139	16669	11596	5073	2696	–
24888	**6543**	**514478**	**252633**	**261846**	**210913**	**4250**
5930	1400	159165	72083	87082	34538	4250
8087	313	30562	3826	26736	18975	–
10285	4243	322471	175444	147028	156462	–
587	587	2280	1280	1000	937	–
92448	**19077**	**1943709**	**1528365**	**415344**	**313824**	**34880**
38172	8414	884715	777311	107403	93072	34880
3292	300	11645	3092	8553	12916	–
50984	10363	1047349	747962	299388	207836	–
–	–	–	–	–	–	–

单位:万元　　　　　　　　　　　　　　8－06　续表

项　　目	Item	营业收入 Revenue of Business	其中:主营业务收入 Main Revenue of Business	主营业务成本 Main Cost of Business	主营业务税金及附加 Main Sales Tax and Extra Charges
批发零售贸易业企业合计	**Total**	**112303838**	**110129754**	**104668068**	**211935**
1. 内资企业	**Domestic－funded Enterprises**	**107282669**	**105188601**	**100089731**	**199982**
国有企业	State－owned Enterprises	6975009	6952188	6435789	77307
集体企业	Collective－owned Enterprises	795941	783674	768096	1248
股份合作企业	Cooperative Enterprises	19131	18921	17732	64
联营企业	Joint Ownership Enterprises	254974	254974	234982	269
国有联营企业	State Joint Ownership Enterprises	30407	30407	27535	46
集体联营企业	Collective Joint Enterprises	34195	34195	33353	－
国有与集体联营企业	Joint State－collective Enterprises	57634	57634	54807	51
其他联营企业	Other Joint Ownership Enterprises	132739	132739	119286	173
有限责任公司	Limited Liability Corporations	45541488	45161132	42921318	58237
国有独资公司	State－funded Corporations	2270002	2268008	2246505	225
其他有限责任公司	Other Limited Liability Corporations	43271486	42893125	40674813	58012
股份有限公司	Share－holding Corporations Ltd.	13512938	11943474	11222563	14370
私营企业	Private Enterprises	40124550	40016227	38436039	48212
私营独资企业	Private－funded Enterprises	709685	707755	668214	954
私营合伙企业	Private Partnership Enterprises	54601	54588	52300	33
私营有限责任公司	Private Limited Liability Corporations	38673563	38571579	37080534	44011
私营股份有限公司	Private Share－holding Corporations Ltd.	686701	682306	634992	3214
其他企业	Other Enterprises	58639	58012	53212	275
2. 港、澳、台商投资企业	**Enterprises With Investment from Hong Kong, Macao and Taiwan**	**1159756**	**1153289**	**1059106**	**2430**
合资经营企业(港或澳、台资)	Joint－venture Enterprises (With Funds from Hong Kong, Macao and Taiwan)	304468	301756	273647	741
合作经营企业(港或澳、台资)	Coorperative Enterprises (With Funds from Hong Kong, Macao and Taiwan)	61799	61799	51722	317
港、澳、台商独资经营企业	Enterprises With Sole Investment from Hong Kong, Macao and Taiwan	787498	783745	729786	1331
港、澳、台商投资股份有限公司	Share－holding Corporations Ltd. With Investment from Hong Kong, Macao and Taiwan	5991	5989	3952	42
3. 外商投资企业	**Enterprises With Foreign Investment**	**3861413**	**3787864**	**3519232**	**9523**
中外合资经营企业	Joint－venture Enterprises	2590349	2546763	2463392	3172
中外合作经营企业	Cooperation Enterprises	7211	5838	4625	21
外资企业	Enterprises With Sole Foreign Investment	1263853	1235263	1051214	6331
外商投资股份有限公司	Share－holding Corporations Ltd. With Foreign Investment	－	－	－	－

continued (10000 yuan)

销售费用 Cost of Sales	管理费用 Administration Cost	财务费用 Financil Cost	营业利润 Management Profits	利润总额 Total Profits	应交所得税 Income Tax	应付职工薪酬（本年贷方累计发生额） Salary Payable to Employees
2591569	**1345622**	**755607**	**1516623**	**1652730**	**414873**	**1081040**
2391084	**1229562**	**726928**	**1444296**	**1576865**	**388709**	**996741**
59522	103907	10580	313508	306759	71775	70678
10693	6910	14280	21938	23012	1117	5258
192	489	33	621	1004	253	414
5858	2930	1666	9703	9682	2342	1288
339	250	-174	2412	2388	605	198
7	38	868	362	362	–	41
1161	282	-10	1342	1346	341	576
4352	2360	982	5587	5587	1397	472
1254204	465705	215792	699652	798423	183486	499709
9898	12723	7019	-4615	2653	1994	8109
1244307	452982	208773	704267	795770	181493	491600
332130	186681	166838	209406	227954	64186	163847
725435	460906	317538	188772	209251	65491	254184
25578	10237	11322	-6374	-5364	1630	9667
777	1138	603	-257	-204	2	490
676973	436468	300121	187874	207547	61667	234123
22106	13064	5492	7529	7272	2191	9905
3048	2035	202	697	780	59	1363
58947	**30088**	**3300**	**6584**	**9548**	**4609**	**29082**
16934	7890	-59	6383	9431	1730	10988
1932	3795	100	3932	3961	1000	2698
39931	16607	3218	-3740	-3855	1872	15101
151	1796	41	10	11	7	295
141538	**85972**	**25380**	**65743**	**66317**	**21555**	**55217**
56112	30725	10797	18068	18810	5591	24037
1884	31	-2	384	396	–	363
83542	55217	14585	47291	47111	15964	30817
–	–	–	–	–	–	–

8－07 全市限额以上批发零售贸易企业

Main Financial Indicators of Enterprises Above Designated

单位:万元

项　目	Item	法人企业数(个) Number of Enterprises (unit)	年末资产负债 Assets and Liabilities 流动资产合计 Circulating Funds	#存　货 Inventory	固定资产原价 Orginal Value of Fixed Assets
总　计	**Total**	**3392**	**40856187**	**6309927**	**3340107**
一、批发业	**Wholesale**	**2670**	**35335047**	**4877062**	**2129747**
农畜产品批发业	Wholesale of Farm and Animal Products	33	479964	84446	25020
食品、饮料、烟草制品批发	Wholesale of Food, Beverages and Tobaccos	139	3003451	335676	307338
纺织、服装及日用品批发	Wholesale of Textile Products, Garments, Shoes and Caps	482	4611905	710329	366699
文化、体育用品及器材批发	Wholesale of Cultural and Sports Goods	67	698563	195966	72765
医药及医疗器材批发	Wholesale of Medicines and Medical Appliances	91	1650232	335432	92524
矿产品、建材及化工产品批发	Wholesale of Mineral Products, Building and Chemical Materials	1300	20117893	2478302	1001245
机械设备、五金交电及电子产品批发	Wholesale of Machinery, Hardware and Electronic Products	471	4326404	686004	250685
其中:汽车、摩托车及零配件批发	Wholesale of Automobiles, Motorcycle and Parts	65	649430	99226	29878
其他批发	Other	82	441450	50246	13328
二、零售业	**Retail Trade**	**722**	**5521140**	**1432865**	**1210360**
综合零售	Comprehensive Retail Trade	93	2485062	547788	562035
食品、饮料及烟草制品专门零售	Specialism Retail of Food, Beverages and Tobaccos	23	45185	16411	7318
纺织、服装及日用品专门零售	Specialism Retail of Textile Products, Garments, Shoes and Caps	52	169696	80927	126660
文化、体育用品及器材专门零售	Specialism Retail of Cultural and Sports Goods	39	238924	102070	102044
医药及医疗器材专门零售	Specialism Retail of Medicines and Medical Appliances	46	144159	42392	18559
汽车、摩托车、燃料及零配件专门零售	Specialism Retail of Automobiles, Motorcycle, Fuels and Parts	356	1857956	530384	294258
其中:汽车零售	Specialism Retail of Automobiles	225	1757282	512791	244512
家用电器及电子产品专门零售	Specialism Retail of Household Electric Applianes, and Electronic Products	79	501354	98330	36236
五金家具及室内装修材料专门零售	Specialism Retail of Hardware and Upholstery Materials	20	40328	9421	37291
无店铺及其他零售	Other Retail Trade	14	38477	5143	25958

财务状况按国民经济行业分(2011 年)

Size in Wholesale and Retail Sale Trade by Sector(2011)

(10000 yuan)

累计折旧 Accumulated Depreciation	#本年折旧 Depreciation	资产总计 Total Assets	负债合计 Total Liabilities	所有者权益合计 Creditors' Equity	实收资本 Capital Hold	#国家资本 State Capital
1094815	**200133**	**52543988**	**40261716**	**12282272**	**7117123**	**1108774**
735865	**132297**	**45394870**	**34776670**	**10618200**	**5943171**	**998567**
8141	1339	559801	460570	99230	65905	5732
102097	16116	3852183	2421073	1431110	598049	125197
141566	25052	5720734	4357365	1363369	745029	9364
26534	3967	1011372	613988	397383	148818	70701
38957	7226	1886842	1460065	426778	196067	29664
325459	58844	26334702	20936842	5397860	3360603	714787
89020	18839	5530745	4093446	1437299	754851	43121
10587	2481	1118848	806305	312543	229744	2000
4030	893	493199	429284	63915	73208	–
358950	**67836**	**7149118**	**5485046**	**1664072**	**1173952**	**110207**
185909	30950	3155373	2466082	689291	366366	14059
2728	746	61710	37866	23844	18740	3186
17560	4397	324737	239745	84992	118622	749
19672	2144	379303	277635	101668	68096	5080
7914	1605	164006	128205	35800	72570	52141
94405	21023	2339931	1817133	522798	333336	27492
74775	18339	2171662	1727832	443830	277552	15639
11859	2641	582695	439111	143584	130770	–
9077	2540	82018	42541	39477	42080	–
9826	1790	59346	36728	22618	23374	7500

单位:万元

8-07 续表

项　目	Item	营业收入 Revenue of Business	其中:主营业务收入 Main Revenue of Business	主营业务成本 Main Cost of Business	主营业务税金及附加 Main Sales Tax and Extra Charges
总　计	**Total**	**112303838**	**110129754**	**104668068**	**211935**
一、批发业	**Wholesale**	**99009353**	**97080946**	**92881202**	**166810**
农畜产品批发业	Wholesale of Farm and Animal Products	776455	774624	740486	496
食品、饮料、烟草制品批发	Wholesale of Food, Beverages and Tobaccos	7421648	7298589	6275077	86963
纺织、服装及日用品批发	Wholesale of Textile Products, Garments, Shoes and Caps	11016532	10888693	10166117	10258
文化、体育用品及器材批发	Wholesale of Cultural and Sports Goods	1338413	1328791	1262249	1850
医药及医疗器材批发	Wholesale of Medicines and Medical Appliances	4169834	4120443	3817455	5912
矿产品、建材及化工产品批发	Wholesale of Mineral Products, Building and Chemical Materials	60443204	58894432	57591648	31394
机械设备、五金交电及电子产品批发	Wholesale of Machinery, Hardware and Electronic Products	11842659	11775677	11058279	14192
其中:汽车、摩托车及零配件批发	Wholesale of Automobiles, Motorcycle and Parts	2852155	2848968	2693589	2250
其他批发	Other	1963500	1962589	1934012	15713
二、零售业	**Retail Trade**	**13294485**	**13048809**	**11786866**	**45125**
综合零售	Comprehensive Retail Trade	3588707	3443448	2969535	22307
食品、饮料及烟草制品专门零售	Specialism Retail of Food, Beverages and Tobaccos	104681	103084	72235	707
纺织、服装及日用品专门零售	Specialism Retail of Textile Products, Garments, Shoes and Caps	313153	294069	221170	1595
文化、体育用品及器材专门零售	Specialism Retail of Cultural and Sports Goods	384601	380482	319440	5933
医药及医疗器材专门零售	Specialism Retail of Medicines and Medical Appliances	303808	300751	233820	1079
汽车、摩托车、燃料及零配件专门零售	Specialism Retail of Automobiles, Motorcycle, Fuels and Parts	7372958	7334625	6917504	9389
其中:汽车零售	Specialism Retail of Automobiles	6150915	6113213	5753075	8250
家用电器及电子产品专门零售	Specialism Retail of Household Electric Appliances, and Electronic Products	977000	946943	855724	2507
五金家具及室内装修材料专门零售	Specialism Retail of Hardware and Upholstery Materials	95522	93149	69189	1090
无店铺及其他零售	Other Retail Trade	154056	152258	128250	519

continued (10000 yuan)

销售费用 Cost of Sales	管理费用 Administration Cost	财务费用 Financil Cost	营业利润 Management Profits	利润总额 Total Profits	应交所得税 Income Tax	应付职工薪酬（本年贷方累计发生额）Salary Payable to Employees
2591569	**1345622**	**755607**	**1516623**	**1652730**	**414873**	**1081040**
1785844	**991041**	**675612**	**1260960**	**1396268**	**334146**	**704549**
11272	10346	11041	2055	6746	1185	3996
404567	127156	34071	454453	493469	117648	156995
327846	215634	73638	215271	210736	44850	154521
25022	24900	3080	31653	31218	3846	15451
134672	73582	24477	140246	140355	29383	57184
511300	349269	451729	291715	360824	99520	172997
364775	181056	46911	154489	154666	36441	138498
123535	19638	6085	8867	9936	2073	17997
5962	8825	30394	-29146	-1977	1253	4752
805725	**354581**	**79995**	**255663**	**256462**	**80727**	**376492**
370978	130206	14864	127323	132190	39018	146450
22530	7919	228	683	1983	933	11479
53892	27617	8446	-10373	-12937	2857	26084
29796	18724	8326	1169	938	1221	17843
38619	14198	1626	14611	14705	4153	20585
176452	118654	41385	113916	110291	29294	113815
146215	111243	39812	97116	94010	25573	100552
83752	25256	3343	3735	3607	2313	33625
12386	6555	1589	3717	3712	315	2951
17320	5453	188	883	1972	623	3660

8－08 分地区限额以上
The Situation of Wholesale

单位:万元

项　　目 Item	全　市 Total	市　区 Urban District	#萧山区 Xiaoshan
商品销售总额 Total Sales of Commodities	126634702	121447324	13061412
企业法人数(个) Number of Enterprises(unit)	3392	2961	469
从业人员年平均人数(人) Annual Average Number of Staff and Worhers(person)	196172	179409	17702
流动资产合计 Circulating Funds	40856187	39295333	4815893
固定资产合计 Fixed Assets	2292551	2151661	220835
主营业务收入 Main Revenue of Business	110129754	105578619	11907528
主营业务成本 Main Cost of Business	104668068	100381994	11185096
主营业务税金及附加 Business Tax and Extra Charges	211935	193848	20759
本年应交增值税 Value Added Tax Payable	983558	777148	102080
利润总额 Total Profits	1652730	1628606	292275

批发零售业情况
and Retail Trade by Region

(10000 yuan)

#余杭区 Yuhang	桐庐县 Tonglu	淳安县 Chun'an	建德市 Jiande	富阳市 Fuyang	临安市 Lin'an
5884416	777406	284875	574504	2464111	1086482
329	81	31	57	182	80
10615	2587	3101	2672	4918	3485
2056824	250011	90627	255946	733793	230477
146276	31805	10322	15191	56048	27525
5347174	680222	275882	513785	2171578	909669
5139133	649103	231250	485532	2064204	855985
6852	2857	716	1400	11421	1694
29796	31374	6519	8137	149542	10839
26480	5450	1355	-304	4619	13004

8-09 全市限额以上住宿业和餐饮业

Main Financial Indicators of Lodging and Catering Services

单位:万元

项　　目	Item	法人企业数(个) Number of Enterprises (unit)	年末资产负债 Assets and Liabilities		
			流动资产合计 Circulating Funds	# 存　货 Inventory	固定资产原价 Orginal Value of Fixed Assets
总　计	**Total**	**853**	**1779243**	**125200**	**2559379**
(一)按登记注册类型分组	**Grouped By Registered Type**				
1. 内资企业	**Domestic-funded Enterprises**	**815**	**1185021**	**60947**	**2038793**
国有企业	State-owned Enterprises	69	107216	5118	288308
集体企业	Collective-owned Enterprises	25	24758	928	111262
股份合作企业	Cooperative Enterprises	3	2947	193	2851
联营企业	Joint Ownership Enterprises	3	7980	189	6647
国有联营企业	State Joint Ownership Enterprises	-	-	-	-
集体联营企业	Collective Joint Enterprises	-	-	-	-
国有与集体联营企业	Joint State-collective Enterprises	1	3990	102	6045
其他联营企业	Other Joint Ownership Enterprises	2	3990	87	602
有限责任公司	Limited Liability Corporations	208	429281	15023	959791
国有独资公司	State-funded Corporations	4	32531	769	113056
其他有限责任公司	Other Limited Liability Corporations	204	396751	14253	846735
股份有限公司	Share-holding Corporations Ltd.	16	96897	4454	106981
私营企业	Private Enterprises	488	512534	34471	556319
私营独资企业	Private-funded Enterprises	33	11705	1064	9964
私营合伙企业	Private Partnership Enterprises	11	1980	153	8011
私营有限责任公司	Private Limited Liability Corporations	427	420120	20842	502162
私营股份有限公司	Private Share-holding Corporations Ltd.	17	78729	12413	36181
其他企业	Other Enterprises	3	3408	571	6634
2. 港、澳、台商投资企业	**Enterprises With Investment from Hong Kong, Macao and Taiwan**	**19**	**433188**	**40033**	**357880**
合资经营企业(港或澳、台资)	Joint-venture Enterprises (With Funds from Hong Kong, Macao and Taiwan)	10	384170	39166	299402
合作经营企业(港或澳、台资)	Coorperative Enterprises (With Funds from Hong Kong, Macao and Taiwan)	-	-	-	-
港、澳、台商独资经营企业	Enterprises With Sole Investment from Hong Kong, Macao and Taiwan	9	49018	867	58479
港、澳、台商投资股份有限公司	Share-holding Corporations Ltd. With Investment from Hong Kong, Macao and Taiwan	-	-	-	-
3. 外商投资企业	**Enterprises With Foreign Investment**	**19**	**161034**	**24221**	**162706**
中外合资经营企业	Joint-venture Enterprises	8	133262	22703	117038
中外合作经营企业	Cooperation Enterprises	2	17495	262	24237
外资企业	Enterprises With Sole Foreign Investment	8	10024	1243	21255
外商投资股份有限公司	Share-holding Corporations Ltd. With Foreign Investment	1	254	14	176
(二)按国民经济行业分组	**Grouped By Sector**				
正餐	Dinner	383	401166	38168	283722
快餐	Short Order	19	47674	21577	69118
饮料及冷饮服务	Beverages and Services	15	5027	721	1652
其他餐饮业	Others	11	11789	321	5663

财务状况按注册类型、行业分(2011 年)

Enterprises Above Designated Size by Status of Registration and Sector(2011)

(10000 yuan)

累计折旧 Accumulated Depreciation	#本年折旧 Depreciation	资产总计 Total Assets	负债合计 Total Liabilities	所有者权益合计 Creditors' Equity	实收资本 Capital Hold	#国家资本 State Capital
887827	**130662**	**4357682**	**3009089**	**1348593**	**1601700**	**372394**
695552	**97184**	**3216244**	**2155827**	**1060417**	**1422777**	**354458**
125907	12476	307982	153584	154397	124029	122256
43909	4726	118053	81421	36632	43400	–
1749	216	5057	4005	1052	1150	–
3865	291	10856	3830	7026	5391	3691
–	–	–	–	–	–	–
–	–	–	–	–	–	–
3859	285	6262	1361	4902	3691	3691
6	6	4593	2469	2124	1700	–
279302	43653	1435396	950234	485162	366242	147417
10755	4674	194558	168130	26428	35600	15600
268546	38979	1240838	782104	458734	330642	131817
50291	3811	217175	62415	154760	112028	81073
187154	31665	1111523	893703	217821	767913	21
3404	618	21160	12765	8395	7700	–
2575	279	7824	7505	319	2241	–
168997	27530	961178	782791	178387	740512	21
12178	3239	121362	90643	30719	17460	–
3375	347	10202	6635	3567	2624	–
142054	**14240**	**688855**	**480546**	**208309**	**84447**	**17937**
128333	10682	589002	395459	193543	57381	17937
–	–	–	–	–	–	–
13721	3558	99853	85088	14766	27066	–
–	–	–	–	–	–	–
50222	**19238**	**452583**	**372716**	**79867**	**94476**	**–**
36182	17304	376943	288785	88158	61161	–
4816	612	37769	25297	12472	18850	–
9077	1316	37287	58489	(21201)	13505	–
147	6	584	146	438	960	–
86267	20460	795870	596357	199513	673851	22495
35747	14320	144979	112203	32775	26847	–
1037	150	6413	4193	2221	1855	245
2708	229	15625	6256	9369	3745	21

单位:万元　　　　8－09　续表

项　　目	Item	营业收入 Revenue of Business	主营业务收入 Main Revenue of Business	主营业务税金及附加 Business Tax and Extra Charges
总　　计	**Total**	**2899118**	**2855411**	**137213**
(一)按登记注册类型分组	**Grouped By Registered Type**			
1.内资企业	**Domestic－funded Enterprises**	**1768974**	**1741241**	**94991**
国有企业	State－owned Enterprises	193433	187455	9547
集体企业	Collective－owned Enterprises	41050	40604	2314
股份合作企业	Cooperative Enterprises	3273	3232	180
联营企业	Joint Ownership Enterprises	9329	9329	508
国有联营企业	State Joint Ownership Enterprises	－	－	－
集体联营企业	Collective Joint Enterprises	－	－	－
国有与集体联营企业	Joint State－collective Enterprises	4054	4054	224
其他联营企业	Other Joint Ownership Enterprises	5275	5275	284
有限责任公司	Limited Liability Corporations	522174	512621	27732
国有独资公司	State－funded Corporations	32175	31884	1764
其他有限责任公司	Other Limited Liability Corporations	489999	480737	25969
股份有限公司	Share－holding Corporations Ltd.	101156	100284	5065
私营企业	Private Enterprises	889434	878593	49085
私营独资企业	Private－funded Enterprises	28349	28316	1561
私营合伙企业	Private Partnership Enterprises	6714	6714	359
私营有限责任公司	Private Limited Liability Corporations	656342	648926	36725
私营股份有限公司	Private Share－holding Corporations Ltd.	198030	194637	10440
其他企业	Other Enterprises	9124	9124	560
2.港、澳、台商投资企业	**Enterprises With Investment from Hong Kong, Macao and Taiwan**	**608370**	**596124**	**12844**
合资经营企业(港或澳、台资)	Joint－venture Enterprises (With Funds from Hong Kong, Macao and Taiwan)	583808	572952	11537
合作经营企业(港或澳、台资)	Coorperative Enterprises (With Funds from Hong Kong, Macao and Taiwan)	－	－	－
港、澳、台商独资经营企业	Enterprises With Sole Investment from Hong Kong, Macao and Taiwan	24562	23172	1307
港、澳、台商投资股份有限公司	Share－holding Corporations Ltd. With Investment from Hong Kong, Macao and Taiwan	－	－	－
3.外商投资企业	**Enterprises With Foreign Investment**	**521775**	**518046**	**29378**
中外合资经营企业	Joint－venture Enterprises	452344	450574	25622
中外合作经营企业	Cooperation Enterprises	5072	5072	290
外资企业	Enterprises With Sole Foreign Investment	63418	61460	3413
外商投资股份有限公司	Share－holding Corporations Ltd. With Foreign Investment	941	941	53
(二)按国民经济行业分组	**Grouped By Sector**			
正餐	Dinner	865929	860401	47332
快餐	Short Order	467002	464879	26375
饮料及冷饮服务	Beverages and Services	11871	11703	523
其他餐饮业	Others	23348	22129	983

continued (10000 yuan)

销售费用 Cost of Sales	管理费用 Administration Cost	财务费用 Financil Cost	营业利润 Management Profits	利润总额 Total Profits	应交所得税 Income Taxes Payable	应付职工薪酬（本年贷方累计发生额）Salary Payable to Employees
681418	**489673**	**82630**	**123321**	**142902**	**42892**	**414514**
471909	**383668**	**61434**	**8634**	**28675**	**16171**	**283956**
59651	56046	2580	9380	9693	2271	44691
12866	13861	2356	-2382	-2333	193	6786
1019	757	26	-150	-171	7	748
2750	3650	44	711	712	2	2083
-	-	-	-	-	-	-
-	-	-	-	-	-	-
1328	1642	-10	13	17	2	619
1423	2007	55	698	695	-	1464
149857	146867	26714	-8557	-5733	3390	103921
9757	12389	4145	-3229	-1536	317	7268
140100	134478	22569	-5327	-4197	3073	96653
33396	18009	395	3732	20600	1515	21648
210376	142178	28905	5092	4806	8752	102461
7001	3094	308	955	931	173	3521
1431	774	341	-190	-218	36	791
173808	130882	26005	-16761	-14911	3456	79839
28137	7427	2252	21089	19003	5087	18310
1994	2301	414	807	1100	41	1620
64515	**53095**	**10542**	**76465**	**77197**	**14316**	**39164**
56474	46923	9071	75061	75616	14316	34885
-	-	-	-	-	-	-
8041	6172	1471	1404	1581	-	4280
-	-	-	-	-	-	-
144994	**52910**	**10654**	**38222**	**37030**	**12405**	**91394**
111161	45339	7185	41805	41135	12388	77496
1092	2316	1088	-421	-409	-	1486
32740	5140	2363	-2767	-3318	17	12148
-	115	17	-394	-377	-	264
199240	90306	15339	18961	34172	8598	105250
126765	34293	2098	48393	46605	12478	76104
3037	2752	126	1536	-422	125	1630
2770	2446	15	2530	2528	761	4427

8-10 全市限额以上住宿业和餐饮业经营按登记注册类型分(2011)

Management Conditions of Lodging and Catering Services Enterprises Above Designated Size by Status of Registration(2011)

单位:万元 (10000 yuan)

项目	Item	法人企业(个) Number of Enterprises (unit)	营业收入 Revenue of Business	#客房收入 Revenue of Guest Rooms	#餐饮收入 Revenue of Catering Services	#商品销售收入 Revenue of Goods Sales
总计	**Total**	**853**	**2429123**	**546958**	**1747792**	**21729**
1. 内资企业	**Domestic - funded Enterprises**	**815**	**1754978**	**465507**	**1175510**	**18676**
国有企业	State - owned Enterprises	69	192087	78070	86906	2025
集体企业	Collective - owned Enterprises	25	41603	25473	11545	242
股份合作企业	Cooperative Enterprises	3	3267	1356	1736	17
联营企业	Joint Ownership Enterprises	3	9329	4739	3566	78
国有联营企业	State Joint Ownership Enterprises	-	-	-	-	-
集体联营企业	Collective Joint Enterprises	-	-	-	-	-
国有与集体联营企业	Joint State - collective Enterprises	1	4054	1690	1681	78
其他联营企业	Other Joint Ownership Enterprises	2	5275	3049	1885	-
有限责任公司	Limited Liability Corporations	208	513485	183718	282408	7823
国有独资公司	State - funded Corporations	4	32175	12398	16833	140
其他有限责任公司	Other Limited Liability Corporations	204	481310	171320	265575	7682
股份有限公司	Share - holding Corporations Ltd.	16	101023	17186	77648	2030
私营企业	Private Enterprises	488	885086	153015	704941	6461
私营独资企业	Private - funded Enterprises	33	28618	3209	23891	79
私营合伙企业	Private Partnership Enterprises	11	6702	811	5547	116
私营有限责任公司	Private Limited Liability Corporations	427	654902	137777	493499	6240
私营股份有限公司	Private Share - holding Corporations Ltd.	17	194864	11219	182004	27
其他企业	Other Enterprises	3	9099	1951	6761	-
2. 港、澳、台商投资企业	**Enterprises With Investment from Hong Kong, Macao and Taiwan**	**19**	**156318**	**60358**	**83740**	**170**
合资经营企业(港或澳、台资)	Joint - venture Enterprises (With Funds from Hong Kong, Macao and Taiwan)	10	132035	53506	67415	99
合作经营企业(港或澳、台资)	Coorperative Enterprises (With Funds from Hong Kong, Macao and Taiwan)	-	-	-	-	-
港、澳、台商独资经营企业	Enterprises With Sole Investment from Hong Kong, Macao and Taiwan	9	24284	6852	16325	72
港、澳、台商投资股份有限公司	Share - holding Corporations Ltd. With Investment from Hong Kong, Macao and Taiwan	-	-	-	-	-
3. 外商投资企业	**Enterprises With Foreign Investment**	**19**	**517827**	**21092**	**488542**	**2883**
中外合资经营企业	Joint - venture Enterprises	8	450186	17214	426831	2729
中外合作经营企业	Cooperation Enterprises	2	3886	2488	776	151
外资企业	Enterprises With Sole Foreign Investment	8	62814	1390	59996	3
外商投资股份有限公司	Share - holding Corporations Ltd. With Foreign Investment	1	941	-	941	-

8-11 全市限额以上住宿业和餐饮业经营按国民经济行业分(2011年)

Management Conditions of Lodging and Catering Services Enterprises Above Designated Size by Sector(2011)

单位:万元 (10000 yuan)

项 目	Item	法人企业(个) Number of Enterprises (unit)	营业收入 Revenue of Business	#客房收入 Revenue of Guest Rooms	#餐饮收入 Revenue of Catering Services	#商品销售收入 Revenue of Goods Sales
总 计	**Total**	**853**	**2429123**	**546958**	**1747792**	**21729**
住宿业	**Lodging**	**425**	**1068021**	**517480**	**442728**	**10294**
旅游饭店	Restaurants for Junketing	282	935403	427449	410216	10002
一般旅馆	General Hotel	142	127826	88468	29390	292
其他住宿服务	Other Lodging	1	4792	1563	3122	-
餐饮业	**Catering Services**	**428**	**1361101**	**29478**	**1305064**	**11435**
正餐	Dinner	383	858897	29449	806414	11039
快餐	Short Order	19	466470	-	465001	-
饮料及冷饮服务	Beverages and Services	15	11917	-	11108	397
其他餐饮业	Others Catering Services	11	23817	30	22542	-

8-12 个体工商业登记注册情况(2011年末)
Statistics of Individual Owned Business(End of 2011)

项目	Item	全市 Whole City 合计 Total	全市 Whole City #城镇 Urban	市区 Urban District 合计 Total	市区 Urban District #城镇 Urban
户数(户)	**Number of Households (household)**	**311703**	**227300**	**215618**	**176278**
农、林、牧、渔业	Farming, Forestry, Animal Husbandry and Fishery	4435	1618	3095	1282
采矿业	Mining and Quarrying	95	26	13	2
制造业	Manufacturing	21468	7768	11243	4407
电力、燃气及水的生产和供应业	Production and Supply of Electricity, Gas and Water	110	73	55	46
建筑业	Construction	905	433	519	305
交通运输、仓储和邮政业	Transportation, Storage and Post	6668	3976	3565	2504
信息传输、计算机服务和软件业	Information Transmission, Computer Services and Software	604	491	453	424
批发和零售业	Wholesale and Retail Trade & Catering Services	214017	164212	154361	131160
住宿和餐饮业	Lodging and Catering	26200	19745	16751	14153
房地产业	Real Estate	222	205	198	189
租赁和商务服务业	Renting and Business Service	2439	1989	1855	1522
居民服务和其他服务业	Service for the Residents and Other Service Sector	32559	25119	22230	19145
卫生、社会保障和社会福利业	Health Care, Sports & Social Welfare	344	255	144	126
文化、体育和娱乐业	Culture, Sports and Entertainment	1332	1131	887	799
其他行业	Others	305	259	249	214
从业人员(人)	**Employed Persons(person)**	**703094**	**486803**	**451844**	**372194**
农、林、牧、渔业	Farming, Forestry, Animal Husbandry and Fishery	11477	3535	6362	2314
采矿业	Mining and Quarrying	542	136	36	2
制造业	Manufacturing	74588	23300	26474	8909
电力、燃气及水的生产和供应业	Production and Supply of Electricity, Gas and Water	190	121	67	54
建筑业	Construction	3289	1095	1496	553
交通运输、仓储和邮政业	Transportation, Storage and Post	10165	6426	5237	3898
信息传输、计算机服务和软件业	Information Transmission, Computer Services and Software	1288	1097	967	918

8－12 续表 continued

项　目	Item	全　市 Whole City		市　区 Urban District	
		合　计 Total	#城　镇 Urban	合　计 Total	#城　镇 Urban
批发和零售业	Wholesale and Retail Trade & Catering Services	411366	293073	279495	235138
住宿和餐饮业	Lodging and Catering	71735	57049	44144	38944
房地产业	Real Estate	362	331	321	304
租赁和商务服务业	Renting and Business Service	37429	36456	36051	35367
居民服务和其他服务业	Service for the Residents and Other Service Sector	74957	59440	47791	42745
卫生、社会保障和社会福利业	Health Care, Sports & Social Welfare	846	652	401	363
文化、体育和娱乐业	Culture, Sports and Entertainment	4040	3423	2377	2164
其他行业	Others	820	669	625	521
注册资金(万元)	**Capital Registered (10000 yuan)**	**1952637**	**1440315**	**1184180**	**982619**
农、林、牧、渔业	Farming, Forestry, Animal Husbandry and Fishery	115747	39790	70390	28958
采矿业	Mining and Quarrying	4845	1455	97	27
制造业	Manufacturing	196676	74314	87053	39895
电力、燃气及水的生产和供应业	Production and Supply of Electricity, Gas and Water	589	316	191	146
建筑业	Construction	32675	15650	17456	12803
交通运输、仓储和邮政业	Transportation, Storage and Post	70589	49653	41862	35634
信息传输、计算机服务和软件业	Information Transmission, Computer Services and Software	3047	2438	1957	1860
批发和零售业	Wholesale and Retail Trade & Catering Services	1040135	858661	696944	622822
住宿和餐饮业	Lodging and Catering	220630	186337	130189	119899
房地产业	Real Estate	777	591	725	556
租赁和商务服务业	Renting and Business Service	23172	17205	15529	12054
居民服务和其他服务业	Service for the Residents and Other Service Sector	215462	168756	106233	93416
卫生、社会保障和社会福利业	Health Care, Sports & Social Welfare	3660	2874	1670	1524
文化、体育和娱乐业	Culture, Sports and Entertainment	22863	20803	12558	11945
其他行业	Others	1770	1472	1326	1080

8－13　私营企业登记注册情况（2011年末）
Statistics of Private Owned Business（End of 2011）

项　目	Item	全　市 Whole City		市　区 Urban District	
		合　计 Total	#城　镇 Urban	合　计 Total	#城　镇 Urban
户数（户）	**Number of Households（household）**	**181128**	**130897**	**151937**	**120797**
农、林、牧、渔业	Farming, Forestry, Animal Husbandry and Fishery	2535	873	1512	682
采矿业	Mining and Quarrying	187	34	32	14
制造业	Manufacturing	41123	13894	27220	11037
电力、燃气及水的生产和供应业	Production and Supply of Electricity, Gas and Water	353	79	92	37
建筑业	Construction	8921	7091	7731	6495
交通运输、仓储和邮政业	Transportation, Storage and Post	3166	2131	2735	1932
信息传输、计算机服务和软件业	Information Transmission, Computer Services and Software	9937	9350	9492	9097
批发和零售业	Wholesale and Retail Trade & Catering Services	61830	50236	54591	47198
住宿和餐饮业	Lodging and Catering	2605	2162	2185	1916
房地产业	Real Estate	4824	3780	3831	3123
租赁和商务服务业	Renting and Business Service	23375	21704	21993	20718
居民服务和其他服务业	Service for the Residents and Other Service Sector	8623	7025	7683	6482
卫生、社会保障和社会福利业	Health Care, Sports & Social Welfare	296	237	260	209
文化、体育和娱乐业	Culture, Sports and Entertainment	1206	1118	1089	1042
其他行业	Others	12147	11183	11491	10815
从业人员（人）	**Employed Persons（person）**	**1636678**	**1214413**	**1298511**	**1115203**
农、林、牧、渔业	Farming, Forestry, Animal Husbandry and Fishery	15050	5167	7329	3361
采矿业	Mining and Quarrying	2918	576	673	174
制造业	Manufacturing	433513	143112	208654	108165
电力、燃气及水的生产和供应业	Production and Supply of Electricity, Gas and Water	2696	732	563	377
建筑业	Construction	82797	70108	69625	62124
交通运输、仓储和邮政业	Transportation, Storage and Post	25708	19198	19984	15459
信息传输、计算机服务和软件业	Information Transmission, Computer Services and Software	104428	101099	102481	99769

8－13 续表 continued

项目	Item	全市 Whole City		市区 Urban District	
		合计 Total	#城镇 Urban	合计 Total	#城镇 Urban
批发和零售业	Wholesale and Retail Trade & Catering Services	509538	446990	464568	423586
住宿和餐饮业	Lodging and Catering	31140	28251	26543	24955
房地产业	Real Estate	37906	32859	30109	26888
租赁和商务服务业	Renting and Business Service	211400	202531	201571	194695
居民服务和其他服务业	Service for the Residents and Other Service Sector	63999	55854	57820	51950
卫生、社会保障和社会福利业	Health Care, Sports & Social Welfare	2552	2124	2219	1856
文化、体育和娱乐业	Culture, Sports and Entertainment	10921	10215	9816	9509
其他行业	Others	102112	95597	96556	92335
注册资金(万元)	**Capital Registered (10000 yuan)**	**53905023**	**40983169**	**45297521**	**36980258**
农、林、牧、渔业	Farming, Forestry, Animal Husbandry and Fishery	523747	155662	317722	113350
采矿业	Mining and Quarrying	88200	28782	12457	9990
制造业	Manufacturing	11793513	4387320	7970100	3364579
电力、燃气及水的生产和供应业	Production and Supply of Electricity, Gas and Water	89269	23132	24219	10059
建筑业	Construction	3778339	2998632	3238921	2633692
交通运输、仓储和邮政业	Transportation, Storage and Post	692425	485804	566487	416218
信息传输、计算机服务和软件业	Information Transmission, Computer Services and Software	1884873	1815445	1829867	1792962
批发和零售业	Wholesale and Retail Trade & Catering Services	11220133	9660709	10021076	9049388
住宿和餐饮业	Lodging and Catering	569719	455086	404182	355509
房地产业	Real Estate	5500365	4643338	4444683	3838290
租赁和商务服务业	Renting and Business Service	11880668	11083159	11340455	10674262
居民服务和其他服务业	Service for the Residents and Other Service Sector	1400292	1131517	1223356	1033187
卫生、社会保障和社会福利业	Health Care, Sports & Social Welfare	51108	50036	41830	41168
文化、体育和娱乐业	Culture, Sports and Entertainment	259603	244791	237824	233823
其他行业	Others	4172769	3819756	3624342	3413781

主要统计指标解释

社会消费品零售额 指各种经济类型的批发零售贸易业、住宿餐饮业对城乡居民和社会集团的消费品零售额总和。这个指标反映通过各种商品流通渠道向居民和社会集团供应的生活消费品来满足他们生活需要,是研究人民生活,社会消费品购买力、货币流通等问题的重要指标。社会消费品零售额包括:(1)售给城乡居民作为生活用的商品和修建房屋用的建筑材料;(2)售给机关、团体、学校、部队、企业、事业单位的职工食堂各种食品、燃料;(3)售给部队干部、战士生活用的粮食、副食品、衣着品、日用品、燃料;(4)售给来华的外国人、华侨、港澳台同胞的消费品;(5)售给社会集团的办公用品、纸张、帐册、文印用品、计算工具、书刊杂志和奖品;公共用品和纺织品、针织品;学校用的教学用具;文体用品;非专用的劳动保护用品,如工作服、套袖、围裙、手套、毛巾、肥皂等;日用百货和杂品,包括职工食堂用的餐具、炊具、设备和清洁卫生工具等;家具、设备、日用电器、电讯设备、电影器材和照相器材等;取暖用的设备和燃料、防暑、降温的饮料;非生产经营用的交通工具如小轿车、面包车、工具车、卡车和油料;零星修理的各种零配件、材料、工具、建筑材料等;举办各种招待会、茶话会、宴会用的烟酒茶和各种食品及馈赠的礼品;从公费医疗经费中开支的中、西药品、中药材和医疗器材以及其他非生产性设备和用品。

限额以上批发零售贸易业 指批发贸易业年主营业务收入在2000万元及以上,零售贸易业年主营业务收入在500万元及以上的各种经济类型商贸企业。

商品销售总额 指对本企业(单位)以外的单位和个人出售(包括对国(境)外直接出口)的商品金额。这个指标反映批发零售贸易业在国内市场上销售商品以及出口商品的总量。商品销售总额包括:(1)售给城乡居民和社会集体团消费用的商品;(2)售给工业、农业、建筑业、运输邮电业、批发零售贸易业、餐饮业、服务业等作为生产、经营使用的商品;(3)售给批发零售贸易业作为转卖或加工后转卖的商品;(4)对国(境)外直接出口的商品,不包括:出售本企业(单位)自用的废旧包装用品,未通过买卖行为付出的商品,经本单位介绍,由买卖双方直接结算,本单位只收取手续费的业务,购货退出的商品以及商品损耗和损失等。

Explanatory Notes on Main Statistical Indicators

Total Retail Sales of Consumer Goods referring to the sum of retail sales of consumer goods sold by wholesale and retail, catering and lodging to urban and rural residents and social groups. This indicator is used to show the supply of consumer goods through various channels to households and institutions, and is very important for the study on people's livelihood, on the purchasing power of consumer goods and on the circulation of money. The retail sales of consumer goods include: (1) commodities sold to urban and rural residents for their daily use and building materials sold to them for the construction or repair of houses; (2) food and fuels sold to canteens of institutions, enterprises, schools and military units; (3) grains and non-staple food, clothing, daily articles and fuels sold to military personnel; (4) consumer goods sold to foreigners, overseas Chinese, and Chinese compatriots form Taiwan, Hong Kong and Macao during their stay in the mainland of China; (5) commodities sold to social groups. included under this heading arc : office appliances, paper, account books, printing articles, calculaters, newspapers, magazines and prizes; public articles, textiles and knitgoods; realias for schools; cultural and sports articles; working articles for unspecial use i. e. working clothes, raglan sleeves, gloves, towels and soaps; commidities and miscellaneous goods for daily use i. e. dishwares, cookers and cleaning articles for canteens of institutions, enterprises, schools; furnishings, appliances, communications facilities , film and photograph equipments and materials; heating facilities, fuels and beverages; vehicles (exclude for business use) such as cars, microbuses, trucks and oils; parts , fittings, instruments and building materials, tobaccoes, alcohols, teas, foods for all kinds of reception meetings and banquets and prizes for presenting; Chinese and Western medicines, herbs and medical facilities expenditured by medical insurance fund and other non - production goods and equipments.

Wholesale And Retail Trade Above Designated Size wholesale trade, with year main business revenue over 20 million yuan of different status of registration; retail sale trade, with year main business revenue over 5 million yuan of different status of registration.

Total Sales of Commodities refer to selling of commodities by the establishments to other establishments and individuals (including direct export). This indictor is used to show the total value of sales of commodities at domestic markets and export. The total sales include: (1) commodities sold to urban and rural residents and social groups for their consumption; (2) commodities sold to establishments in industry, agriculture, construction, transportation, post and telecommunications, wholesale and retail trades, catering trade and public utility for their production and operation; (3) commodities sold to wholesale and retail establishment for re - selling, with or without further processing; and (4) commodities for direct export to other countries. Excluded are selling of waste packaging materials used by the establishments (units) themselves, commodities transferred without buying or selling procedures, commission income from brokerage in transactions whose settlement is directly handled by buyers and sellers, rejected commodities in the purchase, loss in commodities, etc.

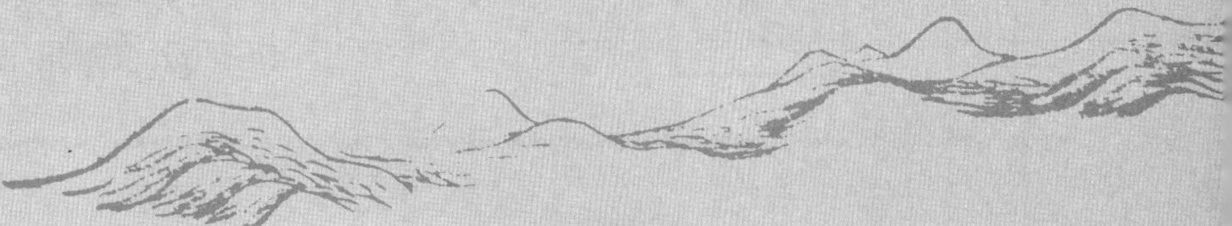

第 九 篇
CHAPTER-9

对外经济、旅游
FOREIGN TRADE AND TOURISM

9

对外经济、旅游
Foreign Trade and Tourism

主要统计指标
Major Statistical Indicators

协议利用外资金额	Total Contracted Foreign Investments	81.71	亿美元	(USD 100 million)
为上年	As Compared with the Preceding Year	106.0	%	(%)
实际利用外资金额	Foreign Investments Actually Used	47.22	亿美元	(USD 100 million)
为上年	As Compared with the Preceding Year	108.4	%	(%)
进出口总额	Total Imports and Exports	639.72	亿美元	(USD 100 million)
为上年	As Compared with the Preceding Year	122.2	%	(%)
# 出口总额	Total Exports	415.21	亿美元	(USD 100 million)
为上年	As Compared with the Preceding Year	117.5	%	(%)
接待境外旅游	Number of Foreign Tourists	306.31	万人次	(10000 person-times)
为上年	As Compared with the Preceding Year	111.1	%	(%)
旅游外汇收入	Total Foreign Exchange Earnings from International Tourism	19.6	亿美元	(USD 100 million)
为上年	As Compared with the Preceding Year	115.8	%	(%)

9－01 主要年份外商直接投资情况
Foreign Direct Investment in Main Years

单位：万美元 (USD 10000)

年份 Year	项目个数(个) Number of Projects (unit)	协议总投资额 Total Investments of Agreements	协议利用外资金额 Foreign Investments of Agreements	实际利用外资金额 Foreign Investments Actually Used
1978				
1979				
1980	3	153	128	
1981				
1982				
1983	2	356	100	
1984	9	6932	2697	
1985	21	6638	1731	907
1986	9	5722	2017	683
1987	10	2685	1256	1470
1988	23	6781	2734	696
1989	34	3897	1569	1860
1990	68	7817	3951	751
1991	121	11107	5551	2129
1992	583	125224	60915	9678
1993	1078	222325	121947	35713
1994	624	174406	110541	41098
1995	427	136662	90207	42659
1996	221	108150	70982	53651
1997	174	51682	27888	41187
1998	216	98219	51400	38425
1999	212	83416	56742	42025
2000	315	89781	64548	43093
2001	483	154447	103023	50324
2002	587	247888	96720	52186
2003	869	432660	200104	100850
2004	802	629727	307746	140982
2005	756	770941	400503	171274
2006	747	1080602	537986	225536
2007	574	854907	558059	280181
2008	483	862523	622788	331154
2009	554	948323	696486	401370
2010	545	1188055	770911	435627
2011	500	1291015	817108	472230

9-02 外商直接投资分行业情况(2011年)
Foreign Direct Investment by Sector(2011)

单位:万美元 (USD 10,000)

行业 Sector	项目数(个) Projects (unit)	占总数% Proportion (%)	合同外资 Total Contracted Foreign Investments	占总数% Proportion (%)	实际引资 Foreign Investments Actually Used	占总数(%) Proportion (%)
合计 Total	**500**	**100.00**	**817108**	**100.00**	**472230**	**100.00**
第一产业 Primary Industry			**46**	**0.01**	**4487**	**0.95**
农业 Agriculture					2771	0.59
第二产业 Secondary Industry	**176**	**35.20**	**310499**	**37.99**	**183224**	**38.79**
采矿业 Mining & Quarrying			1148	0.14	1910	0.40
制造业 Manufacturing	169	33.80	295395	36.15	178279	37.75
电子 Electronics	2	0.40	3550	0.43	2836	0.60
建筑业 Construction	5	1.00	10406	1.27	199	0.04
第三产业 Tertiary Industry	**324**	**64.80**	**506563**	**62.01**	**284519**	**60.25**
交通运输、仓储、邮电通信业 Transportation, Storage and Post	3	0.60	20645	2.53	4165	0.88
信息传输、计算机服务和软件业 Information Transmission, Computer Service and Software	64	12.80	98231	12.02	29547	6.26
批发和零售贸易、餐饮业 Whole sale and Retail Tvade. Catering Services	112	22.40	68358	8.37	41223	8.73
房地产业 Real Estate	14	2.80	170062	20.81	162787	34.47
租赁及商务服务业 Renting and Business Service	50	10.00	62228	7.62	21962	4.65
科学研究和综合技术服务业 Scientific research and comprehensive technology Services	69	13.80	73294	8.97	21136	4.48
其他行业 Others	12	2.40	13745	1.69	3699	0.78

9-03 外商投资企业分国别(地区)情况(2011年)

Foreign - Funded Enterprises by Region or Territory(2011)

单位:万美元 (USD 10000)

国别(地区)	Country (territory)	历年累计 Accumulated			2011年 In Year 2011			
		项目(个) Projects (unit)	总投资额 Total Investments	协议外资金额 Total Contracted Foreign Investments	项目(个) Projects (unit)	总投资额 Total Investments	协议外资金额 Total Contracted Foreign Investments	实际引资 Foreign Investments Actually Used
合计	**Total**	**11081**	**9609552**	**5791603**	**500**	**1291015**	**817108**	**472230**
#香港	#Hong Kong	4611	5192412	3262910	263	870084	587906	331261
澳门	Macao	67	69947	39817	1	10680	5395	3845
台湾	Taiwan	1376	320943	169357	22	19352	5323	2982
日本	Japan	699	401145	197589	29	41670	15100	15970
美国	U. S. A	1459	842218	474178	64	60196	31523	13213
新加坡	Singapore	281	360432	204082	14	81831	40405	21517
澳大利亚	Australia	172	86111	52567	5	12549	10561	599
泰国	Thailand	36	12762	3446		-37	-37	14
意大利	Italy	193	128097	61008	5	23751	6364	3377
荷兰	Netherlands	79	65254	24334	3	687	3699	1945
西班牙	Spain	65	57312	22966	4	-70	531	2944
马来西亚	Malaysia	72	29351	15730	2	79	80	79
韩国	Republic of Korea	279	84664	49140	13	7362	6378	1258
法国	France	112	68271	36926	3	3745	3114	2580
玻利维亚	Bolivia	12	1770	1262	-	-	-	-
加拿大	Canada	184	83192	50284	10	9135	3859	570
英国	Britain	168	168694	92146	6	8811	7300	1593
奥地利	Austria	20	13094	6612	-	-	-	44
波兰	Poland	4	240	147	-	-	-	-
洪都拉斯	Honduras	6	1118	563	-	-	-	-
德国	Germany	183	94946	49623	7	5932	5396	761
英属维尔京群岛	The British Virgin Islands	514	997580	556044	19	69404	43436	30161

9-04 外商直接投资分区县(市)情况

Foreign Direct Investment by Region

单位:万美元 (USD 10000)

区 域	Region	批准项目数(个) Number of Projects(unit)		协议利用外资金额 Total Contracted Foreign Investments		实际利用外资金额 Foreign Investments Actually Used	
		2011 年 In Year 2011	历年累计 Accumulated Until the End of 2011	2011 年 In Year 2011	历年累计 Accumulated Until the End of 2011	2011 年 In Year 2011	历年累计 Accumulated Until the End of 2011
全 市	**Total**	**500**	**11081**	**817108**	**5791603**	**472230**	**3018000**
市 区	Urban District	441	9200	701632	4978505	405378	2634693
上 城	Shangcheng	30	574	42568	313162	17726	149097
下 城	Xiacheng	23	658	58516	305246	27589	139002
江 干	Jianggan	27	588	50829	329226	21838	126405
拱 墅	Gongshu	33	793	51742	357474	54028	212661
西 湖	Xihu	52	807	51712	331423	23620	178124
高新(滨江)区	Hi-Tech(Binjiang)	50	887	93699	616592	57502	384524
萧 山	Xiaoshan	73	1337	90105	559710	48019	293702
余 杭	Yuhang	73	1288	79620	499751	41816	233611
桐 庐	Tonglu	25	463	23154	146709	13093	70631
淳 安	Chun'an	10	168	21256	140026	10271	62927
建 德	Jiande	9	209	10900	95471	3278	28074
富 阳	Fuyang	9	653	36135	263915	26074	137161
临 安	Lin'an	6	388	24031	166977	14136	84514

9－05 国内招商引资分区县(市)情况
Domestic Attract Investment by Region

单位:亿元 (100 million yuan)

区 域 Region	批准项目数(个) Number of Projects(unit)		实际引进资金 Foreign Investments Actually Used	
	2011 年 In Year 2011	2010 年 In Year 2010	2011 年 In Year 2011	2010 年 In Year 2010
全 市 Total	**3766**	**5847**	**720.57**	**650.27**
市 区 Urban District	2482	5621	610.88	552.27
上 城 Shangcheng	265	381	75.56	71.51
下 城 Xiacheng	598	905	92.45	84.73
江 干 Jianggan	296	351	83.54	73.87
拱 墅 Gongshu	896	2083	92.94	83.21
西 湖 Xihu	658	990	80.96	71.43
高新(滨江)区 Hi－Tech(Binjiang)	303	276	68.08	66.98
萧 山 Xiaoshan	194	240	49.98	43.17
余 杭 Yuhang	127	148	38.18	32.08
桐 庐 Tonglu	89	69	21.83	19.47
淳 安 Chun'an	60	48	21.78	19.47
建 德 Jiande	45	50	22.15	19.36
富 阳 Fuyang	42	32	22.04	20.02
临 安 Lin'an	48	27	21.89	19.68

9-06 国家级开发区建设发展情况(2011 年末)

The Construction of National - Class Development Zones(End of 2011)

项　目	Item	合计 Total	杭州经济技术开发区 Hangzhou Economic and Technological Development Zone	杭州高新技术开发区 Hangzhou High - tech Development Zone	杭州之江国家旅游度假区 Hangzhou Zhijiang National Tourism and Holiday Resort	萧山经济技术开发区 Xiaoshan Economic and Technological Development Zone
规划面积(平方公里)	Area of planning (sq. km)	372.74	34	12.64	156	170.1
已开发面积(平方公里)	Area of Development (sq. km)	87.6	41.16	12.64	11.74	22.06
有偿出让土地面积(平方公里)	Area of Being Sold (sq. km)	57.31	18.29	9.59	9.19	20.24
累计由开发区投入基础设施款(亿元)	Investments in Infrastructure (100 million yuan)	577.31	240.38	167.27	95.51	74.15
年末批准进区企业(个)	Number of Enterprises Approved (unit)	11939	4781	6259		899
其中:三资企业(个)	Foreign Investments Enter - prises (unit)	1771	646	491	90	544
累计协议利用外资(亿美元)	Foreign Investments of Agree-ments (USD 100 million)	209.44	89.16	60.88	16.6	42.8
累计实际利用外资(亿美元)	Foreign Investments Actually Used (USD 100 million)	120.06	48.21	36.95	10.1	24.8
年末投产企业个数(个)	Number of Enterprises in Pro-duction or Operation (unit)	6456	2450	1780		2226
当年销售收入(亿元)	Sales Revenue (100 million yuan)	4337.67	1500.98	2200	6.69	630
当年工业总产值(现价)(亿元)	Gross Industrial Output Value (100 million yuan)	3547.84	1499.91	1365	52.93	630
当年实现利税(亿元)	Fulfilled Profits and Tax (100 million yuan)	504.97	183.97	271.00		50.00
当年出口创汇(亿美元)	Foreign Exchange Earmings of Export (USD 100 million)	102.61	52.61	32.00		18
当年财政收入(亿元)	Financial Revenue (100 million yuan)	204.46	92.64	54.3	10.02	47.5

9-07 主要年份进出口情况
Imports and Exports in Main Years

单位:亿美元 (USD 100 million)

年份 Year	进出口 Exports And Imports 总值 Total Value	进出口 为上年% As Compared with the Preceding Year(%)	出口 Exports 总值 Total Value	出口 为上年% As Compared with the Preceding Year(%)	进口 Imports 总值 Total Value	进口 为上年% As Compared with the Preceding Year(%)
1978						
1979						
1980						
1981						
1982						
1983						
1984						
1985						
1986						
1987						
1988						
1989	0.84		0.50		0.34	
1990	1.45	172.6	0.99	198.0	0.46	135.3
1991	2.18	150.3	1.48	149.5	0.70	152.2
1992	3.42	156.9	2.16	146.0	1.26	180.0
1993	8.73	255.3	4.92	227.8	3.81	302.4
1994	34.96	400.5	26.11	530.7	8.85	232.3
1995	45.18	129.2	33.18	127.1	12.00	135.6
1996	43.52	96.3	31.11	93.8	12.41	103.4
1997	48.83	112.2	37.43	120.3	11.40	91.8
1998	59.73	122.3	44.16	118.0	15.57	136.6
1999	73.40	122.9	50.79	115.0	22.61	145.3
2000	104.76	142.7	69.65	137.1	35.11	155.3
2001	112.98	107.9	72.84	104.6	40.14	114.3
2002	131.07	116.0	84.81	116.4	46.26	115.3
2003	182.38	139.2	109.55	129.2	72.83	157.4
2004	244.96	134.3	151.75	138.6	93.21	128.0
2005	298.70	121.9	198.04	130.5	100.66	108.0
2006	389.09	130.3	262.28	132.4	126.81	126.0
2007	434.26	111.7	299.66	114.3	134.60	106.2
2008	480.65	110.7	336.14	112.2	144.51	107.4
2009	404.20	84.1	271.80	80.9	132.40	91.6
2010	523.55	129.5	353.37	130.0	170.18	128.6
2011	639.72	122.2	415.21	117.5	224.50	131.9

9－08 进出口情况(2011年)
Imports and Exports(2011)

单位:亿美元 (USD 100 million)

项目	Item	2011年 In Year 2011	2010年 In Year 2010	为上年(%) As Compared with year 2010 (%)
全市进出口总值(海关口径)	Total Exports And Imports	639.72	523.55	122.2
一、出口总额	Exports	415.21	353.40	117.5
1.国有企业	State－owned Enterprises	83.87	79.14	106.0
2.三资企业	Foreign Investment Enterprises	138.89	121.03	114.8
(1)中外合作企业	Cooperation Enterprises	0.99	0.97	102.2
(2)中外合资企业	Joint－Venture Enterprises	67.49	56.15	120.2
(3)外商独资企业	Enterprises With Sole Foreign Investment	70.40	63.91	110.2
3.集体企业	Collective－owned Enterprises	17.46	15.30	114.1
4.私营企业	Private Enterprises	174.33	137.43	126.9
二、进口总额	Imports	224.50	170.20	131.9

9－09 外贸出口分区县(市)情况(2011 年)
Export of Foreign Trade by Region(2011)

单位:万美元 (USD 10000)

区 域	Region	出口总值 Exports of This Year	为上年(%) As Compared with the Preceding Year(%)	进口总值 Imports of This Year	为上年(%) As Compared with the Preceding Year(%)
全市合计	**Total**	**4152147**	**117.5**	**2245033**	**131.9**
#不含省属	#Non－provincial	3442122	120.3	1947466	137.8
上 城	Shangcheng	119446	118.7	125834	135.5
下 城	Xiacheng	154594	122.8	188393	132.8
江 干	Jianggan	133205	111.2	22421	126.2
拱 墅	Gongshu	83354	125.0	34004	100.7
西 湖	Xihu	167388	111.0	62107	109.9
高新(滨江)区	Hi－Tech(Binjiang)	319968	133.7	102646	135.8
萧 山	Xiaoshan	898382	121.2	534360	135.8
余 杭	Yuhang	433972	123.5	50930	132.9
桐 庐	Tonglu	86226	130.6	7238	99.6
淳 安	Chun'an	15893	129.5	4566	75.2
建 德	Jiande	86265	112.8	19498	96.7
富 阳	Fuyang	99450	126.3	117125	133.0
临 安	Lin'an	109619	128.8	23110	199.0

9－10　出口企业自营出口前20位排名(2011年)
The List of First Twenty Export Enterprises(2011)

单位:万美元　　(USD 10000)

企业名称	Name of Enterprises	位次 Ranks	出口额 Export Value
东芝信息机器(杭州)有限公司	Toshiba Information Equipment (Hangzhou) Co., Ltd.	1	132545
杭州中策橡胶有限公司	Hangzhou Zhongce Rubber Co. Ltd.	2	102035
杭州华三通信技术有限公司	H3C	3	56204
杭州正泰太阳能科技有限公司	Hangzhou Astronergy Solar energy Technology Co., Ltd.	4	55980
杭州巨星科技有限公司	Hangzhou Greatstar Indnserial Co., Ltd.	5	31844
杭州市轻工工艺纺织品进出口有限公司	Hangzhou Hardicrafts and Textiles Import and Export Corporation	6	30531
博世电动工具(中国)有限公司	Bosch Power Tools(China) Co., Ltd	7	26137
杭州市矢崎配件有限公司	HZ YAZAKI	8	25647
松下电化住宅设备机器(杭州)有限公司	Hangzhou Panasonic Home Appliances Washing Machine Co., Ltd.	9	22015
杭州松下住宅电器设备有限公司	Hangzhou Panasonic Home Appliances Co., Ltd.	10	21744
杭州余杭国际贸易有限公司	Hangzhou Yuhang International Trade Co., Ltd.	11	21634
汇孚集团有限公司	Wellfull Group Co., Ltd.	12	20011
浙江恒逸石化股份有限公司	Zhejiang HengYi Petroleum &Chemical Co., Ltd.	13	19058
浙江新安化工集团股份有限公司	Zhejiang Wynca Chemical Group Co., Ltd.	14	18975
杭州余杭对外贸易有限公司	Hangzhou Yuhang Foreign Trade Co., Ltd.	15	18522
浙江物产国际贸易有限公司	Zhejiang Materials Industny International Co., Ltd.	16	18191
杭州鼎胜进出口有限公司	Hangzhou Dingsheng Import&export Co., Ltd.	17	17144
西子奥的斯电梯有限公司	XiZi Otis Elevator Co., Ltd.	18	17112
浙江杭叉进出口有限公司	Zhejiang HC forklift Import&export Co., Ltd.	19	15781
汉帛(中国)有限公司	Hempel (China) Co. Ltd.	20	15120

9－11 外贸出口主要国别（地区）情况

Export of Foreign Trade by Main Country or Territory

单位:万美元 (USD 10000)

国别（地区）	Country (territory)	2011年 In Year 2011	2010年 In Year 2010	为上年(%) As Compared with the Preceding Year(%)
合 计	**Total**	**4152147**	**3533740**	**117.5**
#香港	#Hong Kong	909245	105078	86.5
台湾	Taiwan	42503	39472	107.7
德国	Germany	254757	229663	110.9
日本	Japan	375692	314672	119.5
美国	U.S.A	778389	714107	109.0
新加坡	Singapore	46405	38629	120.2
澳大利亚	Australia	92366	82154	112.4
泰国	Thailand	50005	35377	141.4
意大利	Italy	148683	127546	116.6
荷兰	Netherlands	142570	105981	134.5
西班牙	Spain	71722	68243	105.1
马来西亚	Malaysia	36772	31966	115.0
韩国	Republic of Korea	91267	69125	132.0
法国	France	103080	88559	116.4
比利时	Belgium	53609	44027	121.7
加拿大	Canada	80000	70324	113.7
英国	Britain	147410	133192	110.7
印度尼西亚	Indonesia	66332	44838	147.9
丹麦	Denmark	29398	26606	110.5
俄罗斯	Russia	96067	71042	135.3

9-12 主要年份旅游事业发展情况
Development of Tourism in Main Years

年 份 Year	旅游总收入（亿元）Total Tourism Revenue (100 million yuan)	国内旅游收入（亿元）Domestic Earnings (100 million yuan)	旅游外汇收入（亿美元）Foreign Exchange Earnings from International Tourism (USD 100 million)	旅游总人数（万人次）Total Tourists (10000 person-times)	国内游客人数（万人次）Domestic Tourists (10000 person-times)
1978			0.07		
1979			0.10		
1980			0.11		
1981			0.13		
1982			0.13		
1983			0.14		
1984			0.15		
1985			0.23		
1986			0.36		
1987			0.38		
1988			0.47		
1989			0.23		
1990			0.48		
1991			0.66		
1992			0.86		
1993			0.80		
1994			1.01		
1995	106.0	94.3	1.45	2148	2104
1996	136.5	122.6	1.67	2055	2009
1997	158.8	142.1	2.01	2150	2100
1998	163.4	146.0	2.10	2172	2121
1999	186.0	166.7	2.37	2266	2207
2000	214.3	190.0	2.92	2376	2305
2001	249.7	218.9	3.37	2592	2510
2002	294.4	254.8	4.77	2758	2652
2003	325.9	290.9	4.22	2862	2776
2004	410.1	361.2	5.97	3139	3016
2005	465.1	403.6	7.58	3417	3266
2006	543.7	471.2	9.09	3864	3682
2007	630.1	548.6	11.19	4320	4112
2008	707.2	617.2	12.96	4773	4552
2009	803.1	708.9	13.80	5324	5094
2010	1025.7	910.9	16.90	6581	6305
2011	1191.0	1063.8	19.60	7487	7181

9-13 主要年份境外旅游者人数

Number of International Tourists in Main Years

单位:人次 (person-times)

年份 Year	合计 Total	外国人 Foreigners	华侨 Overseas Chinese	港澳台同胞 Compatriots from Hong Kong, Macao and Taiwan	平均逗留天数 Average days of Staying
1978	53475	728	728	26648	
1979	84914	44714	1069	39131	2.59
1980	124960	61710	1868	61382	2.70
1981	154745	87727	2004	65014	2.71
1982	152897	89100	2483	61314	2.49
1983	160564	97803	3136	59625	2.18
1984	179200	105771	2514	70915	2.12
1985	238385	156311	7011	75063	2.18
1986	266370	170960	8318	87092	2.38
1987	300603	183477	17048	100078	2.38
1988	349246	149512	39989	159745	2.08
1989	248502	66094	18819	163589	2.08
1990	388345	86621	33593	268131	2.09
1991	390197	136809	23698	229690	2.00
1992	489578	183781	38541	267256	2.03
1993	459620	199796	25184	234640	2.06
1994	337362	201692	11324	124346	2.10
1995	441262	249418	14608	177236	2.06
1996	462313	273477	9991	178845	2.07
1997	504276	288949	10060	205267	2.20
1998	507243	261353	14281	231609	2.20
1999	591853	324625	9250	257978	2.09
2000	707148	400906	-	306242	2.15
2001	819438	447689	-	371749	2.41
2002	1056266	631576	-	424690	2.50
2003	861163	482073	-	379090	2.72
2004	1234063	791616	-	442447	2.59
2005	1513585	1020840	-	492745	2.63
2006	1820171	1236792	-	583379	2.57
2007	2085997	1453650	-	632347	2.67
2008	2213329	1543665	-	669654	2.73
2009	2304045	1572838	-	731207	2.87
2010	2757147	1878528	-	878619	2.94
2011	3063140	2108263	-	954877	2.96

注:从1995年起为全市数。

a) Data in this table has included the tourists of whole municipality since 1995.

9－14　接待境外游客及旅游外汇收入情况
Number of International Tourists and Foreign Exchange Earnings

项　　目	Item	2011 年 In Year 2011	2010 年 In Year 2010	为上年(%) As Compared with the preceding year(%)
全年接待人数总计(人)	**Number of Foreign Tourists(person)**	**3063140**	**2757147**	**111.1**
#外国人	#Foreigners	2108263	1878528	112.2
港澳台同胞	Compatriots From Hong Kong, Macao and Taiwan	954877	878619	108.7
全年接待人天数(人天)	**Total Person－days (person－days)**	**9071404**	**8106012**	**111.9**
#外国人	#Foreigners	6069395	5297569	114.6
港澳台同胞	Compatriots From Hong Kong, Macao and Taiwan	3002009	2802212	107.1
平均逗留天数(天)	**Average Days of Staying (days)**	**2.96**	**2.94**	**100.7**
#外国人	#Foreigners	2.88	2.82	102.1
港澳台同胞	Compatriots From Hong Kong, Macao and Taiwan	3.14	3.19	98.4
旅游外汇总收入(万美元)	**Total Foreign Exchange Earnings From International Tourism (USD 10000)**	**195710**	**169008**	**115.8**

9－15 接待境外游客分国别(地区)情况

Number of International Tourists by Country or Territory

单位:人次 (person－times)

国 别(地区)	Country(territory)	2011年 In Year 2011	2010年 In Year 2010	为上年(%) As Compared with the Preceding Year(%)
合 计	**Total**	**3063140**	**2757147**	**111.1**
#香港	#Hong Kong	360291	332626	108.3
澳门	Macao	30742	22095	139.1
台湾	Taiwan	563844	523898	107.6
日本	Japan	321892	334880	96.1
美国	U. S. A	190442	163485	116.5
新加坡	Singapore	74363	62777	118.5
澳大利亚	Australia	38160	34189	111.6
泰国	Thailand	69303	64023	108.2
意大利	Italy	27658	27690	99.9
荷兰	Netherlands	21454	15831	135.5
西班牙	Spain	26374	24271	108.7
马来西亚	Malaysia	99259	94393	105.2
韩国	Republic of Korea	507422	478999	105.9
法国	France	47290	41533	113.9
德国	Germany	60498	56168	107.7
加拿大	Canada	36993	33884	109.2
英国	Britain	46832	41898	111.8
印度尼西亚	Indonesia	29349	31633	92.8
印度	India	24057	20782	115.8
菲律宾	Filipine	11701	11303	103.5

主要统计指标解释

外商直接投资 是指外国企业和经济组织或个人(包括华侨、港澳台胞以及我国在境外注册的企业)按我国有关政策、法规,用现汇、实物、技术等在我国境内开办外商独资企业、与我国境内的企业或经济组织共同举办中外合资经营企业、合作经营企业或者合作开发资源的投资(包括外商投资收益的再投资)以及经政府有关部门批准的项目投资总额内,企业从境外借入的资金。

进出口总额 海关进出口总额指实际进出我国国境的货物总金额。包括对外贸易实际进出口货物,来料加工装配进出口货物,国家间、联合国及国际组织无偿援助物资和赠送品,华侨、港澳台同胞和外籍华人捐赠品,租赁期满归承租人所有的租赁货物,进料加工进出口货物,边境地方贸易及边境地区小额贸易进出口货物(边民互市贸易除外),中外合资经营企业、中外合作经营企业、外商独资经营企业进出口货物和公用物品,到、离岸价格在规定限额以上的进出口货样和广告品(无商业价值、无使用价值和免费提供出口的除外),从保税仓库提取在中国境内销售的进口货物,以及其他进出口货物。进出口总额以观察一个国家在对外贸易方面的总规模。我国规定出口货物按离岸价格统计,进口货物按到岸价格统计。

境外旅游人数 指来我国参观、访问、旅行、探亲、访友、休养、考察、参加会议和从事经济、科技、文化、教育、体育、宗教等活动的外国人、华侨、港澳和台湾同胞的人数。不包括外国在我国的常驻机构,如使领馆、通讯社、企业办事处的工作人员;来我国常住的外国专家、留学生以及在岸逗留不过夜人员。

境外旅游(外汇)收入 指入境旅游的外国人、华侨、港澳台同胞在中国大陆旅游过程中发生的一切旅游支出,对国家来说就是境外旅游(外汇)收入。

Explanatory Notes on Main Statistical Indicators

Direct Investment by Foreign Entrepreneurs refers to the investments inside China by foreign enterprises and economic organizations or individuals (including overseas Chinese, compatriots from Hong Kong, Macao and Taiwan, and Chinese enterprises registered abroad) , following the relevant policies and laws of China, for the establishment of ventures exclusively with foreign own investment, Sino – foreign joint ventures and cooperative enterprises or for co – operative exploration of resources with enterprises or economic organizations in China. It includes the re – investment of the foreign entrepreneurs with the profits gained from the investment and the funds that enterprises borrow from abroad in the total investment of projects which are approved by the relevant department of the government.

Total Imports and Exports at Customs refer to the value of commodities imported into and exported from the boundary of China. They include the actual imports and exports through foreign trade, imported and exported goods under the processing and assembling trades and materials, supplies and gifts as aid given gratis between governments and by the United Nations and other international organizations, and contributions donated by overseas Chinese, compatriots in Hong Kong, Macao and Chinese foreign citizenship, leasing commodities owned by tenant at the expiration of leasing period, the imported and exported commodities processed with imported materials, commodities trading in border areas (excluding mutual exchange goods) , the imported and exported commodities and articles for public use of the Sino – foreign joint ventures, cooperative enterprises and ventures exclusively with foreign own investment. Also included are import or export of samples and advertising goods for whose CIF or FOB value are beyond the permitted ceiling (excluding goods of no trading or use value and free commodities for export) , imported goods sold in China from bonded warehouses and other imported or exported goods. The indicator of the total imports and exports at customs can be used to observe the total size of external trade in a country. In accordance with the stipulation of Chinese government, imports are calculated at CIF, while exports are calculated at FOB.

International Tourists refer to foreigners, overseas Chinese compatriots from Hong Kong, Macao and Taiwan coming to China for sightseeing, visits, tours, family reunions, vacations, study tours, conferences and other activities of a business, scientific and technological, cultural, educational and religious nature. It does not include representatives and employees of resident institutions of foreign countries in China such as embassies, consulates, news agencies and offices of foreign companies and organizations, nor does it include long – term foreign experts or students residing in China, or persons in transition without spending a night in China.

Foreign Exchange Earnings from International Tourism refer to the total expenditures of foreigners, overseas Chinese, Chinese compatriots from Hong Kong, Macao and Taiwan during their stay in the mainland of China, which are earnings of foreign exchange form international tourism from the point of vies from China.

第 十 篇
CHAPTER-10

财政、金融、保险
FINANCE,BANKING AND INSURANCE

10 财政、金融、保险
Finance, Banking and Insurance

主要统计指标
Major Statistical Indicators

全市财政总收入	Total Financial Revenue	1488.92	亿元	(100 million yuan)
为上年	As Compared with the Preceding Year	119.6	%	(%)
地方财政收入	Financial Revenue of Local Government	785.15	亿元	(100 million yuan)
为上年	As Compared with the Preceding Year	117.0	%	(%)
地方财政支出	Financial Expenditure of Local Government	747.5	亿元	(100 million yuan)
为上年	As Compared with the Preceding Year	121.2	%	(%)
年末金融机构各项存款余额	Balance of Deposits of Financial Institutions at Year-end	18396.57	亿元	(100 million yuan)
为上年	As Compared with the Preceding Year	108.6	%	(%)
#城乡居民储蓄存款余额	Balance of Savings Deposits of Rural and Urban Residents at Year-end	5547.48	亿元	(100 million yuan)
为上年	As Compared with the Preceding Year	111.5	%	(%)
年末金融机构各项贷款余额	Balance of Loans of Financial Institutions at Year-end	16573.74	亿元	(100 million yuan)
为上年	As Compared with the Preceding Year	111.2	%	(%)

10－01 主要年份财政收入及支出

Financial Revenue and Expenditure in Main Years

单位:万元 (10000 yuan)

年 份 Year	财政收入 Financial Revenue		财政支出 Financial Expenditure	
	全 市 Total	市 区 Urban District	全 市 Total	市 区 Urban District
1978	94102	73396	16170	7779
1979	103259	81885	20334	11289
1980	118529	94015	21726	11867
1981	128564	100645	23964	13891
1982	140510	107298	24945	13687
1983	153941	116559	32765	17822
1984	172996	130757	46937	28710
1985	186472	131923	57710	35435
1986	205952	141943	73213	43959
1987	226262	152268	70717	41011
1988	246961	161208	95655	53031
1989	255003	156649	113571	61534
1990	252503	149904	118167	62587
1991	267597	158130	123134	62403
1992	286394	168341	132814	65984
1993	394946	233670	185168	90545
1994	484597	300014	215415	102430
1995	551262	339828	249050	120084
1996	635334	414557	302390	151016
1997	740725	485650	363834	197054
1998	869824	585615	424478	237221
1999	1026577	689394	563524	335243
2000	1428519	970937	734328	445698
2001	1884608	1612225	1049330	849479
2002	2571408	2235021	1410199	1166298
2003	3297091	2861459	1635948	1340463
2004	3957516	3488744	1956282	1602303
2005	5207930	4584112	2383344	1957619
2006	6244906	5484645	2754809	2254347
2007	7884237	6929667	3357153	2747060
2008	9105489	7991043	4196674	3454599
2009	10194264	8965758	4903983	4000324
2010	12454323	10988265	6165836	4988197
2011	14889206	13009046	7475004	5971740

注:从2001年起市区数据包括萧山区和余杭区。

a) Data of urban district include Xiaoshan and Yuhang district since 2001.

10－02 分县(市)
Local Financial

单位:万元

指标 Item	全市 Total 2011	为上年(%) As Compared with Year 2010(%)	市区 Urban District 2011	为上年(%) As Compared with Year 2010(%)
合计 Total	**14889206**	**119.6**	**13009046**	**118.4**
一、地方财政收入 Local Financial Revenue	7851524	117.0	6822765	115.7
(一)税收收入 Tax Revenue	7582715	116.3	6614306	115.1
1.增值税 Value added Tax	1018017	114.1	827524	111.0
2.营业税 Business Tax	2409436	108.9	2134679	107.7
3.企业所得税 Enterprises´Income Tax	1308761	131.9	1181634	131.2
4.企业所得税退税 Company Income Tax Rebates	-		-	
5.个人所得税 Individual Income Tax	510554	130.2	454713	130.4
6.城市维护建设税 City Construction and Maintenance Tax	549604	139.6	487304	140.2
7.耕地占用税 Tax on the Use of Arable Land	103448	76.0	79173	68.3
8.契税 Contract Tax	722185	100.6	638045	98.6
9.房产税 Real Estate Tax	245337	160.9	218417	164.9
10.其他税收 Others Tax	715373	113.4	592817	112.5
(二)非税收入 Non－tax Revenue	268809	139.6	208459	141.4
1.专项收入 Special Revenue	231881	139.1	190660	141.0
其中:教育费附加 Revenue from Extra－Charges for Education	211035	138.8	178853	141.3
排污费 Revenue for Permitting Pollution	14814	106.7	8792	103.2
2.行政事业性收费收入 Income from Administrative Fees	16844	141.8	12654	129.1
3.罚没收入 Penalty and Confiscatory Income	115948	107.1	88660	106.8
4.国有资本经营收入 Seate－owned Assets Profits	－113682	107.9	－98270	109.4
其中:国有计划亏损补贴 Subsides to Loss－making of state－owned Enterprises	－113682	107.9	－98270	109.4
5.国有资源(资产)有偿使用收入 Compensation for the Use of Seate－owned Assets Income	17666	160.5	14709	159.5
6.其他收入 Others Revenue	152	506.7	46	153.3
二、上划中央二税 Revenue of Central Government	4308703	117.6	3731758	115.9
1.消费税 Consumption Tax	1254652	127.1	1249187	127.1
2.增值税 Value－added Tax	3054051	114.1	2482571	111.0
三、中央所得税 Central Government Income Tax	2728979	131.4	2454523	131.0
1.企业所得税 Enterprises Income Tax	1963144	131.9	1772452	131.2
2.个人所得税 Individual Income Tax	765835	130.2	682071	130.4

财政收入(2011年)
Revenue by Region(2011)

(10000 yuan)

#萧山区 Xiaoshan	#余杭区 Yuhang	桐庐县 Tonglu	淳安县 Chun'an	建德市 Jiande	富阳市 Fuyang	临安市 Lin'an
2170200	**1500007**	**771722**	**303030**	**392298**	**260425**	**152685**
1133788	956393	409488	171946	211018	141146	95161
1097469	924912	383246	158630	204153	135025	87355
208220	91346	89936	30787	37992	23727	8051
283738	329168	97383	52096	55213	33100	36965
195143	123018	40696	17541	30959	22436	15495
–	–	–	–	–	–	–
65046	53559	20582	8206	13822	8807	4424
83147	52264	24482	8826	15827	9166	3999
26541	10149	8658	6226	4717	3478	1196
103909	104540	38358	13324	16601	9830	6027
38953	12737	11016	2849	5717	4682	2656
92772	148131	52135	18775	23305	19799	8542
36319	31481	26242	13316	6865	6121	7806
35978	20398	17920	6226	7473	6011	3591
31873	18898	13962	5307	6513	4184	2216
2528	1500	3832	466	960	604	160
–	–	2654	231	200	704	401
13018	15682	7430	6210	6480	3794	3374
-14870	-7000	-3000	–	-7712	-4700	–
-14870	-7000	-3000	–	-7712	-4700	–
2153	2400	1238	649	424	312	334
40	1	–	–	–	–	106
646129	278748	270315	92463	114108	72414	27645
21470	4710	507	101	132	1233	3492
624659	274038	269808	92362	113976	71181	24153
390283	264866	91919	38621	67172	46865	29879
292714	184527	61044	26312	46439	33654	23243
97569	80339	30875	12309	20733	13211	6636

10-03 分县(市)

Local Financial

单位:万元

指 标 Item	全 市 Total		市 区 Urban District	
	2011	为上年(%) As Compared with Year 2010(%)	2011	为上年(%) As Compared with Year 2010(%)
合 计 Total	**7475004**	**121.2**	**5971740**	**119.7**
一、一般公共服务 Expenditure for General Public Services	857578	112.3	671901	111.6
二、国防 Expenditure for National Defense	10475	110.3	8524	110.4
三、公共安全 Expenditure for Public Security	507281	122.0	422390	122.8
四、教育 Expenditure for Education	1320537	124.7	941807	122.0
其中:教育费附加支出 Expenditure on Extra - Charges for Educations	155221	143.6	127617	138.8
五、科学技术 Expenditure for Science and Technology	350657	121.5	291768	119.3
六、文化体育与传媒 Expenditure for Culture, Sports and Media	185042	120.2	157826	117.2
七、社会保障和就业 Expenditure for Social Safety Net and Employment Effort	775422	121.3	635614	119.7
八、医疗卫生 Expenditure for Medical and Health Care	513455	123.1	389812	120.3
九、环境保护 Expenditure for Environmental Protection	141227	101.9	73847	91.0
其中:排污费支出 Sewage Expenses	14786	94.2	9103	100.2
十、城乡社区事务 Expenditure for Urban and Rural Community Affairs	1231576	125.3	1167724	124.6
十一、农林水事务 Expenditure for Agriculture, Forestry and water Conservancy	392344	122.7	203158	116.6
十二、交通运输 Expenditure for Trassportation	212663	122.0	134605	112.8
十三、资源勘探电力信息等事务 Resources exploration eletricity information, etc	282772	88.1	249458	85.3
十四、商业服务业等事务 Cornmercial and service business, etc	200406	125.9	172027	132.0
十五、金融监管支出 Expenditure for Financial Supervision	5355	29.2	4082	22.7
十六、地震灾后恢复重建支出 Expenditure for Post - earthquake Recorery and Reconstruction	23578	70.3	23578	80.3
十七、国土资源气象等事务 Land resources, meteorological services, etc	40875	143.0	29550	125.0
十八、住房保障支出 Expenditure on housing support	60192	188.5	44085	237.4
十九、粮油物资储备等管理事务 Expenditure for Grrain and Ovl Reservation, and Other Materials Management Services	17568	163.9	12347	144.7
二十、储备事务支出 Reserve Affairs Expenditure	3222		3222	
二十一、国债还本付息支出 Repayment and Interest payment of National Debt Expenditures	1545	217.3	681	100.0
二十二、其他支出 Other Expenditure	341234	170.7	333734	171.4

财政支出(2011 年)
Expenditure by Region(2011)

(10000 yuan)

#萧山区 Xiaoshan	#余杭区 Yuhang	桐庐县 Tonglu	淳安县 Chun'an	建德市 Jiande	富阳市 Fuyang	临安市 Lin'an
1097600	**842414**	**227949**	**240155**	**231133**	**468439**	**335588**
121134	109806	25898	33690	29039	52529	44521
2668	1629	530	298	483	33	607
90611	48759	16501	11894	12262	25788	18446
221791	174421	52614	56543	56692	126548	86333
21615	18707	5925	2569	4611	7575	6924
33784	29810	8735	5001	10492	20080	14581
20169	17076	4659	3855	3056	9760	5886
92311	97287	24838	19556	20089	46246	29079
95459	72514	17756	27023	21515	35390	21959
18082	16790	11527	5396	11124	23059	16274
3503	1600	755	–	2389	1229	1310
169211	98391	11327	6877	7604	26249	11795
66900	60608	25575	31920	35223	61986	34482
38662	15968	11363	21800	8727	13358	22810
81019	22765	6047	4571	2771	9886	10039
14423	40060	6813	2283	3696	5384	10203
20	10	70	10	668	346	179
4188	–	–	–	–	–	–
3561	4613	472	914	2226	4060	3653
17835	4565	1830	5902	2125	5882	368
–	120	818	1155	49	52	3147
–	3222	–	–	–	–	–
–	681	556	8	–	–	300
5772	23319	20	1459	3292	1803	926

10-04 主要年份全市金融机构存、贷款余额
Balance of Deposits and Loans of Financial Institutions in Main Years

单位:万元 (10000 yuan)

年份 Year \ 项目 Item	各项存款 Deposits	#城乡储蓄存款 Savings Deposits Of Urban and Rural Residents	#城镇储蓄存款 Savings Deposits of Urban Residents	各项贷款 Loans
1978	86824	20714	17056	136759
1979	108998	28937	22640	135713
1980	180707	40447	30896	174153
1981	226949	51440	38889	236678
1982	262156	67192	50113	216040
1983	303130	86635	64736	236203
1984	388305	115766	85439	329195
1985	484999	159596	115592	580180
1986	635514	222110	153572	769841
1987	776105	302762	207505	967477
1988	839680	351943	241839	1145989
1989	1017087	501592	346318	1338984
1990	1646165	697515	479031	1803266
1991	2036334	904490	616308	2136903
1992	2652966	1144737	763309	2651983
1993	3469954	1563328	1048413	3415527
1994	5061345	2394370	1642498	4450932
1995	7079650	3423379	2448787	5672105
1996	9619291	4638458	3459439	7434243
1997	12251840	5583306	4229591	9388500
1998	14948225	6701158	5155548	11620537
1999	17886717	7425967	5760527	14937506
2000	20884723	7885579	6151084	16866431
2001	26215100	9418400	7396800	20877000
2002	33731500	11834000	9492300	27523800
2003	46527300	15899600	13079600	38187000
2004	57072000	18351700	15016100	48000400
2005	67487200	21916600	17960100	55453000
2006	78555500	25552400	20789600	66038600
2007	93109600	26348300	21154300	84306800
2008	113333500	34765900	27584600	100690500
2009	142842104	42869189	34027871	131133023
2010	170843548	49909744	39352353	150787269
2011	183965719	55474824	43464332	165737441

注:1989 年以前数据均为银行机构存贷款,1990 年及以后年份数据为调整后金融机构存贷款。2003 年起金融机构存贷款为本外币合并数据。

a) Data before 1989 was belonged to banking system, data after 1990 adjusted for deposits and loans of financial institutions, data of 2003 included both RMB and foreign currency.

10-05 主要年份市区金融机构存、贷款余额

Balance of Deposits and Loans of Financial Institutions of Urban District in Main Years

单位:万元 (10000 yuan)

项目 Item / 年份 Year	各项存款 Deposits	#城乡储蓄存款 Savings Deposits of Urban and Rural Residents	#城镇储蓄存款 Savings Deposits of Urban Residents	各项贷款 Loans
1978	58372	13774	13246	101144
1979	73720	18055	17241	98792
1980	134275	24702	23282	121231
1981	172721	31358	29345	170539
1982	198350	39756	37047	142091
1983	226160	50439	46833	155297
1984	293145	66108	61934	194977
1985	359825	89114	82868	418214
1986	458142	115818	106703	557763
1987	565429	156704	142642	714313
1988	610601	180341	163466	846998
1989	737388	256238	229518	1000731
1990	1062574	354316	297390	1271779
1991	1309462	451756	397322	1469671
1992	1695011	572660	479248	1774158
1993	2263969	762234	662234	2298124
1994	3383877	1242379	1085363	3033010
1995	4851774	1853512	1639875	3907199
1996	6828786	2734904	2371657	5350499
1997	8831147	3287475	2873638	6772221
1998	10785066	3905602	3440607	8615412
1999	13051806	4336058	3835542	11462505
2000	15436286	4620235	4101716	13105849
2001	23765400	7976400	6460200	19237800
2002	30638400	10139800	8370100	25476700
2003	42522000	13834200	11693000	30297500
2004	52542100	16014700	13479900	44517600
2005	62249500	19231800	16208400	51455900
2006	72269600	22391800	18737800	61190700
2007	86197300	23124600	19132300	78456200
2008	104930100	30665200	24996500	93838100
2009	131800234	37837816	30801878	121473548
2010	156776515	43676938	35370599	138671334
2011	168052916	48263525	38996516	151756838

注:1989 年以前数据均为银行机构存贷款,1990 年及以后年份数据为调整后金融机构存贷款。2003 年起金融机构存贷款为本外币合并数据。

a) Data before 1989 was belonged to banking system, data after 1990 adjusted for deposits and loans of financial institutions. data of 2003 included both RMB and foreign currency.

10－06　金融机构

Balance of Deposits and

单位:万元

指　标	Item	全市 Total 2011年末 At the End of Year 2011	全市 Total 为上年(%) As Compared with the Preceding Year(%)	市区 Urban District 2011年末 At the End of Year 2011	市区 Urban District 为上年(%) As Compared with the Preceding Year(%)
一、各项存款	**Deposits**	**183965719**	**108.6**	**168052916**	**107.4**
1.单位存款	Deposits of Enterprises	116481031	106.2	108305622	104.7
(1)活期存款	Current Deposits	34833828		30875016	
(2)定期存款	Fixed Deposits	43977906		41875498	
(3)通知存款	Deposits at Notice	5898177		5603363	
(4)保证金存款	Margin Deposits	15632989		14600129	
2.个人存款	Personal Deposits	57366714	114.8	50013222	114.4
(1)储蓄存款	Savings Deposits	55474824	111.5	48263525	110.6
活期储蓄	Current Deposits	20880611	111.6	17684571	115.9
定期储蓄	Fixed Deposits	34594213	108.5	30578954	107.6
(2)保证金存款	Margin Deposits	112532		106516	
(2)结构性存款	Structured Deposits	1779357		1643182	
3.财政性存款	Treasury Deposits	4271762	90.8	3943369	95.2
4.临时性存款	Temporary Deposits	481502	112.2	463377	134.8
5.委托存款	Entrusting Deposits	434521	44.9	420042	41.2
6.其他存款	Other Deposits	4930189	136.5	4907284	137.0
二、各项贷款	**Loans**	**165737441**	**111.2**	**151756838**	**109.9**
1.境内贷款	Domestic Loans	165073293	111.0	151092815	109.7
(1)短期贷款	Short－term Loans	79479590	118.3	71117520	117.1
(2)中长期贷款	Medium and Long term Loans	79567340	104.5	74211698	104.7
(3)融资租赁	Finance lease	3335911	129.6	3335911	129.6
(4)票据融资	Note Financing	2565895	95.9	2308692	83.7
(5)各项垫款	Advance Money	124557	94.0	118994	83.6
2.境外贷款	Foreign Loans	664148	157.9	664023	169.1

注:2011年起指标项目有调整。

本外币存、贷款余额（2011 年末）

Loans of Financial Institutions(End of 2011)

（10000 yuan）

		桐庐县 Tonglu	淳安县 Chun'an	建德市 Jiande	富阳市 Fuyang	临安市 Lin'an
#萧山区 Xiaoshan	#余杭区 Yuhang					
25862027	**13155305**	**2466432**	**1936184**	**2395563**	**5890352**	**3224272**
16167540	7371606	1101329	1034883	1027491	3378748	1632958
4548367	2756263	546022	605485	570586	1437357	799363
5879611	2403774	304309	264364	188271	924102	421361
314020	317608	62420	16680	22129	166394	27191
3683667	964585	65340	12901	96953	663239	194428
9264457	5470499	1227212	819678	1323520	2452405	1530676
9015437	5388797	1204914	811855	1287136	2421212	1486182
2899016	1783636	484897	357278	506420	1088391	759054
6116421	3605161	720017	454577	780716	1332821	727128
11343	13999	5	322	2695	1296	1699
237677	67703	22293	7501	33689	29896	42795
110381	241076	134129	73680	42056	42237	36291
40206	12159	1491	5826	2260	4314	4235
51488	18724	2218			12261	
227955	41241	53	2117	236	387	20112
22218882	**10305382**	**1959045**	**1361340**	**1965151**	**5795175**	**2899892**
22216002	10303455	1959013	1361340	1965130	5795135	2899860
16757778	5525452	900187	542775	1135285	4027014	1756809
5153672	4424537	1029044	813259	811848	1568393	1133099
288436	339082	27114	5306	15694	199729	9361
16116	14383	2668		2303		591
2880	1927	32		21	40	32

a) The indicator items have been adjusted since 2011.

10-07 金融机构人民币
Balance of RMB Deposits, RMB Loans

单位:万元

指 标	Item	全市 Total 2011年	全市 Total 为上年(%) As Compared with the Preceding Year(%)	市区 Urban District 2011年	市区 Urban District 为上年(%) As Compared with the Preceding Year(%)
一、各项存款	**Deposits**	**181154415**	**108.5**	**165396103**	**108.0**
1.单位存款	Deposits of Enterprises	114446650	106.1	106402503	105.4
(1)活期存款	Current Deposits	33293290		29457694	
(2)定期存款	Fixed Deposits	43703205		41601878	
(3)通知存款	Deposits at Notice	5827097		5532283	
(4)保证金存款	Margin Deposits	15513969		14488073	
2.个人存款	Personal Deposits	56722174	114.8	49391597	114.3
(1)储蓄存款	Savings Deposits	54871383	111.6	47682799	110.8
(2)保证金存款	Margin Deposits	110449		104438	
(3)结构性存款	Structured Deposits	1740342		1604361	
3.财政性存款	Treasury Deposits	4271760	90.8	3943368	94.5
4.临时性存款	Temporan Deposits	366834	92.0	349021	91.6
5.委托存款	Entrusting Deposits	428873	44.8	414394	43.7
6.其他存款	Other Deposits	4918124	136.3	4895219	137.1
二、各项贷款	**Loans**	**158889191**	**110.9**	**145027964**	**110.4**
1.境内贷款	Domestic Loans	158808843	110.8	144947741	110.4
(1)短期贷款	Short-term Loans	75660791	118.3	67409590	117.7
(2)中长期贷款	Medium and Long term Loans	77148669	104.2	71799231	104.1
(3)融资租赁	Finance lease	3335911	129.6	3335911	129.6
(4)票据融资	Note Financing	2565712	95.9	2308509	95.6
(5)各项垫款	Advance Money	97759	100.2	94500	99.7
2.境外贷款	Foreign Loans	80348	2194.0	80223	11875.6

注:2011年起指标项目有调整。

存、贷款余额(2011 年末)

of Financial Institutions(End of 2011)

(10000 yuan)

		桐庐县 Tonglu	淳安县 Chun'an	建德市 Jiande	富阳市 Fuyang	临安市 Lin'an
#萧山区 Xiaoshan	#余杭区 Yuhang					
25530925	**13064348**	**2432649**	**1926798**	**2373496**	**5823564**	**3201805**
15873647	7294155	1072016	1027776	1009509	3319644	1615203
4296553	2690779	516722	599156	557473	1379927	782318
5867533	2394244	304309	263630	188271	923756	421361
305520	317608	62420	16680	22129	166394	27191
3662959	964056	65327	12856	92084	661911	193718
9231270	5457749	1222747	817400	1319660	2444761	1526009
8983610	5376241	1200449	809576	1283277	2413765	1481517
11236	13999	5	322	2694	1293	1697
236424	67509	22293	7501	33689	29703	42795
110381	241076	134129	73680	42056	42237	36291
36249	11404	1487	5826	2036	4273	4190
51423	18724	2218			12261	
227955	41241	53	2117	236	387	20112
21387899	**10254243**	**1951412**	**1359025**	**1934094**	**5725376**	**2891320**
21385019	10252316	1951381	1359025	1934073	5725336	2891288
15961120	5479680	892555	540460	1106531	3963419	1748237
5119623	4424537	1029044	813259	811848	1562189	1133099
288317	339045	27114	5306	15694	199729	9361
15959	9055	2668		–		591
2880	1927	32		21	40	32

a) The indicator items have been adjusted since 2011.

10-08 城乡居民储蓄存款余额(2011 年)

Balance of Savings Deposits of Rural and Urban Residents(2011)

单位:万元 (10000 yuan)

地区	Region	总计 Total		城镇居民 Urban Residents		农村居民 Rural Residents	
		2011 年末 At the End of Year 2011	为上年(%) As Compared with the Preceding Year(%)	2011 年末 At the End of Year 2011	为上年(%) As Compared with the Preceding Year(%)	2011 年末 At the End of Year 2011	为上年(%) As Compared with the Preceding Year(%)
全 市	**Total**	**55474824**	**111.15**	**43464332**	**110.45**	**12010492**	**113.76**
市 区	Urban District	48263525	110.50	38996517	110.25	9267008	111.57
萧山区	Xiaoshan	9015437	107.81	5437932	105.96	3577505	110.76
余杭区	Yuhang	5388797	117.10	3179685	116.31	2209112	118.26
桐庐县	Tonglu	1204914	119.09	760946	117.98	443969	121.05
淳安县	Chun'an	811855	121.96	473457	117.09	338398	129.49
建德市	Jiande	1287136	112.95	896120	108.97	391016	123.25
富阳市	Fuyang	2421212	114.30	1442000	111.33	979213	118.96
临安市	Lin'an	1486182	114.55	895293	109.87	590889	122.44

注:2003 年始为本外币合并储蓄存款余额。

a) Data in this table include both RMB and foreign currency since 2003.

10－09 保险业务情况(2011 年)
Development of Insurance Business(2011)

单位:万元 (10000 yuan)

指 标	Item	保险费收入 Premium	赔付金额 Indemnity Expenditure
全市总计	**Total**	**2111021.14**	**623926.27**
为上年%	As Compared with the Preceding Year＝100(%)	118.1	137.0
一、财产保险	Property Insurance	962268.74	452398.84
企业财产险	Enterprise Property Insurance	75978.08	24461.08
家庭财产险	Family Property Insurance	2955.05	965.14
机动车辆险	Transportation Equipment Insurance	717760.52	357838.48
工程险	Project Insurance	10548.57	6154.12
责任险	Responsibilihty Insurance	17594.12	5914.3
信用险	Export Credit Insurance	86191.50	35062.18
保证险	Guarantee Insurance	14798.46	1769.37
船舶险	Shipping Insurance	7846.37	10031.52
货运险	Cargo Insurance	17984.72	7100.64
特殊风险保险	Special Pisks Insurance	4563.95	109.88
农业保险	Agriculture Insurance	5068.93	2539.88
其他险	Other	978.48	452.24
二、人身险	Personal Insurance	1148752.40	171527.43
寿险	Life Insurance	1009731.34	108782.54
意外伤害险	Accidental Insurance	52844.12	10317.16
健康险	Health Insurance	86176.94	52427.73

主要统计指标解释

财政收入 包括:(1)各项税收。主要有增值税、营业税、土地增值税、城市维护建设税、资源税、城市土地使用税、印花税、个人所得税、企业所得税、关税和耕地占用税等。

(2)专项收入包括征收排污费、征收城市水资源费收入,教育费附加收入等。

存款 企业、机关、团体或居民根据可以收回的原则,把货币资金存入银行或其他信用机构保管并取得一定利息的一种信用活动形式。根据存款对象的不同可划分为企业存款、财政存款、机关团体存款、基本建设存款、城镇储蓄存款、农村存款等科目。它是银行信贷资金的主要来源。

贷款 银行或其他信用机构根据必须归还的原则,按一定利率,为企业、个人等提供资金的一种信用活动形式。我国银行贷款分为流动资金贷款、固定资产贷款、城乡个体工商户贷款城乡个体工商户贷款以及农业贷款等科目。

Explanatory Notes on Main Statistical Indicators

Financial Revenue It includes the following main items: (1) various tax revenues, including value added tax, business tax, land value added tax, tax on city maintenance and construction, resources tax, tax on use of urban land, stamp tax, personal income tax, enterprise income tax and tax on occupancy of cultivated land, etc. (2) Special revenues, including revenue collected from imposing fee on sewage treatment, revenue collected from imposing fee on urban water resources, and extra – charges for education, etc.

Deposit is a form of credit by which enterprises, institutions, organizations or households can put money into banks and other credit institutions for safekeeping and interest earning under the principle of free withdrawal. According to different depositors, deposits are divided into enterprise deposits, treasury deposits, deposits of government agencies and organizations, capital construction deposits, urban savings deposits, rural deposits and other deposits. Deposits are major sources of the credit funds of banks.

Loan is a form of credit by which banks and other credit institutions provide funds at certain interest rate to enterprises and individuals in the light of the principle of unconditional repayment. Loans from Chinese banks include circulating capital loans, fixed assets loans, loans to urban and rural individuals engaged in industrial and commercial business and agricultural loans.

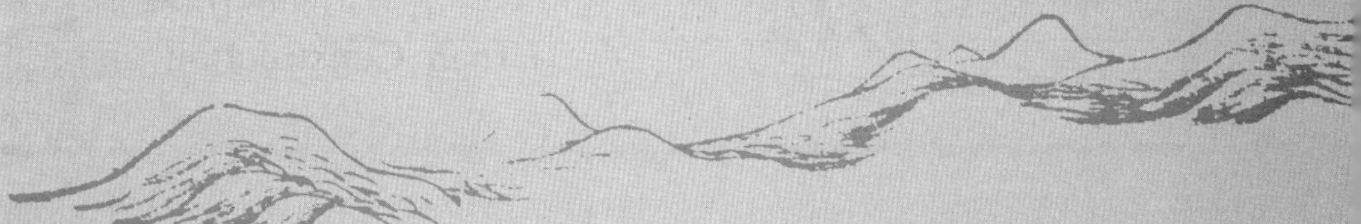

第十一篇
CHAPTER-11

城市建设、环境保护
URBAN CONSTRUCTION AND ENVIRONMENTAL PROTECTION

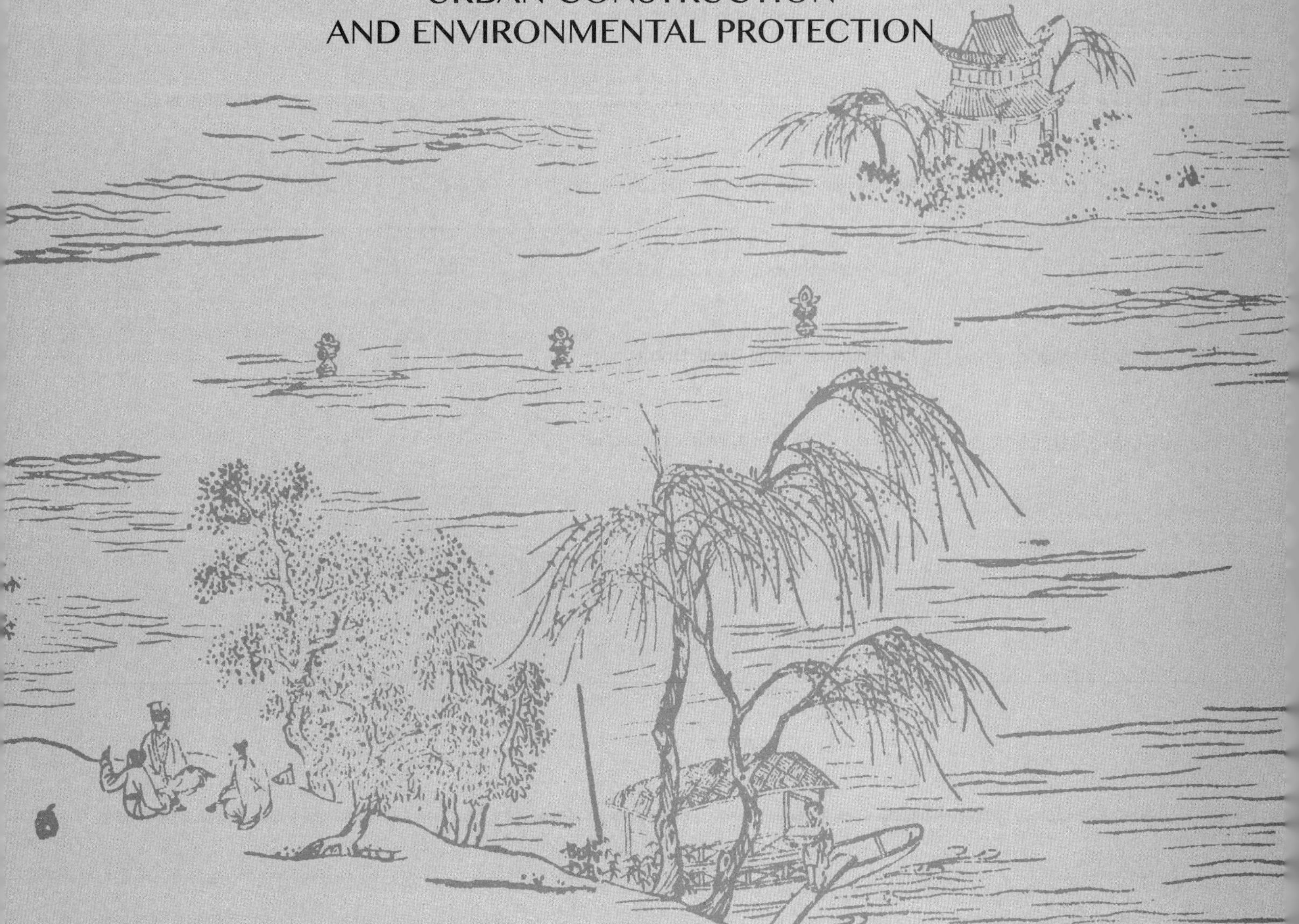

11 城市建设、环境保护
Urban Construction and Environmental Protection

主要统计指标
Major Statistical Indicators

市区建成区面积	Developed Area in Urban District	432.98	平方公里	(sq.km)
市区实有道路面积	Area of Roads in Urban District at Year-end	4900	万平方米	(10, 000 sq.m)
市区用电量	Electricity Consumption of Urban District	432.57	亿千瓦时	(100 million kw/h)
#工业用电	Industrial Electricity Consumption	282.95	亿千瓦时	(100 million kw/h)
生活用电	Electricity Consumption for Residential Use	55.49	亿千瓦时	(100 million kw/h)
市区供水能力	Water-supply Capacity of Urban District	320	万吨/日	(10, 000 tons/day)
市区供水总量	Annual Volume of Tap Water Supplied in Urban District	52660	万吨	(10, 000 tons)
市区气化率	Percentage of Population with Access to Gas in Urban District	100	%	(%)
市区公共绿地面积	Public Green Area in Urban District	5287	公顷	(hectare)
市区空气质量达标天数	The Number of Days of Air Quality Reach the Standards	333	天	(day)

11－01 主要年份市区城市公共交通

Urban Public Transportation in Main Years

指　标	Item	2000	2005	2006	2007	2008	2009	2010	2011
年末运营线路条数（条）	Number of Operating Routes (year－end) (unit)	163	368	381	393	425	441	548	611
年末运营线路总长度（公里）	Length of Operating Routes (year－end) (km)	2016	4902	5172	5416	6190	6462	8594	11106
年末运营公共汽车（辆）	Number of Public Transportation Vehicles(year－end) (unit)	1781	3997	4396	4578	5785	6150	7209	7543
年末运营无轨电车（辆）	Number of Operating Trolleys (unit)	223	189	118	118	118	118	65	54
客运总量（万人次）	Passenger Traffic (10,000 person－times)	57986	70653	78027	88362	102579	112844	127967	126999
全年票款收入（万元）	Income of Tickets (10,000 yuan)	43604	86448	98416	105773	120975	127746	150050	158373
年末实有出租汽车数（辆）	Number of Taxis (year－end) (unit)	6300	8320	8398	8583	9167	9305	9362	10905
年末免费公共自行车数（辆）	Number of free Public Bicycles (year－end) (unit)	－	－	－	－	－	50000	60600	65000

注：运营线路和公共汽车数据2009年前不含萧山、余杭。

a) Data of Operating Routes and public transportation vehicles don′t include Xiaoshan and Yuhang district before 2009.

11－02　主要年份市区城市供电、供水
Urban Electricity and Water Supply in Main Years

指　标	Item	2000	2005	2006	2007	2008	2009	2010	2011
一、城市供电	**Urban Electricity Supply**								
全年用电总量（亿千瓦时）	Total Electricity Consumption (100 million kwh)	60.19	244.78	279.94	313.47	325.75	346.93	392.64	432.57
工业（亿千瓦时）	Industrial Electricity Consumption (100 million kwh)	33.52	172.56	197.61	219.92	221.28	230.20	258.35	282.95
生活（亿千瓦时）	Electricity Consumption for Residential Use (100 million kwh)	9.86	27.98	32.53	36.86	41.15	45.31	50.74	55.49
二、城市供水（自来水）	**Urban Water Supply**								
总售水量（万吨）	Total Annual Volume of Tap Water Saled (10,000 tons)	27510	58332	57518	56906	58452	59291	45666	44335
平均日供水（万吨）	Per Capita Daily Consumption of Tap Water (10,000 tons)	92	201	177	183	187	190	147	144
供水能力（万吨/日）	Capacity of Water Supply (10,000 tons/day)	146	253	256	274	299	320	320	320
供水总量（万吨）	Total Annual Volume of Tap Water Supplied (10,000 tons)	33725	73331	64734	66753	68178	69499	53565	52660
其中：生产用水（万吨）	For Productive Use (10,000 tons)	8100	27327	20258	19519	19354	16671	11479	11884
生活用水（万吨）	For Residential Use (10,000 tons)	19410	35220	33979	33682	35902	37274	30978	22384
用水普及率（%）	Percentage of Population with Access to Tap Water (%)	100	100	100	100	100	100	100	100

注：从2001年起市区数据包括萧山区和余杭区。
a) Data of urban include Xiaoshan and Yuhang district since 2001.

11－03 主要年份市区市政建设

Public Utilities in Urban District in Main Years

指　标	Item	2000	2005	2006	2007	2008	2009	2010	2011
一、市政建设	**Urban Infrastructure**								
建成区面积（平方公里）	Constructed Area (sq. m)	－	314.45	327.45	344.59	367.26	392.73	412.59	432.98
年末实有道路面积（万平方米）	Area of Roads (year－end) (10,000 sq. m)	1183	3175	4216	4185	4258	4485	4754	4900
年末实有道路长度（公里）	Length of Roads (year－end) (km)	1050	1782	1942	1993	2030	2117	2194	2255
年末实有桥梁数（座）	Number of Bridges (year－end) (unit)	291	991	857	848	917	960	1021	1059
排水管道长度（公里）	Length of Drainage Pipelines (km)	1431	2945	2419	3115	3286	3650	3904	4056
城市污水排放量（万立方米）	Volume of Sewage Drained (10,000 cu. m)	27010	55141	44108	47952	61330	57132	43746	44809
城市污水处理总量（万立方米）	the Total Volume of Urban Sewage Treatment (10,000 cu. m)		43352	37758	36918	51808	51433	41733	42781
二、城市液化气	**Urban Liquefied Petroleum Gas**								
供气总量（万吨）	Total Volume of Liquefied Petroleum Gas Supply (10,000 tons)	7.47	15.28	8.54	5.91	8.96	10.11	11.44	11.19
其中:家庭用气（万吨）	Supply for Residential Use (10,000 tons)	5.08	9.51	5.53	3.52	6.63	6.25	5.77	5.93
三、人工煤气及天然气	**Coal Gas and Natural Gas**								
家庭用气总量（万立方米）	Total Volume of Coal Gas Consumed (10,000 cu. m)	4367	3225	3101	4010	4917	7285	10053	11365
家庭用气户数（万户）	Residential Households with Access to Gas (10,000 households)	14.46	25.48	29.50	37.46	43.58	51.84	62.85	72.5
四、全社会气化率　%	**Percentage of Population with Access to Gas** (%)	**95.70**	**99.17**	**100**	**100**	**100**	**100**	**100**	**100**

注:从2001年起市区数据包括萧山区和余杭区。

a) Data of urban include Xiaoshan and Yuhang district since 2001.

11－04　主要年份市区园林绿化
Urban Forestation in Main Years

指　标	Item	2000	2005	2006	2007	2008	2009	2010	2011
一、园林绿化	**Urban Forestation**								
建城区绿化覆盖面积（公顷）	The Green Areas Coveraged in Constructed Areas (hectare)	6083	11734	12490	13284	14177	15686	16483	17336
园林绿地面积（公顷）	Total Area of Parks, Gardens and Green Areas (hectare)	6035	10774	11309	12141	12971	14366	15118	15898
其中：公共绿地（公顷）	Public Green Area (hectare)	976	2564	2926	3486	4078	4676	5017	5287
建城区绿化覆盖率（%）	Rate of the Green Areas Coveraged in Constructed Areas (%)	34.33	37.31	38.14	38.55	38.60	39.94	39.95	40.00
公园景点个数　（个）	Number of Parks and Scenic Resorts (unit)	70	184	106	138	150	165	176	181
公园景点面积（公顷）	Area of Parks and Scenic Resorts (hectare)	489	997	852	1412	1430	1688	1906	2047
二、收费公园、风景点游人量（万人次）	**Number of Visitors to Parks and Scenic Resorts (10,000 persontimes)**	**1916**	**2396**	**2994**	**2976**	**3726**	**3985**	**5314**	**5478**

注：从 2001 年起市区数据包括萧山区和余杭区。

a) Data of urban include Xiaoshan and Yuhang district since 2001.

11－05 环境保护情况(2011年)
Environmental Protection Situation (2011)

单位:%　　(%)

指标名称		Item		全　市 Whole City	市　区 Urban District
工业废水排放量	(万吨)	Industrial Wastewater Emissions	(10,000 tons)	47954.04	20253.08
工业废水中COD排放量	(吨)	COD Emissions in Industrial Wastewater	(tons)	40366.70	18132.95
工业废水中氨氮排放量	(吨)	Ammonia emissions in Industrial wastewater	(tons)	1595.13	748.61
工业二氧化硫产生量	(吨)	Industrial Sulfur Dioxide Produced	(tons)	152742.59	101572.25
工业二氧化硫排放量	(吨)	Industrial Emissions of Sulfur Dioxide	(tons)	91688.39	52193.75
工业氮氧化物排放量	(吨)	Industrial Nitrogen Oxide Emissions	(tons)	83079.03	45633.23
工业烟(粉)尘去除量	(吨)	Industrial Smoke, Powder and Dust Removal	(tons)	4489481	1895660
工业烟(粉)尘排放量	(吨)	Industrial Smoke, Powder and Dust Emissions	(tons)	38296.84	20724.84
一般工业固体废物综合利用率	(%)	Comprehensive Utilization Rate of General Industrial Solid Waste	(%)	92.70	93.65
城市污水集中处理率	(%)	Centralized Treatment Rate of Urban Sewage	(%)	93.61	95.47
城市生活垃圾无害化处理率	(%)	Harmless Treatment Rate of City's Living Garbage	(%)	100	100
空气质量达标(API＜100)天数	(天)	Number of Days of Air Quality Reach the Standards (API＜100)	(days)	-	333
集中式饮用水源地水质达标率	(%)	Compliance Rate of Centralized Sources of Drinking Water	(%)	100	100
COD削减率	(%)	Reduction Rate of COD	(%)	2.81	-
氨氮削减率	(%)	Reduction Rate of Ammonia Nitrogen	(%)	2.35	-
SO2削减率	(%)	Reduction Rate of SO2	(%)	3.44	-
氮氧化物削减率	(%)	Reduction Rate of Nitrogen Oxides	(%)	-0.38	-

主要统计指标解释

自来水生产能力　指年底城建部门管理的自来水厂实际生产能力。

生活用水量　指居民日常生活与公共福利设施的用水量。包括居民、饮食店、旅馆、医院、理发店、浴池、洗衣店、游泳池、商店、学校、机关、部队等单位的用水量。

供气总量　指全年售给各类用户的全部煤气量。包括工业用量、家庭用量和其他用量。

年末实有道路长度　指除土路外,路面经过铺装宽度在3.5米以上的道路,包括高级、次高级道路和普通道路。

城市桥梁　指城市范围内,修建在河道上的桥梁和道路与道路立交、道路跨越铁路的立交桥,以及人行天桥。包括永久性桥和半永久性桥,不包括临时性桥、铁路桥、涵洞。

营运线路长度　指设置的固定营运线路的长度,包括郊区营运线路长度。不包括临时行驶的线路长度。

用水普及率　指城市用水的非农业人口数(不包括临时人口和流动人口)与城市非农业人口总数之比。计算公式为:

$$用水普及率=\frac{城市用水非农业人口数}{城市非农业人口数}\times 100\%$$

城市园林绿地面积　指城市公共绿地、专用绿地、生产绿地、防护绿地、郊区风景名胜区的全部面积。

公共绿地面积　指供游览休息的各种公园、动物园、植物园、陵园以及花园、游园和供游览休息用的林荫道绿地、广场绿地。不包括一般栽植的行道树及林荫道的面积。

Explanatory Notes on Main Statistical Indicators

Production Capacity of Tap Water refers to the actual comprehensive production capacity of the waterworks administered by the urban construction department.

Consumption of water for Residential Use refers to the water consumption of households for daily life and the water consumption of public welfare facilities, including the consumption of restaurants, hotels, hospitals, barber shops, public bathhouses, laundries, swimming pools, shops, schools, institutions, army units and other units.

Volume of Gas Supply refers to the total volume of gas Sold to users in a year, including the volume for industrial use, residential use and other uses.

Length of Roads at the Year – end refers to the length of roads with a paved surface, and with a width of more than 3 – 5 meters, including high quality, medium quality and ordinary roads.

Urban Bridges refers to bridges over river courses, great separated junctions and overpasses in urban areas. Permanent bridges and semi – permanent bridges are included. Temporary bridges, railway bridges and culverts are excluded.

Length in Operation refers to the length of the roads in fixed operation, including the suburb one, but excluding the tomporary ones.

Percentage of Urban Population with Access to Tap Water refers to the ratio of the urban non – agricultural population (excluding temporary and mobile population) with access to tap water to the tolal urban non – agricultural population. The formula is:

$$\text{Percentage of Poputalion with Access to Tap Water} = \frac{\text{Urban Non – agricultural Population with Access to Tap Water}}{\text{Urban Non – agricultural Population}} \times 100\%$$

Area of Urban Gardens and Green Areas refers to the total area of urban public green land, special green land, production green land, protection green land and suburban scenic spots.

Public Green Area refers to green area of various parks, zoos, botanical gardens, cemeteries, amusement parks, tree – flanked boulevards Greenland squares for tourism and relaxing. Areas with trees planted along – side the streets and boulevards are excluded.

第十二篇
CHAPTER-12

科技、教育、文化、卫生、体育

SCIENCE AND TECHNOLOGY,EDUCATION,CULTURE,
PUBLIC HEALTH AND SPORTS

12 科技、教育、文化、卫生、体育

Science and Technology, Education, Culture, Public Health and Sports

主要统计指标

Major Statistical Indicators

高等学校数	Number of Regular Institution of Higher Education	38	个	(unit)
高等学校在校学生数	Number of Students in Regular Institution of Higher Education	44.67	万人	(10, 000 person)
高中在校学生数	Number of Students in Senior High Schools	11.71	万人	(10, 000 person)
初中在校学生数	Number of Students in Junior High Schools	22.35	万人	(10, 000 person)
小学在校学生数	Number of Students in Primary Schools	46.53	万人	(10, 000 person)
医疗病床数	Number of Beds in Health Institutions	4.53	万张	(10, 000 bed)
# 医院	Number of Beds in Hospitals	3.94	万张	(10, 000 bed)
卫生技术人员数	Number of Medical Technical Personnel	6.59	万人	(10, 000 person)
#执业(助理)医师	Number of Registered (Assistant) Doctors	2.58	万人	(10, 000 person)
公共图书馆	Public Library	16	个	(unit)

12－01 全市科技活动情况

The Situation of the City's Scientific and Technological Activities

指　标　　Item		2011	2010
科技活动人员 Scientific and Technological Activities Personnel	(万人) (10,000)	16.58	15.01
每万人口中科技活动人员数 The Number of Scientific and Technological Activities Personnel per 10,000 people	(人) (Person)	190.12	172.55
科技经费投入 Financial Input of Science and Technology	(亿元) (0.1 billion yuan)	354.93	306.67
科技经费投入占 GDP 比重 The Proportion of Financial Input of Science and Technology in GDP	(%) (%)	5.06	5.15
研究与试验发展活动人员 R&D Activities Personnel	(万人) (10,000)	9.91	8.17
全社会每万人口中研究与试验发展活动人员数 The Number of R&D Activities Personnel per 10,000 people in Whole Society	(人) (Person)	113.57	93.85
研究与试验发展经费支出 R&D Financial Expenditure	(亿元) (0.1 billion yuan)	202.35	166.87
研究与试验发展经费支出占 GDP 比重 The Proportion of R&D Financial Expenditure in GDP	(%) (%)	2.88	2.80
专利授权指数 Patent Granted	(项) (Item)	84404	67513
#发明专利授权量 #Invention Patent Granted	(项) (Item)	4511	3238

12-02 规模以上工业企业科技活动情况

The Scientific Activities Situation of Industrial Enterprises Above Designated Size

指 标 Item	2011	2010
有科技活动企业数 (个) The Number of Scientific and Technological Activities Enterprises (Unit)	1662	1541
企业有科技机构 (个) Scientific and Technological Institutions of Enterprises (Unit)	1226	1143
科技活动人员 (人) Scientific Activities Personnel (Person)	83815	72783
#高中级职称人员 (人) #Senior and Intermediate Professional Titles Personnel (Person)	19506	15761
研究与试验发展人员 (万人) R&D Personnel (10,000)	5.45	4.27
每万名从业人员中研究与试验发展活动人员数 (人) The Number of R&D Activities Personnel per 10,000 Employees (Person)	437	356
企业技术开发费支出 (亿元) The Technological Development Expenses of Enterprises (0.1 billion yuan)	180.8	161.84
技术开发费占主营业务收入的比例 (%) The Proportion of Technological Development Expenses in Main Business Income (%)	1.50	1.59
研究与试验发展经费支出 (亿元) R&D Financial Expenditure (0.1 billion yuan)	119.87	101.83
研究与试验发展经费支出占主营业务收入的比例 (%) The Proportion of R&D Financial Expenditure in Main Business Income (%)	1.00	1.00

12－03 分县(市)非私营单位年末人才资源

Trained Personnel Resource of Non－private Units by Region

单位:人 (person)

地　区	Region	人才资源年末数 Number of Trained Personnel Resources		#专业技术人员 Technical Personnel	
		2011	2010	2011	2010
全市	**Whole City**	**1497260**	**1341692**	**591207**	**541569**
市区	Urban District	1289076	1149009	502028	459257
萧山区	Xiaoshan	260947	236904	87061	77235
余杭区	Yuhang	109252	98832	39388	36557
桐庐县	Tonglu	30089	28130	11953	10986
淳安县	Chun'an	22614	21046	10530	9763
建德市	Jiande	32241	29191	13218	11976
富阳市	Fuyang	69841	67540	31329	30936
临安市	Lin'an	53399	46776	22149	18651

12－04　按经济类型分的非私营单位专业技术人员（2011年末）

Technical Personnel of Non－private Units by Ownership（End of 2011）

单位：人　　（person）

地　区	Region	合计 Total	国有 State－owned	集体 Collective－owned	其他 Others
总计	**Total**	**591207**	**225465**	**15474**	**350268**
市区	Urban District	507228	183061	11614	312553
萧山区	Xiaoshan	87061	20484	4303	62274
余杭区	Yuhang	39388	15112	1534	22742
桐庐县	Tonglu	11953	6844	533	4576
淳安县	Chun'an	10530	6660	342	3528
建德市	Jiande	13218	7913	759	4546
富阳市	Fuyang	26129	12063	936	13130
临安市	Lin'an	22149	8924	1290	11935

12－05　分行业非私营单位专业技术人员(2011 年末)

Technical Personnel of Non－private Units by Sector(End of 2011)

单位:人　　　　(person)

行　业	Sector	合计 Total	国有 State－owned	集体 Collective－owned	其他 Others
全市	**Total**	**591207**	**225465**	**15474**	**350268**
农、林、牧、渔业	Farming, Forestry, Animal Husbandry and Fishery	498	139	8	351
采矿业	Mining & Quarrying	271	16	30	225
制造业	Manufacture	109428	3536	515	105377
电力、燃气及水的生产和供应业	Production and Supply of Electricity, Gas and Water	5087	3001	78	2008
建筑业	Construction	72324	3421	477	68426
交通运输、仓储和邮政业	Transportation, Storage, Post & Telecommunications	8606	3403	415	4788
信息传输、计算机服务和软件业	Information Transmission, Computer Services and Software	45274	3237	51	41986
批发和零售贸易	Wholesale & Retail Trade	22256	2871	418	18967
住宿和餐饮业	Lodging and Catering	6781	814	328	5639
金融业	Banking	39294	7713	-	31581
房地产业	Real Estate	16097	1596	282	14219
租赁与商务服务业	Renting and Business Service	12886	4096	1173	7617
科学研究、技术服务与地质勘查业	Scientific Research, Technical Service and Geological Prospecting	57069	25597	690	30782
水利、环境和公共设施管理业	Water Conservancy, Environment and Public Utility	7152	2471	139	4542
居民服务和其他服务业	Service for the Residents and Other	752	358	48	346
教育	Education	107441	96666	3900	6875
卫生、社会保障和社会福利业	Health Care, Sports & Social Welfare	63392	52529	6851	4012
文化、体育和娱乐业	Culture, Sports and Entertainment	12096	10836	41	1219
公共管理和社会组织	Public Management and Social Organizations	4503	3165	30	1308

12－06 文化事业
Number of Institutions

单位:个

指 标	Item	全 市 Total	市 区 Urban District	#萧山区 Xiaoshan
剧 场	Theaters	11	10	－
剧 团	Opera Troupes	21	17	1
文化馆	Cultural Centers	15	10	1
文化站	Cultural Stations	190	94	29
图书馆	Libraries	15	10	1
博物馆	Museums	65	54	8
展览馆	Exhibition Buildings	1	1	－

12－07 分县(市)艺术表演团体
Basic Statistics on Performance of

指 标	Item	全 市 Total 2011	全 市 Total 为上年(%) As Compared with the Preceding Year(%)	市 区 Urban District 2011	市 区 Urban District 为上年(%) As Compared with the Preceding Year(%)
艺术表演场所演出场次 (场)	Number of Performances in Artistic Performance Place (scene)	5066	106.1	5028	107.6
艺术表演场所演出收入 (万元)	Income of Performances in Artistic Performance Place (10000 yuan)	1695	116.1	1683	116.7
剧团演出场次 (场)	Number of Performances of Opera Troupes (scene)	6817	93.1	5938	94.8
#农 村 (场)	#Rural Areas (scene)	3738	139.1	2934	166.9
剧团演出观众人数(万人次)	Number of Spectators of Opera Troupes (10000 person－times)	684	99.9	528	95.5
剧团演出收入 (万元)	Income of Performances of Opera Troupes (10000 yuan)	7865	128.1	7428	129.4

单位数(2011 年)
for Culture(2011)

(unit)

#余杭区 Yuhang	桐庐县 Tonglu	淳安县 Chun'an	建德市 Jiande	富阳市 Fuyang	临安市 Lin'an
2	–	–	–	–	1
1	1	–	1	1	1
1	1	1	1	1	1
19	14	23	16	25	18
1	1	1	1	1	1
4	2	1	4	3	1
–	–	–	–	–	–

演出情况(2011 年)
Art Troupes by Region(2011)

#萧山区 Xiaoshan	#余杭区 Yuhang	桐庐县 Tonglu	淳安县 Chun'an	建德市 Jiande	富阳市 Fuyang	临安市 Lin'an
–	441	–	–	–	–	38
–	13	–	–	–	–	12
100	263	158	–	280	85	356
80	230	148	–	230	70	356
20	18	22	–	38	7	89
76	150	130	–	60	80	167

12－08 全市专利申请与授权情况（2011 年）

Patent Application and Authorization（2011）

单位：件　　　　（item）

地　　区	Region	专利申请合计 Patent Applications	专利申请发明 Inventions	专利申请实用新型 Utility Models	专利申请外观设计 Designs	专利授权合计 Patent Applications Granted	专利授权发明 Inventions	专利授权实用新型 Utility Models	专利授权外观设计 Designs
全市	**Whole City**	**40890**	**9717**	**18783**	**12390**	**29249**	**4511**	**14556**	**10182**
市区	Urban District	33507	9032	15532	8943	23510	4057	12211	7242
上城区	Shangcheng	1657	309	840	508	1272	103	732	437
下城区	Xiacheng	3314	893	1148	1273	2228	467	878	883
江干区	Jianggan	5544	1643	2552	1349	4197	572	1971	1654
拱墅区	Gongshu	1616	309	941	366	1005	99	590	316
西湖区	Xihu	7740	3653	3127	960	4246	1674	2037	535
高新（滨江）区	Hi－Tech（Binjiang）	3116	1148	1013	955	2606	790	1013	803
萧山区	Xiaoshan	5687	531	3468	1688	4068	177	2757	1134
余杭区	Yuhang	4833	546	2443	1844	3888	175	2233	1480
桐庐县	Tonglu	1327	83	578	666	1221	25	527	669
淳安县	Chun'an	545	48	324	173	330	22	104	204
建德市	Jiande	978	95	114	769	657	42	89	526
富阳市	Fuyang	2269	225	1541	503	1980	261	1085	634
临安市	Lin'an	2266	236	694	1336	1551	104	540	907

12-09 主要年份市区文化事业单位数
Cultural Institutions of Urban District in Main Years

单位:个 (unit)

年份 Year	电影院 Cinemas	剧团 Opera Troupes	剧场 Theaters	文化馆 Cultural Centers	文化站 Cultural Stations	图书馆 Libraries	博物馆 Museums
1978	7	13	6	5	–	2	1
1979	8	14	7	5	27	2	1
1980	8	15	7	5	37	2	1
1981	8	17	7	6	40	2	1
1982	9	17	7	6	45	3	1
1983	9	15	3	6	46	3	1
1984	9	15	4	6	49	3	1
1985	8	16	9	6	47	3	2
1986	8	15	8	6	48	3	2
1987	8	15	9	6	38	3	2
1988	7	14	9	6	50	3	2
1989	7	14	9	6	48	2	2
1990	9	14	9	5	48	3	2
1991	10	14	8	5	48	3	2
1992	11	14	8	5	48	3	6
1993	10	14	9	5	42	3	6
1994	11	13	9	5	48	3	6
1995	11	13	9	5	67	3	6
1996	10	13	8	5	55	3	6
1997	10	13	8	5	52	3	6
1998	9	13	8	6	55	3	7
1999	9	13	6	6	52	3	8
2000	8	12	6	6	52	3	9
2001	49	14	11	8	89	5	11
2002	–	14	10	8	90	4	11
2003	19	14	11	13	92	4	11
2004	18	14	14	8	93	5	12
2005	16	15	10	8	94	7	12
2006	16	15	10	8	94	8	12
2007	16	15	10	8	92	9	12
2008	18	15	11	8	92	9	13
2009	15	16	11	8	95	11	34
2010	25	17	11	8	96	11	54
2011	23	17	10	10	94	10	54

注:从2001年起市区数据包括萧山区和余杭区。

a) Data of urban include Xiaoshan and Yuhang district since 2001.

12－10 主要年份高等学校基本情况

Basic Statistics on Regular Institutions of Higher Education in Main Years

单位:人 (person)

年 份 Year	学校数(个) Number of Schools(unit)	在校学生数 Number of Students	教职员工数 Teachers and Staff	#专职教师 Number of Full－time Teachers
1978	9	13319	8966	3946
1979	12	17518	10182	4458
1980	13	23545	12400	5278
1981	13	28936	13090	5359
1982	13	25821	14363	6067
1983	14	27443	15267	6172
1984	16	31384	15889	6387
1985	20	36996	17507	7247
1986	22	40051	18968	7845
1987	21	39922	18965	7876
1988	21	40787	19582	8133
1989	21	40330	19680	8107
1990	21	39866	19495	8075
1991	21	42192	19489	7737
1992	19	43787	19841	7561
1993	19	51063	19787	7561
1994	19	59109	19903	7703
1995	20	63124	19883	7799
1996	20	66023	19693	7824
1997	20	69391	19540	7793
1998	17	76546	19320	7723
1999	18	89109	20136	8135
2000	32	122386	23791	10477
2001	33	174894	25805	11866
2002	34	224048	27307	13605
2003	35	269798	34508	18141
2004	36	313599	33325	18445
2005	36	351918	34816	19583
2006	36	373563	36929	21375
2007	36	392770	38843	23197
2008	36	409559	39762	24017
2009	36	429774	40420	24765
2010	37	434811	41582	25003
2011	38	446721	42222	25735

注:在校学生数包括各高校研究生。

a) Number of students include graduate students in all schools.

12－11 主要年份中等专业学校基本情况
Basic Statistics on Specialized Secondary Schools in Main Years

单位:人 (person)

年 份 Year	学校数(个) Number of Schools(unit)	在校学生数 Number of Students	教职员工数 Teachers and Staff	#专职教师 Number of Full－time Teachers
1978	26	8711	3044	1080
1979	27	11093	2601	1124
1980	26	9453	2450	1101
1981	35	7309	3122	1276
1982	37	8284	3694	1529
1983	37	10516	3716	1604
1984	42	13419	4194	1758
1985	46	16527	5095	1959
1986	50	19114	5641	2336
1987	52	20929	6081	2623
1988	51	22117	6144	2741
1989	54	23302	6602	2888
1990	55	23564	6679	2948
1991	55	23331	6584	2770
1992	55	26373	6786	2825
1993	56	30336	6732	2780
1994	57	36079	6881	2840
1995	57	42784	6851	2888
1996	58	49593	6789	2904
1997	57	51752	6731	2896
1998	56	55796	6554	2746
1999	50	52272	5023	2272
2000	28	45238	2950	1421
2001	26	32763	2053	1051
2002	14	26255	1251	566
2003	13	21735	1058	457
2004	11	21262	869	416
2005	10	20344	893	443
2006	8	12540	410	184
2007	8	8927	414	194
2008	8	5514	345	152
2009	8	4016	233	65
2010	6	3999	348	151
2011	5	4071	369	154

12-12 主要年份高中基本情况
Basic Statistics on Senior High Schools in Main Years

单位:人 (person)

年份 Year	学校数(个) Number of Schools(unit)	在校学生数 Number of Students	专职教师数 Number of Full-time Teachers
1978	352	102815	5235
1979	182	58866	3471
1980	151	43661	3173
1981	118	34606	2825
1982	113	35136	2740
1983	111	38580	2740
1984	105	43167	2781
1985	104	47510	3016
1986	95	46379	2972
1987	92	44697	3006
1988	89	42196	2947
1989	88	39994	2898
1990	86	39829	2922
1991	82	37809	2896
1992	74	34620	2791
1993	72	32483	2641
1994	75	35720	2673
1995	72	40771	2880
1996	70	43692	3135
1997	69	47975	3388
1998	75	55688	3693
1999	82	64459	4172
2000	85	73049	4745
2001	88	79632	5262
2002	81	91635	6126
2003	77	108116	6879
2004	81	115303	7510
2005	80	120883	8041
2006	82	124177	8421
2007	80	122939	8542
2008	76	120294	8646
2009	75	118057	8751
2010	72	116983	8871
2011	71	117089	9061

12-13 主要年份初中基本情况

Basic Statistics on Junior Middle Schools in Main Years

单位:人　　　　(person)

年份 Year	学校数(个) Number of Schools(unit)	在校学生数 Number of Students	专职教师数 Number of Full-time Teachers
1978	254	247209	11978
1979	363	208484	11020
1980	369	204073	10695
1981	359	194024	10015
1982	367	193135	10107
1983	370	190221	9948
1984	368	192971	9679
1985	361	196889	9799
1986	376	199638	9821
1987	385	195426	10264
1988	380	170079	10055
1989	376	151223	9825
1990	382	160111	9564
1991	387	185590	10020
1992	367	212022	10603
1993	365	203896	10876
1994	371	205388	11495
1995	373	216300	12058
1996	374	229466	12810
1997	368	227809	13370
1998	359	222191	13493
1999	339	239174	13723
2000	330	269484	14529
2001	314	285203	15685
2002	315	282951	15758
2003	316	268824	15836
2004	303	252291	16042
2005	289	241374	16205
2006	263	235527	16374
2007	262	238252	16591
2008	260	244464	16965
2009	252	241899	17317
2010	245	236014	17795
2011	246	223545	17652

12-14 主要年份小学基本情况

Basic Statistics on Primary Schools in Main Years

单位:人 (person)

年份 Year	学校数(个) Number of Schools(unit)	在校学生数 Number of Students	教职员工数 Number of Teachers and Staff	#专职教师数 Number of Full-time Teachers
1978	4959	605137	24103	22291
1979	4850	577811	25089	23220
1980	4781	560244	25388	22902
1981	4668	525503	22468	20832
1982	4528	479264	22213	20289
1983	4417	444301	20842	18945
1984	4345	427763	20496	18500
1985	4286	414839	20945	18415
1986	4250	413507	20796	18464
1987	4205	405856	21067	18751
1988	4137	426842	21658	19236
1989	4106	459162	22660	20177
1990	4077	460514	20542	18099
1991	3972	453055	20781	18369
1992	3654	450496	21452	19067
1993	3473	477026	22141	19775
1994	3352	504867	22751	20462
1995	3172	513988	23743	21380
1996	3006	525674	24553	22197
1997	2762	538390	25269	23022
1998	2395	532845	25718	23499
1999	1996	512874	26350	24120
2000	1659	485679	25938	23876
2001	1354	467982	25535	23179
2002	1197	456535	25425	23138
2003	1044	448969	25304	22955
2004	897	447971	25396	23066
2005	791	458942	25793	23541
2006	605	459529	26040	23848
2007	437	456152	26455	24251
2008	418	452143	26894	24743
2009	417	445132	27445	25424
2010	408	453897	27881	25709
2011	409	465289	27862	26395

12－15　主要年份幼儿园基本情况
Basic Statistics on Kindergartens in Main Years

单位:人　　　　(person)

年　份 Year	园　数(个) Kindergartens(unit)	在园幼儿数 Number of Children	教职员工数 Teachers and Staff	#教　师 Number of Full－time Teachers
1978	266	37597	2570	1439
1979	216	59245	3731	2201
1980	518	82182	4763	3398
1981	676	82808	5275	3691
1982	853	95733	6357	4269
1983	1034	95676	6271	4135
1984	1749	112095	7238	4900
1985	1743	115766	7360	5278
1986	1607	118792	7898	5659
1987	1678	133773	8622	6335
1988	1541	139883	9221	6608
1989	1397	132947	9595	6849
1990	1526	136277	9808	7167
1991	1422	150982	10472	7388
1992	1431	133773	9240	6487
1993	1328	171005	10779	7886
1994	1470	165860	10718	7891
1995	1493	149497	10102	7943
1996	1437	150587	10203	7625
1997	1504	146530	10480	7743
1998	1695	153035	10691	7956
1999	1787	156372	10719	8107
2000	2037	168414	11740	8770
2001	1249	174204	11447	7880
2002	1268	175891	11988	8086
2003	1285	176862	13702	9076
2004	1098	186472	14991	9544
2005	1188	188991	16161	10288
2006	1188	195552	17550	11053
2007	1071	212754	19330	12168
2008	1037	235867	21193	12917
2009	972	246336	22970	14211
2010	969	267352	25525	15203
2011	970	271128	27458	16023

12－16 高等学校

Basic Statistics on Regular

单位:人

单位名称	Item	在校学生数 Number of Students	
		2011	为上年(%) As Compared with the Preceding Year(%)
全　市	**Total**	**404909**	**102.30**
市　区	**Urban District**	**385215**	**102.36**
浙江大学	Zhejiang University	22664	100.47
杭州电子科技大学	Hangzhou Dianzi University	16116	100.64
浙江工业大学	Zhejiang Univesity of Technology	21645	100.41
浙江理工大学	Zhejiang Sci－Tech University	17022	102.23
浙江农林大学	Zhejiang Forestry University	13469	102.79
浙江中医药大学	Zhejiang University of Traditional Chinese Medicine	5441	107.11
杭州师范大学	Hangzhou Normal University	13630	110.54
浙江工商大学	Zhejiang Gongshang University	14918	101.15
中国美术学院	China Academy of Art	8645	100.07
中国计量学院	China Institute of Metrology	13307	106.89
浙江科技学院	Hangzhou Application Engineering and Technology College	14825	104.24
浙江广播电视大学	Zhejiang Radio & TV University	8487	80.26
浙江水利水电专科学校	Zhejiang Water Conservancy and Hydroelectricity College	7551	105.98
浙江财经学院	Zhejiang Institute of Finance and Economics	12525	105.74
浙江警察学院	Zhejiang Police College	2775	76.43
浙江传媒学院	Zhejiang Institute of Media and Communications	10037	104.29
浙江树人大学	Zhejiang Shuren University	14441	100.82
浙江大学城市学院	Zhejiang University City College	13470	98.69

注:本表不含在校研究生。

基本情况(2011 年)
Institutions of Higher Education(2011)

(person)

本年招生数 Number of New Students Enrollment	本年毕业生数 Number of Graduates	教职员工数 Number of Teachers and Staff 合计 Total	其中:专职教师 Full - time Teachers	2012 年预计毕业生 Number of Students Will Graduate in 2012
117892	**104486**	**42222**	**38278**	**110700**
112826	**99849**	**40316**	**36402**	**106022**
5594	4964	8192	5440	5563
4174	4076	1586	1551	4352
5149	5134	2731	2382	5539
4322	3976	1715	1710	4472
3511	3016	1465	1440	3238
1477	1085	858	857	1356
3996	2710	2301	2145	2700
3836	3745	1643	1643	3852
2283	2213	1059	1021	2214
3467	2574	1284	1203	3153
3912	3035	1190	1190	3460
3403	4741	231	231	1759
2900	2379	597	591	1868
3522	2782	1223	1223	2971
534	1375	383	383	1172
2936	2337	973	973	2488
4061	3599	804	804	3867
3322	3027	1014	1014	3322

a) Data in this table does not contain post - graduate students.

12－17 普通中学及职业

Basic Statistics on Senior, Junior

单位:人

指 标	Item	全 市 Total	市 区 Urban District	#萧山区 Xiaoshan
高 中	**Senior High Schools**			
学校数(所)	Number of Schools(unit)	71	48	9
在校学生数	Number of Students	117089	69753	22698
为上年(%)	As Compared with the Preceding Year (%)	100.09	100.20	101.64
本年招生数	Number of New Students Enrollment	39225	23604	7667
本年毕业生数	Number of Graduates	38579	23142	7442
#专职教师	#Full－time Teachers	9061	5752	1741
2012 年预计毕业生数	Number of Students Will Graduate in 2012	38965	23033	7378
初 中	**Junior High Schools**			
学校数(所)	Number of Schools(unit)	246	149	42
在校学生数	Number of Students	223545	144250	46949
为上年(%)	As Compared with the Preceding Year (%)	94.72	97.04	94.40
本年招生数	Number of New Students Enrollment	72770	48317	15812
本年毕业生数	Number of Graduates	78431	46957	16113
#专职教师	#Full－time Teachers	17652	11392	3418
2012 年预计毕业生数	Number of Students Will Graduate in 2012	76016	47267	15378
职业中学	**Vocational Schools**			
学校数(所)	Number of Schools(unit)	37	20	4
在校学生数	Number of Students	71909	45120	15342
为上年(%)	As Compared with the Preceding Year (%)	102.00	103.05	106.52
本年招生数	Number of New Students Enrollment	25734	15827	5518
本年毕业生数	Number of Graduates	21221	13014	4130
专职教师数	Full－time Teachers	3925	2399	579
2012 年预计毕业生数	Number of Students Will Graduate in 2012	22203	14267	4653

中学基本情况(2011 年)
High Schools and Vacational Schools(2011)

(person)

#余杭区 Yuhang	桐庐县 Tonglu	淳安县 Chun'an	建德市 Jiande	富阳市 Fuyang	临安市 Lin'an
10	3	4	5	6	5
13358	7067	7561	9549	13571	9588
102.07	99.94	100.37	101.59	101.13	96.41
4452	2320	2584	3131	4468	3118
4349	2270	2505	2993	4283	3386
967	519	508	634	975	673
4617	2472	2425	3237	4529	3269
34	14	17	24	21	21
29475	12181	13537	16042	23234	14301
96.90	88.85	91.76	91.48	91.90	88.92
9947	3696	4090	4883	7391	4393
8825	4930	5152	6334	9158	5900
2432	967	1135	1237	1702	1219
9654	4540	5028	5850	8121	5210
4	2	4	3	4	4
9506	2884	4276	3885	10065	5679
104.19	110.24	99.51	88.42	104.43	98.46
3344	1214	1604	1417	3767	1905
2614	724	1392	1633	2888	1570
555	179	205	196	558	388
3002	719	1241	1173	2963	1840

12－18 小学、幼儿园及特殊
Basic Statistics on Primary Schools,

单位:人

指 标	Item	全 市 Total	市 区 Urban District	#萧山区 Xiaoshan
小 学	**Primary Schools**			
学校数(所)	Number of Schools(unit)	409	235	82
班数(班)	Number of Classes(unit)	12074	8252	2499
在校学生数	Number of Students	465289	328992	106357
为上年(%)	As Compared with the Preceding Year (%)	102.51	104.20	101.97
本年招生数	Number of New Students Enrollment	86319	62897	19119
本年毕业生数	Number of Graduates	73465	48454	16917
教职员工数	Number of Teachers and Staff	27862	18632	5140
#专职教师	#Full－time Teachers	26395	17749	4871
2012 年预计毕业生数	Number of Students Will Graduate in 2012	74605	50647	16598
幼儿园	**Kindergartens**			
园数(个)	Number of Kindergartens(unit)	970	607	205
班数(班)	Number of Classes(unit)	9152	6463	1726
在园幼儿数	Number of Children	271128	197658	53443
教职员工数	Number of Teachers and Staff	27458	21133	5359
#教师	#Full－time Teachers	16023	12142	3033
盲聋哑学校	**Schools for the Blind,Deaf and Deaf－mute**			
学校数(个)	Number of Schools(unit)	2	1	－
在校学生数	Number of Students	558	303	－
本年招生数	Number of New Students Enrollment	78	42	－
本年毕业生数	Number of Graduates	110	75	－
专职教师	Number of Full－time Teachers	146	86	－
弱智学校	**Schools for Weaken in Intelligence**			
学校数(个)	Number of Schools(unit)	11	7	1
在校学生数	Number of Students	877	695	157
本年招生数	Number of New Students Enrollment	132	99	16
本年毕业生数	Number of Graduates	94	78	－
专职教师	Number of Full－time Teachers	223	180	48
工读学校	**Reformatory Schools**			
学校数(个)	Number of Schools(unit)	1	1	－
在校学生数	Number of Students	138	138	－
本年招生数	Number of New Students Enrollment	62	62	－
本年毕业生数	Number of Graduates	64	64	－
专任教师总数	Number of Full－time Teachers	44	44	－

教育基本情况(2011 年)

Kindergartens and Special Education(2011)

(person)

#余杭区 Yuhang	桐庐县 Tonglu	淳安县 Chun'an	建德市 Jiande	富阳市 Fuyang	临安市 Lin'an
43	25	37	27	47	38
1755	618	620	589	1215	780
74139	22412	19152	22523	43428	28782
105.60	100.82	94.28	94.02	101.12	100.22
14667	4036	2960	3550	7961	4915
9605	3905	4037	4912	7549	4608
4010	1397	1775	1524	2693	1841
3832	1265	1704	1437	2514	1726
10731	3840	3826	4585	7029	4678
76	82	60	36	109	76
1149	417	371	431	814	656
37445	12464	7134	12284	24060	17528
3542	1089	463	998	2248	1527
2257	615	201	676	1378	1011
–	–	–	–	1	–
–	–	–	–	255	–
–	–	–	–	36	–
–	–	–	–	35	–
–	–	–	–	60	–
1	1	–	1	1	1
44	43	–	24	51	64
16	10	–	4	9	10
–	2	–	–	6	8
10	4	–	4	18	17
–	–	–	–	–	–
–	–	–	–	–	–
–	–	–	–	–	–
–	–	–	–	–	–
–	–	–	–	–	–

12 - 19 各级成人教育

Basic Statistics on

单位:人

指　标	Item	成人高等学历教育 Higher Education for Adults	职工高校 Staff and Workers College	广播电视大学 Broadcasting and Television College	普通高校成人高等学历教育 Adult Higher Education in Ordinary Universities
全　市	**Total**				
学校数(所)	Number of Schools(unit)	4	3	1	-
在校学生数	Number of Students	112407	4833	8487	99018
为上年(%)	As Compared with the Preceding Year (%)	95.39	-	80.3	-
本年招生数	Number of New Students Enrollment	48969	2413	3403	43132
本年毕业生数	Number of Graduates	50283	2734	4741	42800
教职员工数	Number of Teachers and Staff	603	357	231	-
#专职教师	#Full - time Teachers	299	225	67	-
市　区	**Urban District**				
学校数(所)	Number of Schools(unit)	4	3	1	-
在校学生数	Number of Students	109005	4833	8487	95616
为上年(%)	As Compared with the Preceding Year(%)	94.38	-	80.3	-
本年招生数	Number of New Students Enrollment	47493	2413	3403	41656
本年毕业生数	Number of Graduates	49901	2734	4741	42418
教职员工数	Number of Teachers and Staff	603	357	231	-
#专职教师	#Full - time Teachers	299	225	67	-

基本情况（2011 年）
Various Adult Education(2011)

(person)

其它机构 Other Agencies	成人中等学历教育 Adult Secondary Education	成人中等专业 Adult Secondary Specialized	成人中学 Secondary Schools for Adults	成人技术培训学校 Technical Schools for Adults
-	69	8	61	211
69	34461	25032	9429	421178
-	131.14	102.05	538.49	99.39
21	12279	12279	-	-
8	13892	10493	3399	332801
15	986	730	256	2273
7	428	363	65	1284
-	37	8	29	100
69	30712	25032	5680	346873
-	123.38	104.88	553.61	99.48
21	12279	12279	-	-
8	13389	10493	2896	251678
15	912	730	182	1510
7	421	363	58	780

12－20 主要年份医疗卫生机构数

Number of Health Institutions in Main Years

单位：个 (unit)

年 份 Year	全市合计 Total	#医 院 Hospitals	市区合计 Urban District	#医 院 Hospitals
1978	1361	421	689	45
1979	1390	426	696	50
1980	1381	425	675	51
1981	1476	424	749	51
1982	1540	432	798	56
1983	1540	435	800	58
1984	1574	437	807	54
1985	1582	404	787	47
1986	1636	407	826	53
1987	1693	420	865	55
1988	1710	438	878	55
1989	1721	443	882	57
1990	1738	440	890	58
1991	1789	441	889	58
1992	1767	436	885	58
1993	1730	403	882	68
1994	1717	416	882	72
1995	1712	414	883	72
1996	1712	416	893	83
1997	1711	411	891	81
1998	1491	419	757	89
1999	1530	400	789	85
2000	1599	396	853	85
2001	1496	391	1072	191
2002	1817	116	1277	88
2003	1901	99	1323	73
2004	1985	114	1396	87
2005	2196	127	1604	97
2006	2570	134	1886	107
2007	2607	138	1872	104
2008	2544	141	1813	108
2009	2687	144	1887	111
2010	2819	151	1906	113
2011	2958	167	1992	122

注：从 2001 年起市区数据包括萧山区和余杭区。2002 年起医院数据不包括卫生院。

a) Data of urban include Xiaoshan and Yuhang district since 2001. From 2002, the figures of hospitals exclude health centers.

12－21 主要年份医疗病床数

Number of Beds in Health Institutions in Main Years

单位:张 (bed)

年 份 Year	全 市 Total	#医 院 Hospitals	市 区 Urban District	#医 院 Hospitals
1978	14042	11704	6588	5789
1979	15124	12682	7335	6282
1980	16317	13478	8244	6940
1981	17408	13576	9646	7185
1982	17179	14350	9194	7580
1983	17338	14584	9411	7833
1984	17694	14691	9536	7867
1985	19637	15010	11095	7933
1986	20555	16035	11657	8448
1987	21465	16770	12203	8863
1988	23394	17954	13204	9651
1989	24111	18363	13581	9773
1990	24121	18879	13219	10041
1991	24966	19444	13968	10437
1992	25606	20243	14206	10821
1993	25653	20884	14058	10982
1994	25984	20870	14231	11045
1995	26684	21360	14731	11336
1996	28141	22217	15427	12132
1997	26616	22341	15076	12190
1998	27327	23110	15530	12766
1999	26713	22952	14988	12691
2000	27166	23303	15496	13068
2001	27063	23520	20523	17770
2002	27609	22797	21200	18667
2003	29144	22036	22641	18205
2004	31738	24444	25008	20338
2005	33251	25907	26732	21931
2006	33972	27186	27172	23184
2007	36928	29987	29884	25664
2008	38114	31416	30663	26882
2009	40226	33094	32412	28031
2010	42828	36148	34693	30639
2011	45291	39363	36633	33291

注:从 2001 年起市区数据包括萧山区和余杭区。

a) Data of urban include Xiaoshan and Yuhang district since 2001.

12 - 22 医疗卫生

Number of Health

单位:个

指　标	Item	全　市 Total	市区 Urban District
总　计	**Total**	**2958**	**1992**
一、医院	Number of Hospitals	167	122
1. 综合医院	General Hospitals	88	66
2. 中医医院	Hospitals of Chinese Medicine	25	13
3. 中西医结合医院	Chinese Therapeutics with Western	3	3
4. 专科医院	Specialized Hospitals	49	38
口腔医院	Hospitals for Mouth	7	5
眼科医院	Hospitals for Eye	1	1
肿瘤医院	Tumor Hospitals	2	1
妇产(科)医院	Hospitals for Pregnant Woman	6	5
儿童医院	Children Hospitals	1	1
精神病医院	Mental Hospitals	3	2
传染病医院	Hospitals for Infectious Diseases	1	1
骨科医院	Orthopaedics Hospitals	6	3
康复医院	Healing Hospitals	7	6
整型外科医院	Plastic Hospitals	2	2
美容医院	Beauty Hospitals	5	5
其他专科医院	Other Special Hospitals	8	6
5. 护理院	Nursing Centers	2	2
二、疗养院	Sanatoriums	7	4
三、社区卫生服务中心(站)	Health Service Centers for Community	1204	828
1. 社区卫生服务中心	Health Service Centers	126	95
2. 社区卫生服务站	Health Service Stations	1078	733
四、卫生院	Health Service Centers	119	18
1. 街道卫生院	Rural Township Hospitals in Subdistrict	6	0
2. 乡镇卫生院	Rural Township Hospitals in Country	113	18
五、门诊部	Clinics	233	199
六、诊所、卫生所、医务室、护理站	Other Health Care Institutions	1141	768
七、急救中心(站)	First - aid Centers(stations)	10	4
八、采供血机构	Blood Supplying Agencies	3	2
九、妇幼保健院(所、站)	Maternity and Child Care Centers(stations)	9	4
十、专科疾病防治所(所、站)	Specialized Centers for Disease Prevention and Control(stations)	6	1
十一、疾病预防控制中心	Centers for Disease Prevention and Control	15	10
十二、卫生监督所	Institutions of Public Health Inspection	14	9
十三、医学科学研究机构	Research Institutions of Medical Science	1	1
十四、医学在职培训机构	Medical Training Organization for Incumbent	7	4
十五、健康教育所(站、中心)	Education Center for Health(stations)	2	1
十六、其他卫生机构	Other Health Care Institutions	20	17

机构数（2011 年）
Institutions（2011）

（unit）

#萧山区 Xiaoshan	#余杭区 Yuhang	桐庐县 Tonglu	淳安县 Chun′an	建德市 Jiande	富阳市 Fuyang	临安市 Lin′an
546	**333**	**161**	**132**	**168**	**253**	**252**
25	9	5	6	9	9	16
19	4	4	4	5	2	7
3	1	1	2	1	4	4
–	–	–	–	–	–	–
3	3	–	–	3	3	5
1	–	–	–	–	1	1
–	–	–	–	–	–	–
–	–	–	–	–	1	–
–	–	–	–	–	–	1
–	–	–	–	–	–	–
–	1	–	–	1	–	–
–	–	–	–	–	–	–
–	1	–	–	1	–	2
–	–	–	–	1	–	–
1	–	–	–	–	–	–
–	–	–	–	–	–	–
–	1	–	–	–	1	1
1	1	–	–	–	–	–
–	–	–	–	–	3	–
1	189	93	49	37	135	62
305	20	2	2	1	25	1
29	169	91	47	36	110	61
276	–	11	21	22	16	31
18	–	–	–	–	3	3
–	–	11	21	22	13	28
18	28	2	–	12	7	13
23	102	47	48	80	76	122
166	1	–	3	1	1	1
2	–	–	–	1	–	–
1	1	1	1	1	1	1
–	–	–	1	1	2	1
–	1	1	1	1	1	1
1	1	1	1	1	1	1
1	–	–	–	–	–	–
–	1	–	1	1	–	1
1	–	–	–	–	–	1
1	–	–	–	1	1	1

12－23 医疗病床
Number of Beds in

单位:张

指　　标	Item	全　市 Total	市区 Urban District
总　　计	**Total**	**45291**	**36633**
一、医院	Number of Hospitals	39363	33291
1. 综合医院	General Hospitals	25022	20863
2. 中医医院	Hospitals of Chinese Medicine	6493	5134
3. 中西医结合医院	Chinese Therapeutics with Western	1055	1055
4. 专科医院	Specialized Hospitals	6743	6189
口腔医院	Hospitals for Mouth	67	47
眼科医院	Hospitals for Eye	40	40
肿瘤医院	Tumor Hospitals	1374	1374
妇产(科)医院	Hospitals for Pregnant Woman	898	878
儿童医院	Children Hospitals	862	862
精神病医院	Mental Hospitals	1514	1320
传染病医院	Hospitals for Infectious Diseases	600	600
骨科医院	Orthopaedics Hospitals	335	155
康复医院	Healing Hospitals	549	509
整型外科医院	Plastic Hospitals	161	161
美容医院	Beauty Hospitals	94	94
其他专科医院	Other Special Hospitals	249	149
5. 护理院	Nursing Centers	50	50
二、疗养院	Sanatoriums	863	363
三、社区卫生服务中心(站)	Health Service Centers for Community	2842	2551
1. 社区卫生服务中心	Health Service Centers	2797	2551
2. 社区卫生服务站	Health Service Stations	45	–
四、卫生院	Health Service Centers	1030	218
1. 街道卫生院	Rural Township Hospitals in Subdistrict	85	–
2. 乡镇卫生院	Rural Township Hospitals in Country	945	218
五、门诊部	Clinics	20	10
六、诊所、卫生所、医务室、护理站	Other Health Care Institutions	–	–
七、急救中心(站)	First－aid Centers(stations)	19	–
八、采供血机构	Blood Supplying Agencies	–	–
九、妇幼保健院(所、站)	Maternity and Child Care Centers(stations)	644	200
十、专科疾病防治所(所、站)	Specialized Centers for Disease Prevention and Control(stations)	510	–
十一、疾病预防控制中心	Centers for Disease Prevention and Control	–	–
十二、卫生监督所	Institutions of Public Health Inspection	–	–
十三、医学科学研究机构	Research Institutions of Medical Science	–	–
十四、医学在职培训机构	Medical Training Organization for Incumbent	–	–
十五、健康教育所(站、中心)	Education Center for Health(stations)	–	–
十六、其他卫生机构	Other Health Care Institutions	–	–

数(2011 年)

Health Institutions(2011)

(bed)

#萧山区 Xiaoshan	#余杭区 Yuhang	桐庐县 Tonglu	淳安县 Chun'an	建德市 Jiande	富阳市 Fuyang	临安市 Lin'an
5184	**3160**	**1226**	**1039**	**1992**	**2568**	**1833**
4525	2260	906	800	1386	1400	1580
3655	1270	746	614	908	773	1118
656	300	160	186	194	547	272
–	–	–	–	–	–	–
214	660	–	–	284	80	190
–	–	–	–	–	–	20
–	–	–	–	–	–	–
–	–	–	–	–	–	–
–	–	–	–	–	–	20
–	–	–	–	–	–	–
–	520	–	–	194	–	–
–	–	–	–	–	–	–
–	105	–	–	50	–	130
174	–	–	–	40	–	–
–	–	–	–	–	–	–
–	–	–	–	–	–	–
40	35	–	–	–	80	20
–	30	–	–	–	–	–
60	–	–	–	–	500	–
371	700	65	–	8	218	–
371	700	20	–	8	218	–
–	–	45	–	–	–	–
218	–	175	130	258	75	174
–	–	–	–	–	14	71
218	–	175	130	258	61	103
10	–	–	–	–	–	10
–	–	–	–	–	–	–
–	–	–	–	10	–	9
–	–	–	–	–	–	–
–	200	80	109	30	225	–
–	–	–	–	300	150	60
–	–	–	–	–	–	–
–	–	–	–	–	–	–
–	–	–	–	–	–	–
–	–	–	–	–	–	–
–	–	–	–	–	–	–
–	–	–	–	–	–	–

12－24 卫生事业

Number of Medical

单位:人

指　　标	Item	全　　市 Total	市　　区 Urban District
总　　计	**Total**	**79292**	**64177**
一、卫生技术人员	Number of Medical Technical Personnel	65869	53008
1. 执业(助理)医师	Registered (Assistant) Doctor	25773	20566
执业医师	Registered Doctor	23421	19053
助理医师	Assistant Doctor	2352	1513
2. 注册护士	Registered Nurse	25231	20949
3. 药剂师	Druggist	4544	3452
4. 技师人员	Checking Member	2905	2370
5. 其他	Others	6358	4800
二、其他技术人员	Other Medical Technical Personnel	3756	3237
三、管理人员	Managerial Personnel	3809	3151
四、工勤人员	Logistics Worker	5858	4781

人员数(2011 年)

Technical Personnel(2011)

(person)

萧山区 Xiaoshan	余杭区 Yuhang	桐庐县 Tonglu	淳安县 Chun'an	建德市 Jiande	富阳市 Fuyang	临安市 Lin'an
8966	**6349**	**2693**	**1846**	**3128**	**4609**	**2839**
7558	5452	2339	1638	2638	3777	2469
3143	1948	842	677	973	1560	1155
2642	1645	672	566	834	1326	970
501	303	170	111	139	234	185
2677	1875	782	483	1041	1237	739
503	389	199	165	247	269	212
296	232	106	75	120	127	107
844	918	385	204	226	525	218
445	225	65	61	35	195	163
358	222	148	46	170	220	74
605	450	141	101	285	417	133

12－25　主要年份卫生技术人员

Number of Medical Technical Personnel in Main Years

单位:人　　　　(person)

年份 Year	全市 Total	执业(助理)医师 Number of Registered (Assistant) Doctors	注册护士 Registered Nurses	市区 Urban District	执业(助理)医师 Number of Registered (Assistant) Doctors	注册护士 Registered Nurses
1978	19059	7375	3483	10867	4346	2510
1979	20060	7539	3536	11779	4733	2632
1980	21110	8311	3885	12376	5179	2804
1981	22737	9284	4139	13697	5946	3032
1982	23558	9883	4369	14221	6204	3193
1983	24914	10833	4562	15213	6990	3352
1984	25648	11291	4817	15807	7393	3487
1985	25593	11503	5071	15840	7644	3705
1986	26489	12623	5391	16543	8239	3940
1987	27663	12369	5805	17361	8329	4156
1988	28676	13674	6938	18022	8710	4801
1989	29791	14177	7348	18619	9146	5085
1990	30990	14483	7822	19231	9374	5397
1991	32169	14858	8153	19630	9494	5610
1992	32628	14842	8417	19690	9373	5736
1993	33172	15181	8643	19708	9499	5797
1994	33964	15465	8979	19907	9472	5940
1995	34245	16465	9531	19943	9607	6249
1996	34946	16789	9794	20695	9889	6508
1997	35423	17112	10019	20728	9902	6571
1998	35857	16022	10577	21035	9452	6788
1999	35256	16668	10587	20519	9610	6856
2000	35487	16317	11186	20344	9050	7300
2001	36643	16994	11576	28293	12968	9343
2002	37193	16092	11922	28818	12332	9653
2003	39019	16614	12460	30299	12731	10161
2004	39816	16770	13248	30886	12894	10840
2005	42353	17833	14514	33206	13802	12034
2006	45375	18831	15557	35904	14689	12986
2007	49780	20701	17455	39860	16290	14601
2008	52379	21223	18702	42015	16747	15556
2009	56270	22753	20997	45219	17996	17530
2010	61117	24345	23418	49232	19414	19481
2011	65869	25773	25231	53008	20566	20949

注:从2001年起市区数据包括萧山区和余杭区。
a) Data of urban include Xiaoshan and Yuhang district since 2001.

12－26 体育运动情况(2011年)
Basic Statistics on Sports Activities(2011)

单位:人 (person)

指 标	Item	2011年	为上年(%) As Compared with the Preceding Year(%)
一、体委工作人员数	**Workers in Sports Commissions**	**991**	**100.8**
#教练员	#Full－time Coaches	75	100.0
二、等级裁判员发展人数	**Number of Referees in Grades**	**366**	**130.7**
#女	#Female	108	98.2
一级裁判员	First Grade Referees	－	－
二级裁判员	Second Grade Referees	366	130.7
三级裁判员	Third Grade Referees	－	－
三、等级运动员发展人数	**Number of Athletes in Grades**	**341**	**106.6**
#女	#Female	132	88.6
一级运动员	First Grade Athlete	－	－
二级运动员	Second Grade Athlete	341	106.6
三级运动员	Third Grade Athlete	－	－

主要统计指标解释

文化事业机构　指从事专业文化工作和为专业文化工作服务的独立建制的单独核算的单位。不包括这些单位另外举办独立核算的其他机构和各部门的业余文化组织。

艺术表演团体　指从事戏曲、音乐、舞蹈、杂技等专业艺术表演，有独立帐户，实行单独核算的团体。不包括半工半艺、半农半艺和民间职业剧团。

普通高等学校　指按照国家规定的设置标准和审批程序批准举办，通过国家统一招生考试，招收高中毕业生为主要培养对象，实施高等教育的全日制大学、独立设置的学院和高等专科学校、短期职业大学。

成人高等学校　指按照国家有关规定审批，招收通过全国成人高教统一招生考试的具有高中毕业或同等学历的在职从业人员利用脱产、半脱产、业余或函授等多种形式对其实施高等学历教育，培养高等教育专科或本科毕业水平的专门人才，修业年限、课程设置和总学时数均按高等学历教育要求付诸实施的学校。包括广播电视大学、职工高等学校、农民高等学校、管理干部学院、教育学院、独立设置的函授学院等。

小学学龄儿童入学率　指调查范围内已入小学学习的学龄儿童占校内外学龄儿童总数（包括弱智儿童在内，但不包括盲聋哑儿童）的比重。计算公式：

$$小学学龄儿童入学率=\frac{已入学的小学学龄儿童数}{校内外小学学龄儿童总数}*100\%$$

等级运动员人数　指经考核正式批准授予等级运动员称号的人数。运动员等级分为国际级运动健将、运动健将、一级运动员、二级运动员、三级运动员、少年级运动员。

等级裁判员人数　指经考核正式批准授予等级裁判员称号的人数。裁判员等级分为国际裁判、国家级裁判、一级裁判、二级裁判、三级裁判。

卫生机构　卫生机构是指从卫生行政部门取得《医疗机构执业许可证》，或从民政、工商行政、机构编制管理部门取得法人单位登记证书，为社会提供医疗保健、疾病控制、卫生监督等服务或从事医学科研、医学教育等卫生单位和卫生社会团体。不包括卫生行政机构、香港和澳门特别行政区以及台湾所属卫生机构。

卫生技术人员　卫生技术人员包括执业（助理）医师、注册护士、药剂人员、检验和影像技师（士、员）等卫生专业人员。

执业（助理）医师、执业（中）药师和注册护士　执业（助理）医师、执业（中）药师和注册护士是指领取医师、药师执业证书和注册护士证书的人员。不包括从事管理工作的医师、药师和护士。

Explanatory Notes on Main Statistical Indicators

Cultural Institutions refer to units which have their own organizational system and independent accounting system and specialize in or serve cultural development. They exclude other establishments run by these cultural institutions and amateur cultural groups established by various departments.

Art Troupe refers to the troupe which is engaged in drama, opera, music, dance, acrobatics or other art performance, opens independent accounts with banks and has self – supporting accounting system; excluding the troupes which are engaged partly in industrial or agricultural activities, partly in art performance and the professional troupes organized by the people.

Regular Institutions of Higher Learning refer to educational establishments set up according to the government evaluation and approval procedures, enrolling graduates from senior secondary schools and providing higher education courses and training for senior professionals, They include full – time universities, colleges, high professional schools and short – term professional universities.

Institutions of Higher Learning for Adults refer to educational establishments, set up in line with relevant rules approved by the government, enrolling staff and workers with senior secondary school or equivalent education, and providing higher education courses in many forms of full – time, part – time, space – time, or correspondence for adults. Professionals thus trained receive a qualification equivalent to graduates studying regular courses at regular universities, colleges and professional colleges. Institutions of higher learning for adults include Radio and TV universities, schools of high education for staff and workers and peasants, colleges for management cadres, pedagogical colleges, independent correspondence colleges.

Enrollment Rate of Primary School – age Children refer to the proportion of school – age children enrolled at schools to the total number of school – age children both in and outside schools (including retarded children, but excluding blind, deaf and mute children). The formula is:

$$\text{Enrollment Rate of Primary School – age Children} = \frac{\text{Total primary School – age Children at Schools}}{\text{Total Primary School – age Children Both at and Outside Schools}}$$

Number of Athletes in Grades refers to the number of athletes who have been given titles through examination. The titles of athletes include international masters of sports, masters of sports, first – grade, second – grade and third – grade sportsmen and young athletes.

Number of Referees in Grades refers to the number of referees who have been given titles after examination. They are classified as international referees, national referees and referees of the first, second and third grades.

Health Institutions refers to the Institutions and Society organization that get the registered license of health and medical institution from the health adiministration department, or get the registered license of units from civil administration department, industry and business administration and organization management department, and offers medical treatment, controlling of disease, supervision of sanitation. Health institution excludes health administration department and Institutions of Hong Kong, Macao, and Taiwan.

Medical Technical Personnel include registered (Assistant) doctor, registered nurse, druggist, checking members and photo artificer.

Registered (Assistant) Doctor, Registered Druggist and Registered Nurse refers to the personnel who get the licence of doctor, druggist and nurse, the management staff excluded.

第十三篇
CHAPTER-13

人民生活、物价、民政
PEOPLE'S LIVELIHOOD,PRICE INDICES AND CIVIL ADMINISTRATION

13 人民生活、物价、民政
People's Livelihood, Price Indices and Civil Administration

主要统计指标
Major Statistical Indicators

全市非私营单位在岗职工工资总额	Total Wages of Staff and Workers of Non-private Units	1122.28	亿元	(100 million yuan)
#国有单位	State-owned Units	372.85	亿元	(100 million yuan)
全市非私营单位在岗职工平均工资	Annual Average Wages of Staff and Workers of Non-private Units	54408	元	(yuan)
#国有单位	State-owned Units	79657	元	(yuan)
市区城镇居民人均年可支配收入	Per Capita Annual Disposable Income of Urban Households of Urban District	34065	元	(yuan)
为上年	As Compared with the Preceding Year	113.4	%	(%)
农民人均年纯收入	Per Capita Annual Net Income of Rural Households	15245	元	(yuan)
为上年	As Compared with the Preceding Year	115.6	%	(%)
市区居民消费价格指数	Consume Price Index of Urban District	104.8	上年=100	(Preceding Year=100)
市区商品零售价格指数	Commodity Retail Price Index of Urban District	104.4	上年=100	(Preceding Year=100)
工业品出厂价格指数	Ex-factory Price Index of Industrial Products	104.7	上年=100	(Preceding Year=100)

13－01 主要年份市区城镇住户调查情况

Basic Conditions of Urban Households in Main Years

年份 Year	调查户数（户） Number of Households Surveyed（household）	平均每户人口（人） Average Household Size（person）	平均每户就业人数(人) Average Number of Employed Persons Per Household(person)	年人均可支配收入(元) Per Capita Annual Disposable Income（yuan）	年人均消费性支出(元) Per Capita Annual Living Expenditure（yuan）	人均住房使用面积（平方米） Per Capita Living Space in City Areas（sq. m）
1978	28	4.20	2.89	338	301	
1979	28	4.19	2.77	396	365	
1980	28	4.18	2.79	521	491	
1981	100	3.97	2.37	540	513	
1982	100	3.90	2.35	532	532	
1983	100	3.90	2.42	578	535	8.8
1984	100	3.90	2.36	729	679	9.3
1985	150	3.53	2.26	1026	908	9.7
1986	150	3.49	2.27	1169	1072	9.9
1987	150	3.42	2.25	1260	1118	10.6
1988	200	3.41	2.16	1565	1515	10.6
1989	200	3.40	2.15	1764	1615	10.6
1990	200	3.37	2.15	1985	1685	10.9
1991	200	3.40	2.20	2128	1894	10.8
1992	200	3.28	2.14	2580	2296	11.1
1993	200	3.21	2.10	3525	3183	11.2
1994	200	3.31	2.10	5249	4559	11.9
1995	200	3.20	2.05	6301	5559	11.7
1996	200	3.20	2.00	7206	6095	11.9
1997	200	3.14	1.99	7896	6766	12.4
1998	300	3.12	1.93	8465	7235	14.1
1999	300	3.11	1.92	9085	7424	14.6
2000	300	3.10	1.83	9668	7790	14.9
2001	440	2.98	1.72	10896	8968	15.5
2002	500	2.93	1.53	11778	9215	16.3
2003	500	2.92	1.51	12898	9950	17.2
2004	500	2.92	1.48	14565	11213	17.8
2005	600	2.84	1.42	16601	13438	20.7
2006	600	2.81	1.44	19027	14472	21.0
2007	600	2.72	1.45	21689	14896	21.6
2008	600	2.75	1.29	24104	16719	22.4
2009	600	2.68	1.25	26864	18595	23.1
2010	600	2.70	1.25	30035	20219	23.2
2011	600	2.71	1.32	34065	22642	25.3

注:从2001年起市区数据包括萧山区和余杭区。

a) Data of urban include Xiaoshan and Yuhang district since 2001.

13－02　市区城镇居民家庭平均每人全年现金收支

Per Capita Annual Cash Income and Expenditure of Urban Residents

单位:元　　　　(yuan)

项　目 Item	1995	2000	2005	2010	2011
家庭总收入 Total Income	**9120.88**	**9709.45**	**18761.51**	**33810.11**	**38275.50**
一、工薪收入 Income from Wages	6776.28	7074.79	12961.40	21074.58	23760.42
1.工资及补贴收入 Bonus and Subsidy	6446.59	6702.84	12235.25	20712.77	23039.80
2.其他劳动收入 Other Income of Staff & Workers From Their Working Units	329.69	371.95	726.15	361.81	720.62
二、经营净收入 Income of Staff & workers in Other－owned Units	277.48	235.69	1041.05	1650.75	1607.48
三、财产性收入 Property Income	131.78	116.93	585.72	2189.12	2586.76
四、转移性收入 Transfer Income	1935.34	2282.04	4173.33	8895.66	10320.84
#养老金或离退休金 Annuities & Retirement Pension	1705.17	1751.49	3384.69	7689.32	8697.74
#赡养收入 Supporting Income	15.07	23.99	47.71	276.57	270.56
#捐赠收入 Income from Donation	118.51	230.73	353.99	377.14	527.64
其中:可支配收入 Disposable Income	9085	9668	16601	30034.99	34065.09
借贷收入 Credit Income	**1680.13**	**2157.36**	**4289.05**	**23064.64**	**24311.98**
#提取储蓄存款 Money Drawn from Bank	1464.73	1869.60	3779.11	21892.88	23586.37
#借入款 Money Borrowed	85.35	62.28	118.70	17.87	120.24
家庭总支出 Total Expenditure	**6531.96**	**9169.32**	**17260.06**	**29955.68**	**33510.21**
消费性支出 Living Expenditure	5558.62	7789.68	13437.58	20218.98	22642.10
其中:服务性消费支出 Service Living Expenditure	－	－	3832.72	5426.97	6229.99
非消费性支出 Other Non－Living Expenditure	973.34	1379.64	3822.48	9736.70	10868.11
1.购买商品住宅及建房支出 Expenditure for House－purchasing	731.72	751.68	435.25	1852.46	2741.36
2.赡养支出 Supporting Expenditure	54.52	108.60	345.31	1695.31	1646.84
3.捐赠支出 Living Expenditure	123.79	455.76	920.25	1851.01	1707.23
4.各种非储蓄性保险支出 Expenditure for Non－saving Insurance	4.99	28.80	42.99	241.83	380.99
5.社会保障支出 Expenditure for Social Security	－	－	1739.65	2963.13	3476.48
#个人交纳的养老基金 Annuities	－	－	618.20	1087.76	1278.48
#个人交纳的住房公积金 Accumulated Expenditure for House－purchasing	－	－	872.86	1404.53	1538.60
#个人交纳的医疗基金 Expenditure for Medical Treatment	－	－	199.24	376.18	560.08
借贷支出 Expenditure for Credit	**1319.42**	**2154.60**	**4547.79**	**27961.46**	**29976.37**
#存入储蓄款 Saving in Bank	1007.63	1658.52	3298.06	25550.75	27018.63
#借出款 Money Lent	54.89	42.00	28.10	0.15	0.60
#储蓄性保险支出 Expenditure for Saving Insurance	25.99	109.80	190.63	232.59	386.10
期末手存现金 Per Capita Cash in Hand at Year－end	**512.68**	**1374.96**	**2255.52**	**783.14**	**1043.92**

13－03　2011年市区城镇居民家庭人均现金收支(按收入水平分组)

Per Capita Annual Cash Income and Expenditure of Urban Residents in 2011(Grouped by Income Level)

单位:元　　(yuan)

项　目 Item	总平均 Average	按可支配收入分组 Grouped by Disposable Income				
		20%低收入户 20% Lowest Income House－holds	20%较低收入户 20% Low Income House－holds	20%中间收入户 20% Middle Income House－holds	20%较高收入户 20% High Income House－holds	20%最高收入户 20% Highest Income House－holds
家庭总收入 Total Income	**38275.50**	**17027.22**	**26828.15**	**34349.64**	**44985.29**	**77257.40**
一、工薪收入 Income from Wages	23760.42	9720.58	16446.63	19056.14	26745.29	53094.03
二、经营净收入 Income of Staff & workers in Other－owned Units	1607.48	1044.22	974.71	689.77	1740.35	3994.23
三、财产性收入 Property Income	2586.76	1090.95	1096.23	1374.09	2903.87	7333.94
四、转移性收入 Transfer Income	10320.84	5171.47	8310.59	13229.65	13595.79	12835.20
其中:可支配收入 Disposable Income	34065.09	14397.32	23698.95	30550.03	40245.69	69781.54
借贷收入 Credit Income	**24311.98**	**9695.87**	**12718.55**	**19565.00**	**30609.17**	**56019.79**
家庭总支出 Total Expenditure	**33510.21**	**16808.06**	**21894.93**	**25948.40**	**40373.25**	**70699.65**
消费性支出 Living Expenditure	22642.10	12384.02	16073.46	19584.87	28619.07	41285.69
其中:服务性消费支出 Service Living Expenditure	6229.99	3388.04	4168.64	5259.39	7824.20	11870.02
非消费性支出 Other Non－Living Expenditure	10868.11	4424.04	5821.47	6363.53	11754.18	29413.96
1. 购买商品住宅及建房支出 Expenditure for House－purchasing	2741.36	135.90	645.19	154.56	2965.74	11317.16
2. 赡养支出 Supporting Expenditure	1646.84	1096.57	740.88	466.09	1088.28	5306.25
3. 捐赠支出 Living Expenditure	1707.23	640.37	1242.72	1559.77	2146.92	3382.19
4. 各种非储蓄性保险支出 Expenditure for Non－saving Insurance	380.99	50.25	141.85	315.66	594.45	954.15
5. 社会保障支出 Expenditure for Social Security	3476.48	2330.70	2714.83	3216.61	4064.87	5573.99
借贷支出 Expenditure for Credit	**29976.37**	**9769.32**	**17225.73**	**27979.40**	**37544.22**	**65975.96**
期末手存现金 Per Capita Cash in Hand at Year－end	**1043.92**	**865.23**	**943.03**	**878.12**	**639.60**	**1975.62**

13－04 主要年份市区城镇居民家庭人均消费性支出

Per Capita Annual Living Expenditure of Urban Residents in Main Years

单位:元 (yuan)

项目 Item	1995	2000	2005	2010	2011
消费性支出 Total Living Expenditure	**5558.62**	**7789.68**	**13437.58**	**20218.98**	**22642.10**
食品类 Food	2774.32	3303.48	4682.40	7790.18	8354.70
粮食 Grain	235.38	206.76	249.84	394.25	473.57
油脂类 Oil and Fats	49.08	56.88	72.50	149.80	173.78
肉禽及制品 Meat, Poultry and Related Products	554.87	514.56	574.29	984.02	1197.37
蛋类 Eggs	57.23	43.80	55.16	99.67	122.87
水产品类 Aquatic Products	395.19	514.20	466.42	808.88	851.61
菜类 Vegetables	266.63	302.88	364.56	664.29	723.61
酒和饮料 Liquor and Beverage	146.63	192.12	298.47	485.20	497.23
干鲜瓜果类 Dried and Fresh Melons and Fruits	211.93	214.44	335.20	609.96	701.23
在外用餐 Out－dining	368.60	531.00	1232.68	2032.78	2015.35
衣着类 Clothing	665.02	645.00	1298.53	2061.36	2261.21
家庭设备用品及服务 Facilities, Articles and Service	491.46	626.50	673.50	955.98	1052.29
医疗保健 Medicine and Medical Service	145.11	444.12	983.06	994.16	1026.95
交通和通信 Transportation and Communication	280.01	547.51	2234.02	3909.61	4678.29
教育文化娱乐服务 Education, Cultural and Recreation Service	433.13	1079.11	1970.11	2088.77	2613.71
居住 Residence	488.03	701.04	1150.69	1853.18	1944.75
杂项商品和服务 Miscellaneous Commodities and Service	281.53	442.92	445.26	565.73	710.20

13－05　2011年市区城镇居民家庭人均全年消费性支出（按收入水平分组）

Per Capita Annual Living Expenditure of Urban Residents in 2011（Grouped by Income Level）

单位:元　　　　　　　　　　　　　　　　　　　　　　　　　　　　（yuan）

项　　目 Item	总平均 Average	按可支配收入分组 Grouped by Disposable Income				
		20%低收入户 20% Lowest Income House－holds	20%较低收入户 20% Low Income House－holds	20%中间收入户 20% Middle Income House－holds	20%较高收入户 20% High Income House－holds	20%最高收入户 20% Highest Income House－holds
消费性支出 Total Living Expenditure	**22642.10**	**12384.02**	**16073.46**	**19584.87**	**28619.07**	**41285.69**
食品类 Food	8354.70	5648.17	7495.61	8646.68	9662.58	11287.30
粮食 　Grain	473.57	384.81	447.09	501.31	505.11	558.01
油脂类 　Oil and Fats	173.78	146.02	171.92	194.33	196.59	166.56
肉禽及制品 　Meat,Poultry and Related Products	1197.37	1015.95	1190.13	1337.42	1308.96	1174.82
蛋类 　Eggs	122.87	91.02	119.79	130.04	145.95	137.62
水产品类 　Aquatic Products	851.61	602.87	852.24	938.00	942.35	991.81
菜类 　Vegetables	723.61	606.52	724.6	837.27	772.31	698.72
酒和饮料 　Liquor and Beverage	497.23	317.88	452.8	504.87	544.47	729.76
干鲜瓜果类 　Dried and Fresh Melons and Fruits	701.23	389.78	610.58	752.57	848.65	1012.00
在外用餐 　Out－dining	2015.35	1023.52	1473.52	1818.47	2391.62	3797.13
衣着类 Clothing	2261.21	990.38	1640.58	1935.97	2808.61	4481.53
家庭设备用品及服务 Facilities,Articles and Service	1052.29	349.06	710.48	940.43	1311.14	2243.78
医疗保健 Medicine and Medical Service	1026.95	616.67	878.87	1091.85	1081.32	1609.08
交通和通信 Transportation and Communication	4678.29	1919.36	1947.09	2622.14	6881.73	11615.93
教育文化娱乐服务 Education, Cultural and Recreation Service	2613.71	1515.68	1862.61	2207.79	3361.69	4647.80
居住 Residence	1944.75	1141.08	1186.52	1471.63	2719.17	3648.25
杂项商品和服务 Miscellaneous Commodities and Service	710.20	203.63	351.70	668.39	792.84	1752.02

13－06 主要年份市区城镇居民家庭平均每百户耐用消费品拥有量

Number of Major Durable Consumer Goods Owned Per 100 Urban Households in Main Years

项　目 Item		1995	2000	2005	2010	2011
摩托车 Motorcycle	（辆）(unit)	1.50	3.60	11.00	4.51	4.12
助力电动车 Electric－bicycle	（辆）(unit)			28.67	42.37	45.95
家用汽车 Family Car	（辆）(unit)		0.70	12.83	22.83	31.24
微波炉 Micro－wave Oven	（个）(unit)		39.00	68.17	78.76	73.53
普通电话 Telephone	（部）(set)		95.00	99.83	89.62	84.71
移动电话 Mobile Phone	（部）(set)		19.00	178.67	193.59	211.00
淋浴热水器 Water Heater	（台）(unit)	43.50	81.30	92.33	99.43	103.44
洗衣机 Washing Machine	（台）(unit)	93.50	96.33	94.17	96.23	96.26
电冰箱 Refrigerator	（台）(unit)	103.50	101.67	100.00	102.28	102.50
家用电脑 Personal Computer	（台）(unit)		23.00	74.50	99.02	109.70
彩色电视机 Color TV Set	（台）(unit)	102.30	146.67	182.67	179.19	176.88
组合音响 Music Center	（套）(set)	12.00	28.67	37.83	30.00	25.48
摄像机 Video Recorder	（架）(unit)		3.33	7.50	11.09	11.59
照相机 Camera	（架）(unit)	54.00	64.67	59.00	54.76	62.07
空调器 Air Conditioner	（台）(unit)	43.00	104.00	183.33	214.61	212.03

13－07 主要年份全市农村住户调查情况

Basic Conditions of Whole Municipality Rural Households in Main Years

年份 Year	调查户数(户) Number of Households Surveyed (household)	平均每户人口(人) Average Number of Residents per Household (person)	平均每户劳动力(人) Average Number of Laborers Per Household (person)	农民人均年纯收入(元) Per Capita Annual Net Income of Rural Households (yuan)	人均生活费支出(元) Per Capita Annual Living Expenditure (yuan)	人均居住面积(平方米) Per Capita Floor Space (sq. m)
1978				162		
1979				204		
1980	60	4.72	2.93	250	287	23.3
1981	60	4.60	2.70	333	294	25.2
1982	60	4.43	2.73	405	328	26.3
1983	170	4.55	2.85	395	355	29.9
1984	170	4.44	2.81	510	416	31.7
1985	420	4.40	2.88	624	542	29.9
1986	620	4.39	2.88	675	601	31.3
1987	620	4.34	2.86	820	714	33.1
1988	620	4.26	2.87	996	925	35.5
1989	620	4.17	2.85	1117	1011	36.8
1990	620	4.16	2.89	1171	923	39.6
1991	620	4.03	2.81	1308	1018	38.0
1992	620	4.01	2.81	1493	1129	37.5
1993	540	3.91	2.76	1748	1276	37.1
1994	630	3.85	2.35	2267	1884	37.8
1995	630	3.87	2.30	3012	2373	40.5
1996	630	3.81	2.77	3482	2772	42.2
1997	630	3.87	2.86	3785	2762	42.0
1998	630	3.87	2.88	4006	2858	46.2
1999	630	3.80	2.80	4209	2851	48.0
2000	630	3.61	2.59	4894	3393	49.0
2001	630	3.57	2.53	5330	3909	52.0
2002	630	3.53	2.53	5708	4444	52.7
2003	670	3.48	2.53	6250	5142	54.7
2004	670	3.48	2.54	6950	5608	58.9
2005	1100	3.34	2.34	7655	6004	66.0
2006	1100	3.63	2.52	8515	6901	66.5
2007	1100	3.60	2.61	9549	7568	68.0
2008	1100	3.56	2.58	10692	8446	69.7
2009	1100	3.57	2.59	11822	9065	70.7
2010	1100	3.58	2.59	13186	10267	71.2
2011	1100	3.46	2.49	15245	12125	72.5

13－08　主要年份全市农村居民家庭人均纯收入

Per Capita Annual Gross and Net Income of Whole Municipality Rural Households in Main Years

单位:元　　　　(yuan)

项　目 Item	1995	2000	2005	2010	2011
全年纯收入 Net Income	**3012**	**4894**	**7655**	**13186**	**15245**
1. 劳动者的工资性收入 Laborers´Remuneration	896	2045	3347	7777	9079
2. 家庭经营收入 Income from Household Business Operation	1960	2363	3358	4049	4478
#农业收入 Income from Farming	578	1016	1858	1005	1159
林业收入 Income from Forestry	142	71	311	365	445
牧业收入 Income from Animal Husbandry	397	382	310	223	271
渔业收入 Income from Fishery	24	31	185	73	45
工业收入 Income from Industry	112	262	392	473	469
建筑业收入 Income from Construction	77	102	228	345	430
交通、运输、仓储及邮电业收入 Transportation, Posts, Storage and Telecommunication	136	163	483	517	532
批发和零售贸易、餐饮业收入 Income from Retail Wholesale & Trade and Catering Services	118	150	391	699	742
社会服务业收入 Social Serve Trade	59	73	127	210	205
3. 转移性收入 Transfer Income	83	312	481	719	945
#在外人口寄回或带回 Income of Going out to Work	5	21	93	101	133
农村外部亲友赠送 Present from Rural Friends and Relatives	9	7	133	23	58
4. 财产性收入 Property Income	73	174	469	641	743
#土地征用补偿收入 #Compensation for Confiscating Land	6	100	243	190	206

13－09　主要年份全市农村居民家庭人均支出

Per Capita Gross Expenditure of Whole City's Rural Households in Main Years

单位:元　　　　(yuan)

项　目 Item	1995	2000	2005	2010	2011
全年总支出 Gross Expenditure	**3457**	**3789**	**8043**	**13439**	**15941**
生活消费支出 Living Expenditure	**2373**	**3393**	**6004**	**10227**	**12125**
1. 食品 Food	1213	1392	2145	3333	4076
#在外饮食 #Out－dining	43	83	221	487	570
食品加工费 Food－processing	13	15	11	12	8
2. 衣着 Clothing	169	169	381	609	819
3. 居住 Residence	396	694	1143	2603	2845
#住房 #Housing	284	509	724	1855	2144
电费 Electricity	22	56	110	255	282
燃料 Fuel	53	38	77	126	155
4. 家庭设备、用品及服务 Household Facilities, Articles and Services	155	163	307	512	645
5. 医疗保健 Medicines and Medical Services	99	329	474	623	753
#医药卫生保健用品 #Medicines	39	99	189	252	226
医疗保健服务费 Medicines Services	58	64	256	371	528
6. 交通和通讯 Transportation and Communications	102	204	680	1451	1865
#交通工具 #Vehicles	67	123	158	784	857
交通费 Traffic	18	36	83	90	94
邮电费 Postage	4	62	219	264	242
7. 文教娱乐用品及服务 Cultural, Educational and Recreational Articles and Services	156	318	735	934	861
文化教育娱乐用品 Cultural, Educational and Recreational Articles	43	70	114	227	268
文化教育娱乐服务 Culrural, Educational and Recreational Services	113	248	621	546	593

单位:元 13－09 续表 continued (yuan)

项 目 Item	1995	2000	2005	2010	2011
#学杂费 #Tuition and Incidental Expenses	94	210	430	344	175
技术培训费 Technical Training Expenses	5	5	32	31	48
文娱费 Recreational and Cultural Expenses	11	9	22	53	45
8.其他商品和服务 Other Commodities and Services	84	124	139	202	261
家庭经营费用支出 Expenditure of Household Business Operation	**681**	**427**	**1157**	**1285**	**1831**
种植业生产支出 Expenditure of Farming	199	183	245	279	404
林业生产支出 Expenditure of Forestry	3	10	71	87	143
牧业生产支出 Expenditure of Animal Husbandry	267	121	168	184	377
渔业生产支出 Expenditure of Fishery	4	10	116	48	11
工业生产支出 Expenditure of Industry	62	61	276	449	313
建筑业生产支出 Expenditure of Construction	3	3	35	74	149
运输业生产支出 Expenditure of Transportation	64	29	141	175	128
批发和零售贸易、餐饮业支出 Expenditure of Wholesale and Retail Trade & Catering Services	53	6	84	53	129
服务业支出 Expenditure of Services Trade	5	1	9	8	52
其他经营支出 Others	22	3	12	6	16
购置生产用固定资产支出 Expenditure of Purchasing Fixed Assets	**135**	**86**	**202**	**121**	**178**
税费支出 Expenditure of Taxes	**23**	**50**	**31**	**10**	**10**
其他非借贷性支出 Others Expenditure not for Loans	**235**	**206**	**649**	**1079**	**1477**
#寄给和带给在外人口 Posting and Giving to People Outside	6	23	396	260	168
赠送农村外部亲友 Present to Rural Friends and Relatives	7	8	7	7	8
附:生产用固定资产累计折旧 Depreciation of Fixed Assets for Production	**63**	**79**	**218**		

13－10　主要年份全市农村居民家庭平均每百户耐用消费品拥有量

Number of Major Durable Consumer Goods Owned Per 100 Rural Households in Main Years

项　　目	Item	1995	2000	2005	2010	2011
自行车　（辆）	Bicycle　（Unit）	209	183	124	127	107
洗衣机　（台）	Washing Machine（Unit）	14	34	62	85	78
电冰箱　（台）	Refrigerator　（Unit）	23	46	72	98	93
摩托车　（辆）	Motorcycle　（Unit）	13	38	73	66	41
黑白电视机（台）	Black and White TV Set（Unit）	73	57	17	4	2
彩色电视机（台）	Color TV Set　（Unit）	34	86	141	186	192
照相机　（架）	Camera　（Unit）	4	7	14	23	22
抽油烟机　（台）	Smoke Exhauster（Unit）	4	17	39	62	57
吸尘器　（台）	Dust Collector　（Unit）	2	3	5	10	9
空调机　（台）	Air Conditioner（Unit）	1	8	12	111	120

13-11 主要年份全市非私营单位在岗职工工资总额

Total Wages of Fully Employed Staff and Workers of Non-private Units in The Whole City in Main Years

单位:万元 (10000 yuan)

年份 Year	总计 Total	国有 State-owned	集体 Collective-owned	其他 Other
1978	43775	32730	11045	
1979	52127	38651	13476	
1980	67918	49461	18457	
1981	72896	52581	20315	
1982	75584	55325	20259	
1983	78336	57716	20620	
1984	102223	72149	29385	689
1985	130114	90643	38482	989
1986	157471	111010	45230	1231
1987	180077	127353	50512	2212
1988	230868	163863	63525	3480
1989	253956	180706	68230	5020
1990	277910	203212	70253	4445
1991	313906	227438	78827	7641
1992	377614	272098	89429	16087
1993	534537	367062	118634	48841
1994	772236	525936	159864	86436
1995	890488	598524	170638	121326
1996	973592	647327	171227	155038
1997	1073862	722182	173502	178178
1998	1112718	719249	127584	265885
1999	1180947	755073	102906	322968
2000	1267524	784396	80911	402217
2001	1481659	899920	65534	516205
2002	1614676	1026645	65820	522211
2003	1867776	1174126	64820	628830
2004	2188159	1367229	71112	749818
2005	2970200	1617671	88226	1264303
2006	3811735	1825613	99009	1887113
2007	4954813	2202920	130443	2621450
2008	6416424	2551401	149362	3715661
2009	7549145	2871075	171367	4506703
2010	9330552	3335202	201537	5793813
2011	11222834	3728461	230166	7264206

注:1998 年以前为全市职工工资总额。

a) Data on total wage bill before 1998 refer to wages of staff and workers.

13－12 主要年份市区非私营单位在岗职工工资总额

Total Wages of Fully Employed Staff and Workers of Non－private Units in Urban District in Main Years

单位:万元 (10000 yuan)

年份 Year	总计 Total	国有 State－owned	集体 Collective－owned	其他 Other
1978	28256	21727	6529	
1979	34318	26164	8154	
1980	45574	33920	11654	
1981	48809	35856	12953	
1982	50959	37898	13061	
1983	52909	39848	13061	
1984	69135	51057	17498	580
1985	87774	63830	23100	844
1986	105995	77989	26936	1070
1987	121003	89233	29728	2042
1988	152859	113227	36474	3158
1989	167055	123862	38759	4434
1990	182985	139337	40061	3587
1991	209052	157279	45778	5995
1992	253653	186961	52890	13802
1993	359041	254742	63921	40378
1994	521669	360273	87807	73589
1995	615450	422101	92980	100369
1996	683244	462364	94061	126819
1997	762957	521029	84456	147472
1998	803264	532561	74852	195851
1999	864418	559707	61417	243294
2000	949872	594435	47580	307857
2001	1279749	756669	49687	473393
2002	1398222	866806	48691	482724
2003	1617504	996961	44920	575624
2004	1859164	1162299	50943	645921
2005	2584779	1380262	64558	1139959
2006	3338568	1562198	72670	1703700
2007	4317965	1882616	101388	2333961
2008	5679543	2180009	117583	3381951
2009	6665279	2425106	147894	4092280
2010	8238017	2814874	169969	5253173
2011	9954506	3158169	193784	6602554

注:从 2001 年起市区数据包括萧山区和余杭区,1998 年以前为职工工资总额。

a) Data of urban include Xiaoshan and Yuhang district since 2001, data on total wage bill before 1998 refer to wages of staff and workers.

13－13　主要年份全市非私营单位在岗职工年平均工资

Average Annual Wages of Fully Employed Staff and Workers of Non－private Units in Main Years

单位:元　　　　(yuan)

年　份 Year	总　计 Total	国有 State－owned	集体 Collective－owned	其他 Other
1978	597	634	509	
1979	643	694	531	
1980	777	832	660	
1981	783	824	693	
1982	791	823	714	
1983	813	840	745	
1984	1036	1080	943	1006
1985	1266	1302	1188	1287
1986	1469	1531	1336	1561
1987	1616	1682	1469	1685
1988	1986	2063	1806	2129
1989	2173	2259	1961	2416
1990	2382	2504	2078	2582
1991	2586	2710	2252	3123
1992	3071	3236	2600	3571
1993	4220	4479	3404	4949
1994	6118	6565	4750	6936
1995	7156	7546	5604	8266
1996	7966	8336	6178	9199
1997	9108	9522	6905	10519
1998	10555	11180	7720	10826
1999	12187	12972	8938	11883
2000	14257	15441	10150	13401
2001	18319	21119	13831	15394
2002	21418	24739	15090	17685
2003	24668	29121	18154	19757
2004	28891	35507	24010	21879
2005	31069	40483	23964	24332
2006	32791	44664	21845	26641
2007	36496	53343	26095	29300
2008	40193	56802	30698	33823
2009	43947	63602	36625	36953
2010	48772	71579	42929	41378
2011	54408	79657	49117	46932

注:1998 年以前为全市职工年平均工资。

a) Data on total wage bill before 1998 refer to average wages of staff and workers.

13－14 主要年份市区在岗职工年平均工资

Average Annual Wages of Fully Employed Workers of Urban District in Main Years

单位:元 (yuan)

年 份 Year	全社会 Whole society	非私营单位 Non－private	国有 State－owned economic	集体 Collective－owned	其他 Other
1978		642	673	558	
1979		692	730	593	
1980		814	868	688	
1981		810	847	724	
1982		809	845	719	
1983		835	869	746	
1984		1071	1119	954	1012
1985		1316	1348	1235	1290
1986		1536	1589	1401	1519
1987		1690	1744	1545	1692
1988		2073	2135	4897	2119
1989		2261	2340	2031	2381
1990		2486	2587	2179	2691
1991		2706	2812	2350	3233
1992		3233	3385	2719	3658
1993		4561	4816	3565	5115
1994		6597	7024	4978	7254
1995		7786	8154	5928	8658
1996		7851	9032	6689	9888
1997		10048	10319	7624	11299
1998		11512	11865	8298	12339
1999		13225	13698	9391	13545
2000		15454	16373	10370	15017
2001	18205	18962	21916	14573	16018
2002	19749	22091	25720	15295	18279
2003	20113	25535	30334	18074	20563
2004	22235	30719	37585	24291	23488
2005	22645	32166	41977	24220	25440
2006	23581	33967	46509	21971	27751
2007	25489	37991	55675	25774	30746
2008	27863	41501	58696	31097	35252
2009	30480	45149	65118	38096	38423
2010	34330	49938	73130	43804	42850
2011	38837	55958	81867	50891	48725

注:市区全社会在岗职工平均工资包括所有国有、集体、股份制、三资和私营单位,但不包含个体工商户。

a) The average annual wage of fully employed workers of the whole society in urban district includes all state－owned, collective－owned, share holding, foreign－funded and private enterprises, but excludes individual businesses.

13-15 全市非私营单位从业人员劳动报酬(2011年)

Laborers' Remuneration of Employed Persons in Non-private Units(2011)

单位:万元 (10000 yuan)

项目 Item	年末单位从业人员劳动报酬 Laborers' Remuneration of Employed Persons at Year-end	在岗职工工资总额 Total Wages of Fully Employed Staff and Workers	劳务派遣人员报酬 The Labor Dispatch Personnel Compensation	其他从业人员劳动报酬 Laborers' Remuneration of Other Employed Persons	#在岗职工平均工资(元/人) Average Wage of Fully Employed Staff and Workers (yuan/person)
全市总计 Total	**13050619**	**11222834**	**1241751**	**586035**	**54408**
其中:企业 Enterprises	10144657	8510404	1143765	490488	49536
事业 Institutions	2006533	1848874	82847	74812	78730
机关 Agencies and Organizations	815509	787495	14523	13491	88956
民间非营利组织 Non-profit Organizations	41992	36534	298	5160	36888
其他 Other	41928	39527	318	2084	34549
市区总计 Urban District	**11649473**	**9954506**	**1144410**	**550556**	**55958**
其中:企业 Enterprises	9271571	7746633	1055327	469611	51329
事业 Institutions	1662285	1522260	74835	65190	82219
机关 Agencies and Organizations	639599	617096	13744	8760	93802
民间非营利组织 Non-profit Organizations	36652	31402	280	4970	37779
其他 Other	39365	37116	225	2025	35463
上城区 Shangcheng	**1359355**	**1148359**	**145642**	**65354**	**83042**
下城区 Xiacheng	**1636485**	**1435069**	**112503**	**88913**	**81863**
江干区 Jianggan	**787658**	**663321**	**62279**	**62058**	**45534**
拱墅区 Gongshu	**816083**	**637280**	**145254**	**33549**	**52068**
西湖区 Xihu	**1788163**	**1399521**	**305994**	**82647**	**54703**
高新(滨江)区 Hi-Tech (Binjiang)	**1165474**	**1063776**	**76091**	**25607**	**70170**
萧山区 Xiaoshan	**2073319**	**1957572**	**55655**	**60092**	**41263**
余杭区 Yuhang	**948369**	**883092**	**46213**	**19064**	**49702**
桐庐县 Tonglu	**207240**	**192451**	**7794**	**6996**	**45001**
淳安县 Chun'an	**167147**	**148580**	**14095**	**4472**	**49637**

单位:万元　　13－15　续表　continued　　(10000 yuan)

项　　目 Item	年末单位从业人员劳动报酬 Laborers´Remuneration of Employed Persons at Year－end	在岗职工工资总额 Total Wages of Fully Employed Staff and Workers	劳务派遣人员报酬 The Labor Dispatch Personnel Compensation	其他从业人员劳动报酬 Laborers´Remuneration of Other Employed Persons	#在岗职工平均工资(元/人) Average Wage of Fully Employed Staff and Workers(yuan/person)
建德市 Jiande	**204718**	**193514**	**4414**	**6790**	**47287**
富阳市 Fuyang	**468060**	**401737**	**54972**	**11351**	**45106**
临安市 Lin´an	**353982**	**332046**	**16066**	**5870**	**40933**
按国民经济行业分组 Grouped by Sector					
农、林、牧、渔业 Farming, Forestry, Animal Husbandry and Fishery	5636	5544	–	92	36303
采矿业 Mining and Quarrying	8596	7980	593	24	36093
制造业 Manufacturing	3356915	3020453	264986	71476	42901
电力、煤气及水的生产和供应业 Production and Supply of Electricity, Gas and Water	186975	171386	14435	1154	92641
建筑业 Construction	1942396	1176721	477824	287851	31477
交通运输、仓储及邮政业 Transportation, Storage and Post	518861	451644	60591	6626	60475
信息传输、计算机服务和软件业 Information Transmission Computer Service and Software	663767	608944	48752	6071	101268
批发与零售业 Wholesale & Retail Trade	817789	691953	105454	20382	53799
住宿和餐饮业 Lodging and Catering	256425	236438	9351	10637	31960
金融业 Banking and Insurance	1056335	974665	56283	25387	155414
房地产业 Real Estate	333586	310075	9981	13530	53584
租赁与商务服务业 Renting and Business Service	372682	319785	44251	8646	46189
科学研究、技术服务与地质勘查业 Scientific Research, Technical Service and Geological Prospecting	584104	534497	21560	28047	70111
水利、环境和公共设施管理业 Water Conservany, Environment and Public Utility	173736	128170	28521	17046	42753
居民服务和其他服务业 Service for the Residents and Other	32846	25668	5832	1345	40711
教育 Education	1027152	967347	33332	26473	74903
卫生、社会保障和社会福利业 Health Care, Sports and Social Welfare	652184	581385	30414	40385	84393
文化、体育与娱乐业 Culture, Sports and Entertainment	132956	116350	12031	4575	72281
公共管理与社会组织 Public Management and Social Organizations	927680	893829	17562	16289	82209

13 - 16 全市国有单位从业人员劳动报酬(2011 年)

Laborers´Remuneration of Employed Persons for State - owned Units(2011)

单位:万元 (10000 yuan)

项目 Item	年末单位从业人员劳动报酬 Laborers´Remuneration of Employed Persons at Year - end	在岗职工工资总额 Total Wages of Fully Employed Staff and Workers	劳务派遣人员劳动报酬 The Labor Dispatch Personnel Compensation	其他从业人员劳动报酬 Laborers´Remuneration of Other Employed Persons	#在岗职工平均工资(元/人) Average Wage of Fully Employed Staff and Workers (yuan/person)
总计 Total	**4089546**	**3728461**	**245901**	**115184**	**79657**
按隶属关系分 Grouped by Subordination					
中央属 Central	853284	748234	97463	7587	100204
省　属 Provincial	1156620	1035476	69759	51385	84388
市　属 Municipal	604453	551322	38544	14587	74326
县及县以下 At and below County Level	1436645	1358151	37738	40756	71300
其他 Other	38544	35279	2397	868	58486
按企业、事业、机关分组 Grouped by Enterprises, Institutions and Agencies					
企业 Enterprises	1367181	1182410	151279	33492	74277
事业 Institutions	1893432	1746482	79878	67073	80196
机关 Agencies and Organizations	815509	787495	14523	13491	88956
民间非营利组织 Non - profit Organizations	9813	8843	55	915	46079
其他 Other	3610	3232	166	213	49271
按国民经济行业分组 Grouped by Sector					
农、林、牧、渔业 Farming, Forestry, Animal Husbandry and Fishery	2694	2654	-	40	40331
采矿业 Mining & Quarrying	324	324	-	-	30819
制造业 Manufacturing	123902	117637	2628	3637	61803

项目 Item	年末单位从业人员劳动报酬 Laborers' Remuneration of Employed Persons at Year－end	在岗职工工资总额 Total Wages of Fully Employed Staff and Workers	劳务派遣人员劳动报酬 The Labor Dispatch Personnel Compensation	其他从业人员劳动报酬 Laborers' Remuneration of Other Employed Persons	#在岗职工平均工资(元/人) Average Wage of Fully Employed Staff and Workers (yuan/person)
电力、煤气及水的生产和供应业 Production and Supply of Electricity, Gas and Water	125382	111634	13640	108	117262
建筑业 Construction	79941	62243	9889	7809	76259
交通运输、仓储及邮政业 Transportation, Storage and Post	279467	246127	30225	3114	62204
信息传输、计算机服务和软件业 Information Transmission Computer Service and Software	87222	69248	17940	34	120098
批发与零售业 Wholesale & Retail Trade	79864	74512	4835	517	93868
住宿和餐饮业 Lodging and Catering	37980	32271	4805	904	39201
金融业 Banking and Insurance	179500	161681	8662	9156	151090
房地产业 Real Estate	35261	31923	2065	1272	63441
租赁与商务服务业 Renting and Business Service	158559	118337	37955	2268	44612
科学研究、技术服务与地质勘查业 Scientific Research, Technical Service and Geological Prospecting	281741	262766	8827	10148	82683
水利、环境和公共设施管理业 Water Conservany, Environment and Public Utility	86748	69460	11415	5873	51871
居民服务和其他服务业 Service for the Residents and Other	19175	13910	4460	805	49553
教育 Education	938261	886250	31702	20308	79986
卫生、社会保障和社会福利业 Health Care, Sports and Social Welfare	571780	513261	27656	30863	89932
文化、体育与娱乐业 Culture, Sports and Entertainment	110977	95263	11670	4044	77305
公共管理与社会组织 Public Management and Social Organizations	890771	858961	17526	14283	87071

13－17 全市集体单位从业人员劳动报酬(2011年)

Laborers´ Remuneration of Employed Persons for Collective－owned Units(2011)

单位:万元 (10000 yuan)

项目 Item	年末单位从业人员劳动报酬 Laborers´ Remuneration of Employed Persons at Year－end	在岗职工工资总额 Total Wages of Fully Employed Staff and Workers	劳务派遣人员劳动报酬 The Labor Dispatch Personnel Compensation	其他从业人员劳动报酬 Laborers´ Remuneration of Other Employed Persons	#在岗职工平均工资(元/人) Average Wage of Fully Employed Staff and Workers (yuan/person)
总计 Total	**249320**	**230166**	**8449**	**10704**	**49117**
按企业、事业分组 Grouped by Enterprises and Institutions					
企业 Enterprises	155815	146680	5837	3299	44142
事业 Institutions	89139	80823	2580	5737	61980
机关 Agencies and Organizations	－	－	－	－	－
民间非营利组织 Non－profit Organizations	2726	1058	33	1635	41988
其他 Other	1640	1606	－	34	47241
按国民经济行业分组 Grouped by Sector					
农、林、牧、渔业 Farming, Forestry, Animal Husbandry and Fishery	234	234	－	－	22452
采矿业 Mining & Quarrying	1736	1733	－	3	31563
制造业 Manufacturing	15622	14538	784	301	34541
电力、煤气及水的生产和供应业 Production and Supply of Electricity, Gas and Water	2545	2543	－	2	139709
建筑业 Construction	7478	5697	870	911	33910
交通运输、仓储和邮政业 Transportation, Storage and Post	45064	43877	914	273	68892
信息传输、计算机服务和软件业 Information Transmission Computer Service and Software	1864	1500	239	124	54956
批发与零售业 Wholesale & Retail Trade	8976	8605	141	229	47834
住宿和餐饮业 Lodging and Catering	6984	6569	250	165	27258
金融业 Banking and Insurance	－	－	－	－	－
房地产业 Real Estate	8787	8036	387	364	73125
租赁与商务服务业 Renting and Business Service	46277	45439	267	572	34814
科学研究、技术服务与地质勘查业 Scientific Research, Technical Service and Geological Prospecting	9135	7286	1658	190	73157
水利、环境和公共设施管理业 Water Conservancy, Environment and Public Utility	7965	6404	287	1275	32705
居民服务和其他服务业 Service for the Residents and Other	2072	1930	7	135	37401
教育 Education	34563	32382	672	1509	64776
卫生、社会保障和社会福利业 Health Care, Sports and Social Welfare	48956	42396	1958	4602	65934
文化、体育与娱乐业 Culture, Sports and Entertainment	394	371	17	6	37130
公共管理与社会组织 Public Management and Social Organizations	670	627	－	43	46081

13－18 全市其他非私营单位从业人员劳动报酬(2011年)

Laborers´ Remuneration of Employed Persons for Other Non－private Units(2011)

单位:万元 (10000 yuan)

项目 Item	年末单位从业人员劳动报酬 Laborers´ Remuneration of Employed Persons at Year－end	在岗职工工资总额 Total Wages of Fully Employed Staff and Workers	劳务派遣人员劳动报酬 The Labor Dispatch Personnel Compensation	其他从业人员劳动报酬 Laborers´ Remuneration of Other Employed Persons	#在岗职工平均工资(元/人) Average Wage of Fully Employed Staff and Workers (yuan/person)
合计 Total	**8711754**	**7264206**	**987401**	**460147**	**46932**
按登记注册类型分 Grouped by Ownership					
内资 Domestic－funded Enterprises	6015888	4874560	751823	389506	45649
港、澳、台商投资 Enterprises with Investment from Hong Kong, Macao and Taiwan	1104979	994035	94374	16570	48804
外商投资 Enterprises with Foreign Investment	1590887	1395611	141205	54071	50513
按企业、事业分组 Grouped by Enterprises, Institutions and Agencies					
企业 Enterprises	8621661	7181315	986650	453697	47072
事业 Institutions	23961	21569	390	2002	53628
民间非营利组织 Non－profit Organizations	29453	26633	209	2610	34441
其他 Other	36678	34689	152	1837	33211
按国民经济行业分组 Grouped by Sector					
农、林、牧、渔业 Farming, Forestry, Animal Husbandry and Fishery	2708	2656	－	52	34722
采矿业 Mining and Quarrying	6537	5924	593	21	38046
制造业 Manufacturing	3217391	2888279	261574	67538	42424
电力、煤气及水的生产和供应业 Production and Supply of Electricity, Gas and Water	59048	57210	795	1043	65026
建筑业 Construction	1854977	1108781	467065	279131	30462

单位:万元　　13－18　续表　continued　　(10000 yuan)

项目 Item	年末单位从业人员劳动报酬 Laborers' Remuneration of Employed Persons at Year－end	在岗职工工资总额 Total Wages of Fully Employed Staff and Workers	劳务派遣人员劳动报酬 The Labor Dispatch Personnel Compensation	其他从业人员劳动报酬 Laborers' Remuneration of Other Employed Persons	#在岗职工平均工资(元/人) Average Wage of Fully Employed Staff and Workers (yuan/person)
交通运输、仓储和邮政业 Transportation, Storage and Post	194331	161640	29453	3238	56230
信息传输、计算机服务和软件业 Information Transmission Computer Service and Software	574681	538195	30573	5913	99494
批发与零售业 Wholesale & Retail Trade	728949	608835	100478	19636	51213
住宿和餐饮业 Lodging and Catering	211461	197598	4296	9568	31197
金融业 Banking and Insurance	876835	812984	47620	16231	156304
房地产业 Real Estate	289539	270115	7529	11894	52210
租赁与商务服务业 Renting and Business Service	167846	156009	6030	5807	52606
科学研究、技术服务与地质勘查业 Scientific Research, Technical Service and Geological Prospecting	293229	264445	11075	17708	60848
水利、环境和公共设施管理业 Water Conservancy, Environment and Public Utility	79023	52306	16819	9898	35752
居民服务和其他服务业 Service for the Residents and Other	11599	9829	1364	406	32959
教育 Education	54328	48715	957	4656	36499
卫生、社会保障和社会福利业 Health Care, Sports and Social Welfare	31448	25728	800	4920	47751
文化、体育与娱乐业 Culture, Sports and Entertainment	21585	20716	345	524	56385
公共管理与社会组织 Public Management and Social Organizations	36240	34241	36	1963	34451

13－19 主要年份市区消费价格指数

Consumer Price Indices of Urban District in Main Years

（上年＝100） (Preceding Year＝100)

年 份 Year	居民消费价格指数 General Consumer Price Index	商品零售价格指数 General Retail Price Index
1978	100.1	100.1
1979	100.4	100.9
1980	100.8	109.3
1981	102.0	102.0
1982	102.0	102.3
1983	102.1	102.3
1984	103.1	103.1
1985	117.2	117.5
1986	106.0	106.1
1987	110.5	111.3
1988	121.9	123.4
1989	117.8	118.2
1990	104.6	104.4
1991	107.5	106.9
1992	110.4	110.2
1993	121.4	117.3
1994	121.5	118.8
1995	116.5	113.3
1996	110.5	107.2
1997	106.7	102.4
1998	101.8	99.8
1999	100.4	98.2
2000	100.8	98.3
2001	99.5	95.3
2002	98.8	97.9
2003	99.5	98.1
2004	102.5	101.6
2005	101.7	100.3
2006	101.2	100.2
2007	103.5	103.1
2008	104.9	106.0
2009	98.6	98.6
2010	103.9	103.7
2011	104.8	104.4

13－20 市区居民消费价格指数(2011 年)

Consumer Price Indices in Urban District(2011)

(上年＝100)　　　　(Preceding Year＝100)

项　　目	Item	指数 Indices
居民消费价格总指数	**Consumer Price Indices**	**104.8**
一、食品	**Food**	**110.7**
1. 粮食	Grain	110.1
2. 淀粉及制品	Starches and Tubers	99.4
3. 干豆类及豆制品	Bean and Its Products	120.3
4. 油脂	Oil and Fat	118.7
5. 肉禽及其制品	Meal Poultry and Their Products	120.1
6. 蛋	Eggs	115.7
7. 水产品	Aquatic Products	112.3
8. 菜	Vegetables	99.8
9. 调味品	Flavoring	103.4
10. 糖	Sugar	108.1
11. 茶及饮料	Tea and Beverages	106.3
12. 干鲜瓜果	Dried and Fresh Melons and Fruits	113.8
13. 糕点饼干面包	Cake、Biscuit and Bread	108.7
14. 液体乳及乳制品	Milk and Its Products	106.3
15. 在外用膳食品	Outward Dinner	107.6
16. 其他食品	Other Food	109.9
二、烟酒及用品	**Tobacco、Liquor and Articles**	**100.9**
1. 烟草	Tobacco	100.1
2. 酒	Liquor	103.4
三、衣着	**Clothing**	**106.1**
1. 服装	Garments	106.0
2. 衣着材料	Clothing Material	120.7

(上年 = 100)　　13 - 20　续表　continued　　(Preceding Year = 100)

项　　目	Item	指　　数 Indices
3. 鞋袜帽	Shoes, Socks and Hats	105.9
4. 衣着加工服务费	Clothing Processing Service	108.1
四、家庭设备用品及维修服务	**Household Facilities, Articles and Repair Service**	**104.2**
1. 耐用消费品	Durable Consumer Goods	101.6
2. 室内装饰品	Interior Decorations	100.0
3. 床上用品	Bed Articles	108.6
4. 家庭日用杂品	Daily Use Household Articles	102.0
5. 家庭服务及加工维修服务	Household and Repair Service	116.6
五、医疗保健和个人用品	**Medical Articles and Personal Articles**	**103.6**
1. 医疗保健	Medical Care	103.5
2. 个人用品及服务	Personel Articles and Service	104.0
六、交通和通信	**Transportation and Communication**	**98.4**
1. 交通	Transportation	98.3
2. 通信	Communication	98.6
七、娱乐教育文化用品及服务	**Recreation, Education and Culture Articles**	**100.1**
1. 文娱用耐用消费品及服务	Durable Consumer Goods and Recreation Service	92.1
2. 教育	Education	100.0
3. 文化娱乐类	Cultural and Recreational Articles	104.9
4. 旅游	Tourism and Outgoing	103.0
八、居住	**Residence**	**104.8**
1. 建房及装修材料	Construction and Upholstery Materials	104.1
2. 住房租金	House Renting	103.9
3. 自有住房	Private Owned Houses	106.3
4. 水、电、燃料	Water, Electricity and Fuels	101.5

13－21　市区零售价格指数(2011年)

Retail Price Indices in Urban District(2011)

(上年=100)　　　　(Preceding Year=100)

项　目	Item	指数 Indices
商品零售价格总指数	**Retail Price Indices**	**104.4**
一、食品	**Food**	**110.9**
1.粮食	Grain	110.2
2.淀粉及制品	Starches and Tubers	98.6
3.干豆类及豆制品	Bean and Its Products	121.7
4.油脂	Oil and Fat	118.9
5.肉禽及其制品	Meal Poultry and Their Products	120.2
6.蛋	Eggs	115.7
7.水产品	Aquatic Products	111.9
8.菜	Vegetables	99.8
9.调味品	Flavoring	103.4
10.糖	Carbohydrate	109.2
11.干鲜瓜果	Dried and Fresh Melons and Fruits	113.3
12.糕点饼干面包	Cake、Biscuit and Bread	108.6
13.液体乳及乳制品	Milk and Its Products	106.7
14.在外用膳食品	Outward Dinner	107.8
15.其他食品	Other Food	109.9
二、饮料、烟酒	**Beverages,Tobacco and Liquor**	**102.0**
1.茶及饮料	Tea and Beverages	105.8
2.烟草	Tobacco	100.1
3.酒	Liquor	103.3
三、服装、鞋帽	**Garments,Shoes and Hats**	**105.7**
1.服装	Garments	105.7
2.鞋袜帽	Shoes,Socks and Hats	106.0
3.其他	Other	102.0
四、纺织品	**Textiles**	**112.7**
1.衣着材料	Clothing Material	120.7
2.床上用品	Bed Articles	107.6
五、家用电器及音像器材	**Household Electric Appliances,Audio and Video Equipment**	**97.0**
1.家庭设备	Household Equipment	99.6
2.文娱用耐用消费品	Durable Consumer Goods for Entertainment	91.6

(上年＝100)　　13－21　续表　continued　　(Preceding Year＝100)

项　目	Item	指数 Indices
3. 专业音像器材	Audio and Video Equipment	96.9
六、文化办公用品	**Stationery and Office Supplies**	**98.2**
七、日用品	**Commodities**	**101.8**
1. 日用百货	General Merchandise for Daily Use	101.3
2. 日用杂品	Sundries for Daily Use	100.8
3. 洗涤用品	Washing Articles	101.3
4. 其他日用品	Other Commodity	103.9
八、体育娱乐用品	**Sports and Entertainment Goods**	**100.6**
1. 体育用品	Sports Goods	100.9
2. 娱乐用品	Entertainment Goods	100.5
九、交通、通信用品	**Transportation and Communications Articles**	**93.3**
1. 交通运输机械	Transportation Vehicles	93.9
2. 通讯器材	Equipment of Communication	89.4
十、家具	**Funishings**	**105.4**
十一、化妆品	**Cosmetics**	**101.8**
十二、金银珠宝	**Jewellery**	**107.9**
十三、中西药品及医疗保健用品	**Chinese and Western Medicine, Health Care Articles**	**105.5**
1. 医疗器具及用品	Medical Instruments and Articles	102.9
2. 中药材及中成药	Chinese Medicinal Materials and Chinese Traditional Medicine	116.1
3. 西药	Western Medicine	98.7
4. 保健器具及用品	Articles for Health Care	109.1
十四、书报杂志及电子出版物	**Books, Newspapers, Magazines and Electron Publications**	**102.9**
1. 教材及参考书	Teaching Materials and Reference Books	101.1
2. 书报杂志	Books, Newspapers and Magazines	107.8
3. 电子音像制品	Electronic Music and Film Products	100.0
十五、燃料	**Fuels**	**109.3**
1. 煤炭及制品	Coal and Coal Products	103.6
2. 石油及制品	Oil and Oil Products	110.2
十六、建筑材料及五金电料	**Construction Materials and Hardware**	**104.4**
1. 建筑装潢材料	Construction and Upholstery Materials	105.2
2. 五金电料	Hardware and Electric Materials	102.6

13－22 工业生产者出厂价格分类指数
Industrial Producer Ex－Factory Price Indices in Main Years

(上年＝100)　　(Preceding Year＝100)

项目 Item	1999	2000	2005	2010	2011
工业生产者出厂价格总指数 Industrial Producer Ex－factory General Price Index	**96.9**	**100.3**	**103.5**	**104.9**	**104.7**
一、按轻重工业分 Grouped by Industries					
轻工业 Light Industry	**95.8**	**99.3**	**101.8**	**105.0**	**105.5**
以农产品为原料 Made from Agricultural Products	96.9	99.9	102.0	103.9	104.6
以非农产品为原料 Made from Non－agricultural Products	95.3	98.0	101.7	106.0	106.9
重工业 Heavy Industry	**98.0**	**101.1**	**105.6**	**104.7**	**104.2**
采掘 Mining & Quarrying Industry	－	99.5	103.0	114.0	116.6
原料 Raw Materials Industry	99.0	104.4	107.7	110.7	108.7
加工 Manufacturing Industry	97.6	98.9	104.3	102.5	102.8
二、按二大部类分 Grouped by Means of Producting and Consumer Goods					
生产资料 Means of Production	**97.9**	**101.9**	**104.8**	**106.2**	**105.1**
采掘 Mining	－	99.6	103.0	114.0	116.6
原料 Raw Materials	98.4	103.8	110.7	114.5	110.6
加工 Manufacture	97.7	100.3	101.6	103.9	103.3
生活资料 Consumer Goods	**95.7**	**97.5**	**101.2**	**101.0**	**103.7**
食品 Foods	98.8	96.4	101.6	100.1	104.3
衣着 Clothing	95.2	101.1	101.4	102.4	104.5
一般日用品 Articles for Daily Use	94.9	97.8	101.7	100.8	103.9
耐用消费品 Durable Consumer Goods	94.8	94.5	99.5	100.9	101.5

(上年＝100)　　13－22　续表　continued　　(Preceding Year＝100)

项　目 Item	1999	2000	2005	2010	2011
三、按工业部门分 Grouped by Industrial Sector					
冶金工业 Metallurgical Industry	95.6	104.0	104.8	108.0	107.1
电力工业 Power Industry	99.8	96.0	106.2	105.2	102.0
煤炭及炼焦工业 Coal and Coking Industry	99.8	107.9	102.1		–
石油工业 Petroleum Industry	108.1	131.6	124.7	117.0	110.5
化学工业 Chemical Industry	97.2	101.1	106.0	111.9	109.3
机械工业 Machine Building Industry	94.9	96.7	102.9	100.8	101.3
建材材料工业 Building Materials Industry	103.1	103.0	91.7	109.3	109.8
森林工业 Timber Industry	96.6	96.9	101.4	101.6	102.0
食品工业 Food Industry	98.0	95.8	100.6	100.1	105.1
纺织工业 Textile Industry	97.3	107.3	103.4	107.5	105.1
缝纫工业 Tailoring Industry	96.3	100.5	101.5	102.2	105.6
皮革工业 Leather Industry	91.6	98.0	101.4	102.9	101.9
造纸工业 Paper Industry	96.2	102.9	100.3	104.6	102.0
文教艺术用品工业 Cultural, Educational & Handicrafts Articles	90.4	98.7	99.7	97.3	100.9
其它工业 Others	101.1	103.6	102.2	104.7	109.0

13-23 工业生产者购进价格分类指数

Industrial Producer Purchasing Price Indices in Main Years

(上年=100) (Preceding Year=100)

项目 Item	1999	2000	2005	2010	2011
工业生产者购进价格指数 Industrial Producer Purchasing Price Index	**97.2**	**107.4**	**106.9**	**112.1**	**110.8**
燃料动力类 Fuel and Power	103.0	108.0	116.4	111.3	110.6
黑色金属材料类 Ferrous and Metals	96.3	102.7	105.2	108.6	107.0
1. 钢材 Rolled -steel	94.9	103.2	104.9	108.2	106.6
2. 其他 Other	98.2	101.0	105.7	113.0	113.1
有色金属材料及电线类 Non-ferrous Metals and Electric Wire	97.6	108.0	111.2	129.3	113.4
化工原料类 Chemical Raw Materials	97.6	111.0	110.1	113.3	114.3
木材及纸浆类 Wood and Paper Pulps	95.5	104.5	101.0	106.4	104.0
建筑材料及非金属类 Building Materials	98.2	100.6	102.3	108.8	116.8
其他工业原材料及半成品类 Other Industrial Raw Materials and Semi-products	97.2	111.0	103.6	109.8	107.2
农副产品类 Farm and Sideline Products	95.0	104.0	103.9	114.1	112.8
纺织原料类 Textile Raw Materials	89.4	104.7	99.9	110.4	110.5

13－24　住宅销售价格指数

Sales Price Indices of Houses in Main Years

月份　Month	新建住宅 New Residential Building		其中:新建商品住宅 New Residential Commodities Building		二手住宅 The Second－hand House	
	上月＝100	上年同期＝100 Preceding Year＝100	上月＝100	上年同期＝100 Preceding Year＝100	上月＝100	上年同期＝100 Preceding Year＝100
全年　Annual Total	**－**	**100.6**	**－**	**100.7**	**－**	**100.5**
一月　January	101.6	100.8	101.7	100.9	100.3	104.4
二月　February	100.8	101.6	100.9	101.8	100.2	104.6
三月　March	99.9	101.4	99.9	101.6	100.1	103.7
四月　April	100.1	98.8	100.1	98.8	99.7	100.1
五月　May	100.0	99.0	100.0	99.0	99.8	100.4
六月　June	100.0	99.3	100.0	99.3	100.0	100.5
七月　July	99.9	100.0	99.9	100.0	99.7	100.7
八月　August	100.0	101.8	100.0	101.8	99.6	100.4
九月　September	99.9	101.2	99.9	101.2	99.6	100.0
十月　October	99.6	101.5	99.6	101.5	98.5	98.1
十一月　November	99.7	101.3	99.7	101.3	99.1	97.7
十二月　December	99.3	101.0	99.3	101.0	98.6	95.6

注:按国家统计局每月公布的城市房价数据整理。

Note:The data was organized by the urban housing prices which were pubushed monthly by National Bureall of Statistics of China.

13－25 优抚对象

Number of Persons Enjoying

单位:人

指　　标 Item	全　市 Total	市　区 Urban District	#萧山区 Xiaoshan
享受定期抚恤金人数 Number of Persons Receiving Periodical Commiseration	634	194	89
烈属 Number of Martyr Kinsfolk	291	71	32
牺牲军人家属 Number of the Sacrifice Soldiers	109	34	12
病故军人家属 Number of Kinsfolks of the Illness－died Soldiers	234	89	45
享受定期补助人数 Number of Persons Enjoying Regular Subsidies	14084	3216	1477
其中:红军失散人员 Number of Persons be Scattered of the Red Army	1	－	－
在乡复员军人 Rural Demobilized Soldier	3675	1126	449
抗日 The War of Resistance Against Japan	33	18	2
优待优抚对象带病回乡退伍军人 Number of Rural Veterans with Illness Receiving Subsiders	5991	792	556
优待优抚对象户数 Number of Households Receiving Subsiders	29165	10296	3317
优待军属户数 Number of Households Sacrifice Soldiers	7688	3421	1100

人员情况(2011 年)
Public Subsidies(2011)

(person)

#余杭区 Yuhang	桐庐县 Tonglu	淳安县 Chun'an	建德市 Jiande	富阳市 Fuyang	临安市 Lin'an
57	93	90	86	112	59
21	39	55	54	39	33
11	22	6	11	29	7
25	32	29	21	44	19
1186	1511	1524	2049	3097	2687
–	–	1	–	–	–
496	535	409	355	636	614
3	5	–	–	1	9
203	602	961	1232	619	1785
2463	2609	2420	3550	4434	5856
822	615	510	945	765	1432

13－26 市、县级社会

Basic Statistics on Institutions and

单位：个

指标	Item	全市 Total	市区 Urban District	#萧山区 Xiaoshan
合计	**Total**	**2325**	**1576**	**231**
按活动区域分	**Grouped by Region**			
地级社团	City－level Societies	641	641	－
县级社团	County－level Societies	1684	935	231
按性质分	**Grouped by Category**			
科技与研究	Technology and Research	135	96	1
生态环境	Ecological Environment	55	8	2
教育	Education	104	52	4
卫生	Health	101	63	14
社会服务	Social Services	281	182	17
文化	Culture	227	146	35
体育	Sport	187	145	8
法律	Law	16	11	－
工商业服务	Industry and Business Services	388	276	20
宗教	Religion	32	20	5
农业及农村发展	Agricure and Rural Development	163	56	22
职业及从业组织	Vocational and Business Organizations	166	105	1
国际及涉外组织	International and Foreign Organizations	2	－	－
其他	**Other**	**468**	**416**	**102**

团体机构情况(2011 年)
Organizations at County Level(2011)

(unit)

#余杭区 Yuhang	桐庐县 Tonglu	淳安县 Chun'an	建德市 Jiande	富阳市 Fuyang	临安市 Lin'an
221	**124**	**108**	**167**	**193**	**157**
–	–	–	–	–	–
221	124	108	167	193	157
4	–	4	6	13	16
3	37	2	4	2	2
15	37	3	6	1	5
7	13	6	8	5	6
62	26	30	18	21	4
8	11	7	21	31	11
22	–	4	22	12	4
1	–	1	2	2	–
89	–	10	16	46	40
2	–	3	4	4	1
6	–	28	19	41	19
2	–	10	25	4	22
–	–	–	–	2	–
–	**–**	**–**	**16**	**9**	**27**

13 - 27 社会办福利院情况(2011 年)
Basic Statistics on Welfare Homes(2011)

指标 Item	单位(个) Homes (unit)	年末职工人数(人) Staff and Workers (person)	年末床位数(张) Beds (bed)	年末在院人数(人) Persons Housed (person)	#老人(人) Seniors(person)
全市 Total	**254**	**2687**	**33561**	**14768**	**13610**
市区 Urban District	150	2101	22465	9852	8988
#萧山区 Xiaoshan	34	289	5859	1852	1765
余杭区 Yuhang	29	187	3122	710	664
桐庐县 Tonglu	13	130	1817	1583	1552
淳安县 Chun'an	23	83	1737	768	753
建德市 Jiande	22	161	2159	1007	927
富阳市 Fuyang	17	92	2627	670	576
临安市 Lin'an	29	120	2756	888	814

13－28 社会保障分县(市)情况(2011年)

Social Security by Region(2011)

单位:人 (persons)

指标 Item	城镇基本养老保险参保人数 Number of Persons in the Basic Pension Program	基本养老保险参保职工 Number of Employed Persons in the Basic Pension Program	基本医疗保险参保人数 Number of Persons in the Basic Medical Insurance Program	工伤保险参保人数 Number of Persons in the Work－injure Insurance Program	生育保险参保人数 Number of Persons in the Bear Insurance Program	失业保险参保人数 Number of Persons in the Unemployment Insurance Program
全　市 Total	**4281172**	**3657862**	**3863347**	**3552801**	**2543800**	**2775332**
市　区 Urban District	3537383	3023704	3254132	2912793	2157602	2441669
#萧山区 Xiaoshan	901714	812167	565469	669045	464265	466995
余杭区 Yuhang	473414	416360	436775	417061	262849	310000
桐庐县 Tonglu	112586	95055	91458	94671	57121	46693
淳安县 Chun'an	82575	68610	79606	76823	39807	37102
建德市 Jiande	143715	115245	100528	85456	65040	65446
富阳市 Fuyang	254741	225409	204639	253540	148542	144305
临安市 Lin'an	150172	129839	132984	129518	75688	40117

13－29 近年来社会保障情况
Social Security in Recent Years

单位:万人 (10000 persons)

指标 Item	2000	2005	2006	2007	2008	2009	2010	2011
城镇登记失业人员 Number of the Registered Unemployed Persons in Urban	5.6	6.09	6.30	5.96	5.45	5.64	4.85	4.4
城镇登记失业率(%) The Registered Rate of Unemployment in Urban (%)	3.48	3.71	3.46	3.21	3.02	2.99	2.19	1.86
失业人员再就业 The Re－employed Persons of Unemployment	14.69	13.09	12.08	13.1	12.59	15.56	15.54	13.17
城镇基本养老保险参保人数 Number of Persons in the Basic Pension Program in Urban	123.69	227.58	253.34	280.49	318.11	342.24	383.97	428.12
#基本养老保险参保职工 Number of Employed Persons in the Basic Pension Program	81.96	185.32	208.87	233.15	267.6	288.29	325.88	365.79
失业保险参保人数 Number of Persons in the Unemployment Insurance Program	96.66	118.36	145.77	170.09	202.41	215.68	243.98	277.53
基本医疗保险参保人数 Number of Persons in the Basic Medical Insurance Program	-	187.71	208.5	237.74	274.59	298.31	345.24	386.33
工伤保险参保人数 Number of Persons in the Work－injure Insurance Program	47.86	111.03	132.09	201.64	245.82	274.15	314.95	355.28
生育保险参保人数 Number of Persons in the Bear Insurance Program	63.99	96.41	128.89	155.64	181.68	199.80	228.53	254.38
城乡居民养老保险(障)人数 Number of Persons in the Urban and Rural old－age Security						15.82	106.3	112.35
城乡居民参加医疗保险人数 Number of urban and rural residents participated in medical insurance	-	350.6	370.65	369.7	369.18	346.95	408.32	392.69

注:城乡居民参加医疗保险人数:2009 年前为参加新型农村合作医疗的人数。

a) Number of urban and rural residents participated in medical insurance: before 2009, it was the number of people who participated in new rural cooperative medical insurance.

主要统计指标解释

从业人员劳动报酬 指各单位在一定时期内直接支付给本单位全部从业人员的劳动报酬总额。

在岗职工工资总额 指各单位在一定时期内直接支付给本单位全部在岗职工的劳动报酬总额。

工资总额的计算原则应以直接支付给职工的全部劳动报酬为根据。各单位支付给本单位全部职工的劳动报酬,不论是计入成本的还是不计入成本的,不论是以货币形式支付还是以实物形式支付的,不论是单位自筹的资金还是上级(或政府财政部门)下拨的资金,不论是厂级单位筹集的资金还是下属车间(科室)及附属经营单位筹集的资金,均应列入工资总额计算的范围。

在岗职工平均工资 指各单位的在岗职工在一定时期内平均每人所得的货币工资额。它表明一定时期内在岗职工工资收入的高低程度,是反映在岗职工工资水平的主要指标。计算公式为:

$$在岗职工平均工资=\frac{报告期实际支付的全部在岗职工工资总额}{报告期全部在岗职工平均人数}$$

城镇居民家庭总收入 指被调查的城镇居民家庭全部收入。包括经常或固定得到的收入和一次性收入,不包括周转性收入。如:提取银行存款、向亲友借入款、收回借出款以及其他各种暂收款。

城镇居民家庭可支配收入 指被调查的城镇居民家庭在支付个人所得税、个人交纳的社会保障支出之后,所余下的实际收入。

计算公式为:可支配收入=总收入-个人所得税-个人交纳的社会保障支出

城镇居民家庭消费性支出 指被调查的城镇居民家庭用于日常生活的全部支出,包括购买商品支出和文化生活、服务等非商品性支出。不包括罚没、丢失款和缴纳的各种税款(如个人所得税、牌照税、房产税等),也不包括个体劳动者生产经营过程中发生的各项费用。

农村居民家庭纯收入 指农村常住居民家庭总收入中,扣除从事生产和非生产经营费用支出、缴纳税款和上交承包集体任务金额以后剩余的,可直接用于进行生产性、非生产性建设投资、生活消费和积蓄的那一部分收入。它是反映农民家庭实际收入水平的综合性的主要指标。农民家庭纯收入,既包括从事生产性和非生产性的经营收入,又包括取自在外人口寄回带回和国家财政救济、各种补贴等非经营性收入;既包括货币收入,又包括自产自用的实物收入。但不包括向银行、信用社和向亲友贷款等属于借贷性的收入。

计算公式为:

纯收入=总收入-家庭经营费用支出-生产用固定资产折旧-税收-上交集体承包任务

离休、退休、退职人员 指正式办理了离休、退休、退职手续,并享受相应的离休、退休、退职待遇的人员。

保险福利费用 指企业、事业、机关单位在工资以外实际支付给职工和离休、退休、退职人员个人以及用于集体的劳动保险和福利费用。

社会福利事业单位 指集中收养社会孤、老、残、幼的机构。包括由民政部门管理的社会福利院、儿童福利院、精神病人福利院和城镇集体办的福利院,以及农村集体举办的敬老院。

社会福利事业单位收养人数 包括民政部门管理和城镇及农村集体举办的社会福利事业单位中收养的老人,少年儿童,缺乏生活自理能力的残疾人员和精神病人。

商品零售价格指数 是反映城乡商品零售价格变动趋势的一种经济指数。零售物价的调整变动直接影响到城乡居民的生活支出和国家的财政收入,影响居民购买力和市场供需平衡,影响消费与积累的比例。因此,计算零售价格指数,可以从一个侧面对上述经济活动进行观察和分析。

居民消费价格指数 是反映一定时期内城乡居民所购买的生活消费品价格和服务项目价格变动趋势和程度的相对数。是综合了城市居民消费价格指数和农民消费价格指数计算取得。利用居民消费价格指数,可以观察和分析消费品的零售价格和服务价格变动对城乡居民实际生活支出的影响程度。

工业品出厂价格指数 是反映全部工业产品出厂价格总水平的变动趋势和程度的相对数。其中除包括工业企业售给商业、外贸、物资部门的产品外,还包括售给工业和其他部门的生产资料以及直接售给居民的生活消费品。通过工业生产价格指数能观察出厂价格变动对工业总产值的影响。

Explanatory Notes on Main Statistical Indicators

Labour Remuneration refers to total payment by various units to their employees during a certain period of time, including total wage bill of permanent workers and staff and remuneration payment to other employees.

Total Wages of Fully Employed Staff and Workers refer to the total remuneration payment to fully employed staff and workers in various units during a certain period of time. The calculation of total wages is based on the total remuneration payment to the staff and workers. Therefore, all the wages and salaries and other payments to staff and workers are included in the total wages regardless of their sources, category, and forms (in kind or cash). (Total wages of staff and workers in this yearbook include only total wages of fully employed staff and workers, excluding the living allowances distributed to those who have left their working units while keeping their labour contract/employment relation unchanged).

Average Wage of Fully Employed Staff and Workers refers to the average wage in money terms per person during a certain period of time for fully employed staff and workers in enterprises, institutions, and government agencies, which reflects the general level of wage income during a certain period of time and is calculated as follows:

$$\text{Average Wage of Fully Employed Staff and Workers} = \frac{\text{Total wages of Fully employed staff and workers in Reference Period}}{\text{Average Number of Fully employed Staff and workers in Reference period}}$$

Total Income of Urban Households refers to the total actual income of the sample households, including regular or fixed income and occasional income. The income of a circulating nature such as withdrawal from bank deposit, loans borrowed from relatives or friends, repayment of loans received and various temporary collection of many is excluded.

Disposable Income of Urban Households refers to total income minus income tax, personal contribution to social security and subsidy for keeping diaries in being a sample household. The following formula is used:

Disposable Income = total households income – income tax – personal contribution to social security

Expenditure for Consumption of Urban Households refers to total expenditure of the sample households for consumption in daily life, including expenditure for various commodities and expenses for non – commodity items such as culture and service, etc., but excluding fines and confiscation, loss, tax payments (such as income tax, license tax, real estates tax, etc.) and various expenses by individual laborers for business purposes.

Net Income of Rural Households refers to the total income of the permanent residents of the rural households during a year after the deduction of the expenses for productive and non – productive business operation, the payment for taxes and productive constriction, for consumption in daily life and for savings deposit. It is a comprehensive indicator to show the actual level of the income of the peasants' household. The net income of the rural households includes not only the income from the productive and non – productive business operation, but also the income from the non – business operation, such as the money remitted or brought back by the members of the household who are in other places, the government relief payment and various subsidies. It includes not only the money income, but also the income in kind. But the income from borrowing from banks, friends and relatives is excluded.

Retired and Resigned Person refers to the persons who have form ally gone through the formalities for their retirement or quitting work and enjoy the corresponding treatments.

Insurance an d welfare Funds refers to labour insurance and welf are funds paid by enterprises, organizations and institutions to their staff and workers as well as retired and resigned persons in addition to their wages and salaries.

Social Welfare Institutions refer to institutions taking care of old people without children, handicapped people and orphans. They include social welfare institutions run by civil affairs departments, children welfare institutions, social welfare institutions for mental patients, and collective – owned old people's home in rural areas.

Number of People Taken in by social welfare Institutions refers to the number of old people, children, totally dependent handicapped people and mental patients taken in by social welfare institutions run by civil affairs departments and those run by collective units in urban and rural areas.

Retail price Index reflects the general change in retail prices of commodities. The change and adjustment in retail prices directly affect the living expenditure of urban and rural residents, government revenue, purchasing power of residents and the equilibrium of market supply and demand, and the ratio of consumption to accumulation. Therefore, the calculation of retail price index is useful to analyze the changes of the above economic activities.

Consumer Price Index reflects the trend and degree of changes in prices of consumer goods and services purchased by urban and rural residents, and is a composite index derived from the urban consumer price index and the rural consumer price index. Consumer price index can be used to analyze the impact of consumer price change on actual expenditure for living cost of urban and rural residents.

Ex – factory price index of Industrial Products reflects the trend and degree of changes in general ex – factory prices of all industrial products, including sales of industrial products by and industrial enterprise to all units outside the enterprise, as well as sales of consumer goods to residents. It can be used to analyze the impact of ex – factory prices on gross industrial output value.

中国统计出版社最新图书简目

（仅供参考，以最后出书为准）

统计资料

中国统计年鉴－2012
2012中国发展报告
中国劳动统计年鉴－2012
中国建筑业统计年鉴－2012
中国商品交易市场统计年鉴－2012
中国民政统计年鉴－2012
中国科技统计年鉴－2012
中国高技术产业统计年鉴－2012
全国农产品成本收益资料汇编－2012
大中型批发零售和住宿餐饮企业统计年鉴－2012
中国农村住户调查年鉴－2012（中、英文）
第二次全国R&D资源清查资料汇编－工业企业卷
2010年中国第六次人口普查公报

中国统计摘要－2012
中国第三产业统计年鉴－2012
中国社会统计年鉴－2012
中国人口和就业统计年鉴－2012
中国房地产统计年鉴－2012
中国贸易外经统计年鉴－2012
中国农村统计年鉴－2012
中国教育经费统计年鉴－2010
中国科学技术协会统计年鉴－2012
中国城市（镇）生活与价格年鉴－2012
中国农村全面建设小康监测报告－2012
中国零售和餐饮连锁企业统计年鉴－2012

国际统计年鉴－2012
中国区域经济统计年鉴－2012
中国城市统计年鉴－2009
中国工业经济统计年鉴－2012
中国能源统计年鉴－2012
2012中国地区经济监测报告
中国农产品价格调查年鉴－2012
中国农村贫困监测报告－2012
工业企业科技活动资料－2012
中国县（市）社会经济统计年鉴－2012
第二次全国R&D资源清查资料汇编－综合卷
中国民族统计年鉴2011、2012

2012年省级综合统计年鉴系列

北京 天津 河北 山西 内蒙古
河南 湖北 湖南 广东 广西
辽宁 吉林 黑龙江 上海 江苏
海南 重庆 四川 贵州 云南
浙江 安徽 福建 江西 山东
西藏 陕西 甘肃 青海 宁夏
新疆 新疆生产建设兵团

2012年市（县）级综合统计年鉴系列

天津滨海新区
运城 忻州 临汾 呼和浩特
上海浦东新区
杭州 宁波 绍兴 台州 温州
厦门经济特区 南昌 上饶
十堰 荆州 咸宁 长沙 广州
石家庄 唐山 邯郸 太原 大同
包头 沈阳 大连 长春 吉林市
苏州 无锡 常州 徐州 南通
金华 嘉兴 衢州
济南 青岛 潍坊 郑州
东莞 惠州 深圳 桂林 南宁
贵阳 昆明 庆阳 西安
长治 阳泉 晋城 朔州 晋中
四平 哈尔滨 黑龙江垦区
盐城 镇江 江阴 丹阳
福州 福州经济技术开发区
洛阳 三门峡 南阳 武汉 宜昌
柳州 来宾 河池 海口 成都 绵阳
兰州 银川 乌鲁木齐

2010年人口普查资料系列

中国2010年人口普查资料
浙江 安徽 福建 江西 山东
西藏 陕西 甘肃 青海 宁夏
中国分县2010年人口普查资料
北京 天津 河北 山西 内蒙古
河南 湖北 湖南 广东 广西
新疆 新疆生产建设兵团
中国分乡镇、街道2010年人口普查资料
辽宁 吉林 黑龙江 上海 江苏
海南 重庆 四川 贵州 云南
河南省各市2010年人口普查资料丛书
中国分民族2010年人口普查资料

“十一五”规划教材

非参数统计 医学统计学
多元统计分析 经济计量学教程
统计数据处理概论
企业经营管理统计
统计学：从数据到结论
概率论与数理统计 统计学
应用时间序列分析
质量管理统计方法 社会统计学
市场调查与预测
国民经济核算教程（国民经济统计学）
现代金融投资统计分析
统计指数理论及应用
多元统计分析实验
统计学原理（非统计专业使用）
概率论与数理统计（经济、管理类专业使用）

重点图书

挑大学选专业2012—高考志愿填报指南　　挑大学选专业2012—考研择校指南

欲购以上图书请与中国统计出版社发行部联系
电话：(010)63376907，63376908　同榻行书店电话：68783171，68783172
通讯地址：北京市西城区三里河月坛南街57号　邮政编码：100826
网址：http://csp.stats.gov.cn

浙江预防医学

ZHEJIANG JOURNAL OF PREVENTIVE MEDICINE

月刊 1989年9月创刊 第24卷 第9期 2012年9月

主 管
浙江省科学技术协会
主 办
浙江省预防医学会
协 办
浙江省疾病预防控制中心
出 版
浙江预防医学杂志编辑部
社 长
丛黎明
主 编
丛黎明
副主编
韩晓军 陈 坤 莫世华
地址：浙江省杭州市江干区机场路137号
邮编：310004
电话：(0571)87115497
传真：(0571)87115497
E-mail：zjyfyx@mail.hz.zj.cn
http：//www.zjyfyxzz.com
印 刷
浙江新中商务印刷有限公司
发 行
浙江预防医学杂志编辑部
广告经营许可证号
3300004000063
中国标准刊号
ISSN 1007－0931
CN 33－1200/R
定 价
每期 6.00元
全年 72.00元

论 著

综 述

疾病预防与控制

卫生监测与监督

ISSN1007-0
CN33-120

浙江预防医学

ZHEJIANG YUFANG YIXUE

Sep.2012 Vol.24,No.9 2012年9月 第24卷 第9期

浙江省科学技术协会主管
浙江省预防医学会主办

ZJPM

ZHEJIANG JOURNAL OF PREVENTIVE MEDICINE

《中国核心期刊数据库》
全文收录期刊
《中国学术期刊（光盘版）》
全文收录期刊
《中文科技期刊数据库》
全文收录期刊

9
201

ISSN 1007-0931
9 771007 093005 09

中华预防医学会系列杂志
SERIAL JOURNAL OF CHINESE PREVENTIVE MEDICINE ASSOCIATION

浙江预防医学 二〇一二年九月 第二十四卷 第九期 中华预防医学会系列杂志